P9-BJY-039

INDEXING AND ABSTRACTING IN THEORY AND PRACTICE

F. W. LANCASTER

1991

UNIVERSITY OF ILLINOIS

GRADUATE SCHOOL OF LIBRARY AND INFORMATION SCIENCE

249 ARMORY BUILDING / 505 EAST ARMORY STREET

CHAMPAIGN ILLINOIS 61820-6291

Copyright © 1991 by F.W. Lancaster

All rights reserved.
No part of this publication may be reproduced, stored
in a retrieval system, or transmitted,
in any form or by any means,
electronic, mechanical, photocopying, recording, or otherwise,
without prior written permission of the author.

Distributed exclusively by the
University of Illinois
Graduate School of Library and Information Science
249 Armory Building / 505 East Armory Street
Champaign, IL 61820-6291
USA

ISBN 0-87845-083-1

Designed by Bob Chapdu, IntelliText Corp., Champaign, IL 61826, USA. Typeset
in Garamond Book by the Publications Office, Graduate School of Library and
Information Science, University of Illinois. Printing and binding by Cushing-
Malloy Inc., Ann Arbor, MI 48107, USA.

INDEXING AND ABSTRACTING
IN
THEORY AND PRACTICE

CONTENTS

Appendices

PREFACE

My interest in indexing and abstracting dates back to 1957-1959 when I served as editor of an in-house abstracts bulletin produced by Tube Investments Limited, Birmingham, England. The main stimulus for producing the present book occurred in 1986. I was asked to prepare a course in indexing and abstracting for the Arab League Documentation Centre and discovered that no book then available dealt with the subject in the way I wanted to present it. Good books on subject indexing did exist but most were either out-of-date or espoused one particular indexing method. Excellent books on abstracting were (and are) available and this work should be considered to complement these rather than to replace them. While a few books endeavored to treat indexing and abstracting together, I felt that they did not cover the subject comprehensively and, in any case, tended to deal with the two topics as separate activities, whereas I wanted to stress their similarities rather than their differences.

This book, then, is intended primarily as a text to be used in teaching indexing and abstracting in schools of library and information science. Nevertheless, I hope it may be of some value to all individuals and institutions involved in information retrieval and related activities, including librarians, managers of information centers, and database producers.

Indexing is closely related to the subject of vocabulary control, but this topic is not dealt with in detail here because it is covered in my book *Vocabulary Control for Information Retrieval*. While I concentrate on indexing and abstracting as practiced by published indexing and abstracting services (in paper or electronic form), rather than library catalogs, the principles are the same, and I hope that the book may be of interest and value to those concerned with improving subject access in online catalogs.

At various stages in the preparation of this text I received considerable help from three graduate assistants, Jill Byttner, Lorraine Haricombe and Beverly Rauchfuss, and I must offer my sincere thanks to them, and also to Kathy Painter, who put the text into machine-readable form.

F. W. Lancaster
University of Illinois
Urbana, April 1990

List of Exhibits

1

Introduction

THE MAIN PURPOSE of indexing and abstracting is to construct *representations* of published items in a form suitable for inclusion in some type of *database*. This database of representations could be in printed form (as in an indexing/abstracting publication such as *Chemical Abstracts* or the *Engineering Index*), in machine-readable form (in which case the database will often be roughly equivalent to a printed service), or in card form (as in a conventional library catalog).

The role of the indexing/abstracting operations within the larger framework of information retrieval activities in general is illustrated in Exhibit 1. First, the producer of the database selects from the population of newly published documents those that meet certain criteria for inclusion in the database. The most obvious criterion is the subject dealt with, but others, such as type of document, language, or source, may also be important. For those databases that deal primarily with articles from journals, the selection criteria will usually focus on the journal rather than the article; that is, certain journals will be covered and others not (although some journals may be indexed in their entirety and others selectively). To a large extent the coverage of many databases is governed by considerations of cost-effectiveness. Particularly in the case of databases dealing with a highly specialized field, only those journals that publish most on the subjects of interest will be included.

The items selected for inclusion in the database must be "described" in various ways. Descriptive cataloging procedures (not explicit in Exhibit 1) identify authors, titles, sources, and other bibliographic elements, indexing procedures identify the subject matter dealt with, and abstracting may be used to summarize the contents of the item. The terms used in indexing will frequently be drawn from some form of controlled vocabulary, such as a thesaurus (the "system vocabulary" of Exhibit 1), but may instead be "free" terms (e.g., drawn from the document itself). These description activities create document representations in a form suitable for inclusion in the database. The documents themselves will usually go to a different type of database (document store) such as the shelves of a library.

Members of the community to be served use the database primarily to satisfy various information needs. To do this they must convert an information need into some form of "search strategy," which may be as simple as selecting a single term to consult in a printed index or card catalog, or may involve the combining of many terms into a more elaborate

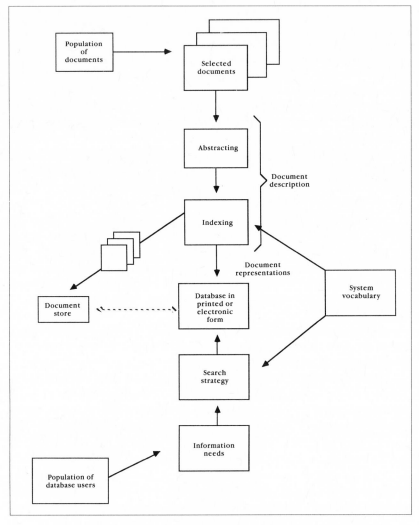

Exhibit 1
The role of indexing and abstracting in the larger information retrieval picture

and sophisticated strategy used to interrogate a database through a computer terminal.

In searching a database, of course, one wants to find items that are useful in satisfying some information need, and to avoid retrieving items that are not useful. Terms such as "relevant" and "pertinent" are frequently used to refer to "useful" items, and these terms have been defined in several different ways. There is a lot of disagreement as to what "relevance" and "pertinence" really mean (Lancaster, 1977). In this book I will consider as synonymous the expressions "useful," "pertinent," and "relevant to an information need." That is, a pertinent (useful) item is one that contributes to the satisfaction of some information need.

The information retrieval problem is depicted graphically in Exhibit 2. The entire rectangle represents a database and the items it contains. The plus (+) items are those that a hypothetical requester would find useful in satisfying some current information need, and the minus (−) items are those that he would judge not useful. For any particular information need there will be many more − items than + ones. Indeed, if the diagram were drawn "to scale," one would expect that the 11 useful items might be accompanied by a whole wall of useless ones. The problem is to retrieve as many as possible of the useful items and as few as possible of the useless ones.

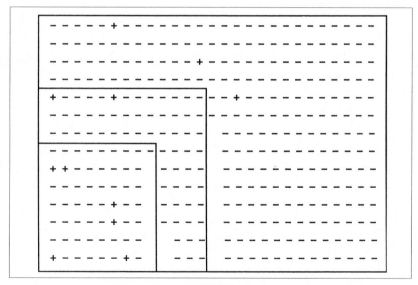

Exhibit 2
The problem of retrieving pertinent items from a database

The smaller of the two interior rectangles of Exhibit 2 represents the results of a search performed in the database. It retrieved 57 items, of which 6 were useful and 51 not useful. The ratio of useful items to total items retrieved (6/57 or about 10 percent in this case) is usually referred to as a *precision ratio*. The ratio commonly used to express the extent to which all the useful items are found is the *recall ratio*. In this case the recall ratio is 6/11 or about 54 percent.

To improve recall in this situation one would probably need to search more broadly. This is depicted in the larger of the two interior rectangles. Through searching more broadly, recall has been raised to 8/11 (73 percent)), but precision has declined further to 8/112 or about 7 percent. It is an unfortunate characteristic of the information retrieval situation that an improvement in recall will usually cause a deterioration in precision and vice versa.

Exhibit 2 suggests another phenomenon. It might be possible to search sufficiently broadly to find all the useful items (i.e., achieve 100 percent recall), but precision would probably be intolerable. Furthermore, the larger the database the less tolerable will be a low precision. While a user might be willing to look at abstracts of, say, 57 items to find 6 useful ones, he may be much less willing to examine 570 abstracts for 60 useful ones. With very large databases, then, it becomes increasingly difficult to achieve an acceptable level of recall at a tolerable level of precision.

In this book I use the term *recall* to refer to the ability to retrieve useful items and *precision* to refer to the ability to avoid useless ones. There are other measures of the performance of searches in a database (see, for example, Robertson [1969]), some more mathematically exact, but *recall* and *precision* give the general picture and still seem to be the obvious measures to use to express the results of any search that simply divides a database into two parts (retrieved and not retrieved).*

It is clear from Exhibit 1 that many factors determine whether a search in a database is successful or not. These include the coverage of the database, indexing policy, indexing practice, abstracting policy and practice, the quality of the vocabulary used to index, the quality of the search strategies, and so on. This book makes no attempt to deal with all of these factors (although they are all interrelated) but focuses on the important activities of document description or, at least, those concerned with the content of documents.

---

*A search that ranks output in order of "probable relevance" requires a somewhat different measure that in effect compares the ranking achieved with some ideal ranking.

2

Indexing Principles

While the title of this book refers to "indexing," the scope is actually restricted to subject indexing and to abstracting. Subject indexing and abstracting are closely related activities in that both involve preparing a representation of the subject matter of documents. The abstractor writes a narrative description or summary of the document, while the indexer describes its contents by using one or several index terms, usually selected from some form of controlled vocabulary.

The main purpose of the abstract is to indicate what the document is about or to summarize its contents. A group of index terms can serve the same purpose. For example, the following set of terms gives a fairly good idea of what is dealt with in some hypothetical report:

Information Centers
Resource Sharing
Union Catalogs
Cooperative Cataloging
Online Networks
Interlibrary Loans

In a sense, such a list of terms can be considered to act as a kind of mini-abstract. It would serve such a purpose if all the terms were listed together in a published index or were printed out to represent an item retrieved from some database as a result of a computer search.

More obviously, the terms assigned by an indexer serve as access points through which a bibliographic item can be located and retrieved in a subject search in a published index or machine-readable database. Thus, in a printed index, one should be able to find the hypothetical item mentioned earlier under any one of the six terms. In a computer-based retrieval system, of course, one would expect to be able to find it under any one of these terms or, indeed, any combination of them.

The distinction between indexing and abstracting is becoming increasingly blurred. On the one hand, a list of index terms can be printed out to form a mini-abstract. On the other, the text of abstracts can be stored in a computer-based system in such a way that searches can be performed on combinations of words occurring in the text. Such abstracts can be used instead of index terms, to allow access to the items, or can supplement the access points provided by the index terms. To some extent this changes the role of the abstractor, who must now be concerned not only with writing a good clear description of the contents of a document but also with creating a record that will be an effective representation for retrieval purposes.

If indexing and abstracting were looked upon as fully complementary activities, the character of the indexing operation might change somewhat. For example, the indexer could concentrate on assigning terms that supplement the access points provided in the abstract. However, such complementarity must be fully recognized and understood by the user of the database. Otherwise a set of index terms alone would give a very misleading picture of the content of an item.

Length of Record

One of the most important properties of a representation of subject matter is its length. The effect of record length is illustrated in the example of Exhibit 3. At the left are various representations of the content of a journal article in the form of narrative text; at the right are two representations in the form of lists of index terms.

The title is a general indication of what the article is about. The brief abstract gives more detail, indicating that survey results are presented in the article and identifying the major questions addressed. The extended abstract carries this further, identifying all of the survey questions and giving the size of the sample used in the study.

The more information given, the more clearly the representation indicates the scope of the article and the more likely it is to indicate to a reader whether or not it satisfies some information need. For example, one might be looking for articles mentioning U.S. attitudes toward various Arab leaders. The title gives no indication that this specific topic is discussed and the brief abstract, by focusing on other topics, suggests that it may not be. It is only the extended abstract that shows that the article includes information on this subject.

The longer the representation, too, the more access points it provides. If title words were the only access points, this item would probably be missed in many searches for which it might be considered a valuable response. As the length of the representation is increased, so is the retrievability of the item. Only with the extended abstract, presumably, would one be likely to retrieve this item in a search for information on U.S. attitudes toward Arab leaders.

Title
Nationwide public opinion survey of U.S. attitudes on the Middle East)

Abstract (brief)

A telephone survey held in 1985 presents views on such matters as: U.S. aid to Israel and to Egypt; whether the U.S. should side with Israel, the Arab nations, or neither; whether the PLO should participate in a peace conference; and whether an independent Palestinian State is a prerequisite for peace.

Abstract (expanded)

Telephone interviews were conducted in 1985 with 655 Americans sampled probabilistically. Answers were obtained to the following questions: is the establishment of a Palestinian State essential for peace; should U.S. aid to Israel and Egypt be reduced; should the U.S. participate in a peace conference that includes the PLO; should the U.S. favor neither Israel nor the Arab nations but maintain friendly relations with both? Opinions were also expressed on major Middle East leaders (Hussein, Arafat, Peres, Mubarak, Fahd, Assad), especially their peace efforts, and whether or not respondents felt they had enough information on the various national groups in the region.

Indexing (selective)
PUBLIC OPINION
TELEPHONE SURVEYS
UNITED STATES
ATTITUDES
MIDDLE EAST

Indexing (exhaustive)
PUBLIC OPINION
TELEPHONE SURVEYS
UNITED STATES
ATTITUDES
MIDDLE EAST
ISRAEL
EGYPT
ARAB NATIONS
PALESTINE
 LIBERATION
 ORGANIZATION
PEACE CONFERENCES
PEACE
PALESTINIAN STATE
FOREIGN AID
POLITICAL LEADERS

Exhibit 3
Effect of record length on retrievability

The same situation applies to indexing. The selective indexing, involving only five terms, gives a very general indication of what the article is about (roughly equivalent, in this case, to the title) and a very limited level of access. The more exhaustive indexing provides a much better indication of the specific subject matter dealt with, as well as allowing many more access points.

Steps in Subject Indexing

Subject indexing involves two principal steps:

1. Conceptual analysis, and
2. Translation.

These are intellectually quite separate, although they are not always clearly distinguished and may actually occur simultaneously.

Conceptual analysis, first and foremost, involves deciding what a document is about—that is, what it covers. The terms listed on the right of Exhibit 3 represent this author's conceptual analysis of a particular article—what he considered it to be about.

This statement on conceptual analysis is oversimplified. Subject indexing is usually performed to meet the needs of a particular audience— the users of a particular information centre or of a particular publication. Effective subject indexing involves deciding not only what a document is about but also why it is likely to be of interest to a particular group of users. In other words, there is no one "correct" set of index terms for any item. The same publication could be indexed rather differently in different information centers and should be indexed differently if the groups of users are interested in the item for different reasons.*

The indexer, then, must ask several questions about an item:

1. What is it about?
2. Why has it been added to our collection?
3. What aspects will our users be interested in?

The point is well illustrated in Exhibit 4. This hypothetical example refers to a report issued by the National Aeronautics and Space Administration (NASA) and dealing with a manned space flight. When NASA adds this report to its own database, it will presumably be interested in all facets and may index it exhaustively, trying to cover all of the aspects, perhaps at a fairly general level. One section of the report may deal with the clothing used by the astronauts, mentioning some new synthetic rubber compounds used in part of the clothing. This makes the report of interest to a rubber company. When added to this company's collection, however, the report will be indexed quite differently. Highly specific terms will be used to index the new compounds and the general term SPACE SUITS may be used to indicate the particular application of the compounds. A

---

*Dabney (1986) recognized this in the distinction he makes between document-oriented and request-oriented indexing. It is also implicit in the "gedanken" approach advocated by Cooper (1978).

metals company may be interested in this report for another reason: it mentions a new welding technique developed to join some alloys in the construction of the space vehicle. Here it is indexed under the welding terms, the appropriate metals terms and perhaps the general application term SPACE VEHICLES. The rubber company indexes the report quite differently from the metals company and neither set of terms resembles the more exhaustive list used by NASA itself.

This is as it should be. The more specialized the clientele of an information center, the more likely it is that the indexing can and should be tailored to the precise interests of the group. It is only in more general institutions—e.g., general academic libraries—that one might expect to find one organization indexing an item in exactly the same way as another.

There is an important lesson to be learned from this. Indexers need to know much more than the principles of indexing. In particular, they must be thoroughly familiar with the interests of the community served and the information needs of members of that community. Indeed, it will usually be desirable that the indexer should not remain "behind the scenes" but should also work in other capacities, including that of a reference librarian.

NASA Technical Report Describing a New Manned Space Mission

NASA	Rubber Company	Metals Company
——— Exhaustive ——— indexing ——— covering ——— all aspects ——— at a ——— somewhat ——— general level ——— ——— ——— ———	——— New ——— synthetic ——— rubber ——— compounds ——— SPACE SUITS	——— New ——— welding ——— techniques ——— and ——— metals ——— involved SPACE VEHICLES

Exhibit 4
Example of item indexed from various points of view

Aboutness

In the previous discussion no attempt was made to define "about": the expression "is about" was merely a synonym for "covers." That is, "what a document is about" was used to mean the same as "what a document covers." These expressions may not be very precise and the terms "about" and "covers" are not easily defined. Nevertheless, they are expressions that seem acceptable to most people and to be understood by them. It is not my intention to enter into a philosophical discussion on the meaning of "about" or "aboutness." A number of authors have already done so. In so doing, they have failed to clarify the situation, at least as far as the task of subject indexing is concerned. Beghtol (1986) and Hutchins (1978) both draw upon text linguistics in discussing the subject, Maron (1977) adopts a probabilistic approach, and Swift et al. (1978) are careful to point out that aboutness in indexing may not coincide with the aboutness that searchers for information are concerned with. Most recently, Frohmann (1990) has used the work of Wittgenstein for criticizing some approaches to indexing theory. Wilson (1968) goes so far as to imply that subject indexing faces "intractable" problems because it is so difficult to decide what a document is about. But do we really need to understand "aboutness" in order to index effectively? Is it not enough to be able to recognize that a document is of interest to a particular community because it contributes to our understanding of topics x, y, and z? The recognition that it does contribute in this way exemplifies the process we have called "conceptual analysis," while the process of "translation" involves a decision on which of the available labels best represent x, y, and z.

"Concept" is another word that some writers like to philosophize around (see, for example, Dahlberg [1979]). In this book I use it to refer to a topic discussed by an author. "Conceptual analysis," then, means nothing more than identifying the topics discussed in a document. Preschel (1972) has a very practical approach. She takes "concept" to mean "indexable matter" and defines "conceptual analysis" as "indexer perception of indexable matter." Also practical is Tinker (1966):

> By assigning a descriptor [i.e., an index term] to a document, the indexer asserts that the descriptor has a high degree of relevance to the content of the document; that is, he asserts that the meaning of the descriptor is strongly associated with a concept embodied in the document, and that it is appropriate for the subject area of the document. (Page 97)

Wooster (1964) is even more pragmatic. He refers to indexing as assigning terms "presumably related in some fashion to the intellectual content of the original document, to help you find it when you want to."

I find nothing wrong with these pragmatic definitions or descriptions of subject indexing. Purists will no doubt quibble with them on the grounds that such expressions as "indexable matter," "relevance," "meaning," "associated with," "concept," "appropriate for," "related to," and "intellectual content" are not precisely defined to everyone's satisfaction. However, if one must reach agreement on the precise definition of terms before pursuing any task one is unlikely to accomplish much—in indexing or any other activity.

Weinberg (1988) hypothesizes that indexing fails the researcher because it deals only in a general way with what a document is "about" and does not focus on what it provides that is "new" concerning the topic. She maintains that this distinction is reflected in the difference between "aboutness" and "aspect," between "topic" and "comment" or between "theme" and "rheme." She fails to convince that these distinctions are really useful in the context of indexing or that it might be possible for indexers to maintain such distinctions.

Swift et al. (1978) discuss the limitations of an aboutness approach to indexing in the social sciences. They recommend indexing documents according to the "problems" to which they seem to relate. It is difficult to see how the distinction they make differs from the distinction, made earlier in this chapter, between what an item deals with and why a particular user or group of users might be interested in it. Crowe (1986) maintains that the indexer should address the "subjective viewpoint" of the author. One of her examples deals with the topic of depression which can be discussed in books or articles from several different viewpoints (e.g., treatment through psychotherapy, through drug therapy, and so on). Again, it is difficult to see how this differs from normal indexing practice—e.g., the National Library of Medicine's use of subheadings.

Breton (1981) claims that engineers make little use of databases because indexers label items with the names of materials or devices while engineers are more likely to want to search for their attributes or the functions they perform. In other words, they would like to locate a material or device that satisfies some current requirement (for strength, conductivity, corrosion resistance, or whatever) without being able to name it. This is not a condemnation of subject indexing per se but of the indexing policies adopted by the majority of database producers. If a new material or alloy described in a report is said to have a certain tensile strength, the property may be indexed (e.g., by assigning the term TENSILE STRENGTH) but the particular value of the property (i.e., the strength attainable) would not be indexed by most database producers, although it may well be mentioned in the abstract. Of course, there is no reason why values could not be indexed (e.g., the term TENSILE STRENGTH might be subdivided into twenty more specific terms, each one representing a range of tensile strength values) and they would be in certain databases, such as a company's indexes to its own contract files, indexes to data compilations, or certain patent databases. Some of Breton's objections, then, could be countered by indexing at a much higher level of specificity. Functions can also be indexed as long as the possible functions of a device are identified by an author, and appropriate terms exist in the vocabulary of the database, but it is altogether unreasonable to expect the indexer to be able to recognize applications not specifically claimed by the author.

It has become fashionable in recent years to view the information retrieval problem as primarily one of matching the "anomalous state of knowledge" of a requester with the more "coherent" state of knowledge of authors (see, for example, Belkin et al. [1982]), the implication being that the problems lie more with system output (searching) than with input. This is somewhat misleading. If one accepts that indexing is most effective when oriented toward the needs of a particular group of users, the indexer's role is to predict the types of requests for which a particular document is likely to be a useful response. This is probably more difficult than predicting what types of documents are likely to be useful responses to a particular request, which is in a sense what the searcher's function is. One could argue, then, that the "anomalous" state of knowledge applies more to the input side of the retrieval system than it does to the output. Olafsen and Vokac (1983) make the point clearly:

> The indexer has to make guesses at what questions the future user of the system will put. Regardless of how cleverly the guesswork is construed, they are still guesses, while the user approaches the system with his own concrete question, and his associations may be different from those of the indexer. (Page 294)

They too oversimplify in referring to user questions as "concrete" when, in fact, many will be far from it. Nevertheless, they are probably correct in implying that the problems of effective input to a retrieval system exceed the output problems. As Fairthorne (1958) pointed out many years ago: "Indexing is the basic problem as well as the costliest bottleneck of information retrieval."

In some indexing applications it may be possible to be rather more precise on what should be considered "indexable." In discussing the indexing of an encyclopedia, for example, Preschel (1981) offers the following guidelines:

> All text information of a substantive nature should be indexed. "Substantive" is here defined as information that covers 8-10 text lines or that is unique or outstanding and will almost certainly not occur elsewhere in the encyclopedia. (Page 2)*

In other situations it is not always possible to be so precise.

Translation

Translation, the second step in subject indexing, involves the conversion of the conceptual analysis of a document into a particular set of index terms. In this connection, a distinction can be made between indexing by extraction (derivative indexing) and indexing by assignment. In indexing by extraction, words or phrases actually occurring in a document are selected to represent its subject matter. For example, the item in Exhibit 3 might be indexed with the following terms:

PUBLIC OPINION
TELEPHONE SURVEYS
UNITED STATES
ATTITUDES
MIDDLE EAST
ISRAEL
EGYPT
AID
PEACE

all of which appear in the title or abstract. An early form of derivative indexing, known as Uniterm, used only single words to represent subject matter. If strictly observed, the Uniterm system brought some strange results, such as the splitting of Middle East into MIDDLE and EAST.

Assignment indexing involves assigning terms to a document from a source other than the document itself. The terms could be drawn from the indexer's head—e.g., an indexer might decide that the terms FOREIGN AID and FOREIGN RELATIONS, which do not appear explicitly in either abstract, might be good terms to use with the item in Exhibit 3.

More commonly, assignment indexing involves trying to represent the substance of the conceptual analysis by the use of terms drawn from some form of controlled vocabulary.

Controlled Vocabularies

A controlled vocabulary is basically an authority list. In general, an indexer can only assign to a document terms that appear on the list adopted

---

*This quotation, from an unpublished work, is reproduced by permission of Funk & Wagnalls.

by the agency for whom he works. Usually, however, the controlled
vocabulary is more than a mere list. It will generally incorporate some
form of semantic structure. In particular, this structure is designed to:

1. control synonyms by choosing one form as the standard and referring
   from all others;
2. distinguish among homographs. For example, TURKEY (COUNTRY) is a
   term quite distinct from TURKEY (BIRD); and
3. bring or link together those terms whose meanings are most closely related.
   Two types of relationships may be explicitly identified: the hierarchical
   and the nonhierarchical (or *associative*) relationship. For example, the
   term WORKING WOMEN is related hierarchically to WOMEN (as a species
   of this term) and to HOUSEWIVES (also a species of the term WOMEN),
   as well as being associated with such terms as EMPLOYMENT or SINGLE
   PARENT FAMILIES, which appear in quite different hierarchies.

Three major types of controlled vocabularies can be identified:
bibliographic classification schemes (such as the *Dewey Decimal
Classification*), lists of subject headings, and thesauri. All attempt to present
terms both alphabetically and "systematically." In the bibliographic
classifications, the alphabetical arrangement is secondary, in the form of
an index to the major arrangement, which is hierarchical. In the thesaurus,
the overt arrangement of terms is alphabetical but a covert hierarchical
structure is built into the alphabetical list through the use of cross-
references. The traditional list of subject headings is similar to the thesaurus
in that it is alphabetically based. It differs from the thesaurus because it
incorporates an imperfect hierarchical structure and fails to distinguish
clearly between the hierarchical and the associative relationship. All three
types of vocabulary control synonyms, distinguish among homographs, and
group related terms together, but they use somewhat different methods
to achieve these ends.

A more complete discussion of these matters can be found in the
author's *Vocabulary Control for Information Retrieval* (second edition,
Arlington, VA., Information Resources Press, 1986).

Indexing as Classification

In the literature of library and information science, a distinction is
sometimes made among the three terms *subject indexing, subject
cataloging,* and *classification. Subject cataloging* usually refers to the
assignment of subject headings to represent the overall contents of complete
bibliographic items (books, reports, periodicals, and so on) within the
catalog of a library. *Subject indexing* is a term used more loosely; it may
refer to the representation of the subject matter of parts of complete

bibliographic items as in the case of an index at the back of a book. Thus, a library may "catalog" a book under the subject heading DOGS to indicate its overall subject matter; the detailed contents of the book are only revealed by the back-of-the-book *subject index*. This distinction between the terms *subject cataloging* and *subject indexing*, one referring to complete bibliographic items and the other to parts of items, is artificial, misleading, and inconsistent. The process by which the subject matter of bibliographic items is represented in published databases—printed or machine-readable form—is almost invariably referred to as *subject indexing*, whether overall items or their parts are being discussed. Thus, the *subject index* to, say, *Chemical Abstracts* might refer to complete books or complete technical reports as well as referring to parts of bibliographic items (chapters in books, papers within conference proceedings, articles in periodicals). On the other hand, libraries may choose to represent parts of books (e.g., chapters or papers) within the catalog; this is usually referred to as *analytical cataloging*. When applied to subject matter, this activity would be *analytical subject cataloging*.

The situation is even more confusing when the term *classification* is considered. Librarians tend to use the word to refer to the assignment of class numbers (drawn from some classification scheme—e.g., Dewey Decimal [DDC], Universal Decimal [UDC], Library of Congress [LC]) to bibliographic items, especially for the purpose of arranging these items on the shelves of libraries, in filing cabinets, and so on. But the subject catalog of a library can be either alphabetically based (an *alphabetical subject catalog* or a *dictionary catalog*) or arranged according to the sequence of some classification scheme (a *classified catalog*). Suppose a librarian picks up a book and decides that it is about "birds." He might assign the subject heading BIRDS to this item. Alternatively, he might assign to it the class number 598.2. Many people would refer to the first operation as *subject cataloging* and to the second as *classification*, a completely nonsensical distinction. More confusion occurs when one realizes that *subject indexing* may involve the use of a classification scheme or that a printed subject index might follow the sequence of some classification scheme.

These terminological distinctions are quite meaningless and only serve to cause confusion. The fact is that *classification*, in the broadest sense, permeates all of the activities associated with information storage and retrieval. Part of the terminological confusion is caused by failure to distinguish between the *conceptual analysis* and the *translation* stages in indexing.

Suppose that an information specialist picks up some bibliographic item and decides that this item deals with the subject of "robots." The intellectual activity involved in the decision is the same whatever the item dealt with—book, part of book, periodical, article in a periodical, conference proceedings, conference paper, or whatever. The information specialist has *classified* the item—i.e., put it into the conceptual class of "items discussing robots."

As previously discussed, the process of *translation* involves the representation of the conceptual analysis by means of a term or terms drawn from some vocabulary. A term assigned to a bibliographic item is merely a *label* identifying a particular class of items. This label could be the English word *robots,* drawn from a thesaurus, a list of subject headings or from the document itself, an equivalent word in another language, or a label such as 629.892 drawn from some classification scheme.

The process of deciding what some item is about and of giving it a label to represent this decision is conceptually the same whether the label assigned is drawn from a classification scheme, a thesaurus, or a list of subject headings, whether the item is a complete bibliographic entity or a portion of it, whether the label is subsequently filed alphabetically or in some other sequence (or, in fact, not filed at all), and whether the object of the exercise is to organize items on shelves or records in catalogs, printed indexes, or machine-readable databases.

In the field of information storage and retrieval, document *classification* refers to the formation of classes of items on the basis of their subject matter. Thesauri, subject headings, and bibliographic classification schemes are primarily lists of the *labels* by which these classes are identified and, perhaps, arranged. The process of searching for information involves deciding which classes to consult in a printed index, card catalog, or machine-readable database. A search can involve the examination of a single class (e.g., everything appearing under the heading ROBOTS) or it can involve combinations of classes (e.g., items appearing under ROBOTS and also under ARTIFICIAL INTELLIGENCE). How much combination is possible, or how easily various classes can be combined, is very much dependent on the format of the tool used for searching, especially on whether it is in printed or electronic form.

In short, *subject indexing* is conceptually identical to *subject cataloging*. The activity involved is that of *subject classification*—i.e., forming classes of objects on the basis of their subject matter. In this text, the term *subject indexing* or even *indexing* is used as a matter of convenience to refer to all activities of subject classification.

Specificity of the Vocabulary

Exhibit 5 shows a conceptual analysis prepared for a journal article, and the translation of this conceptual analysis into three different types of vocabulary. The article deals with the use of robots in industry, specifically their use in manufacturing and materials handling applications. It also discusses the use of artificial intelligence techniques in the design and operation of robots, as well as the special problems involved in getting robots to move properly (i.e., problems of locomotion). In most respects, the conceptual analysis can be translated effectively into any one of the vocabularies. The only real problem presented is the idea of locomotion. None of the vocabularies seems to include a term appropriate to cover the movements of a mechanism, such as a robot. It could be argued, however, that the problems of robot locomotion are really the problems of human locomotion (i.e., one of designing robots that have as much flexibility of movement as humans do), and this idea can be expressed clearly in the Dewey Decimal Classification (DDC) and Library of Congress Subject Headings (LCSH). The INSPEC thesaurus appears to lack an appropriate term to cover the idea of locomotion.

It should be noted that the ideas conveyed by the conceptual analysis in Exhibit 5 are covered *collectively* by the groups of terms listed under the three vocabularies. For example, the five DDC class numbers, taken together, cover the subject matter of this article clearly and completely, although there is no one-to-one relationship between the individual elements of the conceptual analysis and the DDC terms. DDC lacks the specific term "industrial robots." Nevertheless, the combination 629.892 and 670.427 certainly conveys the idea of robots in manufacturing operations, just as 629.892 combined with 621.86 conveys the idea of robots as materials-handling devices; 629.892 with 006.3, the idea of artificial intelligence applied to robots; and 629.892 with 612.76, the idea of robot locomotion simulating human locomotion.

Putting aside the idea of locomotion, which does not appear in INSPEC, the conceptual analysis in Exhibit 5 is covered equally completely and specifically in each vocabulary when entire groups of terms are considered. At the single term level, of course, differences do exist. If only one term could be assigned to this article, LCSH and INSPEC would be better than DDC since they can distinguish industrial robots from robots in general.

This example illustrates two important points. First, the type of controlled vocabulary (classification scheme, subject headings, thesaurus) is not the most important factor affecting the translation stage of indexing. Much more important are the scope (coverage) and specificity of the vocabulary. In this indexing exercise, DDC and LCSH come out better than INSPEC which lacks a locomotion term. The second point illustrated is that, while specificity is a very important property of a controlled vocabulary, it can be achieved in different ways in different vocabularies. In particular, it is important to consider the properties of *combinations* of index terms rather than the properties of single terms.

Conceptual Analysis	Dewey Decimal Classification	Library of Congress Subject Headings	INSPEC Thesaurus
Industrial robots	629.892 Robots (automatons)	ROBOTS, INDUSTRIAL	INDUSTRIAL ROBOTS
Artificial intelligence	006.3 Artificial intelligence	ARTIFICIAL INTELLIGENCE	ARTIFICIAL INTELLIGENCE
Manufacturing operations	670.427 Mechanization and automation of factory operations	MANUFACTURING PROCESSES	MANUFACTURING PROCESSES
Materials handling	621.86 Materials handling equipment	MATERIALS HANDLING	MATERIALS HANDLING
Locomotion	612.76 Locomotion (human physiology)	HUMAN LOCOMOTION	

Exhibit 5
Conceptual analysis translated into
three controlled vocabularies

Consider, as an example, an article discussing mental health services. Vocabulary *A* contains the specific descriptor MENTAL HEALTH SERVICES, while Vocabulary *B* has the term HEALTH SERVICES but not the more specific term. Nevertheless, *B* also includes the term MENTAL HEALTH, so the idea of "mental health services" can be specifically covered by indexing under HEALTH SERVICES and MENTAL HEALTH. With regard to this topic, then, vocabulary *B* is as specific as *A*. Vocabularies *C* and *D* are less specific: *C* contains the term MENTAL HEALTH but has no health services term while *D* contains HEALTH SERVICES but lacks a mental health term, so neither one has the ability to express specifically the idea "mental health services." When it comes to searching the systems represented by the various vocabularies, it should be possible to achieve effective results in *A* and *B*, but it will be impossible to restrict the search in *C* and *D*—either everything on mental health or everything on health services will be retrieved.

3

Indexing Practice

An indexer rarely has the luxury of being able to read a document carefully
from cover to cover. The requirement that he index a certain number of
items per day will usually dictate that he must accept less than a complete
reading. A combination of reading and "skimming" is usually advocated.
The parts to be carefully read will be those likely to tell the most about
the contents in the shortest period of time: the title, abstract, summary
and conclusions. Section headings and captions to illustrations or tables
are also worth more attention. The rest of the text should be skimmed
to ensure that the more condensed parts give an accurate picture of what
the item is about. Nevertheless, the indexer should usually take into account
the entire document (parts read, parts skimmed) and the terms assigned
should reflect the whole. The exception would be the case in which only
part of the document (e.g., a lengthy multitopical item) is of interest to
the user group to be served.

Jones (1976), quoting Anderson (1971), points out that some parts
of a document are especially rewarding to an indexer: "Opening paragraphs
(in chapters or sections) and opening and closing sentences of paragraphs
seem to be particularly rich in indexable words." This agrees with the
findings of Baxendale (1958) in her work on the development of procedures
for the automatic indexing of documents.

The international standard on subject indexing (ISO 5963-1985 [E])
offers further guidance on the examination of the document:

> A complete reading is often impracticable, nor is it always necessary,
> but the indexer should ensure that no useful information has been
> overlooked. Important parts of the text need to be considered carefully,
> and particular attention should be paid to the following:
>
> a) the title;
> b) the abstract, if provided;
> c) the list of contents;
> d) the introduction, the opening phrases of chapters and paragraphs,
>   and the conclusion;
> e) illustrations, diagrams, tables and their captions;

f) words or groups of words which are underlined or printed
in an unusual typeface.

All these elements should be scanned and assessed by the indexer
during his study of the document. Indexing from the title alone is
not recommended, and an abstract, if available, should not be regarded
as a satisfactory substitute for an examination of the text. Titles may
be misleading; both titles and abstracts may be inadequate; in many
cases neither is a reliable source of the kind of information needed
by an indexer. (Page 2)*

In their comprehensive study of how indexers actually operate, Oliver
et al. (1966) discovered that the majority do follow a read/scan approach:

The largest group of indexers (about 85 percent of the total) stated
that they routinely examine the entire document. However, these
indexers stressed that certain sections of the document were examined
more carefully than others. These sections included the abstract,
introduction, summary, conclusion, methodology, findings, and charts
and graphs. If one or more of these "condensed" sections were
considered adequate by the indexer, he might lightly scan, or simply
"page through" other parts of the document. The major reasons given
for looking at the body of the document were to see if anything was
overlooked, to facilitate greater depth in indexing, and to clarify any
doubts or questions. (Page 4-14)

One assumption underlying all of this is that the item to be indexed
can be read. As the international standard (ISO 5963-1985 [E])) points
out, different procedures will apply to other types of item:

Non-print documents, such as audio-visual, visual and sound media,
including realia, call for different procedures. It is not always possible
in practice to examine a record in its entirety (for example by running
a film). Indexing is then usually carried out from a title and/or synopsis,
though the indexer should be allowed to view or hear a performance
of the medium if the written description is inadequate or appears to
be inaccurate. (Page 2)

The reason for examining the document, of course, is to decide what
to include in the indexing (in the terms of Preschel [1972], this is the
identification of the "indexable matter"). As suggested in Chapter 2, to
do this effectively the indexer must know a great deal about the interests
of the community served by the index. Within a particular organization,
indexers may be instructed to look for certain predefined elements in a
document; if these occur they must be covered in the indexing. Depending

*The excerpts from ISO 5963 appearing in this chapter are reproduced by permission
of the International Organization for Standardization.

on the type of organization, such essential elements might include: materials of construction, temperatures involved, age group involved, educational level, and so on. In some cases the more essential elements may be preprinted onto an indexing form to remind the indexer that the appropriate terms must be used if they apply to a particular document. For example, the National Library of Medicine uses "checktags" of this kind to account for age groups, gender, types of animals used in experiments, and so on.

This "conceptual analysis" stage of indexing should not be influenced by the characteristics of the vocabulary to be used in the translation stage. That is, the indexer must first decide what topics need to be represented; only later (momentarily perhaps) should he consider whether or not the vocabulary can represent these topics adequately. Put somewhat differently, an indexer should not ignore a topic because he knows or suspects that it cannot be expressed adequately. It is possible that a careful examination of the vocabulary may prove him wrong in this. Moreover, an important function of the indexer is to improve the controlled vocabulary by bringing its inadequacies to the attention of those responsible for its maintenance. This is unlikely to occur if the indexer is encouraged to "think" in the controlled terms. In this respect I am in complete disagreement with ISO 5963, which states that: "Both analysis and transcription should be performed with the aid of indexing tools such as thesauri and classification schemes." The transcription, to be sure, cannot be performed without such tools, but the analysis should be completely independent of them.

A related factor to bear in mind is that the terminology used by an author may not correspond exactly to the terms of the controlled vocabulary. Even though author terms and controlled terms coincide, the way they are used may differ. For example, an author may use the term EPIDEMIOLOGY in a rather loose way, but the vocabulary may define the term much more precisely and the assignment of the term, although used by the author, may be erroneous. It is the ideas dealt with by an author, rather than the words used, that must be indexed.

Exhaustivity of Indexing

Factors affecting the performance of an information retrieval system that are directly attributable to indexing can be categorized as follows:

1. Indexing policy.
2. Indexing accuracy
   Conceptual analysis
   Translation

Policy decisions are established by the managers of the information service, and are thus outside the control of the individual indexer; the accuracy factors are under the individual indexer's control.

The major policy decision is that relating to the exhaustivity of the indexing, which roughly corresponds to the number of terms assigned on the average. The effect of exhaustivity was illustrated earlier in Exhibit 3. Exhaustive indexing implies the use of enough terms to cover the subject matter of a document rather completely. Selective indexing, on the other hand, implies the use of a much smaller number of terms to cover only the central subject matter of a document. The more terms used to index a document the more accessible it becomes and, presumably, the more it will be retrieved. An information center will want to index exhaustively if its users frequently ask for comprehensive searches to be performed. A requester wanting to find all items dealing in any way with the PLO will expect to retrieve the item depicted in Exhibit 3, but this will be possible only if the indexing has been fairly exhaustive.

Policy decisions on exhaustivity should not take the form of absolute limits on the number of terms to be assigned. Rather, the policy might suggest a range of terms—e.g., "most items will be indexed with 8 to 15 terms." In a large information center, dealing with many different types of documents, the policy may vary with type of document. For example, the information center of a large company might establish a policy as follows:

Company's own technical reports	15-25 terms
Other technical reports	10-15 terms
Patents	15-20 terms
Journal articles	5-10 terms

and so on. Alternatively, the policy could be based on subject matter, the subjects of most interest to the company being indexed with most terms.

Although a database indexed exhaustively will tend to allow for comprehensive searches (high recall),* exhaustive indexing is likely to be more expensive than selective indexing. Moreover, exhaustive indexing will cause lower precision in searching. That is, more items will be retrieved that a requester judges not pertinent to his information need. This may occur for two reasons:

> 1. "False associations" will increase with the number of terms assigned. For example, the item in Exhibit 3 might be retrieved in a search on telephone surveys in Egypt, but it has nothing whatever to do with this topic.

---

*This has been demonstrated on numerous occasions, most recently by Boyce and McLain (1989).

2. The more terms used to index an item, the more it will be retrieved in response to search topics dealt with in only a very minor way. The item in Exhibit 3 is likely to be retrieved in a search for articles discussing political leaders of Arab states, but the person requesting such a search may decide that it contributes so little to this topic that it can hardly be considered useful.

The idea of "exhaustivity" can also apply to a retrieval system operating on the basis of searchable text (see Chapter 13). The title of the item in Exhibit 3 is not a very exhaustive representation of its subject matter. The exhaustivity increases with the number of words in the representation.

The term *depth* is frequently used to refer to the number of terms assigned to a document. That is, *depth* is used in place of *exhaustivity*. Both terms are imprecise and can be misleading. To better understand the effect of increasing the number of terms used to index a document, one may consider it as having two dimensions, as illustrated in Exhibit 6. Let us say that an indexer is able to identify ten related topics discussed in the item. One can regard this as the breadth of coverage of the document. If the indexer attempts to cover all of these topics, the indexing can be considered *exhaustive* (i.e., it is an exhaustive representation of the subject matter). The more topics covered the more exhaustive is the indexing. On the other hand, the fewer topics covered the more *selective* the indexing. Clearly, exhaustive indexing will require the use of more terms.

The second dimension of the document, from the indexing point of view, is referred to as *specificity* in Exhibit 6. That is, some of the topics identified could be indexed at more than one level of specificity. Suppose that the first topic is "architecture of cathedrals." This might be indexed under the term ECCLESIASTICAL ARCHITECTURE, which is not completely specific. To increase specificity the indexer might add a second term, CATHEDRALS. The joint use of the two terms precisely represents the topic of discussion. On the other hand, addition of DOMESTIC ARCHITECTURE would increase exhaustivity rather than specificity because it is introducing a new concept into the indexing.

In other words, the addition of further index terms might increase the exhaustivity of a representation or might increase its specificity. Therefore, while it is true to say that "exhaustivity" roughly corresponds to the number of terms assigned, no exact one-to-one relationship exists between exhaustivity and number of terms. In this book, *exhaustivity* refers to the breadth of coverage in indexing as illustrated in Exhibit 6. *Depth* is a less satisfactory term because it denotes the opposite of breadth and is more appropriately applied to the specificity dimension illustrated in Exhibit 6.

The number of terms assigned to a document is really a cost-effectiveness consideration. Generally speaking, the more exhaustive the indexing the greater the cost and there is little sense in indexing more exhaustively than warranted by the needs of the users of the service. (In actual fact, of course, this is an oversimplification. In dealing with a lengthy document, an indexer may need more time to cover the subject matter exhaustively. In other cases, it may be faster to use many terms rather than try to select fewer from a group in which the terms may be closely related or even overlap in meaning. In general, however, the more terms used the more expensive it will be to enter them into the database and process them subsequently. Moreover, increasing the number of terms will add substantially to the costs of indexes in card or printed form.) A high level of exhaustivity will be needed if many requests are made for really comprehensive searches. If comprehensive searches are the exception rather than the rule, a much lower level of exhaustivity will suffice.

Exhibit 7 demonstrates the law of diminishing returns as applied to indexing. For the hypothetical information service illustrated, the assignment of x terms on the average will satisfy about 80 percent of user needs. To raise this to 90-95 percent would require much greater exhaustivity in the indexing. Where point X lies on such a curve, and what x represents in number of terms, will depend very much on considerations that are system specific. The managers of an information service prepare guidelines on exhaustivity of indexing that derive from their knowlege of the needs of users. These tend to be based on intuition, although controlled experiments could be conducted in which samples of information needs are matched against a collection of documents indexed with varying numbers of terms.

Of course, the idea of an optimum level of exhaustivity applying to all items in a database is somewhat misleading since widely different optima would apply to different items depending on the requests actually made by system users (Maron, 1979). Optimum exhaustivity is entirely request dependent.

The number of terms assigned to a document is a critical factor in determining whether or not a particular item will be retrieved. But other related factors also come into play. Most obviously, one expects that the number of items retrieved will decline as more terms are combined in an *and* relationship in a search strategy. Clearly, the extent to which terms can be combined successfully in a search strategy is heavily dependent on the number of terms used in indexing. To take a trivial example, the combining of three terms ($A \cdot B \cdot C$) may retrieve a large number of items when an average of 20 terms per item is used in indexing but is unlikely to retrieve many from a database in which only 3 terms are assigned to each item on the average. The more selective the indexing the more it will be necessary to combine terms in an *or* relationship in order to improve recall. The interactions between exhaustivity of indexing and the characteristics of search strategies have been discussed by Sparck-Jones (1973).

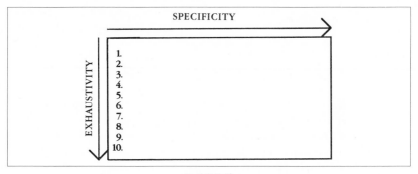

Exhibit 6
The two indexing dimensions of a document

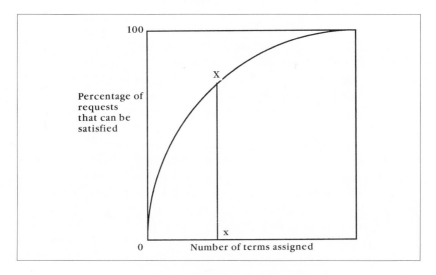

Exhibit 7
Diminishing returns in indexing

In a number of information services indexing may be performed for two somewhat different purposes: (1) to allow access to an item in a printed index, and (2) to allow access to that same item in a machine-readable database. In this situation the indexer may be required to index at some pre-established level of exhaustivity for the latter and to select a subset (perhaps 2-4) of the index terms thus assigned to provide access points in the printed index. The terms in the subset will be those the indexer considers to represent best the most important aspects of the item. This can be considered as a crude form of "weighted" indexing: a term can carry one of two weights—"major" (central subject matter for printed index) or "minor" (all other terms). Weighted indexing is discussed more fully in Chapter 11.

Principle of Specificity

The single most important principle of subject indexing, traceable back to Cutter (1876), is that a topic should be indexed under the most specific term that entirely covers it. Thus an article discussing the cultivation of oranges should be indexed under ORANGES rather than under CITRUS FRUITS or FRUIT.

In general, it is better to use several specific terms rather than a term that is more general. If an article describes the cultivation of lemons, limes, and grapefruit, it is better indexed under the three specific terms rather than the more general CITRUS FRUIT. The term CITRUS FRUIT should be used only for articles discussing citrus fruit in general and for those in which virtually all citrus fruit are discussed. This guideline could be extended to the situation in which several citrus fruit are discussed but not in enough detail (in the indexer's judgment) to warrant use of the specific terms. In some cases, too, the audience served by the indexer may be interested only in certain fruit. In this situation it would be legitimate to index these only and not to include terms for the others.

Some students of indexing make the mistake of indexing redundantly. Having indexed an article on oranges under the term ORANGES, they want also to assign CITRUS FRUIT and even FRUIT. This is quite unnecessary. Indeed, it is poor indexing practice. If the generic terms are assigned every time a specific term is used, it becomes difficult to distinguish general articles from specific ones. For example, the user who searches an index under the term FRUIT should expect to find items on fruit in general rather than items on individual fruit.

In the manual retrieval systems that were the predecessors of computer-based systems, it was in fact necessary to "post up" from specific to generic terms—e.g., the use of the term ORANGES in indexing an item caused CITRUS FRUIT, FRUIT, and even, perhaps, CROPS, to be assigned also. This was done to allow for generic searches. Were it not done, it would be virtually impossible to perform a complete search on, say, all fruit. If a computer-based system is properly designed, however, posting-up in this way should not be necessary, at least when a controlled vocabulary is in use. For example, it should be possible to ask the computer to search on the term FRUIT and everything below it in the hierarchical structure (all of the narrower terms [NTs] in the case of a thesaurus).

In general, then, one would not expect the terms CITRUS FRUIT and ORANGES to be applied to the same item. The only situation in which this combination is justified would involve an article dealing with citrus fruit in general but including a lengthy discussion on oranges, or one on citrus fruit that uses oranges as an example (e.g., the irrigation of citrus fruit with examples drawn from the irrigation of oranges).

The indexer must remember that specificity may be achieved through the use of combinations of terms. If no single term exists, an appropriate combination should be sought in the controlled vocabulary. Some hypothetical examples:

> Medieval French Literature
> indexed under MEDIEVAL LITERATURE and
> FRENCH LITERATURE
> Medical Libraries
> indexed under SCIENCE LIBRARIES and
> MEDICAL SCIENCES
> Canadian Literature
> indexed under LITERATURE and
> CANADA
> Groundnut Oils
> indexed under VEGETABLE OILS and
> GROUNDNUTS

Note that the indexer must look for the most appropriate combination in each case. In theory, Medieval French Literature could be expressed by MEDIEVAL LITERATURE and FRANCE, but the combination of MEDIEVAL LITERATURE and FRENCH LITERATURE expresses the idea more accurately. Likewise, MEDICAL SCIENCES is combined with SCIENCE LIBRARIES rather than LIBRARIES to express the idea of medical libraries, since medical libraries are clearly scientific, and GROUNDNUTS is combined with VEGETABLE OILS rather than OILS since groundnut oil is a vegetable oil.

Sometimes the controlled vocabulary will not include a term at the level of specificity demanded by a particular document. In such a case the indexer must use the most specific term available (e.g., CITRUS FRUIT rather than FRUIT for an article on oranges). He may also want to suggest, to the group maintaining the vocabulary, the need for more specific terms in this category.

Other Guidelines

The process of subject indexing seems to be unsusceptible to precise rules. Beyond the principle of specificity, no real rules for the assignment of terms have been developed, although many exist for what to do with index terms once they are assigned (e.g., establishing the sequence in which they are listed to form headings in a printed index). A number of "theories" of indexing have been put forward, and several have been reviewed by Borko (1977), but these tend not to be true theories and they offer little practical help for the indexer.

Fugmann (1979, 1985) has presented several axioms of "indexing and information supply" but not all of these are directly related to indexing per se. The only real indexing principle put forward, referred to as "mandatory indexing," states that an indexer is to use the most appropriate terms available to describe the subject matter discussed in a document. Since this will usually mean the most specific terms, this is essentially a restatement of the principle of specificity. Most of Fugmann's axioms are really factors affecting the performance of information retrieval systems rather than elements of indexing theory, although several have implications for indexing. For example, the axiom of definability relates to the ability to define an information need clearly and unambiguously. This can obviously be extended to the ability to define the subject matter of documents clearly and unambiguously. Fugmann's axiom of predictability states that the success of a search in a retrieval system depends largely on the predictability with which subject matter is described, which points to the importance of consistency in indexing. The axiom of fidelity states that another factor affecting performance is the ability to precisely and accurately describe subject matter (of information needs and, by extension, documents), which relates more to the vocabulary used to index than it does to indexing itself.

In fact, I have not been able to find any real theories applicable to the process of indexing although there are some theories (see, for example, Jonker [1964]) that relate to the characteristics of index terms. Furthermore, I believe that it is possible to identify only two fundamental rules of indexing, one related to the conceptual analysis stage and the other to the translation stage, as follows:

1. Include all the topics known to be of interest to the users of the information service that are treated substantively in the document.
2. Index each of these as specifically as the vocabulary of the system allows and the needs or interests of the users warrant.

Of course these rules are subject to interpretation. For example, what does "substantively" really mean? One possible guideline would be that topic *x* should be indexed if it is felt that the majority of users seeking information on *x* would find this item of interest. It is clear that "substantively" is not a property that can be expressed or measured in any precise way. Whether or not a particular topic is worth indexing will depend largely on three factors: (1) the amount of information given on the topic, (2) the degree of interest in the topic, and (3) how much information already exists on the topic: a single, brief mention of a compound may be worth indexing if the compound is known to be quite new; years later much more information would be needed to warrant inclusion.

The statement "needs or interests of the users" in the second rule implies that the principle of specificity can and should be modified when it is known that users of a particular system or tool would be better served by indexing a particular topic at a more general level under certain circumstances. For example, in a medical database, articles on veterinary medicine applied to dogs might be indexed under the names of the dog breeds involved. On the other hand, articles discussing the use of dogs in laboratory experiments might simply be indexed under DOGS even though the specific breed might be mentioned.

A corollary to the first rule mentioned above is that topics not discussed in the document should not be covered by the indexer. While this may seem self-evident and trite, it is not necessarily so. Some indexers, particularly those who consider themselves to be subject "experts," may be tempted to see things in a document that the author never intended (e.g., applications of a device beyond those claimed in the document). While it may be an important function of certain information specialists (e.g., those in industry) to bring potential applications to the attention of users of an information service, this is not really the function of the indexer per se. It is much better that he stick to the text and the author's claims. The *ERIC Processing Manual* (1980) gives some advice on this:

> Index the document in hand, not the document the writer *would like* to have written or *intends* to write the next time. Do not confuse speculation, or referrals to implications and possibilities, with real content. (Page VII-13)

"Results not claimed by the author," of course, should not be confused with negative results. It will usually be desirable to index the latter. For example, if a study shows that a particular material is not suitable for use in a certain application, the application mentioned should definitely be included in the indexing if other criteria (e.g., how much information is given) are met.

Post-Coordinate Indexes

The subject matter discussed in a document, and represented by index terms assigned to it, is multidimensional in character. Consider, for example, an article discussing labor migration from Mozambique to the mines of South Africa indexed under the following terms:

MOZAMBIQUE
SOUTH AFRICA
MIGRANT WORKERS
MINERS
ECONOMIC RELATIONS

Although the terms are given here in the form of a list, they actually represent a network of relationships:

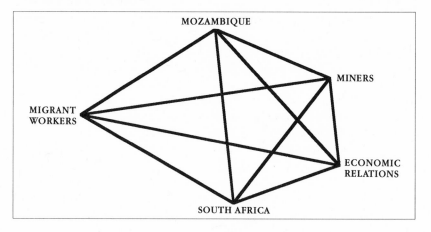

One should be able to retrieve this document in a search involving any single term or any combination of them: any two terms, any three, any four, or all five. An information retrieval system that allows a search to combine terms in any way is frequently referred to as *post-coordinate* (*post-combination* or *manipulative* are other terms that have been used).

Post-coordinate systems emerged in the 1940s, when they were implemented through the use of various types of cards. A modern computer-based system, operated online, can be considered to be a direct descendant of these manual systems. It can be thought of conceptually as a matrix as shown in Exhibit 8.

The files of an online system comprise two major elements:

1. A complete set of document representations: bibliographic reference usually accompanied by index terms or abstract or both.

2. A list of terms showing which documents have been indexed under them (sometimes referred to as an *inverted file* or a *postings file*). The documents are identified by accession numbers as shown in Exhibit 8.

TERMS (CLASSES)	DOCUMENTS														
	1	2	3	4	5	6	7	8	9	10	11	12	13	14	15
A	X									X					
B		X		X		X		X							X
C				X	X						X				
D						X					X				
E	X		X			X	X	X						X	X
F	X														
G		X	X			X						X			
H	X										X		X		
I												X			
J	X		X			X		X						X	X
K	X	X	X			X				X	X	X			
L		X				X		X				X			
M		X			X					X					X
N	X			X	X		X	X				X	X		
O		X	X			X	X								X
P	X			X	X			X	X	X			X		

Exhibit 8
Information retrieval system represented as a matrix

What happens in an online search can be demonstrated through reference to the matrix of Exhibit 8. Suppose the searcher enters the term MOZAMBIQUE at a terminal and that this is represented by *P* in the diagram. The system responds by indicating that seven items have been indexed under the term. The searcher enters MIGRANT WORKERS (*L* in the diagram) and is told that four items appear under this term. If the searcher now asks that *L* be combined with *P,* the system compares the document numbers on these two lists and indicates that three items satisfy the requirement.

When told to do so by the searcher, the computer finds these records by their identifying numbers (4, 8, 10) and displays them or prints them out.

This procedure remains the same no matter how many terms are involved and whatever the logical relationships specified by the searcher. If *F or G* is asked for, the system will indicate that five items satisfy the requirement. The searcher may then ask that this list of five items be combined with the list under *N*—i.e., *(F or G) and N*—resulting in the retrieval of three items.

Of post-coordinate systems it is possible to say that:

1. Terms can be combined in any way when a search is performed.
2. The multidimensionality of the relationships among terms is retained.
3. Every term assigned to a document has equal weight—one is no more important than another (although *weighted indexing,* as discussed in a later chapter, may be used).

These characteristics do not apply to pre-coordinate indexes, which are dealt with in the next chapter.

Indexing Aids

The indexer must have some way of recording the results of the indexing operation. Four possibilities exist:

1. recording on the document itself;
2. completing some kind of form printed on paper;
3. recording on an audiotape; or
4. completing a form displayed online.

In some organizations the indexer merely marks up the document at hand and a typist transcribes the indexer's markings. This mode would usually be appropriate only to situations in which a relatively simple approach to indexing is employed—e.g., the augmentation of titles coupled with the addition of a relatively small number of index terms or codes.

Until online systems became commonplace, it was usual for an indexer to enter terms into a printed form. Exhibit 9, for example, shows the latest version of a form used at the National Library of Medicine. Note the use of "checktags." These are terms potentially applicable to many documents in the database. It is efficient and economical to preprint these on the form so that the indexer need only check off those that are applicable. Not only does this save the indexer time, but it reminds him that these terms must be assigned when they apply to a particular document. Checktags are assigned more consistently than other terms used within MEDLARS (Lancaster, 1968; Funk and Reid, 1983).

① C	⑧ PAGINATION	⑨ LANGUAGE ENG. ___ ___ ___ .	ANONYMOUS A □	⑰ REFS	⑬ SUBJECT NAME

⑩ AUTHOR DATA

⑬ TITLE *(Eng or Transl)*

⑭ TITLE *(Vernac or Translit)*

⑲	⑳				⑫ .AUTHOR
A □ HIST ART	A □ PREGN	J □ CATS	V □ HUMAN	f □ 15th CENT	□ AFFIL
B □ HIST BIOG	B □ INF NEW (to 1 mo)	K □ CATTLE	W □ MALE	g □ 16th CENT	
C □ BIOG OBIT	C □ INF (1–23 mo)	L □ CHICK EMBRYO	X □ FEMALE	h □ 17th CENT	⑫ AUTHOR
G □ MONOGR	D □ CHILD PRE (2–5)	M □ DOGS	Y □ IN VITRO	i □ 18th CENT	□ ABST
H □ ENG ABST	E □ CHILD (6–12)	O □ GUINEA PIGS	Z □ CASE REPT	j □ 19th CENT	
	F □ ADOLESC (13–18)	P □ HAMSTERS	b □ COMP STUDY	k □ 20th CENT	⑭ NIH/PHS GRANT NO.
	G □ ADULT (19–44)	Q □ MICE	c □ ANCIENT	l □ NIH/PHS SUP	
	H □ MID AGE (45–64)	S □ RABBITS	d □ MEDIEVAL	m □ OTHER US GOVT SUP	
	I □ AGED (65 +)	T □ RATS	e □ MODERN	n □ NON-US GOVT SUP	
		U □ ANIMAL			

㉑	
1	
2	
3	
4	
5	
6	
7	
8	
9	
10	
11	
12	
13	
14	
15	
16	
17	
18	
19	
20	
21	
22	
23	
24	
25	
26	
27	
28	
29	
30	
31	

NIH–1416
Rev. 6–80   **INDEXED CITATION FORM**   GPO : 1985 O – 476-504

Exhibit 9
Index form as used by the National Library of Medicine in 1989

In some highly specialized indexing environments it might be possible to preprint the entire controlled vocabulary onto an indexing form, allowing all terms to become essentially checktags. The pioneer of this approach was probably Mooers. Exhibit 10 (from Brenner and Mooers [1958]) shows a typical Mooers indexing form. Note how the descriptors are grouped together systematically. In analyzing a document, the indexer essentially considers every descriptor in the schedule as potentially applicable. In effect, the indexer asks himself the questions posed by the indexing form itself. If, for example, the answer to "are there specific aerodynamic loads?" is "yes" (i.e., the document at hand discusses specific loads), the indexer must account for this by assigning the most appropriate aerodynamic load descriptor or descriptors. The descriptor list, presented in this way, simplifies the indexing process because it takes some of the intellectual burden from the indexer. The potential uses of a document of interest to the organization are represented by the list of "leading" questions which has been carefully compiled by senior scientific personnel. The indexer merely follows the leads given in Exhibit 10.

In the past the U.S. Patent and Trademark Office has developed small retrieval systems restricted to a single class, or limited number of classes, in the patent art. Specialized vocabularies have been devised for these areas, and they are small enough to be printed on a few sheets. Exhibit 11 illustrates part of such a vocabulary for the patent subclass dealing with general purpose digital computers. As with the Mooers descriptor schedules, the entire vocabulary can be easily scanned, preventing the indexer from overlooking an important term, and eliminating the need for entering terms on an indexing sheet. In this case, multiple copies of the term list are available, and a patent is indexed merely by circling the appropriate terms or their codes on a copy of the list. All subsequent processing is clerical. The "microthesaurus" of the Air Pollution Technical Information Center, as described by Tancredi and Nichols (1968), was also designed for use by circling of terms. A portion of the microthesaurus is illustrated in Exhibit 12.

Success has also been achieved in some organizations by having the indexer dictate terms into a tape recorder for future transcription by typists. This approach does have some problems associated with it. Many typing errors may occur when a large technical vocabulary, unfamiliar to the typist, is used, necessitating very careful editing. Some indexers do not work well in this mode because they have trouble remembering which terms they have already assigned to an item.

Increasingly, however, the producers of databases are converting to online indexing procedures. In this mode of operation various formatted displays are presented on the screen and the indexer enters data into the

What material was studied?	Is the process dynamic (rather than static)?	Are there specific aerodynamic loads?	Is structural strength and elasticity involved?
Metals	Vibrations	Lift	Stress and strain
Gases	Transient response	Drag	Plasticity
Plastics	Impact	Moment	Failure
Aluminum	Stability	Gust	Ultimate properties
Magnesium	Velocity	Pressure	Material properties
Titanium		Center of ap-	Aeroelasticity
Air		plication e.g.,	Flutter
		aerodynamic cen-	
		ter, center	
		of pressure,	
		etc.	
What is the type of fluid flow?	**Is it a stability and control problem?**	**Or is there another aerodynamics problem?**	**Is a thermal process involved?**
Fluid flow	Stability	Boundary layer	Thermodynamics
Internal	Control	Aeroelasticity	Thermodynamic constants
flow	Static	Flutter	Combustion
Subsonic	Dynamic trans. resp.	Downwash	Heat transfer
Transonic	Longitudinal	Stall and buffet	Cooling
Supersonic	Lateral	Interference	Convection
Hypersonic	Derivatives	Hydraulics	Conduction
Laminar	Damping	Trajectory	Thermal
Turbulence	Weight and balance	Droplets	Radiation
Slip flow	e.g., center of	Modifying	Aerodynamic heating
Compressi-	gravity, moments of	technique	
bility	inertia, etc.	Performance	
Viscosity			
Vortices			
Shock waves			
Finite span			

Exhibit 10
Typical Mooers indexing form
Reprinted from Brenner & Mooers (1958) by permission of Van Nostrand Reinhold

fields thus displayed. This mode of operation offers significant advantages over its predecessors: the indexer can be prompted in various ways, some indexer mistakes can be recognized by error detection programs and the indexer informed immediately, and the intermediate clerical step of converting the work of the indexer into machine-readable form is avoided. Moreover, it should also be possible for the indexer to switch from an input mode to a retrieval mode. Thus, precedence can be used to guide

```
                 SYSTEM ARCHITECTURE
228              .Plural processors with different
                  internal structures (28/0)
228.1            .Shared memory (28/1)
228.2            .Virtual processor/machine (28/2)
228.3            .Plural (redundant) central processors
                  (28/3)
228.4            .Central processor combined with
                  terminal processor (28/4)
228.5            .Central processor combined with
                  interface processor (28/5)
228.6            .Central processor combined with
                  coprocessor (28/6) *
228.7            .Multiple instruction multiple data
                  (MIMD) (28/7) *
228.8            ..Loosely coupled MIMD (28/8) *
228.9            ..Tightly coupled MIMD (28/9) *
229              .Multiprocessor interconnection (29/0)
229.1            ..Direct (29/1)
229.2            ..Parallel (common bus) (29/2)
229.3            ..Loop (29/3)
229.4            ..Reconfigurable (29/4)
229.41           ..Tree structure (29/A) *
229.5            ..Other specific multiprocessor
                  interconnection (29/5)
230              .Multiprocessor/Processor control (30/0)
230.1            ..Priority assignment (30/1)
230.2            ..Interrupt handling (30/2)
230.3            ..Task assignment (30/3)
230.4            ..Supervisory (master/slave) (30/4)
230.5            ..Other specific multiprocessor control
                  (30/5)
230.6            .Other specific multiprocessor system
                  (30/6)
231              .Mini/Micro/Personal computer (31/0)
231.1            ..Portable (31/1)
231.2            ...Hand-held/Carried on person (31/2)
231.3            ...Other portable computer (31/3)
231.31           ..Other specific mini/micro/personal
                  computer (31/A) *
231.4            .Timeshared (31/4)
231.5            ..Peripheral devices (31/5)
231.6            ..Plural programs (Multiprogrammed)
                  (31/6)
231.7            ..Other specific timeshare (31/7)
231.8            .Pipelined (31/8)
231.9            .Parallel array/Single Instruction
                  Multiple Data (SIMD) (31/9)
232              .Orthogonal (32/0)
232.1            .Virtual (32/1)
232.2            .Adaptive (32/2)
232.21           .Vector processor (32/A) *
232.22           .Data flow (32/B) *
```

Exhibit 11
Portion of a specialized vocabulary on digital computers
as used by the U.S. Patent and Trademark Office
Reproduced by permission of the U.S. Patent and Trademark Office

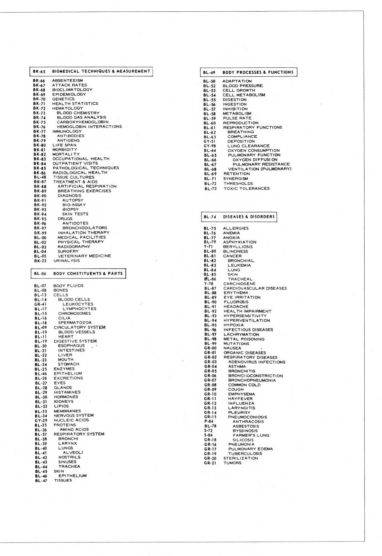

BK-65	BIOMEDICAL TECHNIQUES & MEASUREMENT
BK-66	ABSENTEEISM
BK-67	ATTACK RATES
BK-68	BIOCLIMATOLOGY
BK-69	EPIDEMIOLOGY
BK-70	GENETICS
BK-71	HEALTH STATISTICS
BK-72	HEMATOLOGY
BK-73	BLOOD CHEMISTRY
BK-74	BLOOD GAS ANALYSIS
BK-75	CARBOXYHEMOGLOBIN
BK-76	HEMOGLOBIN INTERACTIONS
BK-77	IMMUNOLOGY
BK-78	ANTIBODIES
BK-79	ANTIGENS
BK-80	LIFE SPAN
BK-81	MORBIDITY
BK-82	MORTALITY
BK-83	OCCUPATIONAL HEALTH
BK-84	OUTPATIENT VISITS
BK-85	PATHOLOGICAL TECHNIQUES
BK-86	RADIOLOGICAL HEALTH
BL-48	TISSUE CULTURES
BK-87	TREATMENT & AIDS
BK-88	ARTIFICIAL RESPIRATION
BK-89	BREATHING EXERCISES
BK-90	DIAGNOSIS
BK-91	AUTOPSY
BK-92	BIO-ASSAY
BK-93	BIOPSY
BK-94	SKIN TESTS
BK-95	DRUGS
BK-96	ANTIDOTES
BK-97	BRONCHODILATORS
BK-99	INHALATION THERAPY
BL-00	MEDICAL FACILITIES
BL-02	PHYSICAL THERAPY
BL-03	RADIOGRAPHY
BL-04	SURGERY
BL-05	VETERINARY MEDICINE
BK-22	URINALYSIS

BL-06	BODY CONSTITUENTS & PARTS
BL-07	BODY FLUIDS
BL-08	BONES
BL-13	CELLS
BL-14	BLOOD CELLS
GR-41	LEUKOCYTES
BL-17	LYMPHOCYTES
BL-15	CHROMOSOMES
BL-16	CILIA
BL-18	SPERMATOZOA
BL-09	CIRCULATORY SYSTEM
BL-10	BLOOD VESSELS
BL-11	HEART
BL-19	DIGESTIVE SYSTEM
BL-20	ESOPHAGUS
BL-21	INTESTINES
BL-22	LIVER
BL-23	MOUTH
BL-24	STOMACH
BL-25	ENZYMES
BL-46	EPITHELIUM
BL-26	EXCRETIONS
BL-27	EYES
BL-28	GLANDS
BL-29	HISTAMINES
BL-30	HORMONES
BL-31	KIDNEYS
BL-32	LIPIDS
BL-33	MEMBRANES
BL-34	NERVOUS SYSTEM
GY-29	NUCLEIC ACIDS
BL-35	PROTEINS
BL-36	AMINO ACIDS
BL-37	RESPIRATORY SYSTEM
BL-38	BRONCHI
BL-39	LARYNX
BL-40	LUNGS
BL-41	ALVEOLI
BL-42	NOSTRILS
BL-43	SINUSES
BL-44	TRACHEA
BL-45	SKIN
BL-46	EPITHELIUM
BL-47	TISSUES

BL-49	BODY PROCESSES & FUNCTIONS
BL-50	ADAPTATION
BL-52	BLOOD PRESSURE
BL-53	CELL GROWTH
BL-54	CELL METABOLISM
BL-55	DIGESTION
BL-56	INGESTION
BL-57	INHIBITION
BL-58	METABOLISM
BL-59	PULSE RATE
BL-60	REPRODUCTION
BL-61	RESPIRATORY FUNCTIONS
BL-62	BREATHING
BL-63	COMPLIANCE
GY-51	DEPOSITION
GY-98	LUNG CLEARANCE
BL-64	OXYGEN CONSUMPTION
BL-65	PULMONARY FUNCTION
BL-66	OXYGEN DIFFUSION
BL-67	PULMONARY RESISTANCE
BL-68	VENTILATION (PULMONARY)
BL-69	RETENTION
BL-71	SYNERGISM
BL-72	THRESHOLDS
BL-73	TOXIC TOLERANCES

BL-74	DISEASES & DISORDERS
BL-75	ALLERGIES
BL-76	ANEMIA
BL-77	ANOXIA
BL-79	ASPHYXIATION
Y-71	BERYLLIOSIS
BL-80	BLINDNESS
BL-81	CANCER
BL-82	BRONCHIAL
BL-83	LEUKEMIA
BL-84	LUNG
BL-85	SKIN
BL-86	TRACHEAL
Y-78	CARCINOGENS
BL-87	CARDIOVASCULAR DISEASES
BL-88	ERYTHEMA
BL-89	EYE IRRITATION
BL-90	FLUOROSIS
BL-91	HEADACHE
BL-92	HEALTH IMPAIRMENT
BL-93	HYPERSENSITIVITY
BL-94	HYPERVENTILATION
BL-95	HYPOXIA
BL-96	INFECTIOUS DISEASES
BL-97	LACHRYMATION
BL-98	METAL POISONING
BL-99	MUTATIONS
GR-00	NAUSEA
GR-01	ORGANIC DISEASES
GR-02	RESPIRATORY DISEASES
GR-03	ADENOVIRUS INFECTIONS
GR-04	ASTHMA
GR-05	BRONCHITIS
GR-06	BRONCHOCONSTRICTION
GR-07	BRONCHOPNEUMONIA
GR-08	COMMON COLD
GR-09	COUGH
GR-10	EMPHYSEMA
GR-11	HAYFEVER
GR-12	INFLUENZA
GR-13	LARYNGITIS
GR-14	PLEURISY
GR-15	PNEUMOCONIOSIS
P-84	ANTHRACOSIS
BL-78	ASBESTOSIS
S-72	BYSSINOSIS
S-84	FARMER'S LUNG
GR-18	SILICOSIS
GR-16	PNEUMONIA
GR-17	PULMONARY EDEMA
GR-19	TUBERCULOSIS
GR-20	STERILIZATION
GR-21	TUMORS

Exhibit 12
Section of microthesaurus of the Air Pollution Technical Information Center
From *American Documentation* (Tancredi & Nichols [1968])
Copyright © 1968 John Wiley & Sons, Inc.
Reprinted by permission of John Wiley & Sons Inc.

certain indexing decisions. That is, the indexer can switch into the database to find out how a particular term has been used in the past or how an earlier document, related to one at hand, was indexed.

Obviously, the controlled vocabulary used by an information service will be a tool of paramount importance to the indexer. It should be organized and displayed in such a way that it gives the indexer positive assistance in the selection of the terms most appropriate to use in a particular situation. While closely related to the subject of indexing, the construction and properties of controlled vocabularies are topics outside the scope of this book. They have been dealt with in detail elsewhere (Lancaster, 1986; Soergel, 1974).

A published thesaurus will usually incorporate a limited *entry vocabulary* in the form of *see, use,* or *see under* references. A large information center may also issue a separate entry vocabulary for in-house use by indexers, searchers, and lexicographers. Such a vocabulary may be available in several forms: card file, loose-leaf, machine-readable for printout or online display, or microfilm. A printed version of the National Library of Medicine (NLM) entry vocabulary was the Integrated Authority File; a specimen page is illustrated in Exhibit 13. The file included definitions or scope notes for descriptors (in upper case). For nondescriptors it presented indexing directions, and it might also give definitions. Foreign terminology was included along with English terms. Note that much of the mapping is one-to-many mapping. Bertielliasis, for instance, must be indexed by the term CESTODE INFECTIONS *and* BERTIELLA. The Integrated Authority File was replaced by NLM's *Medical Subject Headings— Annotated Alphabetic List.* This list shows how various concepts are to be indexed (e.g., microglioma under RETICULOENDOTHELIOSIS) but does not include scope notes (available to indexers in computer printouts but no longer published).

The entry vocabulary concept was carried further at NLM by the issuance of booklets of MEDLARS indexing instructions related to specific subject areas: steroids, pharmacy and pharmacology, respiration physiology, genetics, parasitology, and so on. These described each subject in simple terms, with appropriate illustrations, and discussed the problems involved in indexing in this subject field. Use of the most relevant terms from *Medical Subject Headings* was illustrated and a complete list of these with entry terms and definitions, where appropriate, might be included. Such a booklet was prepared by an indexer who was a subject specialist in the topic involved. These subject-specific indexing booklets are no longer produced by NLM, the only exception being the Tumor Key, which guides indexers to the correct *MeSH* term for various histological types of tumor and cancer.

BERTIELLA (B1)   1967
    genus under Cestoda; tapeworms found
    in primates and occasionally in
    domestic animals and man (MeSH
    definition)

bertielliasis
    Index CESTODE INFECTIONS (IM) (68)
          BERTIELLA (IM) (68)

    Bertolotti's syndrome
        (Ruhl & Sokoloff: A Thesaurus of
        Rheumatology)
        Index SCIATICA (IM) (68)
              SPINAL DISEASES (IM) (68)

BESNOITIASIS (C1,C15) 1968
    syn. globidiosis
    infection with protozoa of the genus
    Besnoitia (Globidium) (MeSH definition)

Bessau's nutrient
    an infant nutrient facilitating the
    growth of intestinal Lactobacillus
    bifidus flora (Gyermekgyogyaszat
    9:299 Oct-Nov 58)
    Index LACTOBACILLUS *growth &
          developement (IM) (68)
          INTESTINES *microbiology (IM) (68)

    beta-inhibitor
        a virus inhibitor which migrates
        electrophoretically with the fast
        gamma globulin or the slow-moving
        beta-globulins (Proc Soc Exp Biol Med
        126:176, Oct 67)
        Index VIRUSES (IM) (68)
              VIRUS INHIBITORS (Prov) (NIM)
                                      (68)

beta-radiography
    utilizes the effect of the emission of
    electrons in the absorption of x-rays
    to produce a charge pattern on an
    insulating plate placed in contact with
    a lead surface (Radiography, Lond 23:
    281, Oct 57)
    Index RADIOGRAPHY (68)

    Betz cells
        cerebral cortical neurons with efferent
        axons in the medullary pyramids
        (J Physiol 166:313, Apr 63)
        Index CEREBRAL CORTEX *cytology (IM)(68)
              NEURONS (IM) (68)

beutacultura (It)
    « submerged cultures »
    Index CULTURE MEDIA (68)

Bewegungsbestrahlung
    « moving-beam irradiation »

Bezold-Jarisch reflex
    respiratory arrest, bradycardia and
    lowering of blood pressure
    Index RESPIRATORY INSUFFICIENCY (IM)(68)
          BRADYCARDIA (IM) (68)
          BLOOD PRESSURE (IM) (68)

BF1 virus
    virus isolated from bovine feces which
    is cytopathogenic for tissue culture
    cells (C R Soc Biol (Par) 153:1653
    1959)
    Index VERTEBRATE VIRUSES (68)

BGA virus
    blue-green algae virus (J Bact 88:771,
    Sep 64)
    Index PLANT VIRUSES (IM) (68)
          ALGAE (NIM) (68)

bharal
    Index ARTIODACTYLA (68)

BHK cells
    cell cultures of hamster cells
    Index TISSUE CULTURE (68)

BICUSPID (A3) 1965
    (premolar) one of the eight teeth in
    man, four in each jaw, between the
    cuspids and the first molars; usually
    has two cusps; replaces the molars of
    the deciduous dentition (MeSH definition)

Biesalski-Mayer technic
    tendon transplant in peroneus
    muscle (Afrigue Fr Chir, Jun-Aug
    54)
    Index TENDONS *transplantation (68)

bigarrure (Fr)
    « mottled enamel »
    Index MOTTLED ENAMEL (68)

Exhibit 13
Specimen entries from a published entry vocabulary

Where a well-established published authority exists on the terminology of a particular branch of medicine, this is accepted by NLM and used as a kind of extension of the system entry vocabulary. Such publications include the *Manual of Tumor Nomenclature and Coding* published by the American Cancer Society, and the *Enzyme Nomenclature* issued by the International Union of Biochemistry.

Published reference works can be of great value to the indexer, most obviously in defining the meaning of unfamiliar terms. Specialized and general dictionaries and encyclopedias, and glossaries of all kinds, will be of particular importance. Bakewell (1987) has produced a list of reference tools of potential use to the indexer. An earlier report on indexing aids in general, by Korotkin et al. (1964), is now very much out of date. In some organizations the work of the indexer may be aided by online access to terminological data banks (*Terminological Data Banks,* 1980).

4

Pre-Coordinate Indexes

The Flexibility Associated with post-coordinate systems is lost when index terms must be printed out on paper or on conventional catalog cards. Printed indexes and card catalogs are *pre-coordinate*; they have the following characteristics:

1. The multidimensionality of the term relationships is difficult to depict.
2. Terms can only be listed in a particular sequence *(A, B, C, D, E)*, which implies that the first term is more important than the others.
3. It is not easy (if not completely impossible) to combine terms at the time a search is performed.

The crudest form of information retrieval system is probably the traditional card catalog as used in libraries. Consider the item mentioned earlier: a book on labor migration from Mozambique to the mines of South Africa. Suppose this were given three subject headings: MOZAMBIQUE, SOUTH AFRICA, and MIGRANT WORKERS. The bibliographic description of the book would appear under all three headings in an alphabetical subject catalog. This makes the book accessible under any one of these headings. However, it will be extremely difficult to perform a search on any *combination* of these terms. For example, a library user looking for books on political or economic relations between Mozambique and South Africa would need to look at all the entries under the heading MOZAMBIQUE or all those under the heading SOUTH AFRICA. Even if he did this, he would not necessarily be able to recognize the pertinent items. If looking under MOZAMBIQUE, he would only be likely to recognize a book as pertinent if it had the term "South Africa" in its title (and vice versa if looking under SOUTH AFRICA), or if the bottom of the catalog card showed the other headings assigned to the book (he would be unlikely to consult these anyway unless he were a very sophisticated catalog user). Another possibility would be to look under all the MOZAMBIQUE entries and all the SOUTH AFRICA entries to try to find titles appearing under both— a very tedious process if many entries are involved.

It is possible to improve this situation in card catalogs by using one heading as subheading (i.e., terms are *pre-coordinated* in an entry). Thus, one might find an entry as follows:

    Mozambique—Economic Relations

or even

    Mozambique—Economic Relations—South Africa

However, subheadings tend to be used rather sparingly in card catalogs and it would be an unusual catalog that put together a whole string* of terms as in the pre-coordinate entry:

    Mozambique, Economic Relations, South Africa, Migrant Workers, Miners

Detailed entries of this type are more likely to appear in printed indexes than they are in card catalogs. In this respect, printed indexes can be considered more effective retrieval tools than conventional card catalogs. In this case, a user could scan the entries under Mozambique to see if any also mention South Africa.

    But an entry such as that illustrated has one obvious problem associated with it: it provides access to the document only for someone searching under the term MOZAMBIQUE and would not allow access in a search relating to South Africa, miners, or migrant workers. To provide additional access points requires that more entries be created for the index.

    There is no way that a printed index can economically provide the level of access to a document provided by a post-coordinate retrieval system. As shown earlier, a post-coordinate system allows access through any *combination* of terms assigned to a document. The number of combinations is $2^n - 1$, where n represents the number of terms. Thus, for an item indexed under five terms, there are $2^5 - 1$ combinations—a total of 31. In theory, then, a printed index could provide for all combinations of 5 terms if it printed 31 entries. It would be economically impractical to create a printed index having so many entries for each item, and the number of entries will increase dramatically with the number of terms—there are 255 combinations of eight terms!

    Moreover, because terms must be printed out one after the other in an entry (i.e., in a linear sequence), printed indexes are governed by *permutation* rather than *combination*. For example, the sequence MOZAMBIQUE, SOUTH AFRICA is not the same as SOUTH AFRICA, MOZAMBIQUE. The number of permutations is *n factorial* where *n* is the number of terms. For example, the number of permutations of eight terms is 40,320 ($8 \times 7 \times 6 \times 5 \times 4 \times 3 \times 2 \times 1$).

---

*Consequently, indexing of this type is sometimes referred to as string indexing (Craven, 1986).

The situation is not quite as dismal for printed indexes as this discussion implies. Various computer programs have been developed for taking a string of terms and generating a set of index entries automatically. One such procedure is known as SLIC (Selective Listing in Combination). The program, devised by Sharp (1966), first arranges the string of terms in alphabetical order. This string (see Exhibit 14) becomes the first index entry. The program then generates all further entries deemed necessary following two simple rules:

1. Terms are always listed in alphabetical order.
2. Redundant sequences are eliminated (e.g., the entry, MIGRANT WORKERS, MINERS, is not needed if, MIGRANT WORKERS, MINERS, SOUTH AFRICA, is already there).

When this rule is followed, the number of entries is reduced from $2^n - 1$ to 2^{n-1}

Economic relations, Migrant workers, Miners, Mozambique, South Africa
Economic relations, Migrant workers, Miners, South Africa
Economic relations, Migrant workers, Mozambique, South Africa
Economic relations, Migrant workers, South Africa
Economic relations, Miners, Mozambique, South Africa
Economic relations, Miners, South Africa
Economic relations, Mozambique, South Africa
Economic relations, South Africa
Migrant workers, Miners, Mozambique, South Africa
Migrant workers, Miners, South Africa
Migrant workers, Mozambique, South Africa
Migrant workers, South Africa
Miners, Mozambique, South Africa
Miners, South Africa
South Africa

Exhibit 14
Entries for a SLIC index

The SLIC method is ingenious in that it allows for all useful juxtapositions of terms, at least as long as the terms are kept in alphabetical order. It also has disadvantages: it still generates a rather large number of entries; to use the index effectively a searcher must mentally rearrange his search terms in alphabetical order (e.g., he can find MIGRANT WORKERS, MOZAMBIQUE but not MOZAMBIQUE, MIGRANT WORKERS); it loses context for terms appearing near the end of the alphabet (e.g., someone looking at all entries under South Africa would have no idea what this item is about).

Other indexes are based on a set of entries arrived at systematically by cycling, rotation, or shunting. In *cycling,* each term in a string is moved to the leftmost position to become an entry point, the remaining terms being listed after it:

ABCDE
BCDEA
CDEAB
DEABC
EABCD

Note that the entry term is followed first by those terms that followed it in the original string and then by the terms that originally preceded it. In a cycled index, the sequence of terms in a string need not be in any obvious order, although they are frequently arranged alphabetically and could be arranged "systematically" (as discussed later).

Rotation is essentially the same as cycling except that the entry term is highlighted in some way (e.g., italicized or underlined) rather than being moved to the leftmost position:

*A*BCDE
A*B*CDE
AB*C*DE
ABC*D*E
ABCD*E*

Cycling and rotation both provide some "context" for a term, but the relationships among some of the terms may still be obscure or ambiguous. An index based on *shunting* uses a two-line display in an attempt to reduce ambiguity (i.e., be more precise in depicting how one term relates to another), as in the examples:

A   B.A
  B.C.D   C.D

The prime example of this, PRECIS, is referred to later.*

A simple method of producing a printed index, based on alphabetical order and the systematic "cycling" of terms to the entry position, as used

*The terminology relating to pre-coordinate indexes is not really standardized. For example, Craven (1986) seems to make no distinction between cycling and rotation.

in *Excerpta Medica* publications, is illustrated in Exhibit 15. Again, the first entry is derived by putting all terms in alphabetical order. The additional entries are derived by moving each term, in turn, to the entry position and listing the other terms after it (always in alphabetical order) as a string of modifiers. While this does not provide for every possible juxtaposition of terms, it does offer some obvious advantages over SLIC: it is more economical (no more entries than the number of terms assigned) and every entry has full "context." With this type of printed index it is possible to recognize two types of terms: those that generate index entries and those that do not. Terms that are not to generate entries are marked in some way by the indexer. Such terms are used as modifiers only. They appear at the end of the string of terms and can be recognized by being out of alphabetical sequence and perhaps being printed in a different typeface (see the "bibliography" example in Exhibit 15).

Economic relations, Migrant workers, Miners, Mozambique, South Africa
Migrant workers, Economic relations, Miners, Mozambique, South Africa
Miners, Economic relations, Migrant workers, Mozambique, South Africa
Mozambique, Economic relations, Migrant workers, Miners, South Africa
South Africa, Economic relations, Migrant workers, Miners, Mozambique

Economic relations, Migrant workers, Miners, Mozambique, South Africa,
Bibliography

Exhibit 15
Entries for an index based on systematic cycling (*Excerpta Medica* model)

The indexes illustrated in Exhibits 14 and 15 assume the use of index terms rather than free text, although in principle they could be produced by computer after programs have been used to extract "significant" phrases from narrative text. Some even simpler approaches to the production of printed indexes have been devised to operate on text and especially on words appearing in the titles of publications. The approaches most commonly used are KWIC (keyword in context), KWOC (keyword out of context), and variations on these.

The KWIC index (Luhn, 1959) is a rotated index most commonly derived from the titles of publications. Each keyword appearing in a title becomes an entry point and is highlighted in some way, usually by being set off at the center of a page as in the example of Exhibit 16. The remaining words in the title are "wrapped around" the keyword. The KWIC index is the simplest approach to the production of printed indexes by computer yet it has some power since each keyword can be viewed in its "context." For example (see Exhibit 16), one can scan down the "crystals" entries to find any that seem to deal with elastic or plastic properties. KWIC indexes normally refer only to some form of document number; it is necessary to look up the number to get full bibliographic details on the item represented.

```
LE TECHNIQUE FOR THE STUDY OF THE ELASTICITY OF CRYSTALS.                                          A SIMP
                  STRUCTURAL IMPERFECTIONS IN QUARTZ CRYSTALS.
             LINEAR COMPRESSIBILITY OF FOURTEEN NATURAL CRYSTALS.
THE LINEAR COMPRESSIBILITY OF THIRTEEN NATURAL CRYSTALS.
                         TRANSLATION GLIDING IN CRYSTALS.
                                         TWINNED CRYSTALS.
                     BENDING CREEP OF ICE SINGLE CRYSTALS.
DIRECT MEASUREMENTS OF THE SURFACE ENERGY OF CRYSTALS.
            THE GROWTH AND DEFORMATION OF ICE CRYSTALS.
RELIMINARY EXPERIMENTS ON THE PLASTICITY OF ICE CRYSTALS.                                      RESULTS OF P
               PROPAGATION OF CLEAVAGE CRACKS IN CRYSTALS.
S. IN DISLOCATIONS AND MECHANICAL PROPERTIES OF CRYSTALS.      THE DIRECT OBSERVATION OF DISLOCATION PAT
AL GRAINS. PETROFABRIC AND INTERFACE STRUCTURE. CRYSTALS.       THE ELASTIC CONSTANTS OF ROCKS IN TERMS O
    DISLOCATIONS AND MECHANICAL PROPERTIES OF CRYSTALS.  TEXTBOOK.
                          DISLOCATIONS IN CRYSTALS. TEXTBOOK.
                  PHYSICAL PROPERTIES OF CRYSTALS.TEXTBOOK.
                          STRENGTH OF CRYSTALS.TEXTBOOK.IN GERMAN.
                         PLASTICITY OF CRYSTALS.TEXTBOOK.
         IMPERFECTIONS IN NEARLY PERFECT CRYSTALS.TEXTBOOK.
         DISLOCATION AND PLASTIC FLOW IN CRYSTALS.TEXTBOOK.
```

(Exhibit continues — KWIC index sample)

Exhibit 16

Sample entries from a KWIC index
Reprinted from the *KWIC Index of Rock Mechanics Literature* by permission of the American Institute of Mining, Metallurgical and Petroleum Engineers, Inc.

Note that the computer program that produces the index identifies keywords through a "reverse" procedure: it recognizes the words that are not keywords (those appearing on a "stop list") and avoids using these as entry points. The stop list contains words that serve a syntactic function (articles, prepositions, conjunctions, and so on) but do not in themselves indicate subject matter. The KWIC index is an inexpensive approach to providing some level of subject access to the contents of a collection. It is useful to the extent that titles are good indicators of content (so it is likely to work better for some subjects or types of materials than for others), although in principle there is no reason why KWIC indexes should not be derived from other text—e.g., sentences from abstracts or even strings of subject headings. Many studies of the value of titles in retrieval have been performed (see Hodges [1983] for a recent example).

The KWOC index is similar to KWIC with the exception that the keywords that become access points are repeated out of context, usually by setting them off in the left hand margin of the page (see Exhibit 17) or using them as though they were subject headings (see Exhibit 18). Sometimes a distinction is made between KWOC indexes and KWAC (keyword and context) indexes. Those who make this distinction would call the indexes illustrated in Exhibits 17 and 18 KWAC indexes. A KWOC index would then be one in which the keyword used as an entry point is not repeated in the title but is replaced by an asterisk (*) or some other symbol. One can find very little justification for this strange practice (using some symbol to replace the keyword) so the distinction between KWOC and KWAC is not a very useful one. Several variations on KWIC/KWOC exist, including Double-KWIC (Petrarca & Lay, 1969).

Related to the KWIC/KWOC family are "permuted term" indexes, best exemplified by the Permuterm index associated with the citation indexes produced by the Institute for Scientific Information. In Permuterm each keyword in a title is associated, one at a time, with each other keyword occurring in that title, as in the following example:

CRYSTALS
ALUMINUM	20071
ANALYSIS	18024
BALANCE	17853
COBALT	00409
DISLOCATIONS	04778
FERRITE	04778
GROWTH	20071
HEXAGONAL	30714

With such an index it is easily possible to correlate keywords in a search—for example, to look down the "crystals" column to see if any title seems to deal with cobalt crystals. Note that all keywords in a title are exhibited in pairwise associations (for instance the common document number, 04778, indicates that "crystals," "dislocations," and "ferrite" all occur in the same title) and that each keyword becomes an entry point in the index: "aluminum" will be an entry point, as will "analysis," "balance," and so on.

Somewhat related to the KWIC/KWOC/permuted group of indexes is the "articulated subject index" exemplified by the subject index to *Chemical Abstracts*. In this type of index a brief narrative description of a document is used to generate entries. This could be a statement written by an indexer or, instead, a title or sentence extracted from the text. Certain words or phrases appearing in this statement are selected as entry points in the index, the remainder of the statement being retained as a modifier to provide the necessary context.

Armstrong and Keen (1982) describe the process of constructing entries for an articulated index as follows:

> Input terms are re-arranged such that each is linked to its original neighbour by a function word or by special punctuation so that the sentence-like structure remains although often re-ordered. (Page 6)

The following simple examples, from Armstrong and Keen, illustrate the principle:

> Indexing of Chemical Periodicals by Researchers
> Chemical Periodicals, Indexing of, by Researchers
> Periodicals, Chemical, Indexing of, by Researchers

Note that the syntax of the original text is retained so that the meaning of the original statement is not obscured. Index statements such as these can be prepared by an indexer following a prescribed set of rules, or computer programs can be written to generate entries of this type (Armitage & Lynch, 1968; Lynch & Petrie, 1973).

One example of the articulated subject index, and in fact the one described in detail by Armstrong and Keen (1982), is NEPHIS (Nested Phrase Indexing System), a system devised by Craven (1977). In the simplest form of NEPHIS, the indexer uses angular brackets to indicate a phrase "nested within" a larger phrase and thus to be used to generate index entries. For example the phrase

> Research Productivity of < **Sleep Researchers**>

will generate the two entries:

> Research Productivity of Sleep Researchers
> Sleep Researchers, Research Productivity of

```
NONEQUILIBRIUM    SCALE EFFECTS FOR NONEQUILIBRIUM CONVECTIVE HE
                  AT TRANSFER WITH SIMULTANEOUS GAS PHASE AND SU
                  RFACE CHEMICAL REACTIONS. APPLICATION TO HYPER
                  SONIC FLIGHT AT HIGH ALTITUDES
                              AD-291 032(K)   $1.60 0025
NONLINEAR         APPLICATION OF VARIATIONAL EQUATION OF MOTION
                  TO THE NONLINEAR VIBRATION ANALYSIS OF HOMOGEN
                  EOUS AND LAYERED PLATES AND SHELLS
                              AD-289 868(K)   $2.60 0667
NONLINEAR         EXTENSIONS IN THE SYNTHESIS OF TIME OPTIMAL OR
                  BANG-BANG NONLINEAR CONTROL SYSTEMS. PART I.
                  THE SYNTHESIS OF QUASI-STATIONARY OPTIMUM NONL
                  INEAR CONTROL SYSTEMS
                              PB 162 547(K)   $4.60 0235
NONLINEAR         EXTENSIONS IN THE SYNTHESIS OF TIME OPTIMAL OR
                  BANG-BANG NONLINEAR CONTROL SYSTEMS. PART I.
                  THE SYNTHESIS OF QUASI-STATIONARY OPTIMUM NONL
                  INEAR CONTROL SYSTEMS
                              PB 162 547(K)   $4.60 0235
NONLINEAR         NONLINEAR FLEXURAL VIBRATIONS OF SANDWICH PLAT
                  ES          AD-289 871(K)   $2.60 0669
NONLINEAR         OPTIMUM NONLINEAR CONTROL FOR ARBITRARY DISTUR
                  BANCES      NASA N62-15890(K)   $2.60 0682
NONRECURRENT      A TECHNIQUE FOR NARROW-BAND TELEMETRY OF NONRE
                  CURRENT PULSES   AD-290 697(K)   $2.60 0577
NONUNIFORM        ELECTROMAGNETIC SCATTERING FROM A SPHERICAL NO
                  NUNIFORM MEDIUM. PART II. THE RADAR CROSS SECT
                  ION OF A FLARE   AD-289 615(K)   $2.60 0747
NONUNIFORM        ELECTROMAGNETIC SCATTERING FROM ASPHERICAL NON
                  UNIFORM MEDIUM. PART I. GENERAL THEORY
                              AD-289 614(K)   $2.60 0748
NORMAL            PROBABILITY INTEGRALS OF MULTIVARIATE NORMAL A
                  ND MULTIVARIATE-T   AD-290 746(K)   $8.60 0760
NORMAL            RESONANCE ABSORPTION OF GAMMA-RAYS IN NORMAL A
                  ND SUPERCONDUCTING TIN
                              AD-289 844(K)   $3.60 0826
NORMS             NORMS FOR ARTIFICIAL LIGHTING
                              AD-290 555(K)   $1.10 0734
NORTH             FACTORS INFLUENCING VASCULAR PLANT ZONATION IN
                  NORTH CAROLINA SALTMARSHES
                              AD-290 938(K)   $7.60 0603
NORTH             SONAR STUDIES OF THE DEEP SCATTERING LAYER IN
                  THE NORTH PACIFIC   PB 162 427(K)   $2.60 0587
NORTH             THE DEVELOPMENT OF RESCUE AND SURVIVAL TECHNIQ
                  UES IN THE NORTH AMERICAN ARCTIC
                              PB 162 410(K)   $12.00 0085
NOSE              THE FLORA OF HEALTHY DOGS. I. BACTERIA AND FUN
                  GI OF THE NOSE, THROAT, AND LOWER INTESTINE
                              LF-2(K)   $2.60 0458
NOZZLE            FABRICATION OF PYROLYTIC GRAPHITE ROCKET NOZZL
                  E COMPONENTS   PB 162 371(K)   $1.10 0351
NOZZLE            FABRICATION OF PYROLYTIC GRAPHITE ROCKET NOZZL
                  E COMPONENTS   PB 162 370(K)   $1.10 0353
NOZZLE            FABRICATION OF PYROLYTIC GRAPHITE ROCKET NOZZL
                  E COMPONENTS   PB 162 372(K)   $2.60 0352
NOZZLE            THIRD SYMPOSIUM ON ADVANCED PROPULSION CONCEPT
                  S SPONSORED BY UNITED STATES AIR FORCE OFFICE
                  OF SCIENTIFIC RESEARCH AND THE GENERAL ELECTRI
                  C COMPANY FLIGHT PROPULSION DIVISION CINCINNAT
                  I, OHIO OCTOBER 2-4, 1962. PLASMA FLOW IN A MA
                  GNETIC ARC NOZZLE   AD-290 082(K)   $2.60 0147
NOZZLES           HEAT TRANSFER AND PARTICLE TRAJECTORIES IN SOL
                  ID-ROCKET NOZZLES   AD-289 681(K)   $5.60 0030
```

Exhibit 17

Example of KWOC index

Reprinted from *U.S. Government Technical Reports,* volume 1, 1963, by permission of
the National Technical Information Service

```
GLYCIDE

     MATERNAL GLYCIDE NORMAL ASSIMILATION, TOMATO BABY, PRECEDENTS
     OF MACROSOMIA AND FETAL MORTALITY. • B SALVADORI,
     G CAGNAZZO, A DELEONARDIS • MINERVA PEDIAT V12 P117,
     11 FEB 60 IT

GLYCINE

     AN INSULIN ASSAY BASED ON THE INCORPORATION OF LABELLED
     GLYCINE INTO PROTEIN OF ISOLATED RAT DIAPHRAGM. •
     K L MANCHESTER, P J RANDLE, F G YOUNG • J ENDOCR V19 P259-62,
     DEC 59

     MAINTENANCE OF CARBOHYDRATE STORES DURING STRESS OF COLD AND
     FATIGUE IN RATS PREFED DIETS CONTAINING ADDED GLYCINE. •
     W R TODD, M ALLEN • USAF ARCTIC AEROMED LAB TECHN REP V57-34
     P1-16, JUNE 60

GLYCINE C14

     RATE OF ASSOCIATION OF S35 AND C14 IN PLASMA PROTEIN FRACTIONS
     AFTER ADMINISTRATION OF NA2S3504, GLYCINE-C14, OR GLUCOSE C14.
     • J E RICHMOND • J BIOL CHEM V234 P2713-6, OCT 59

GLYCOGEN

     GLYCOGEN OF THE ADRENAL CORTEX AND MEDULLA. INFLUENCE OF AGE
     AND SEX. • H PLANEL, A GUILHEM • C R SOC BIOL PAR V153 P844-8,
     1959 FR

     EFFECT OF DIET ON THE BLOOD SUGAR AND LIVER GLYCOGEN LEVEL OF
     NORMAL AND ADRENALECTOMIZED MICE. • B P BLOCK, G S COX •
     NATURE LOND V184 SUPPL 10 P721-2, 29 AUG 59

     LIVER GLYCOGEN AND BLOOD SUGAR LEVELS IN ADRENAL-DEMEDULLATED
     AND ADRENALECTOMIZED RATS AFTER A SINGLE DOSE OF GROWTH
     HORMONE. • C A DE GROOT • ACTA PHYSIOL PHARMACOL NEERL V9
     P107-20, MAY 60

     A MICROMETHOD FOR SIMULTANEOUS DETERMINATION OF GLUCOSE AND
     KETONE BODIES IN BLOOD AND GLYCOGEN AND KETONE BODIES IN
     LIVER. • O HANSEN • SCAND J CLIN LAB INVEST V12 P18-24, 1960

     AN INVERSE RELATION BETWEEN THE LIVER GLYCOGEN AND THE BLOOD
     GLUCOSE IN THE RAT ADAPTED TO A FAT DIET. • P A MAYES • NATURE
     LOND V187 P325-6, 23 JULY 60

     LIVER GLUCOSYL OLIGOSACCHARIDES AND GLYCOGEN CARBON-14
     DIOXIDE EXPERIMENTS WITH HYDROCORTISONE. • H G SIE,
     J ASHMORE, R MAHLER, M H FISHMAN • NATURE LOND V184 P1380-1,
     31 OCT 59

     STUDIES ON GLYCOGEN BIOSYNTHESIS IN GUINEA PIG CORNEA BY
     MEANS OF GLUCOSE LABELED WITH C14. • R PHAUS,
     J OBENBERGER, J VOTOCKOVA • CESK FYSIOL V9 P45-6, JAN 60 CZ

     GLYCOGEN CONTENT AND CARBOHYDRATE METABOLISM OF THE LEUKOCYTES
     IN DIABETES MELLITUS. • G MAEHR • WIEN Z INN MED V40 P330-4,
     SEPT 59 GER

     GLYCOGEN LIVER. AN IATROGENIC ACUTE ABDOMINAL DISORDER IN
     DIABETES MELLITUS. • A SCHOTTE, H K LANKAMP, M FRENKEL •
     NED T GENEESK V103 P2258-62, 7 NOV 59 DUT

     ACUTE GLYCOGEN INFILTRATION OF THE LIVER IN DIABETES MELLITUS.
     2.  THE EFFECTS OF GLUCAGON THERAPY. • A SCHOTTE, H K LANKAMP,
     M FRENKEL • NED T GENEESK V104 P1288-91, 2 JULY 60 DUT
```

Exhibit 18

Alternative format for a KWOC index as used in the *Diabetes-Related Literature Index,*
a supplement to *Diabetes,* volume 12, 1960. Copyright © 1960 by the American Diabetes
Association. Reprinted with permission

Craven builds upon this simple principle by the addition of further symbols and conventions to be used by the indexer to create index entries that are consistent and unambiguous as well as useful. The report by Armstrong and Keen (1982) gives one an appreciation of the capabilities of this relatively simple approach to indexing. Quite similar to NEPHIS is the PASI (Pragmatic Approach to Subject Indexing) system described by Dutta and Sinha (1984).

One other indexing system is worth brief mention. SPINDEX (Selective Permutation Index), which was designed for the indexing of collections of archives, was originally no more than a KWAC or KWOC index (Burke, 1967). In later versions, it was modified to produce two-level index entries consisting of main and qualifying keywords as in the examples ARIZONA, Indian affairs and INDIAN AFFAIRS, Arizona (Cook, 1980). Unfortunately, the *Environmental Periodicals Bibliography* uses the SPINDEX acronym to stand for Subject Profile Index. The American Bibliographical Center uses the same methods in indexing *Historical Abstracts* and *America: History and Life*. This approach is now referred to as ABC-SPINDEX (American Bibliographical Center's Subject Profile Index) to distinguish it from the quite unrelated SPINDEX (Falk & Baser, 1980). It seems virtually identical with the cycled indexes used by *Excerpta Medica* (Falk & Baser, 1980).

Classification in Subject Indexes

All of the indexes discussed so far use approaches that are "alphabetical" rather than "systematic." Other types of indexes require that entries be constructed according to "logical" principles. Such approaches can be traced back to Cutter (1876) who presented rules on such matters as direct versus inverted entry (Ancient History or History, Ancient?). A more sophisticated approach was introduced by Kaiser (1911), who recognized three categories of terms: concretes, processes, and locality terms. "Concretes" are terms that relate to "things," real or imaginary, while "processes" covers activities. Kaiser required that indexing "statements" should arrange terms in a systematic sequence rather than alphabetically. Only three sequences were permitted:

1. Concrete—Process (as in Tubes—Welding or Steel Tubes—Welding)
2. Locality—Process (as in Argentina—Trade)
3. Concrete—Locality—Process (as in Coffee—Brazil—Export)

In order to follow Kaiser's rules, the indexer might have to supply an implicit concrete term. For example, the term *desalination* would become Water—Desalination.

The next major development is attributable to Ranganathan. Although Ranganathan's name is primarily associated with theories of classification and with his own bibliographic classification scheme, the *Colon Classification,* he has also made a significant contribution to modern practice in alphabetical subject indexing. His *chain indexing* is an attempt to arrive at a procedure for systematically developing an alphabetical subject index for a classified catalog (in card or book form). The principles of his classification scheme, and his theories of classification, are beyond the scope of this book. Suffice it to say that a major characteristic of classification schemes constructed on Ranganathan's principles is that of "synthesis" or "number building." That is, the class number that represents some complex subject is arrived at by joining the notational elements that represent more elemental subjects. For example, the topic "manufacture of woollen clothing in Germany in the nineteenth century" might be represented by the notation, *AbCfHYqZb* where *Ab* represents "clothing," *Cf* "woollen," H "manufacture," *Yq* "Germany," and *Zb* "nineteenth century," all of these notational elements being drawn from different parts of the classification scheme and combined in a sequence ("preferred order" or "citation order") specified by the maker of the scheme.

It should be obvious that the alphabetical index to a classified catalog constructed on these principles must be arrived at systematically, otherwise it might appear chaotic and impossible to use. Ranganathan's solution to this problem, chain indexing, involves indexing each step of the hierarchical chain from the most specific to the most general. Thus, an item represented by the class number *AbCfHYqZb* would generate the following index entries:

> Nineteenth century, Germany, Manufacture, Woollen goods,
>   Clothing   *AbCfHYqZb*
> Germany, Manufacture, Woollen goods, Clothing   *AbCfHYq*
> Manufacture, Woollen goods, Clothing   *AbCfH*
> Woollen goods, Clothing   *AbCf*
> Clothing   *Ab*

Clearly, the user of an index of this type must also search according to a predefined sequence of terms. For example, if seeking information on clothing in Germany in the nineteenth century, the searcher would get little help from the index were he to consult the term *clothing.*

In determining the sequence in which class numbers should be combined in an "analytico-synthetic" classification scheme (frequently referred to, somewhat misleadingly, as "faceted"), Ranganathan arrived at five "fundamental categories" and a formula for putting them together. The categories, Personality, Matter, Energy, Space, and Time, are combined in this sequence and the formula is sometimes referred to simply as "PMEST."

Personality is best thought of as "the thing itself," Matter is the material of which the thing is composed, Energy is the action performed on or by the thing, Space is where the action takes place, and Time is when it takes place. The sequence *AbCfHYqZh* observes the PMEST order. It follows, then, that the chain index entry for an item thus categorized will be in the reverse of this order.

Ranganathan's "logical" sequencing of facets in number building can be carried also into alphabetical subject catalogs and indexes. Thus, one could build a logical index entry, following the PMEST formula, as follows:

Clothing: Woollen goods: Manufacture: Germany: Nineteenth Century

Unfortunately, the PMEST formula is a little simplistic. In indexing highly complex subject matter, a particular category may occur more than once (e.g., the stressing of a structure could lead to the cracking of that structure which implies two different occurrences of the "energy" category); some of the categories need to be further subdivided (e.g., to indicate different types of activities); moreover, the PMEST formula does not clearly handle certain attributes that are important in indexing, such as the *properties* of materials.

Nevertheless, Ranganathan's theories have had a profound effect on modern practice in subject indexing. One can see this clearly in the work of Coates (1960) who advocates a catalog or index free from the rigidity of pre-established subject headings. An index entry should be made fully co-extensive with the subject matter discussed, as in the example

Power transmission lines, Overhead, Conductors, Icing, Prevention, Heating

Coates uses a "significance formula" to establish the sequence in which component terms are put together. The basic sequence he adopts is Thing, Part, Material, Action, Property, but this may be modified under certain circumstances. The heading used above, for example, adopts the sequence Thing, Kind, Part, Action, Agent. The procedures developed by Coates were adopted by the *British Technology Index* (later the *Current Technology Index*), of which Coates was the first editor. Some sample entries from this index are shown in Exhibit 19. Note that an item appears only once in the index. Additional approaches are provided through the use of cross references.

Ranganathan's theories can also be considered to have influenced PRECIS (Preserved Context Index System) as developed by Austin (1984). In PRECIS, computer programs generate a complete set of index entries and cross references from a string of terms and instruction codes provided by an indexer for an item. The subject matter of a document is described by a series of terms that are put in a "context-dependent" sequence. Austin and Digger (1977) use the following example:

India, Cotton industries, Personnel, Training

The logic claimed for this is that each term is essentially dependent on the term immediately before it. Thus, *training* applies only to the context of personnel, personnel applies only to the context of cotton industries, and this applies only in the context of India.

In PRECIS, the relationships among component terms in an index entry are presented as a two-line display:

Personnel. Cotton industries. India
    Training

This is justified on the grounds that it provides a practical way of showing, simultaneously, the relationship between the term used as an entry point in the index and the terms that are: (a) of wider context, and (b) of narrower context. In the example above, "Personnel" is modified by "Cotton industries" and "India" to show the broader context while "Training" is displayed as a dependent of "Personnel."

As illustrated in this example, a PRECIS entry has three components:

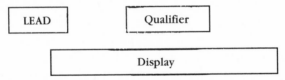

The "lead" term is the entry point in the index and it is printed in bold face, the "qualifier" provides the broader context, and the "display" shows the terms of narrower context. While the lead position will obviously always be occupied, the other positions need not always be.

Entries of the general type illustrated above can be generated by computer from a string of terms presented in a context-dependent sequence. Thus, the string India, Cotton industries, Personnel, Training would generate the following entries:

India
    Cotton industries. Personnel. Training
Cotton industries. India
    Personnel. Training
Training, Personnel, Cotton industries, India

Unfortunately the procedure is not as simple as suggested in this one example. There are many instances in which the sequence in a string of

FABRICS
  Related Headings:
    WEAVING
**FABRICS, Cellulosic ,, Crease resistant : Cross linking :
Dimethylol-1, 3-propylene urea**
  Deferred curing [BP 1,107,796 : Sun Chemical Corp., USA] Dyer,
    Textile Printer, Bleacher & Finisher, 141 (2 May 69) p.614+
FABRICS, Cellulosic ,, Crease resistant : Finishing
  Crease-resist and wash-and-wear finishing. B.C.M. Dorset. Textile
    Manufacturer, 95 (Apr 69) p.156-63
FABRICS, Cellulosic ,, Knitted ,, Crease resistant : Finishing
  Permanent press processes for knitted fabrics. D. Haigh. Hosiery Trade
    J., 76 (May 69) p.127+. il.
FABRICS ; Cellulosic—Nylon : Dyeing, High temperature : Dyes, Reactive
  "Hot-dyeing" reactive dyes on blends [Drimarene X and Drimafon X :
    Sandoz Products Ltd, Horsforth, Leeds] [summary] P.F. Bell. Dyer,
    Textile Printer, Bleacher & Finisher, 141 (2 May 69) p.622+
**FABRICS ; Cellulosic—Polyester fibres : Dyeing, High temperature :
Dyes, Reactive**
  "Hot-dyeing" reactive dyes on blends [Drimarene X and Drimafon X :
    Sandoz Products Ltd, Horsforth, Leeds] [summary] P.F. Bell. Dyer,
    Textile Printer, Bleacher & Finisher, 141 (2 May 69) p.622+
FABRICS, Coated : Clothing. See CLOTHING : Fabrics, Coated
FABRICS : Finishing : Weft straighteners : Control system, Photoelectric
  Fabric straightening [BP 1,107,822] H. Elcken. Dyer, Textile
    Printer, Bleacher & Finisher, 141 (2 May 69) p.612+
FABRICS, Foamback : Laminating
  Versatility the key : different cloths call for different techniques. P.
    Lennox-Kerr. Hosiery Times, 42 (Apr 69) p.107-9. il.
FABRICS ; Man made fibres ,, Pile : Knitting
  Manufacture and use-development of pile fabrics in Du Pont fibres.
    J. Rest & M.R.B. Addison. Hosiery Times, 42 (Apr 69) p.88+. il.
FABRICS ; Mohair : Suitings. See SUITINGS : Fabrics ; Mohair
FABRICS : Tape. See TAPE : Fabrics
**FABRICS, Warp knit : Dyeing, High temperature : Heating : Heat
transfer oil**
  HT process heating in the modern dyehouse [Kestner-Stone-Vapor at
    Nyla-Raywarp, Long Eaton] Dyer, Textile Printer, Bleacher &
    Finisher, 141 (18 Apr 69) p.542+
FABRICS, Warp knit : Knitwear. See KNITWEAR : Fabrics, Warp knit
**FABRICS ; Wool ,, Knitted ,, Shrink resistant : Finishing : Solvents :
Perchloroethylene : Machines**
  'Bentley Rapide' solvent finishing machine for knitwear and piece-goods.
    A.G. Brooks. Hosiery Times, 42 (Apr 69) p.45+. il.
  Milling machine for knitwear [Bentley Rapide] Hosiery Trade J., 76
    (May 69) p.130+. il.

Exhibit 19
Specimen entries from the *British Technology Index*
Reprinted by permission of the Library Association

terms does not in itself illustrate the dependencies unambiguously. In point of fact, a PRECIS indexer must use "operators" (codes tacked onto component terms) in order to represent term relationships unambiguously. For the example used earlier the input string would be

(O) India
(1) cotton industries
(P) personnel
(2) training

where (2) represents "transition action," (P) "object of action, part of key system," (O) "location," and (1) "key system" (object of transitive action). These operators show the "role" that a term plays in relation to other terms (providing a kind of syntax) and thus can be regarded as "role indicators" or "role operators."

Austin and Digger list 26 operators of this type. Clearly, use of such a scheme greatly complicates the indexing operation and adds to its cost and, in fact, a very substantial manual of indexing instructions is needed to implement PRECIS.

Somewhat related to PRECIS is POPSI, the Postulate-based Permuted Subject Indexing system (Bhattacharyya, 1981), which derives from Ranganathan's theories of classification.

The indexing scheme of Farradane (1967, 1980), which predated PRECIS, is similar in that it also uses a scheme of role indicators. Whereas PRECIS uses its roles solely as a means of generating consistent indexing statements by computer, the roles are retained in Farradane's system to show precise relationships among the terms. The relationships are drawn from work on the experimental psychology of thinking by Piaget, Vinacke, Isaacs, and others, and reinforced by the work of Guilford on the "structure of intellect."

Nine explicit relations exist in Farradane's scheme, each represented by an "operator." The complete set of these operators is given in Exhibit 20. The scheme represents stages in the development of thinking drawn from child psychology—i.e., the stages through which a child develops in associating objects and in discriminating among objects. There are two sets of gradation: in associative mechanisms and in discriminating mechanisms. The first associative stage is simple awareness without reference to time; the second is temporary association between ideas; and the third is the fixed (permanent) association of ideas. The stages of discrimination are: simple concurrence (concepts hard to distinguish), not-distinct (concepts having much in common), and distinct conceptualization (concepts that can be completely distinguished).

Indexing statements are constructed by joining terms ("isolates") together by means of these operators. An indexing statement, consisting of terms related by means of operators, is called an "analet." Some simple examples are:

Birds /* Migration
Iron Ore / — Smelting

and a more complex one:

Glass/(Oxygen/)Fluorine/ - Substituting

which represents the substitution of fluorine for oxygen in glass. Two-dimensional display is used where necessary, as:

Beets/ — Storing   The storage of washed
/;   beets
Washing

Rat /* { Sucrose } /—Feeding   Rats fed on sucrose with
        { Coconut Oil }   coconut oil.

Farradane (1977) has compared his relational indexing system with PRECIS, NEPHIS, and POPSI, all of which he refers to loosely as producing "permuted" indexes; he claims that his two-dimensional diagrams can be converted by computer into permuted alphabetical index entries.

		Associative mechanisms		
		Awareness	Temporary association	Fixed association
Discriminatory mechanisms	Concurrent conceptualization	1 /θ Concurrence	4 /* Self-activity	7 /; Association
	Not-distinct conceptualization	2 /= Equivalence	5 /+ Dimensional	8 /(Appurtenance
	Distinct conceptualization	3 /) Distinctness	6 /— Action	9 /: Functional dependence (causation)

Exhibit 20
Farradane's system of relations
Reproduced from Farradane (1980) by permission of Elsevier Science Publishers

The Symbolic Shorthand System (Selye [1966]; Selye & Ember, 1964) is another indexing system that expresses relationships among terms by means of role indicators. The indexer draws terms from a classification scheme comprising 20 main classes organized principally on the basis of body system. Throughout the scheme mnemonic symbols are used to represent subjects. For example, *Adr* represents the adrenal gland, *Hypt* hypothalamus, *BMR* basal metabolic rate, and so on. Selye's basic role indicator is an arrow (←) showing direction of action, as in:

Cer ← ACTH

Effect of adrenocorticotrophic hormone on the brain

or the more complex:

Adr ← Hyp ← ACTH+TX

Effect on the adrenal of hypophysectomy in conjunction with adrenocorticotrophic hormone and thyroxin

Other role indicators show other relationships. For instance, the symbol < is used to indicate content or component (Glu < B represents blood sugar) and the colon (:) is used for the comparison role. Quite complex subject matter can be represented concisely and unambiguously in this system as the following examples show:

R ← ('B/Rb ← R/Duck') /Rat

(Injection of renal substance of duck into a rabbit's blood and injection of serum thus formed into rats, thus producing renal changes)

Glu < B (:Ur) ← CON

(Effect of cortisone on sugar content of blood compared with sugar content of urine)

Level of Coordination

A distinction has been made between pre-coordinate and post-coordinate systems. In point of fact, however, a modern information retrieval system is likely to incorporate pre-coordinate features as well as post-coordinate capabilities. Some pre-coordination is likely to exist in the vocabulary used for indexing. For example, the descriptor POPULATION GROWTH, drawn from a thesaurus, represents the pre-coordination of the terms POPULATION and GROWTH. In some systems, an indexer may be allowed to use certain terms as subheadings of others. Thus, he might create:

POPULATION GROWTH/STATISTICS

Finally, the searcher can freely combine terms in logical relationships—e.g., "retrieve items indexed under POPULATION GROWTH/STATISTICS and also under SOUTH AMERICA."

Some coordination (of concepts or terms representing them) occurs, then, in the characteristics of the vocabulary, and some further coordination may occur at the time of indexing. These can be considered as forms of *pre-coordination* in that the coordination is built into the records that are input into a database. The final level of coordination is that achievable through the manipulation of terms in the conduct of a search (i.e., *post-coordination*).

While this chapter has presented examples of various types of pre-coordinate indexes it certainly has not exhausted the possibilities. A more complete analysis of the characteristics of pre-coordinate indexes can be found in Keen (1977a) and in Craven (1986). Keen (1977b) also discusses the subject of search strategy as applied to such indexes.

Back-of-the Book Indexes

Although many of the principles discussed in this book are valid for indexes of all types, the major focus of attention is the indexing of databases of bibliographic items—post-coordinate indexing for databases in electronic form and pre-coordinate indexing for those in printed form. No attempt is made to present detailed instructions on the indexing of individual books. This topic is well covered elsewhere (e.g., Collison [1972]; Knight [1979]; and in ANSI Z39.4-1984).

5

CONSISTENCY OF INDEXING

IT IS QUITE CLEAR that indexing is a subjective rather than an objective process. Two (or more) individuals may disagree on what some publication is about, what aspects of it deserve indexing, or what terms best describe the topics selected. Moreover, a single individual may make different indexing decisions at different times. *Consistency* in indexing refers to the extent to which agreement exists on the terms to be used to index some document. *Inter-indexer consistency* refers to agreement between or among indexers while *intra-indexer consistency* refers to the extent to which one indexer is consistent with himself.

Several different measures of consistency have been used or proposed; these have been well reviewed by Leonard (1975). Perhaps the most common measure is the simple ratio $AB/(A+B)$, where A represents the terms assigned by indexer a, B represents the terms assigned by indexer b, and AB represents the terms on which a and b agree. Consider the situation depicted in Exhibit 21. Five individuals have indexed the same item with the number of terms assigned varying from four (indexer b) to eight (indexer e). The terms assigned by any pair of indexers can be compared. Hooper (1965) refers to pair consistency values as *consistency pairs* (CPs). For indexers a and b, the CP is 3/6 or .5 (there are six unique terms assigned and three of these are assigned by both). Each pair in the group can be treated in the same way. From the data supplied one can derive the following CPs: *ab*, (.5); *ac*, 4/7 (.57); *ad*, 4/6 (.75); *ae*, 4/9 (.44); *bc*, 3/7 (.43); *bd*, 2/7 (.29); *be*, 4/8 (.5); *cd*, 3/8 (.37); *ce*, 5/9 (.56); *de*, 3/10 (.30).

A measure of intergroup consistency can be obtained by averaging the results for each pair of indexers. For the group $a—e$ the overall consistency is about .47.

If the sequence of terms in Exhibit 21 reflects priority of assignment, one can see that reasonable agreement exists as to the most important terms. All five indexers assign term A and four of the five assign both A and B. Much less agreement exists on the secondary aspects of the document or what terms to assign to these aspects. Note also how the number of terms assigned affects the consistency score: the more terms assigned (at least up to a point), the lower will tend to be the consistency. Zunde and Dexter (1969b) and Rolling (1981) suggest that consistency measures should take into account the importance of various terms to the subject matter of a document. Inconsistency in assignment of minor terms will be much less important than inconsistency in assignment of major terms, and this should be reflected in any scoring method.

a	b	c	d	e
A	A	A	A	A
B	B	C	B	B
C	E	D	C	D
D	F	E	D	E
E		F	H	F
		G		G
				I
				J

Exhibit 21
Terms (A—J) assigned to the same document by five different indexers (a—e)

The data of Exhibit 21 could also represent intra-indexer consistency: the situation where one individual indexes the same document on five different occasions.

Cooper (1969) looks at interindexer consistency in a different way— at the term level. That is, he measures the degree to which a group of indexers agree on the assignment of a particular term to a document. With respect to this term, interindexer consistency is defined as the proportion of indexers who assign the term minus the proportion who do not. In the Exhibit 21 example there is 100 percent agreement on term A, while agreement on B has a value of 60 (80 percent—20 percent), agreement on C a value of 20 (60 percent—40 percent), and so on.

Many studies of interindexer consistency have been performed, although they are not as common now as they once were; they tend to reveal that a high level of consistency is very difficult to achieve. Hooper (1965) summarized 14 different studies and found values ranging from 10 percent to 80 percent. For the six studies in which he was able to recompute the values from the data supplied (to ensure that consistency was calculated in the same way for each), the results ranged from 24 percent to 80 percent.

Factors Affecting Consistency

This variability in consistency scores leads one to ask "what are the factors that have the most effect in determining consistency in indexing?" An attempt is made to identify possible factors in Exhibit 22.

1. Number of terms assigned
2. Controlled vocabulary versus free text indexing
3. Size and specificity of vocabulary
4. Characteristics of subject matter and its terminology
5. Indexer factors
6. Tools available to indexer
7. Length of item to be indexed

Exhibit 22
Possible factors affecting consistency of indexing

The number of terms assigned was already mentioned. If indexers are asked to assign terms in order of perceived "importance" to the subject matter of the document, one would presumably get a fair degree of agreement on the terms at the top of the list. As one goes down the list, this agreement can be expected to decline. Put somewhat differently, one would expect more agreement on what are the main topics of the document than on which of the minor topics are worth inclusion.

But this may be a little simplistic. Exhibit 23 suggests a possible relationship between consistency and number of terms assigned. Assuming that terms are assigned in order of priority, it is hypothesized that agreement may peak at the level of two terms and then begin a gradual decline up to a point when so many terms have been assigned that agreement will again increase. This can be illustrated by the example of Exhibit 24.

Exhibit 24 shows ranked lists of terms assigned by indexers a and b. That is, a believes that A is the most important term, B is the next most important, and so on. Another way of looking at this is to say that, if indexer a could only assign one term to the document that term would be A. Each indexer eventually assigns 16 terms. Note that, while the indexers agree on the top two terms, they do not agree on the number one term. This is not surprising. Many documents involve a relationship between two major concepts. It may be possible to agree on what these concepts are but not to agree on which should take precedence. For example, in an article on welding of titanium, does the metal or the process take precedence? (Of course, such decisions are very much related to the characteristics of the database. In one devoted exclusively to titanium, the term *titanium* has little or no value.) This is a little like betting on greyhounds (or racehorses): it is frequently easier to guess which two dogs will finish in the first two positions than to guess which one will be first.

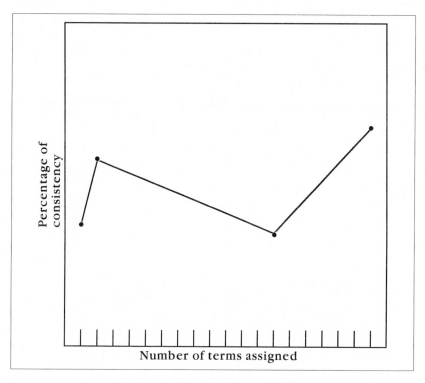

Exhibit 23
Relationship between consistency and number of terms assigned

After all 16 terms have been assigned, perfect agreement has been reached. This is due to a type of "saturation" effect. There are only so many terms that could plausibly apply to any item, at least if these terms are drawn from a controlled vocabulary. If enough terms are assigned, a high consistency will eventually be reached. Note, however, that consistency declines between the two term level and the sixteen term level. For example, after five terms, the CP is 5/6 (.83), after ten terms it is 6/14 (.43), and so on.

The relationship shown in Exhibit 23, then, seems plausible, although it has not been confirmed experimentally. At least the shape of the curve is plausible if the results for many indexers are taken into account. If few indexers were considered, of course, the decline in consistency would probably be less smooth (e.g., greater consistency may exist for four terms than for three).

a	*b*
A	B
B	A
C	D
D	E
E	K
F	C
G	G
H	L
I	M
J	N
K	O
L	P
M	F
N	H
O	I
P	J

Exhibit 24
Effect of number of terms assigned on indexer consistency (two indexers)

Harris et al. (1966) report results that differ somewhat from those hypothesized in Exhibit 23. Consistency was greater after 10 terms than after 5 but declined at the 20 term and 30 term level, increasing again when 40 terms had been assigned. They claimed to have found little evidence of any saturation effect but their indexers were using uncontrolled keywords and not selecting from a limited set of controlled terms. Fried and Prevel (1966) discovered a decline in consistency with the number of terms assigned, but Leonard (1975) found inconclusive evidence on this point— true for one database but not another.

The second factor affecting consistency (Exhibit 22) is the type of vocabulary used in indexing. One of the major advantages claimed for a controlled vocabulary is that it will improve consistency in the representation of subject matter. However, the relationship between vocabulary control and indexer consistency is not as straightforward as it might seem at first sight. Suppose I take a few medical articles and ask a group of high school students to index them. First, I require them to index by extracting words and phrases from the items. I would expect a reasonable level of consistency here. Presumably, the students will behave in more or less the same way that a computer would in this task: they will look for words or phrases that occur frequently and/or appear in the title or other prominent places.

As a second step in this exercise, the students are now asked to translate their free text indexing into terms selected from the National Library of Medicine's *Medical Subject Headings (MeSH)*. Almost certainly, consistency will deteriorate. In this situation the controlled vocabulary will have an adverse effect. This is because the textual expressions selected will not always be identical with the controlled terms. The students will have trouble in selecting the appropriate controlled terms because they lack sufficient knowledge of medicine and its terminology and because some of the controlled terms will have been given a special "meaning" (scope) by the compilers of the vocabulary. A controlled vocabulary should improve consistency of indexing in the long run, but it can only be applied consistently by experienced indexers knowledgeable in the subject matter and fully familiar with the terms.

Another thing to note is that a controlled vocabulary should improve consistency of indexing over a group of documents but may well reduce it at the single document level. That is, the terminology adopted in a particular article should be internally consistent—an author will tend not to use a variety of terms to describe the same topic, at least in articles of a technical or scholarly nature. It is quite possible, however, that two indexers might differ on what controlled term to use to represent this topic. On the other hand, different authors may use different terminology so the controlled vocabulary, by reducing the amount of choice, has a beneficial effect on consistency of indexing over a large group of documents.

It should be noted in passing that a comparison of free text indexing with controlled term indexing is not as simple as it may seem at first sight. A controlled term either is assigned or it is not. With free text indexing, however, one faces the problem of deciding whether or not two expressions are identical. For example, is "electric power" to be considered identical to "electrical power," or how do you score a situation in which one indexer selects the term "medieval French literature" and a second uses both "medieval literature" and "French literature"? This, of course, brings us back to the distinction between conceptual analysis and translation. The effect of these stages on consistency will be mentioned later.

Fugmann (1985) raises a very interesting issue related to consistency. He points out that, while consistency studies focus on selection of terms for a particular document, the seeker of information (searcher) is more concerned about consistency among documents. This implies that a different type of consistency analysis might be useful—one that measures the extent to which the same topic is indexed consistently throughout a database.

The third factor identified in Exhibit 22 is the size and specificity of the vocabulary. The larger the vocabulary, the more specific it is likely to be, and the greater its specificity, the more difficult it will be to use consistently (Tinker, 1966, 1968). For example, two indexers may be more likely to agree that a document is about corrosion than they are to agree on what type of corrosion is discussed.

The finer the shades of meaning that a vocabulary can express, the more difficult it will be to achieve consistency. In his evaluation of MEDLARS, Lancaster (1968) included a small consistency study. He discovered that consistency in the assignment of subject headings *(MeSH)* was 46.1 percent when the results for three indexers were averaged over 16 articles. When subheadings were also used, however, consistency dropped to 34.4 percent. In an earlier study it was found that role indicators had an even more drastic effect in reducing consistency of indexing (Lancaster, 1964), a finding that was confirmed by Mullison et al. (1969).

Slamecka and Jacoby (1963) make a distinction between "prescriptive" and "suggestive" vocabularies. The latter give the indexer some latitude in the choice of terms while the former give the indexer virtually no choice. On the basis of some experiments with vocabularies of different types (subject headings, thesaurus, classification scheme), they concluded that:

> Inter-indexer consistency improves significantly with the use of prescriptive indexing aids containing a minimum of variable semantic relationships among terms. The use of indexing aids which enlarge the indexer's semantic freedom of term choice is detrimental to indexing reliability. Quality of indexing is best improved by vocabularies which formalize relationships so as to uniformly and invariably prescribe the choice of indexing terms. (Page 30)

Note that they appear to consider consistency and quality as more or less equivalent. This point will be discussed in the next chapter.

It is hardly surprising that prescriptive vocabularies produce greater consistency. Indeed, it seems probable that the greatest consistency would be achieved in the assignment of those terms that might be preprinted on an indexing form (as in the case of the "checktags" of the National

Library of Medicine) to remind an indexer that they *must* be used whenever applicable. Leonard (1975) has produced some evidence in support of this as have Funk and Reid (1983).

The fourth factor identified in Exhibit 22 is the nature of the subject matter dealt with and, more particularly, its terminology. One must assume that greater consistency will occur in the indexing of more concrete topics (e.g., physical objects, named individuals), and that consistency will decline as one deals increasingly with abstractions. Nevertheless, Zunde and Dexter (1969a) did not find that consistency increased with "document reading ease."

The fifth factor has to do with the indexers as individuals. One would expect that two indexers with very similar backgrounds (education, experience, interests) will be more likely to agree on what should be indexed than two with widely differing backgrounds. Related to this is the type and extent of training given to the indexers. If all indexers take part in the same rigorous training program, this may serve to reduce the significance of earlier background as a factor influencing consistency. Knowledge of the subject matter dealt with is also important. If two indexers have about the same level of subject expertise, they may be more consistent with each other than would be the case if one is very knowledgeable and the other has only slight acquaintance with the subject matter. More important than subject knowledge per se, however, might be a detailed knowledge of the needs and interests of the users to be served.

Jacoby and Slamecka (1962) found higher consistency among experienced indexers than among beginning indexers in dealing with patents; the experienced indexers also used fewer terms. Leonard (1975) found that consistency increased with the experience of the indexers but found no positive correlation between consistency and educational background of the indexers. That is, improved familiarity with the subject matter (presumed from the educational background) did not increase consistency. Korotkin and Oliver (1964), in an experiment with abstracts in psychology, could detect no significant differences in consistency among two groups of indexers, one familiar with the subject matter and one not. In this case, however, the study was conducted with several artificial constraints that would affect the outcome: no controlled vocabulary was used, abstracts rather than full articles were involved, and indexers were told to assign exactly three terms (no more, no less) to each item.

Another factor identified in Exhibit 22 relates to the tools used by the indexer. If a group of indexers shares a common set of indexing tools (dictionaries, glossaries, handbooks), these may tend to improve consistency among the group. Most important would be some form of *entry vocabulary,* constructed by the information center, that serves to map terms occurring in documents to the appropriate controlled terms.

Finally, the length of the item indexed should affect consistency: the shorter the item, the fewer the terms that might plausibly apply. Not surprisingly, Harris et al. (1966) found that consistency was greater in indexing questions (short textual statements) than it was in indexing journal articles. Rodgers (1961), Fried and Prevel (1966), Leonard (1975), and Horký (1983) also found some evidence of declining consistency with length of item, while Tell (1969) discovered that consistency when indexing from the full text of articles was lower than when indexing from titles or abstracts.

Consistency in Conceptual Analysis Versus Consistency in Translation

The type of consistency study discussed in this chapter blurs the distinction between the conceptual analysis and the translation stages of indexing. However, Preschel (1972) attempted to separate these two stages to determine whether indexers were more likely to agree in their conceptual analysis than they were in the translation into index terms. The results of her investigation indicated that indexers were much more likely to agree on what should be indexed (conceptual analysis) than on how concepts should be described (translation). It is important to recognize, however, that the indexers in this study did not use a controlled vocabulary but made up their own "verbal labels" for topics. Quite different results might have been achieved had the normalizing influence of a controlled vocabulary been present in this study.

Recently, Iivonen (1990) has reported on a study in which distinctions are made among "term," "concept," and "aspect" levels of consistency. At the conceptual level the consistency exceeded consistency at the term level, but "aspect level" consistency was greater still. Unfortunately, the distinction made between "aspect" and "concept" is vague.

Exhibits 25-28 show examples of sets of index terms assigned to articles by two different indexers. In all cases the vocabulary used was the *Thesaurus of ERIC Descriptors*. These are all real examples of alternative approaches to indexing. The indexing was done as part of a homework assignment by students in the Graduate School of Library and Information Science, University of Illinois. The examples were selected from a larger set collected by the author over a period of years. Students were free to choose any articles they wished to index and it was pure chance that more than one student should pick the same article. They are reproduced here because they do illustrate some of the problems involved in achieving agreement among indexers.

Indexer A	**Indexer B**
Major terms	*Major terms*
Crime victims	Assistance (social behavior)
Assistance (social behavior)	Impression formation
Apathy	Participation
Help seeking behavior	Witnesses
Minor terms	*Minor terms*
Crime	Crime prevention
Citizenship	Involvement
Avoidance	Laws
	Social behavior
	Social perception

Exhibit 25
Two approaches to indexing an article entitled
When Bystanders Just Stand By

Exhibit 25 is an extreme example: only one term in common among sixteen assigned. The article deals with the phenomenon of people who refuse to intervene when they witness a crime. Notice how the two indexers view the article from different perspectives—*B* more from the social and legal viewpoint and *A* more from the psychological.

The example of Exhibit 26 is not much better. Among the major terms, the indexers agree on only one. The article deals with a program, offered by a public library, to teach parents of preschool children about literature suitable for that age group. Indexer *B* regards this as preschool education, although it is the parents and not the children who are being educated, while *A* (probably more correctly) interprets it as adult parent education. Indexer *B,* although a student of library science, fails to indicate that the program takes place in a library. Indexer *A,* on the other hand, fails to indicate that the article is related to very young children. Note how closely related terms are selected by the two indexers: *reading interests* versus *reading attitudes, literature appreciation* versus *literary criticism, reading materials* versus *reading material selection.* This illustrates the problems involved in applying a controlled vocabulary that contains many closely related or partially overlapping terms, especially when the indexers are not fully familiar with the intended scope of these terms.

Exhibit 27 shows more consistency in that two of the major terms coincide. Nevertheless, some translation differences are evident here.

Indexer *A* expresses "graduate schools of education" by use of the terms *schools of education* and *higher education,* while *B* selects *schools of education* and *graduate study.* Similarly, where *B* uses *teacher attitudes,* *A* uses *opinions,* and where *B* uses *student-teacher relationship,* *A* uses *interprofessional relationship* and *faculty advisors.*

Indexer A	Indexer B
Major terms	*Major terms*
Children's literature	Children's literature
Library extension	Preschool education
Adult education	Parent aspirations
Parent education	Literary criticism
Reading material selection	
	Minor terms
Minor terms	Early experience
Parent student relationship	Early childhood education
Recreational reading	Reading materials
Literature appreciation	Young children
Reading interests	Reading attitudes
Fiction	Literature
Fantasy	Parent responsibility
Public libraries	

Exhibit 26
Two approaches to indexing an article entitled
A Children's Literature Course for Parents

It is difficult to believe the indexing results of Exhibit 28. There is no term in common among 12 assigned. Again, the problems associated with the use of related and/or overlapping terms are shown clearly here: five "reading" terms are used but they all differ. In this case, however, *A*'s indexing must be regarded as rather poor: the educational level is not indicated and the item is indexed too generally under *audiovisual education* when, specifically, it deals with television. At the time this item was indexed, the term *closed captioned television* did not exist in the thesaurus.

The eight anonymous students whose work is compared in Exhibits 25-28 were not highly experienced indexers, although they were intelligent, interested, and motivated. It is quite likely that indexers of greater experience, especially with greater experience in the use of this thesaurus, would have achieved more consistent results. Nevertheless, these examples do serve to illustrate some of the barriers to consistent indexing.

Exhibit 29 is a different kettle of fish. Here two students have recorded words and phrases representing their conceptual analysis of an article before attempting to translate it into controlled terms. The comparison is very instructive. Apart from the fact that both sets of terms relate to Harlequin romances, they seem to have little in common. *A*'s interpretation is a "soft" and romantic one while *B*'s is, to say the least, harsh. *A* includes only three negative terms (conflict, dominance, resentment) while *B* includes many extreme terms. The fact that such radically different interpretations of the meaning of an article are possible argues, perhaps, for the use of indexing as a tool in psychoanalysis.

Indexer A	Indexer B
Major terms	*Major terms*
Mentors	Mentors
Higher education	Schools of education
Opinions	Graduate study
Schools of education	Teacher attitudes
Minor terms	*Minor terms*
Professional development	Student-teacher relationship
Faculty advisors	Graduate school faculty
Career guidance	Graduate students
Interprofessional relationship	

Exhibit 27
Two approaches to indexing an article entitled
Mentoring in Graduate Schools of Education

While two or more individuals may not agree closely on which terms to assign to a document, this phenomenon is not peculiar to indexing. Saracevic et al. (1988) found that the terms used by different searchers for the same request showed remarkably little overlap.* Moreover, items retrieved by different searchers showed low overlap and each searcher tended to find some relevant items not found by the others. Saracevic suggests the need for multiple searches, by different individuals, for the same request, with the results pooled and ranked—the items retrieved by most searchers at the top of the ranking, those retrieved by only one searcher at the bottom. By the same token, an ideal approach to indexing might involve team effort, with a consensus reached for each document as a result of discussions among a group of indexers. While this approach has been possible in a few highly specialized environments (such as the specialized systems existing within the U.S. Patent and Trademark Office), it is too costly for most applications.

*Fidel (1985) also found that experienced searchers showed little agreement in the selection of terms for use in complex searches. Earlier, Lilley (1954) and Bates (1977) had shown that users of card catalogs also tend not to agree much on what terms to use in searching.

Bates (1986) suggests that indexing is "indeterminate and probabilistic" and that this is more or less inevitable, being "rooted in the nature of the human mind." Rather than bewailing the fact that a high level of consistency in indexing is never likely to be attained, at least when human indexers are involved, we should concentrate on compensating for this at the search end of the process. Searching should not be based on the exact matching of terms but on methods that rank documents by the degree to which they match some form of search statement. Various aids should be available to allow a searcher to select from a variety of methods for generating semantic associations among terms.

Indexer A	Indexer B
Major terms	*Major terms*
Audiovisual education	Captions
Reading research	Television teachers
	Elementary education
Minor terms	
Nontraditional education	*Minor terms*
Reading strategies	Remedial programs
Student motivation	Television curriculum
	Reading skills
	Reading instruction

Exhibit 28
Two approaches to indexing an article entitled
Closed Captioned Television: A New Tool for Reading Instruction

Indexer A	Indexer B
romantic fiction—Harlequin romances	women as readers of contemporary fiction
women's romantic fantasies	Harlequin novels
conflict between men and women	heroines
male/female love relationships	female fantasy
feminine self-perception	masochism—rape
male dominance over women	Gothic novels
romantic novels as outlet for women's	sex roles—stereotyping
resentment	psychoanalysis
	female self image
	narrative
	schizophrenia
	hysteria
	social roles

Exhibit 29
Differences in conceptual analysis for an article entitled
The Disappearing Act: a Study of Harlequin Romances

Consistent indexing is not necessarily the same as indexing of high quality. The quality of indexing is discussed in the next chapter, which also compares quality and consistency.

6

QUALITY OF INDEXING

INDEXING IS NOT an end in itself. "Good" indexing can be defined in a very pragmatic way as indexing that allows items to be retrieved from a database in searches in which they are useful responses and prevents them from being retrieved when they are not. Cooper (1978) carries this somewhat further:

> The assignment of a term to a document is justified if the average utility associated with that assignment is positive and unjustified if it is negative. (Page 110)

He uses the word "utility" here as more or less synonymous with "benefit."

As implied by the relationships depicted in Exhibit 1, several subsystems interact to control the performance of an information retrieval system. Another way of considering this is in terms of a sequence of events governing the performance of a search. This is illustrated in Exhibit 30.

In a typical information center situation, an information need arises in the mind of some customer of the center who discusses this need with an information specialist. The result of this dialogue can be referred to as a *request* (i.e., the specialist's understanding of what the user really wants). On the basis of this request, the information specialist prepares a search strategy using index terms, text words, or some combination of these. The search strategy is then matched against the database (of course, in many cases, the search strategy and the match with the database will be intertwined, since the strategy will be developed interactively online). As a result of the search certain items are retrieved. These may be screened by the searcher to eliminate any that seem obviously irrelevant, and a final set of documents or references is delivered to the user.

It is clear from this diagram that many factors affect the quality of the search as measured, for example, by recall and precision. First and foremost, the searcher needs to understand what the user really wants. If the request is an imperfect representation of the information need, it hardly matters that all other elements—vocabulary, search strategy, indexing, and so on—are satisfactory.

Given that the request is a reasonable approximation of the information need, the next factor affecting performance is the quality of the search

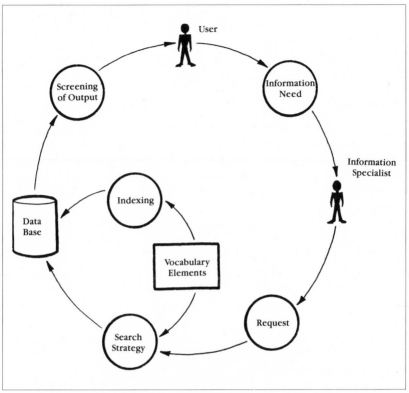

Exhibit 30
Factors affecting the results of a search in a database

strategy. Major influences here are the experience, intelligence, and ingenuity of the searcher. However, the vocabulary of the database also comes into play. If a controlled vocabulary is in use, one cannot search more specifically than the vocabulary allows, although additional specificity may be achieved through use of text words. Unfortunately, it is difficult to think of all the terms necessary to achieve a complete search. The problem in all searching is to try to balance recall and precision. The need is usually to achieve maximum recall but still to operate at an acceptable level of precision.

When the search strategy is matched against the database, clearly, the quality of the database itself is a major factor affecting performance. It is here, of course, that the quality of the indexing comes into play. The vocabulary elements also affect indexing since an indexer cannot use terms that do not exist.

The effectiveness of a "screening" of output, if such an operation is performed, will depend primarily on two factors:

1. How well the searcher understands what the user really wants.
2. How well the document representations stored in the database indicate what the documents are about.

It is not appropriate here to present a detailed analysis of all the factors affecting the performance of a retrieval system (as depicted in Exhibit 30), but only to consider those factors attributable to indexing. An indexing "failure" could occur in the conceptual analysis phase of indexing or in translation.

Conceptual analysis failures could be of two types:

1. Failure to recognize a topic that is of potential interest to the user group served.
2. Misinterpretation of what some aspect of the document really deals with, leading to the assignment of a term (or terms) that are inappropriate.

Translation failures are also of two types:

1. Failure to use the most specific term available to represent some subject.
2. Use of a term that is inappropriate to the subject matter because of lack of subject knowledge or due to carelessness.

In practice, of course, the evaluator of an information system could not draw some of these distinctions. For example, if term X is assigned to an item when it should not be, there is no way of knowing if the indexer misinterpreted what the document is about, did not really understand the meaning or scope of X, or simply assigned this term out of carelessness.

If an indexer fails to assign X when it should be assigned, it is obvious that recall failures will occur. If, on the other hand, Y is assigned when X should be, both recall and precision failures can occur. That is, the item will not be retrieved in searches for x although it should be and will be retrieved in searches for y when it should not be.

The careless omission of a term that should be assigned to a document can have a profound effect on the results of a particular search, even when the term omitted may not seem too important at first sight. Exhibit 31 presents a simple illustration of this, based on one of many examples uncovered by Lancaster (1968) in his evaluation of MEDLARS. The article deals with the effect on growth of the cerebral cortex of being born into darkness and never experiencing light. The indexer covers all the major aspects except that of growth. This simple omission could be very important.

In this case, the article is considered highly relevant to a request for information on factors affecting growth of the central nervous system. The searcher can only use the "growth" term to approach this topic since it is unrealistic to expect that he could predict what the factors might be, so this important article remains unretrieved.

ARTICLE	SEARCH
Topic	*Request*
Effect of visual deprivation on growth of the visual cortex in mice	Factors affecting growth, regeneration and degeneration in the central nervous system
Indexing	*Strategy*
SENSORY DEPRIVATION	CENTRAL NERVOUS SYSTEM (complete
DARKNESS	hierarchy)
CEREBRAL CORTEX	*and* (GROWTH *or* REGENERATION *or*
VISION	DEGENERATION)
MICE	

Exhibit 31
Example of important item missed by simple indexer omission

In the MEDLARS study, Lancaster discovered few examples of indexers using incorrect terms but rather more cases of omissions of important terms by indexers. This is likely to be typical of the situation in other information services.

Recognizing "Good" Indexing

The discussion so far in this chapter implies that quality of indexing can only be judged *ex post facto*—i.e., as a result of experience in the operation of a retrieval system and more particularly its evaluation. To a very large extent this is true. A set of index terms assigned to a document cannot be judged "correct" or "incorrect" in any absolute sense. That is, there is no one "best" set of terms. To claim that such a set exists implies a foreknowledge of all the requests that will be put to the database in which the document is represented.

Nevertheless, errors do occur in indexing and it should be possible for a senior indexer (or "revisor") to spot at least some of these errors before a record is added to a database and thus to impose some quality control over the process. The senior indexer might identify errors of the following types:

1. The indexer contravenes policy, especially policy relating to the exhaustivity of indexing.

2. The indexer fails to use the vocabulary elements in the way in which they should be used (e.g., an incorrect main heading/subheading combination).
3. The indexer fails to use a term at the correct level of specificity. In most cases this will mean that the term selected is not the most specific available.
4. The indexer uses an obviously incorrect term, perhaps through lack of subject knowledge (e.g., *liquid rocket fuels* when it is gaseous fuels that are discussed).
5. The indexer omits an important term.

Usually the revisor will not spend as much time checking the indexing of an item as the indexer spent in the first place. It may be relatively easy to recognize an incorrect term, which is likely to "jump out" at the experienced indexer, but it might be quite difficult to recognize the fact that an important term has been omitted unless it is very obvious (e.g., the term appears in the title).

It is possible to test the work of indexers in a more rigorous way than merely looking over the terms assigned, which is the most that one can expect from a routine checking operation. The most obvious approach is to conduct a simulation of a true evaluation. This can be achieved as follows:

1. Select a group of documents from the normal input stream before these reach the indexers.
2. For each document, compose, say, three questions for which the item can be considered an important response. One question could be based on the central theme of the document while the others would be based on secondary, but still important, themes.
3. Have experienced search analysts construct search strategies for each question. Of course, these would not be the same individuals whose indexing is being studied.
4. Have the items indexed in the normal way.
5. Compare the indexing to the search strategies to determine whether or not the relevant items are retrievable on the terms assigned.

As a method of evaluating the performance of a group of indexers, this procedure should work rather well if the sample of documents is large enough and the best possible search strategies are used. The whole test could take place over a series of weeks. It would be desirable, of course, if the same set of documents was indexed several times, once by each indexer, so that the performance of the indexers could be compared on the same basis, but this may not always be possible because of subject specialization within the group.

Factors Affecting the Quality of Indexing

Regrettably, not much research has been performed on the factors that are most likely to affect the quality of indexing. An attempt has been made to identify such factors in Exhibit 32, but this is based more on common sense or intuition than on hard evidence.

Indexer factors
Subject knowledge
Knowledge of user needs
Experience
Concentration
Reading ability and
  comprehension
	Document factors
	Subject matter
	Complexity
	Language
	Length
	Presentation and
	  summarization

Vocabulary factors Specificity/syntax Ambiguity or imprecision Quality of entry vocabulary Quality of structure Availability of related aids	*"Process" factors* Type of indexing Rules and instructions Required productivity Exhaustivity of indexing *Environmental factors* Heating/cooling Lighting Noise

Exhibit 32
Factors that may affect the quality of indexing
For the idea behind this exhibit the author
is indebted to Oliver et al. (1966).

Indexers should have some familiarity with the subject matter dealt with and understand its terminology, although they need not necessarily be subject experts. Indeed, some organizations have had problems with indexers who are too "expert"—they tend to interpret too much and perhaps to go beyond the claims of the author (e.g., to index a possible application not specifically identified in the article) or even to exhibit prejudices by not indexing claims that they are unwilling to accept. However, lack of subject knowledge may lead to overindexing. Unable to distinguish between two terms, perhaps the indexer assigns both when only one is needed or only one is correct. Loukopoulos (1966) referred to this as indexer *indecision.*

Of course, a special type of expert is the author of a document himself. Some studies of the author as indexer have taken place. For example, Diodato (1981) studied consistency in term selection among three groups: authors, indexers, and readers of mathematics papers. Ebinuma et al. (1983)

translated author-assigned keywords into thesaurus terms and compared these with terms already assigned by experienced indexers. The author-derived indexing seemed to produce better precision but lower recall.

Rasheed (1989) performed a similar study, comparing terms assigned by authors of medical articles with terms assigned by MEDLARS indexers. He found that the indexers assigned many more terms and the terms they used were more specific than those used by authors.

Knowledge of the interests of the users of the database is especially important because "good" indexing should be tailored to the needs of a particular community wherever possible. Years of experience as an indexer should also be a factor affecting quality, as should such characteristics as the individual's ability to concentrate, to read rapidly, and to comprehend quickly. Finally, and perhaps most important of all, a good indexer should enjoy the work. One is unlikely to get good indexing from someone who hates what he is doing.

Document factors also come into play. Some subjects are more difficult to comprehend than others. Usually the theory is much more difficult than the practice, as in the differences between applied mechanics and engineering. Related to this, of course, is the degree of "match" between the subject matter of a document and the knowledge or interests of the indexer.

"Language" can be interpreted in more than one way. Clearly, the indexer who knows no Russian can hardly index Russian articles effectively unless they have unusually clear and complete abstracts in the indexer's own tongue. Another aspect is the clarity of the author's language. Some authors present their thoughts or findings more clearly than others, making the indexer's job less difficult. Finally, there are some presentation factors that will influence how easy it is for the indexer to find out what the document is about: is the title accurate or misleading, is there an abstract or some other summarization and does this fully reflect the contents of the item?

Vocabulary factors can also be expected to influence the quality of indexing. The more specific the vocabulary, the finer the shades of meaning it can express, and the finer the shades of meaning, the more difficult it becomes to make distinctions among closely related terms and to use these terms consistently. Added syntactical elements such as subheadings or role indicators increase specificity and may complicate the indexing task.

Terms that are ambiguous or imprecise (lacking adequate context or scope notes) are difficult to interpret and use correctly and the vocabulary must have a sufficiently complete structure (e.g., the BT/NT/RT structure of the conventional thesaurus) that it guides the indexer to the term most appropriate to represent a particular topic. The size and quality of the entry vocabulary* will also be important, as will the availability of various related aids, such as technical dictionaries or glossaries.

Other factors that may affect quality have to do with the indexing process itself. Some types of indexing, such as the extraction of words or phrases from text, do not require much concentration, intellectual effort, or experience, while other types, particularly those requiring the establishment of precise conceptual relationships (through role or relational indicators), are at the opposite end of the spectrum of difficulty. In general one would expect indexers to perform more effectively when they are given precise rules and instructions rather than operating under laissez-faire conditions. Required productivity should be another significant factor. If required to deal with a specified number of items a day, the indexer may feel under pressure and this may lead to careless errors, especially if the organization expects too much in the way of daily output. Also, exhaustive indexing may require more time than selective indexing.

Finally, indexing requires concentration, and adverse environmental conditions seem likely to have a negative impact on the accuracy of this intellectual task.

Another way of considering factors that affect the quality of indexing is in terms of the difficulties encountered by indexers. Oliver et al. (1966), in an interview survey involving 61 indexers, found that "making decisions about how to best describe the content of documents" was (not surprisingly) the problem most frequently mentioned. Unfortunately, this problem is general, pervasive, and not susceptible to easy solutions. Other significant problems mentioned were "understanding new or unfamiliar material" and lack of appropriate terms in the controlled vocabularies.

Is Quality Related to Consistency?

Quality and consistency are not the same: one can be consistently bad as well as consistently good! Nevertheless, one intuitively feels that consistency and quality should be related. For example, if three indexers tend to agree with each other, but a fourth indexes in a quite different way, one is inclined to believe in the consensus.

In a provocative article, Cooper (1969) questions the value of consistency as an indicator of quality. The point he makes can be illustrated by reference to Exhibit 33. An information center employs four indexers,

---

*An entry vocabulary is a list of nonpreferred terms, occurring in the literature, that are mapped to the appropriate preferred terms through *see* or *use* references. The importance of this is discussed elsewhere by Lancaster (1986).

A—D. B and *C* are quite consistent with each other, but *A* and *D* are both idiosyncratic. However, for one reason or another, *D's* view of the world is closest to that of the users of the center, and the terms he assigns better reflect their interests. One assumes that his indexing is the best, at least for this particular audience. In this case, then, the indexers most consistent

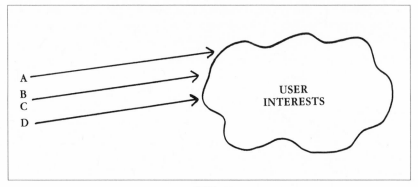

Exhibit 33
Indexer consistency related to user interests

with each other do not produce the best work, although they are not as bad as *A* whose indexing is furthest away from the interests of the users.

While this situation is plausible, it may not be highly so. It is difficult to understand why *B* and *C* would be more consistent with each other unless this reflected the fact that they are the more experienced indexers. If they are, logic suggests that it is these two who would know most about the users. Studies that relate in any way to Cooper's contentions are few and far between. However, Diodato (1981) did find that consistency between authors of mathematics papers and professional indexers was greater than the consistency between authors and readers of the papers.

Leonard (1975) has made the only serious attempt to study the relationship between quality and consistency in indexing. "Quality" was defined in terms of retrieval effectiveness—the ability to retrieve what is wanted and to avoid what is not wanted. Leonard worked with two separate collections of data, subsets from previous evaluation studies. These collections consisted of documents, requests, search strategies, and relevance assessments. For each request it was known which items had been judged relevant and which not. The sets of terms assigned to documents by indexers participating in the study could thus be compared with search strategies previously constructed, allowing the investigator to determine whether or not a particular document would be retrieved by a particular strategy.

The comparison between consistency and retrieval effectiveness proved more difficult than anticipated. A major problem is caused by the fact that the "effectiveness" of indexing is normally associated with the work of a single indexer, while consistency, by definition, is a measure that relates to the work of two or more indexers (Leonard measured group consistency as well as indexer pair consistency). Leonard combined the "effectiveness" scores for two (or more) indexers and then compared this score with the consistency measure for these indexers. The effectiveness score takes into account the number of relevant documents retrieved and the number of irrelevant documents retrieved, and these scores can be combined by averaging the results for the two indexers or by aggregating them. If the aggregation method is used, only unique items are counted, which in effect treats the two indexers as though they were a single individual.

Leonard observed a "moderate to strong" positive relationship between consistency and retrieval effectiveness, with a "clearly defined positive relationship" between consistency and the recall ratio.

The Value of Consistency Studies

The research performed by Leonard (1975) does suggest that a positive relationship exists between consistency and quality of indexing, where "quality" refers to retrieval effectiveness. Even if no such relationship had been discovered, consistency studies still have some value. Hooper (1966) has suggested several applications, including:

1. In the selection or training of indexers. Trainees' indexing is compared with some pre-established standard.
2. In the ongoing quality control of indexing activities.
3. To detect problems in the use of a controlled vocabulary; for example, identification of terms or types of terms that are frequently used inconsistently because of ambiguities or overlapping.
4. To detect any problems that might exist with regard to indexing rules.
5. To determine whether or not consistency may be lower in handling certain subject fields or document types.

In this chapter, quality of indexing has been assumed to mean the same as "retrieval effectiveness" of indexing. Not everyone defines it in this way. Rolling (1981), for example, claims that: "Indexing quality can be defined as the degree of agreement between the terms assigned by the indexer and an 'ideal' or 'optimum' group of terms." He goes on to point out that the ideal is best achieved through some form of expert consensus. The work of one indexer can be compared with the consensus, and he would be "penalized" for not using terms that the experts had agreed on as well as for using terms that had not been agreed on. Rolling, who appears unaware of Leonard's work, claims that effectiveness measures are "not practicable," while consistency studies are "not reliable." He advocates studies of quality, based on the consensus approach, with consistency studies used only to investigate "influences and trends."

Various other investigators have attempted to evaluate indexing outside the context of the retrieval system in which it occurs. For example, White and Griffith (1987) describe an approach in which methods external to the indexing system being studied are used to establish a set of documents judged to be "similar in content." Using sets of this kind (they call them criterial document clusters) as the basis for evaluation, they look at three characteristics of the index terms assigned to items in the set within a particular database:

1. The extent to which terms link related items. The obvious measure of this is the number of terms that have been applied to all or a majority of items in the set. The items can be considered closely linked if several subject terms have been applied to all of them.

2. The extent to which terms discriminate among these sets within the database. The most obvious measure of this is the frequency with which terms that apply to most documents in the set occur in the database as a whole.* Very common terms are not good discriminators. For example, in MEDLINE, the term *human* may apply to every item in a set but is of little value in separating this set from others since it applies to so many items in the database. On the other hand, terms that occur very rarely in the database as a whole will be useful in highly specific searches but of little use in the identification of somewhat larger sets.

3. The extent to which terms discriminate finely among individual documents. Rarity is an applicable measure here also. So is the exhaustivity of the indexing: a term may apply to all items in a set but cannot discriminate among its members; the more additional terms are assigned to each member, the more individual differences can be identified.

To look at quality in this way one must first establish the test sets, retrieve records for the members of each set from some database, and study the characteristics of the terms assigned. White and Griffith used the technique to compare the indexing of their test sets in different databases: MEDLINE was compared with PsycINFO, BIOSIS PREVIEWS, and

*Ajiferuke and Chu (1988) are critical of the discriminating index used by White and Griffith because it fails to take account of the size of the database; they propose an alternative measure that does. In a related paper (Chu and Ajiferuke, 1989), they apply the White/Griffith evaluation criteria, with their own modified discriminating index, to the evaluation of indexing in library science databases.

Excerpta Medica. A comparison of databases in this way is a check on the assumption that test set items are in fact similar in content. White and Griffith used co-citation as the basis for establishing their test sets, although other methods, including bibliographic coupling, could also be used.

The value of this work is limited by the fact that only very small clusters (range of three to eight items) were used. Moreover, the validity of the method as a test of human indexing depends entirely on one's willingness to accept a co-citation cluster as being a legitimate standard. One could make a persuasive argument that it would make more sense to use expert indexers as a standard for judging the legitimacy of the co-citation cluster.

White and Griffith (1987) claim that the method is useful to a database producer as a check on the quality of indexing, and present examples of terms that should perhaps have been used by MEDLINE indexers or added to the controlled vocabulary. However, such "quality" checks can be done more simply: sets of items defined by a particular term or terms (e.g., "superconductors" or "superconductivity" occurring as index terms or text words) can be retrieved from several databases and their indexing compared without the use of co-citation as a standard. In fact, this type of study has also been done by the same group of investigators (McCain et al., 1987). For 11 requests, posed by specialists in the medical behavioral sciences, comparative searches were performed in MEDLINE, Excerpta Medica, PsycINFO, SCISEARCH, and SOCIAL SCISEARCH. In the first three databases the searches were performed on: (a) controlled terms, and (b) natural language. In the citation databases, searches were performed: (a) using the natural language of titles, and (b) using citations to known relevant items as entry points. While the purpose of the investigation was to study the quality of MEDLINE indexing, little was discovered that could be turned into recommendations to the National Library of Medicine on indexing practice, although some recommendations on indexing coverage could be made.

The most important findings of the study were: (1) that the incorporation of natural language approaches into search strategies resulted in significant improvements in recall compared with use of controlled terms only, (2) that citation retrieval should be considered an important adjunct to term-based retrieval because additional relevant items can be found using the citation approach, and (3) that no single database is likely to provide complete coverage of a complex multidisciplinary literature.

7

ABSTRACTS: TYPES AND FUNCTIONS

AN ABSTRACT IS A BRIEF but accurate representation of the contents of a document. A distinction should be made between the words *abstract* and *extract*. An extract is an abbreviated version of a document created by drawing sentences from the document itself. For example, two or three sentences from the introduction followed by two or three from the conclusions or summary might provide a good indication of what a certain journal article is about. A true abstract, while it may include words occurring in the document, is a piece of text created by the abstractor rather than a direct quotation from the author.

Abstracts can be characterized in a number of different ways including length. In Exhibit 3, for example, two different abstracts are presented, one longer than the other. There is absolutely no reason why all abstracts should be approximately the same length. Factors affecting the length of an abstract include the following:

1. *The length of the item being abstracted;*
2. *The complexity of the subject matter;*
3. *The diversity of the subject matter.* For example, an abstract prepared for the proceedings of a conference may need to be rather long if the papers presented cover a wide range of topics;
4. *The importance of the item to the organization preparing the abstract.* As with the exhaustivity of indexing, an industrial information center may want to prepare longer abstracts for the company's own reports than it does for other items;
5. *The "accessibility" of the subject matter.* In a published abstracting service, in particular, it might be sensible to prepare more complete abstracts for items that are less accessible physically (e.g., limited distribution reports or papers presented at conferences) or intellectually (e.g., those written in obscure languages);
6. *Cost.* Longer abstracts are not necessarily more expensive to prepare than short ones. Indeed, it may take much longer to prepare a good condensation of 200 words than one of 500. Nevertheless, it is obvious that the cost of a published abstracting service would increase significantly if the average length of an abstract was increased by, say, 50 percent. Typesetting, paper, and mailing costs would all be affected;
7. *Purpose.* An abstract used primarily to provide access to a document for retrieval purposes might need to be longer to provide sufficient access points.

A very brief abstract (e.g., one that attempts to describe a document by means of a single sentence) is sometimes referred to as an *annotation,* but this is a rather imprecise term.

A distinction is frequently made between indicative abstracts (sometimes called descriptive abstracts) and informative abstracts. The distinction is illustrated in Exhibits 34 and 35 which show two different types of abstract prepared for the item first depicted in Exhibit 3. The indicative abstract simply describes (indicates) what the document is about, whereas the informative abstract attempts to summarize the substance of the document, including the results. That is, an indicative abstract might mention what types of results are achieved in a study but the informative abstract would summarize the results themselves. Cremmins (1982) explains that indicative abstracts may contain information on purpose, scope, or methodology but not on results, conclusions, or recommendations. On the other hand, the informative abstract may include information on purpose, scope, and methods but must also contain results, conclusions, or recommendations. For some purposes, a good informative abstract might act as a reasonable substitute for reading a document. An indicative abstract is unlikely to serve as a substitute in this way. Its main purpose would be to indicate to the reader of the abstract whether or not he would be likely to want to read the original. For obvious reasons, informative abstracts tend to be longer than indicative. They are also more difficult to write. Indeed, while it will usually be possible to write an informative abstract for an experimental study, it may be almost impossible to do so for a theoretical study or an opinion piece. For this reason, informative abstracts occur more frequently in science and technology than they do in the social sciences or humanities.

A single abstract may incorporate indicative and informative elements, depending on the interests of the intended readers. For example, consider a report on air pollution abstracted in a publication intended for chemists. Much of the abstract, covering the environmental aspects, is merely indicative, but a part of it may be truly informative (e.g., presenting results from analyses performed on atmospheric samples). Indicative and informative abstracts may both be included in a single published abstracting service. In general, however, indicative abstracts are more common. Fedosyuk (1978) describes detailed procedures for distinguishing between indicative and informative abstracts using linguistic criteria and even presents an algorithm for this task. While this is ingenious, it is not clear why one would want formal procedures for making such distinctions.

The term *subject slanting* is sometimes used in connection with abstracts. The implication of the term is that the abstract should be "slanted" to the interests of the intended users. That is, in abstracting, as in indexing, a guiding question should be, "Why are our users likely to be interested in this item?" Abstracts prepared by an organization for its own internal use should always be slanted to local needs and interests. The situation is a little more complicated in the case of published abstracting services.

A distinction can be made between services that are discipline-oriented and those that are mission-oriented. The former attempt to serve the needs of a particular discipline (e.g., chemistry, biology, the social sciences) while the latter try to meet the needs of a particular industry or group of individuals (e.g., abstracts for the rubber industry or abstracts for nurses). Subject slanting is more relevant and feasible in the case of mission-oriented services than it is for discipline-oriented, because the interests of users of the former tend to be more homogeneous and specialized than the interests of users of the latter. At least one study has indicated that rather little slanting occurs in published services (Herner, 1959).

> Telephone interviews were conducted in 1985 with 655 Americans sampled probabilistically. Opinions are expressed on whether: (1) the establishment of a Palestinian state is essential for peace in the region; (2) U.S. aid to Israel and to Egypt should be reduced; (3) the U.S. should (a) participate in a peace conference that includes the PLO,(b) favor neither Israel nor the Arab nations, (c) maintain friendly relations with both. Respondents indicated whether or not they had sufficient information concerning various national groups in the region.

Exhibit 34
Indicative abstract

Another type of abstract is the *critical abstract*. Such an abstract is really a "condensed critical review." Applied to reports, journal articles, and other relatively brief items, a critical abstract serves much the same purpose as a critical book review. A critical abstract is evaluative. The abstractor expresses views on the quality of the work of the author and perhaps contrasts it with the work of others. For example, a critical abstract of the item illustrated in Exhibit 3 might mention weaknesses of the methodology used—the way the population was sampled, the size of the sample, the wording of the questions—or compare the results with those of earlier surveys. Because the writers must be true experts, critical abstracts are rather uncommon.

Two publications that do include critical abstracts are *Mathematical Reviews* and *Applied Mechanics Reviews (AMR)*. Exhibit 36 shows a true critical abstract from the latter. Note that the abstract is signed and that it combines descriptive and critical elements. An examination of AMR reveals, however, that true critical abstracts are very much the exception rather than the rule.

> Telephone interviews conducted in 1985 with 655 Americans, sampled probabilistically, brought these results: most (54-56%) think U.S. aid to Israel and Egypt should be reduced; most (65%) favor U.S. participation in a peace conference that includes the PLO; more than 80% consider it important that the U.S. should maintain friendly relations with both Israel and the Arab countries; 70% believe that the U.S. should favor neither side; most (55%) think that the establishment of a Palestinian state is essential to peace in the region. The Israelis are the best known of the national groups and the Syrians the least known. The Arab-Israeli situation is second only to the conflict in Central America among the most serious international problems faced by the U.S.

Exhibit 35
Informative abstract

Nowadays abstracts frequently appear in scholarly journals along with the articles to which they relate; they are usually written by the authors of the articles. In many cases these abstracts are picked up and reproduced by the indexing and abstracting services. Some journals include abstracts in more than one language. For example, several Russian and Japanese journals include English abstracts.

Purpose of Abstracts

Many different purposes of abstracts could be mentioned. First and foremost, perhaps, abstracts facilitate selection. That is, they help the reader decide whether a particular item is likely to be of interest or not. In this way, they save the time of the reader—e.g., by preventing him from acquiring articles that would not be of any interest. In some cases, too, a good informative abstract may actually substitute for the reading of an item that is of interest to the user. Abstracts are particularly useful in illuminating the content of items written in languages unfamiliar to a particular reader.

The printing and distribution of abstracts is effective in keeping people informed of newly published literature in their fields of interest (i.e., providing for *current awareness*). As mentioned earlier, abstracts appearing within the articles or reports to which they relate are useful to an indexer in helping him identify the central subject matter of the item as rapidly as possible. Borko and Bernier (1975) imply that abstracts can substitute for the full text in indexing activities, but this may not always be a desirable practice.

1989. Pao, Y. C., Dept. of Eng. Mech., Univ. of Nebr., Lincoln, **Shy, D. S.**, et al., **On relationship between bulk modulus and relative volume of lung during inflation-deflation maneuvers,** p 136-142, *Journal of Biomechanical Engineering, Transactions of the ASME* v 104, n 2 (May 1982).

The paper presents an equation relating the bulk modulus of the lung to the relative volume during inflation and deflation. The average bulk modulus of the lung was obtained by injecting air via a 6-mm-i.d. cannula in the main lobar bronchus. "Regional lobe" volume changes were measured by roentgen-videographically determined placement of 25 metal markers implanted in the excised lower lobes of three dogs. Whole lobe volumes at various transpulmonary pressures were measured by water displacement. Pressure and volume measurements were used to calculate bulk modulus ($K = \Delta V P/\Delta V$). The "most satisfactory least squares curve-fit" of bulk modulus (K) vs. relative volume (V/V_{max}) was obtained with the equation $K = C/(1 - V/V_{max})^n$. Substituting for bulk modulus. with the equation $K = VdP/dV$, and integrating enabled computer-generated pressure-volume plots. This equation provided a better pressure-volume curve-fit than previously obtained, especially at low values of pressure and volume. Also, as expected, the bulk modulus was smaller at low volume, but the rate of change of modulus was greater during deflation than during inflation.

The authors assumed, without giving sufficient justification, that the "regional lobe" (the area bounded by the 25 markers) included a higher density of airways than the rest of the lobe. Using this assumption, the authors claimed that the modulus and rate of change of modulus were different for parenchyma tissue and the airways during both inflation and deflation. No mention, however, was made of paired t-tests or any other statistical tests. In fact, if they had done a paired t-test, they would have discovered that none of these differences were significant, even at the 90 percent confidence level.

Other sources of error which were not addressed include: the difference in the properties of excised lung and intact lung due to blood in the vessels, surrounding tissue, negative pressure, etc.; the effect of the markers on the pressure-volume relationship; the effect of strain rate on the modulus of lung tissue, which is a viscoelastic material; the time elapsed between regional volume measurement and whole volume measurements (this is important for viscoelastic material); the difference between the true regional ΔV and the measured ΔV; and the differences between the mechanical properties of dog and human lung tissue.

Despite its limitations, the paper presents a step forward in the understanding of mechanical properties of the lung, and, thus, lung diseases. Therefore, it should be of benefit to researchers interested in respiratory mechanics and physiology.

D. S. Feldman, USA

Exhibit 36
Example of a critical abstract
Reprinted from *Applied Mechanics Reviews,* 37, 1984, by permission of the editor

Finally, abstracts now play an important role in computer-based retrieval systems by facilitating the identification of pertinent items and by providing access to stored items (in systems in which the text of abstracts is stored in searchable form).

For certain purposes, a *structured abstract* may be preferred to one in the form of narrative text. A hypothetical example of a "frame" for a structured abstract is shown in Exhibit 37. The subject matter dealt with is that of irrigation. In this case, the abstractor is told to look specifically for the items listed. Abstracting involves putting the appropriate "values" into the frame. That is, for each article, the type of irrigation, soil type, crops involved, climatic conditions, and location are indicated, and codes are used to represent the type of results achieved. This type of abstract has value in the compilation of handbooks summarizing a large number of studies performed in a particular field. However, it would only work for a subject area in which the essential elements would remain more or less the same from one study to another. Zholkova (1975) describes how facet analysis might be used to create a structured abstract but is somewhat unconvincing on the value of this approach.

TYPE OF IRRIGATION	SOIL TYPE	CROPS	CLIMATIC CONDITIONS	PLACE	RESULTS

Exhibit 37
Structured abstract

Terse Literatures

Bernier and Yerkey (1979) have described and illustrated the use of highly abbreviated statements each of which encapsulates the major "point" of some publication. They refer to these generically as "terse literatures" and to the most condensed of these as "ultraterse literatures." One variety is the ultraterse conclusion, a very brief statement on the major conclusion reached in some piece of research. For example:

Theoretical linguistics has had no significant impact on information science

This type of summarization is not an abstract in the conventional sense; nevertheless, terse literatures are certainly related to abstracts. They have a number of potential applications. For example, it would be possible to produce a handbook summarizing what is known about some phenomenon (e.g., disease) as a series of ultraterse statements, each statement linked to a bibliographic reference identifying the source from which it is derived.

Modular Abstracts

In 1964, Herner and Company undertook a study for the National Science Foundation on the feasibility of "modular content analyses" (Lancaster et al., 1965). These had two components: modular abstracts and modular index entries. A specimen is included as Exhibits 38 and 39.

Citation

Rosensweig, R. E., and Beecher, N. Theory for the ablation of fiberglas-reinforced phenolic resin. American Institute of Aeronautics and Astronautics Journal, vol. 1, No. 8, August 1963, pp. 1802-1809.

Annotation

A theoretical model is developed, for a charring and melting composite material, combining glassy ablation and the char layer-molten glass chemical reaction effects.

Indicative

The variables associated with the ablation of a typical resin-glass system are examined. These include glass ablation and plastic pyrolysis, flow in both the reacting and non-reacting parts of the melt, mass loss and heat absorption due to chemical reaction, mass injection effects, and coupling between the external pressure and the assumed chemical reaction. The mathematical development is traced and the approximations utilized are discussed. Parametric examinations are made.

Informative

Pyrolysis, melting, and chemical reaction are taken into account in this theory of the ablation of phenolic-fiberglas. It postulates a very thin, isothermal, surface reaction zone, where the char layer (carbon) formed during the pyrolysis of the organic binder reacts chemically with the molten silica. Other assumptions are conventional.
Calculations for typical IRBM re-entry conditions showed little temperature drop in the reaction zone, 6% maximum and usually less than 1%. Depth of the zone was three orders of magnitude less than the thermal thickness. The unreacting run-off in the melt zone ranged from 40-80% as a function ot the possible reaction enthalpy level. However, more than 99% of the material reaching the reaction zone was affected. At the expected temperatures of 1400-2000°C., the theory assumed the reaction
$$SiO_2 + 3C \rightarrow SiC + 2CO$$
Earlier experiments had yielded the reaction kinetics. Significant effects, up to 25% increase, on the ablation rate appeared only at the lower reaction rates. Changing the reaction enthalpy by a factor of three changed the ablation rate by less than 10%. When compared with a peak re-entry ablation rate, the value given by this theory was reported to be 38% in defect.

Critical

This theory extends the classic work of Bethe and Adams (Avco-Everett Research Lab., Res. Rept. 38, Nov. 1958) on ablation of pure glasses. Thus it treats the problem as concerning carbon-contaminated glass rather than, as is more usual, a char-layer. In the only comparison given between the theory and experimental data, revealing 38% underprediction by the theory, a thorough error analysis was not included. Spalding (Aero. Quart., Aug. 1961, pp. 237-274) and Scala (General Electric Co. (MSVD), Rept. R59SD401, July, 1959; ARS Jnl., June, 1962, pp. 917-924) have treated similar problems.

Exhibit 38
Modular abstracts
Reprinted by permission of Saul Herner

Modular abstracts were intended as full content descriptions of current documents. Each abstract consists of five parts: a citation, an annotation, an indicative abstract, an informative abstract, and a critical abstract. The set was so designed that an abstracting service could process it to conform to its own unique requirements with a minimum of effort: any one of the abstracts could be used intact, or the modules edited to form, for example, a partially indicative, partially informative abstract, or a partially informative, partially critical abstract.

Physical and Mathematical Systems

    Axisymmetric and Blunt Body Systems
    Re-entry Bodies

Environment

    Atmospheric Entry
    Re-entry Conditions
    Space Flight

Mass Transfer

    Ablation, Analytical
    Ablation, Charring
    Ablation, Melting
    Ablation of Glasses
    Chemical Reaction Effects
    Thermal Thickness
    Reaction Zone
    Reaction Thickness
    Gasification Ratio

Thermodynamics

    Coupled Reactions
    Carbon-Silica Reactions

Materials

    Phenolics, Fiberglas Reinforced
    Glass Fibers
    Rocket and Missile Materials
    Ablation Materials
    Reinforced Plastics
    Thermal (Re-entry) Shields
    Phenolic Resin

Means and Methods

    Parametric Analysis

Authors

    Rosensweig, R. E.
    Beecher, N.

Affiliations

    Massachusetts Institute of Technology
    National Research Corporation

Exhibit 39
Modular index entries
Reprinted by permission of Saul Herner

The prime purpose of modular abstracts was to eliminate the duplication and waste of intellectual effort involved in the independent abstracting of the same documents by several services, without any attempt to force "standardized" abstracts on services whose requirements may vary considerably as to form and subject slant. Both abstracts and index entries were prepared by subject specialists, and it was intended that they would reconcile the requirements for speed of publication with the thoroughness of abstracts prepared by experts. Their standardized format and treatment would also reduce repetitive handling and speed the flow of work within recipient abstracting services.

The modular index entries would suggest descriptive terms, drawn

SUMMARY

1. A method is described for the determination of strontium and barium in human bone by radioactivation analysis.

2. Results of analyses of 35 bone samples, from normal persons of both sexes and different ages, are given. The concentrations of barium and strontium were found to be of the order of 7 and 100 µg./g. of ashed tissue respectively.

3. No relationship between sex or disease of individuals with strontium and barium concentration was noted. The concentration of strontium in the age group 0-13 years was significantly lower than that in the group 19-74 years.

4. No significant difference was found in the concentrations of strontium and barium in the various bones of those individuals examined.

5. Results obtained in this survey are discussed and compared with those of other workers.

/00193/
/METHOD/DETERM/STRONTIUM/BONE/HUMANS/RADIOACTIVATION
ANALYSIS/
/00193/
/NO RELAT BETW/STRONTIUM/HUMANS/AND/SEX/OR/DISEASE/
/00193/
/NO RELAT BETW/BARIUM/HUMANS/AND/SEX/OR/DISEASE/
/00193/
/METHOD/DETERM/BARIUM/BONE/HUMANS/RADIOACTIVATION
ANALYSIS/
/00193/
/DETERM/STRONTIUM/BONE/HUMANS/RADIOACTIVATION ANALYSIS/
7 UG PER G ASHED TISSUE/
/00193/
/DETERM/BARIUM/BONE/HUMANS/RADIOACTIVATION ANALYSIS/100
UG PER G ASHED TISSUE/
/00193/
/INCR/STRONTIUM/HUMANS/ADULTS/AGE 19-74/COMP W/CHILD-
REN/0-13/

Exhibit 40
Part 1

Comparison of mini-abstract, author's summary and abstracts from *Chemical Abstracts* and *Biological Abstracts* (see part 2 of exhibit). Reproduced from Lunin (1967) by permission of Drexel University. The abstract from *Biochemical Journal* is reprinted by permission of the Biochemical Society, Portland Scientific Press; the abstract from *Biological Abstracts* by permission of BIOSIS and the abstract from *Chemical Abstracts* by permission of Chemical Abstracts Service. Note that one abstract follows the author's summary very closely and the other is merely a further abbreviation of it.

BA 32: 18857, 1958
18857. SOWDEN, ELEANOR M., and B. R. STITCH. (Med. Res. Council Radiobiol. Res. Unit, Atomic Energy Res. Establishment, Harwell, Didcot, Berks, Eng.) Trace elements in human tissue. 2. Estimation of the concentrations of stable strontium and barium in human bone. Biochem. Jour. 67(1): 104-109. 1957.--A method is described for the determination of strontium and barium in human bone by radioactivation analysis. Results of analyses of 35 bone samples, from normal persons of both sexes and different ages, are given. The concentrations of Ba and Sr were of the order of 7 and 100 µg/g of ashed tissue respectively. No relationship between sex or disease of individuals with Sr and Ba concentration was noted. The concentration of Sr in the age group 1-13 years was significantly lower than that in the group 19-74 years. No significant difference was found in the concentrations of Sr and Ba in the various bones of those individuals examined. Results obtained in this survey are discussed and compared with those of other workers.--Auth. summ.

CA 51: 18184, 1957
II. Estimation of the concentrations of stable strontium and barium in human bone. Eleanor M. Sowden and S. R. Stitch. *Ibid.* 104-9.—A method based on the technique of Harrison and Raymond (*C.A.* 49, 12571g) has been used for the detn. of Sr and Ba in human bone by radioactivation analysis. Results of analyses of 35 bone samples, from normal persons of both sexes and different ages, are given. The concns. of Ba and Sr were found to be of the order of 7 and 100·/g. of ashed tissue, resp. No relation between sex or disease of individuals age group 0-13 yrs. was significantly lower than in the group 19-74 yrs. No significant difference was found in the concns. of Sr and Ba in the various bones of those individuals examined. The results obtained in this survey are discussed and compared with those of other workers.
Roland F. Beers, Jr.

Exhibit 40
Part 2

from representative index vocabularies, that could be used intact, with refinement or with augmentation, to index the abstract derived from the modular package. The representative index vocabularies used as sources for the modular index entries were to be derived from the current indexes or authority lists of the recipient abstracting and indexing services and would thus be reflective of the indexing styles and policies of these services.

A test of the concept was performed in the field of heat transfer, this being a highly interdisciplinary subject of potential interest to a large number of abstracting services. Sets of abstracts/index entries were prepared and submitted to several services for routine processing. The services completed questionnaires to evaluate the concept. It was concluded that it was possible to produce a content analysis, in modular form, that could be used as input to a variety of abstracting services, but that the majority of services were reluctant to relinquish their autonomy in order to participate in the type of clearinghouse implied by the modular approach.

Mini-Abstracts

The term "mini-abstract" is rather imprecise. It could mean merely a short abstract. As used by Lunin (1967), however, the term refers to a highly structured abstract designed primarily for searching by computer. It is, in fact, a kind of cross between an abstract and an index entry, and Lunin defines it as a "machine-readable index-abstract." The terms used in the abstract are drawn from a controlled vocabulary and are put together in a specified sequence. For example, the statement "There is a decreased amount of zinc in the blood of humans with cirrhosis of the liver" would be written:

/DECR/ZINC/BLOOD/HUMANS/CIRRHOSIS/LIVER

Note that the abstractor tries to keep to a sequence of terms as close as possible to the normal sentence structure. The contents of a document may be described in some detail through the use of a series of such stylized statements. While intended primarily to facilitate searching by computer, Lunin's mini-abstracts can also make sense to the intelligent reader. Exhibit 40, taken from Lunin, compares the results of the mini-abstract technique with abstracts from *Biological Abstracts* and *Chemical Abstracts* and with the author's summary.

Telegraphic Abstracts

The term "telegraphic abstract" is also imprecise. It implies a document representation that is presented very parsimoniously: not in complete sentences and resembling a telegram. Indeed it might just be a string of terms without syntax. Lunin's mini-abstracts are telegraphic in style. The term "telegraphic abstract" was used to refer to an essential component in the early computerized retrieval system developed at Western Reserve University (see Chapter 11).

8

WRITING THE ABSTRACT

As WITH INDEXING, one learns to be a good abstractor only through practice. The most that can be done in a book of this type is to give some general guidelines.

Again similar to indexing, the good abstractor will learn to read/skim an item to identify the salient points quickly. Cremmins (1982) discusses in detail how to read an article to pick out the most important points as efficiently as possible and presents some rules for this purpose. Much of this is self-evident and, in any case, different individuals prefer different techniques for getting to the heart of a text.

The characteristics of a good abstract can be summarized as brevity, accuracy, and clarity. The abstractor should avoid redundancy. In particular, the abstract should build upon the information in the title of the item, not duplicate it. For example, the title of the article used as an illustration in Exhibits 3, 34, and 35 is *Nationwide Public Opinion Survey of U.S. Attitudes on the Middle East.* The first line of a published abstract is:

> The results of a survey conducted in February, 1985, of U.S. public attitudes on the Middle East.

Clearly, this adds little to the title except for giving the date. Note how the abstracts in Exhibits 3, 34, and 35 build on the title rather than duplicating it.

The abstractor should also omit other information that the reader would be likely to know or that may not be of direct interest to him. This might include background or historical information—e.g., why a study was undertaken or details of the previous experience of the company conducting the study. Borko and Bernier (1975) stress that the abstractor should indicate what the author did rather than what he tried to do but failed to accomplish or intends to do next.

The shorter the abstract the better, as long as the meaning remains clear and there is no sacrifice of accuracy. Unnecessary words such as "the author" or "the article" can be left out. For example, "This article examines..." can be reduced to "Examines...." Standard abbreviations and acronyms can be used whenever these are likely to be well known to readers (e.g., PLO). In other cases, an abbreviation can be used once its meaning has been defined. For example:

> ...within the framework of European Political Cooperation (EPC). The achievements...by EPC...

Abstracts in some fields of science may use many abbreviations. While this saves space it can reduce intelligibility and actually increase the amount of time required of the reader. Despite the need for brevity, abstracts should be self-contained; a major purpose of the abstract is defeated if a reader needs to consult the original to understand the abstract!

Jargon is best avoided. As Weil et al. (1963) point out, jargon words may mean different things to different groups of readers and may not be understood at all by some people.

Some abstractors feel that they must change the words of an author. While paraphrase is frequently necessary to achieve brevity, nothing is gained by changing the author's words in striving for originality. Indeed it is easy to distort the meaning of the original by deliberately seeking, for stylistic reasons, to find substitute expressions. This point is made forcefully by Collison (1971):

> It is important that the abstractor should use the vocabulary of the author as far as possible; paraphrase is dangerous and can lead the reader to channels of thought not intended by the author. (Page 11)

An abstract is utilitarian and need not be a work of art, although Cremmins (1982) believes that abstracts should have "grace" as well as clarity and precision.

The U.S. national standard on abstracts (American National Standards Institute, 1979) specifies that verbs should be used in the active voice (e.g., "Role indicators reduce recall" rather than "Recall is reduced by role indicators") whenever possible, but that the passive voice may be used for "indicative statements and even for informative statements in which the receiver of the action should be stressed." This qualification is very imprecise and is best forgotten: in most cases the preferred tense will be obvious for stylistic reasons. Borko and Chatman (1963) and Weil (1970) suggest use of the past tense in describing experimental procedures and conditions but the present tense for conclusions derived from the experiments. This is logical: the activities reported by an author are things of the past while the results and conclusions are still with us. Borko and Bernier (1975) are more explicit, recommending active voice and past tense for informative abstracts and passive voice and present tense for indicative.

Weil et al. (1963) have presented a table of hints for abstractors. This is reproduced as Exhibit 41. Their recommendation that the abstractor should essentially work from the specific to the general (findings placed early, "details" next, general statements last) should be viewed with some caution for, in some cases at least, it will produce an abstract that seems

Do	Don't
scan the document purposefully for key facts	
slant the abstract to your audience	change the meaning of the original
tell what was found	comment on or interpret the document
tell why the work was done	
tell how the work was done	mention earlier work
place findings early in the topical sentence	include detailed experimental results
put details in succeeding sentences	describe details of conventional apparatus
place general statements last	
separate relatively independent subjects	mention future work
	begin abstracts with stock phrases
differentiate experiment from hypothesis	use involved phraseology
be informative but brief	use questionable jargon
be exact, concise, and unambiguous	waste words by stating the obvious
use short, complete sentences	say the same thing two ways
use short, simple, familiar words	use noun form of verbs*
avoid unnecessary words	over-use synonyms
use generic expressions when possible	use "high-polymer adjectives"
employ normal technical English	use a choppy, telegraphic style
use direct statements (active voice)	
describe conclusions in the present tense	
use abbreviations sparingly	
avoid cacophony	
cite bibliographical data completely	

Exhibit 41
Hints for abstractors
Reprinted with permission from Weil et al. (1963). *Journal of Chemical Documentation,* 1963, 3, p. 131. Copyright © 1963 American Chemical Society

illogical—e.g., results of an experiment stated before the purpose is given.** The national standard (American National Standards Institute, 1979) gives

*The authors claim that "Separating butadiene from butenes" reads better than "The separation of butadiene from butenes" but this is entirely a personal preference.

**This recommendation really advocates an abstract beginning with an eye-catching headline, rather like a newspaper article. Such a headline might be findings-oriented (especially in the case of a research article) but need not be. This is discussed again later in the chapter.

safer advice when it recommends that the abstract begin with a "topic sentence" (i.e., a central statement of the major thesis). Most of the other recommendations seem eminently sensible, although they apply more to indicative or informative abstracts than to critical. A critical abstract is supposed to "comment on or interpret" and to mention earlier work where this is necessary to put the present work in perspective.

Perhaps the most concise set of abstracting principles is the one issued by the Defense Documentation Center (1968), which is reproduced in Exhibit 42. In a few brief statements this encapsulates the center's rules for what to include, what not to include, how long the abstract is to be, and what type of terminology is to be used. A more complete statement, but still in concise form, is given in a report by Payne et al. (1962). This is reproduced as Appendix 1.

Content and Format

What should be included in an abstract, of course, depends very much on the type of publication involved. A long indicative abstract of some type of research report might mention the objectives of the research, experimental or other procedures used, the types of results achieved (an informative abstract would present the actual results, at least in condensed form), and the author's conclusions on the significance of the results. The treatment of a historical article, on the other hand, would be quite different. The abstract might, for example, emphasize the author's thesis or conclusions, being sure to mention the periods, geographic locations, and individuals involved.

In specialized subject areas, an abstractor may be given precise instructions on certain things to look for in an article and to bring out clearly in the abstract. These might include such varied items as drug dosage, climatic conditions, age of individuals, soil types, equations used, or alloying element involved. Abstracts tend to be easier to write when the subject matter deals with concrete objects and become more difficult to write the more abstract or nebulous the subject.

The majority of abstracts are presented in the conventional format of bibliographic references followed by the text of the abstract. In some publications, however, the abstract precedes the bibliographic references, and the first line of the abstract is highlighted in some way, as in the following example:

LABOUR MIGRATION FROM MOZAMBIQUE TO THE MINES OF SOUTH AFRICA remains a significant element in the economic relationship between these countries. . . .
Brockmann, G. Migrant labour and foreign policy: the case of Mozambique. *Journal of Peace Research,* 22, 1985, 335-344.

This is a more dramatic form of presentation, rather like a newspaper headline, and may attract a reader's attention more readily. Weil et al. (1963) refer to this as a "reader-oriented" abstract, a "topical-sentence first" abstract, or a "findings-oriented" abstract (although the headline need not necessarily relate to findings). If it is suitable, the title of the article could become the headline followed by an amplifying topic sentence.

A complete abstract may be considered to have three parts: the bibliographic *reference* identifying the item abstracted; the *body* of the abstract (the text); and the *signature*. This last element is the attribution of the source of the abstract—e.g., the abstractor's initials, or an indication that the abstract was prepared by the author of the item, is a modified author abstract, or is derived from some other source such as another abstracting service.

Many abstracts seem to fall in the 100-250 word range but, as discussed earlier, it makes sense that the length should vary with such factors as the length of the item itself, its range of subject matter, its perceived importance, its physical availability, and its intellectual accessibility (e.g., items difficult to locate, such as conference papers, or items in obscure languages might be abstracted in more detail than other items). Borko and Bernier (1975) suggest that abstracts of science literature should usually be between one tenth and one twentieth the length of the original.

Sound advice on the sequencing of content is given by Borko and Bernier (1975):

> The body of the abstract can be arranged to save the reader's time. Conclusions placed first may satisfy the reader and save further reading. (S)he may accept or reject the conclusions without needing to know the findings upon which the conclusions were based. Amplifying information should be placed last. Labeling each part of an abstract as, for example, *conclusions, results,* or *procedures,* has been found to be unnecessary; readers understand what part they are reading. The arrangement of parts of the body of an abstract is done for the same purpose that parts of an item in a newspaper are organized—to communicate more information more rapidly.
>
> Paragraphing is not desirable. The abstract is short; it should express a homogeneity of thought, and should be written as a single paragraph. (Page 69)*

The broad types of error that can occur in subject indexing can also occur in abstracting: points that should be included are not and others

*The quotations from Borko and Bernier (1975) are reproduced by permission of Academic Press and the two authors.

OUTLINE

In brief:
1. Always an informative abstract if possible
2. 200-250 words
3. Same technical terminology as in report
4. Contents
    a. Objectives or purpose of investigation
    b. Methods of investigation
    c. Results of investigation
    d. Validity of results
    e. Conclusions
    f. Applications
5. Numerals for numbers when possible
6. Phrases for clauses, words for phrases when possible
7. No unconventional or rare symbols or characters
8. No uncommon abbreviations
9. No equations, footnotes, preliminaries
10. No descriptive cataloging data
11. Security Classification
12. Dissemination controls, if any
13. Review it.

Exhibit 42
Abstracting principles published by the Defense Documentation
Center (1968)
Reproduced by permission of the
Defense Technical Information Center

may be included that are better omitted. Transcription errors can also
occur, especially when formulae or numerical values are involved. The work
of inexperienced abstractors should always be checked and edited by a
more senior person. Borko and Bernier (1975) affirm the value of a good
editor:

> Editors of abstracts seem to develop a sixth sense as to when some
> content of importance is missing. They look for, and expect to see,
> certain categories of information, such as methods and equipment used,
> data collected, and conclusions. (Page 12)

A particular abstracting service will probably adopt some guidelines on
such things as spelling, punctuation, and capitalization. Much of this is
a matter of individual preference so it seems pointless to give examples
here.

To aid the work of the abstractor, particularly in a training program,
it may be desirable to prepare some type of worksheet to prompt the

abstractor on what to look for in a publication. A worksheet* of this kind might include such headings as:

Types and Purpose [Type of investigation, such as experimental, theoretical, review, basic or applied research, development. Purpose: a statement of the problem, a definition of what exactly is investigated.]
Experimental Set-up or Theoretical Model [Salient features, new approaches, hypothesis to be proven, results anticipated when work was begun. What differentiates this work, either experimentally or analytically, from that of other investigators?]
Conditions Examined [Parameters varied, ranges involved, controls imposed.]
Procedures [New techniques utilized, transformations used or developed, how results were obtained.]
Assumptions [What are the direct and indirect assumptions and are they standard?]
Main Conclusions [Author's principal conclusions, other conclusions supported by the data, significant negative results.]
Secondary Conclusions [Minor points, or those in peripheral areas of the investigation, may be reported if they are deemed sufficiently useful. Interpretations and reasonable inferences and extrapolations may be reported. Loose theoretical linkages and speculative questions are not desired.]
Importance or Utility [Importance and competence of the work performed. Potential applications.]
Limitations and Shortcomings [Are the assumptions unduly restrictive or confining? Is the theoretical model too far removed from possible practical application? Are there flaws in the technique? Were limitations imposed on the results by the approach to the problem? What degree of sophistication was employed? Has there been sufficient analysis of the data, particularly with respect to possible errors?]
Critical Comments [Possible fundamental error, and magnitude of the errors. Possible previous publication of this information. Are there any similar investigations and what is the position of the present work in the literature? Which features are particularly praiseworthy? Is the interpretation of results reasonable?]

Clearly not all of these categories will apply to every item to be abstracted and the last three would apply only to critical abstracts. The use of this type of questionnaire approach to abstracting is discussed by Solov'ev (1971).

Some writers have attempted to produce guidelines for abstracting particular types of documents. For example, Solov'ev (1981) suggests that abstracts of doctoral dissertations should address the following points: current significance of the subject, the problem dealt with and the goal of the research, scientific novelty, methodology, results achieved, and conclusions (including implementation of the results).

Although it is somewhat unclear, and thus difficult to interpret in places, the UNHCR Refugee Documentation Centre has compressed the essentials

---

*The headings and descriptions for the worksheet illustrated here are based on those used in the Herner and Company modular abstracts project and are reproduced by permission of Saul Herner.

of abstracting into a single diagram (Exhibit 43). Particularly useful are the evaluation criteria listed on the left of the diagram. Note that the abstract is to be evaluated on the basis of its language and content, its conformity to "house style" (length, structure, spelling and punctuation conventions) and, most importantly, the degree to which it satisfies user needs.

More formal "models" of the abstracting process have been prepared (e.g., by Karasev, 1978). While these may aid our understanding of the steps that an abstractor goes through intuitively, they seem of little practical value to abstractors.

Abstractors

Abstracts can be prepared by authors, other subject specialists, or professional abstractors. Many scholarly journals require authors to prepare abstracts to accompany their papers. Increasingly, these abstracts are adopted by published abstracting services in place of preparing a new abstract.

As in the case of indexing, an abstractor must have some understanding of the subject matter dealt with although he need not be a subject expert. Writing and editing skills are important requirements, and the ability of an abstractor to read and understand quickly is a definite asset.

Borko and Bernier (1975) caution that authors do not necessarily write the best abstracts for their papers. Authors usually lack training and experience in abstracting as well as lacking knowledge of abstracting rules. The more prestigious abstracting publications are usually able to recruit subject specialists as abstractors. These experts may agree to write abstracts in their field of specialization without pay or for a modest honorarium. Borko and Bernier claim that: "Those who are trained in abstracting and are also expert in a field write the best abstracts"—a claim that is difficult to quarrel with. Because these subject specialists are usually volunteers, it may be difficult to get them to abstract promptly. The professional abstractor is expensive but prompt and can do excellent work when dealing with subject areas that are not totally unfamiliar.

At the present time authors and publishers have little incentive for "embroidering" abstracts to make the underlying work seem more attractive than it really is. Price (1983) has argued that this could become a danger in a completely electronic environment (see Chapter 15). Publishers would want to promote use because they would probably be paid on this basis. Authors would want to promote use if this factor became, as it might, a criterion used in promotion and tenure decisions.

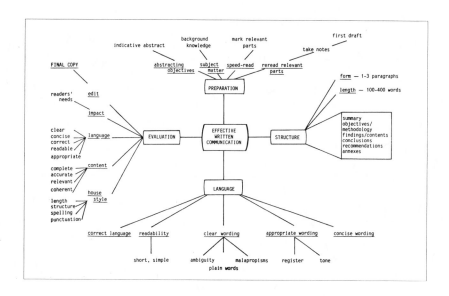

Exhibit 43
Essentials of abstracting
From UNHCR Refugee Documentation Centre (1985) Reproduced by
permission of the UNHCR Centre for Documentation on Refugees

Abstracting and indexing are closely related activities and a strong argument can be made for combining them. It is a small step from the conceptual analysis stage of indexing to the preparation of an acceptable abstract. Moreover, the additional discipline involved in writing the abstract can help in deciding what should be covered in the indexing and what can be omitted. The fact that some combination of reading and skimming is involved in both activities is another reason why it is efficient to combine them in a single individual wherever it is practical to do so.

Quality and Consistency in Abstracting

No two abstracts for a document will be identical when written by different individuals or by the same individual at different times: what is described may be the same, but how it is described will differ. Quality and consistency are a bit more vague when applied to abstracts than when applied to indexing. There seem to be two major facets of quality:

1. Are the major "points" of the document brought out in the abstract?
2. Are these points described accurately, succinctly, and unambiguously?

To some extent, then, the quality of abstracting may be judged according to criteria that are very similar to those used in the evaluation of indexing. The first step in abstracting, as in indexing, is really conceptual analysis— what points should be brought out?—and the second step is the translation of this conceptual analysis into readable text.

The quality of the conceptual analysis, presumably, can be judged against the content-related instructions of the organization for which the abstract is prepared. For example:

1. Is the purpose and scope of the work covered?
2. Are the results indicated or summarized?
3. Are the author's conclusions summarized?
   and so on.

The consistency between two abstracts can then be judged, at this conceptual level, on the degree to which the abstractors have agreed on what points to include.

Judging the quality of the "translation" phase of abstracting is a bit more tricky, because accuracy, ambiguity, and brevity are somewhat subjective criteria. Nevertheless, it is possible for a senior abstractor to use these in judging the work of more junior people. Consistency applied to the translation phase of abstracting should not be a major concern: it should be possible to make the same point in several different ways, each accurate and ambiguous and, perhaps, equally brief.

	Full text	Abstracts
Number of items judged relevant	12	15
Number of items judged nonrelevant	38	35
TOTAL	50	50

Exhibit 44
Hypothetical results from a test of relevance predictability

The ultimate test of a good abstract is simply "does it allow a reader to accurately predict whether or not the item abstracted is relevant to his present interests or not?" For a particular reader, and a particular information need, it is possible to test this on the basis of, say, 50 abstracts printed out as the result of an online search. The results of the study might be those presented in Exhibit 44: the abstracts suggested that 15 items might be relevant but only 12 turned out to be. Moreover, if it is discovered that not all of the 12 judged relevant from text were also judged relevant from the abstracts, the abstracts have failed in both ways: they suggested some items to be relevant when they were not and others not to be relevant when they were.

Of course, this kind of study is somewhat difficult to do. Moreover, the results apply only to a particular user and information need; change the user or information need and the results change. Most users of abstracting services, or of online databases, will have experienced the situation, perhaps fairly frequently, in which an abstract whets the appetite for a document that subsequently turns out to be quite different from what was expected. In these cases, then, the abstracts have failed these users although they might have served other users quite adequately.

The value of abstracts in predicting the relevance of documents to a particular user is discussed in more detail in the next chapter. While several relevance predictability studies have been performed, investigations of the activities of abstractors are few and far between. In fact, more work may have been done on the evaluation of extracting than on the evaluation of abstracting. For example, both Rath et al. (1961b) and Edmundson et al. (1961) discovered that humans were not very consistent (with each other or with themselves) in selecting from a text the sentences that were judged to be the best indicators of its content.

Edmundson et al. (1961) suggest several possible approaches to the evaluation of abstracts:

1. intuitive, subjective judgment;
2. comparison with an "ideal" abstract;
3. determining to what extent test questions about a document can be answered from the abstract;
4. retrievability of the document by the abstract.

Clearly, abstracts are evaluated by editors and others working within information centers or publishing houses, presumably by the intuitive method. It would seem likely that, as more and more use is made of text searching in place of human indexing, the "retrievability" approach to evaluation becomes increasingly important. The criteria for judging an abstract on "retrievability" are not necessarily the same as those used to judge it on the basis of relevance predictability (see "Compatibility Issues" discussion).

Vinsonhaler (1966) proposes behavioral methods for judging the quality of abstracts on the basis of "content validity" or "predictive validity." In a content validity study, the subjects judge the degree to which the document and the abstract are "similar," using perhaps a seven-point similarity scale. Alternatively, a test may be used to determine to what extent an abstract discriminates between documents, especially when the subject matter of the documents may be quite similar. To measure discriminability, Vinsonhaler proposes a test in which subjects examine a particular document and then try to identify the appropriate abstract from a booklet of abstracts. One test of predictive validity determines to what extent decisions made on the similarity of abstracts agree with similarity decisions made on the basis of the documents themselves: if the abstracts are "good," groupings of abstracts on the basis of similarity should coincide with groupings of the documents on the basis of similarity. The second test of predictive validity is more conventional: the extent to which abstracts correctly predict the relevance of documents is determined. Vinsonhaler suggests a crossover test in which one group of subjects judges the relevance of a set of documents to a search request statement and then, after a suitable time interval, does the same thing with the abstracts of the documents. The second group of subjects works in reverse sequence, judging abstracts first and documents second.

Mathis (1972) has proposed that abstracts be evaluated on the basis of a "data coefficient" *(DC)*. The *DC* is expressed by the formula *C/L,* where *C* is a "data retention factor" and *L* a "length retention factor." *C* is a measure of the extent to which all of the "concepts" (Mathis refers to them as "data elements") of the document are retained in the abstract. *L* is simply the number of words in the abstract divided by the number in the document. The *DC* is a numerical value, the higher the value the better. It favors concentration and compression: ability to retain all of the essential elements of the text in the fewest words. The value can be improved by either increasing the number of data elements present or reducing the number of words in the abstract. Mathis suggests that a *DC* value below one would indicate an abstract of unacceptable quality. The approach is ingenious although it is entirely dependent on the ability to identify "data elements." Mathis proposes that they can be identified through syntactic criteria.

As with any other type of text, abstracts can be evaluated on the basis of "readability" using standard readability formulae. Dronberger and Kowitz (1975) used the Flesch Reading Ease formula to compare abstracts from *Research in Education* with the reports from which they were derived. The abstracts were found to have significantly lower readability levels, presumably due to their lack of redundancy. Similarly, King (1976), using a "cloze" criterion, found abstracts from *Child Development Abstracts* to be less readable than the items on which they were based.

Borko and Bernier (1975) have provided what is perhaps the most comprehensive list of possible criteria for the evaluation of abstracts, as follows:

1. A global rating of quality (by human judges).
2. The extent to which the ANSI or some other standard is observed (also a major component in the approach to evaluation recommended by Mathis (1972).
3. The inclusion of significant information and the exclusion of unimportant information.
4. Lack of errors.
5. Consistency of style and readability.
6. Relevance predictability.
7. Ability to serve as a surrogate for the original (informative abstracts).
8. Adequacy as a source of index terms.

Obviously, the list represents various levels of criteria. For example, criteria 3-5 would presumably all have to be taken into account in any "global" rating. One approach to the evaluation of the extent to which an abstract can serve in place of the original (criterion 7) is to compare the ability of groups of individuals to answer questions based on (a) abstracts and (b) full text. Studies of this type have been reported by Payne et al. (1962).

In fact, the Payne studies involved three different approaches to evaluation:

1. *Consistency.* Subject specialists were used to compare abstracts on the basis of similarity in the amount of information given.
2. *The amount of text reduction achieved.*
3. *Utility.* Students answered technical questions based on papers in their area of specialization. Some students read the papers, others only the abstracts. Answers of the two groups were compared.

Compatibility Issues

Thirty years ago the sole reason for writing abstracts was to create a representation of a document to be read by humans. However, abstracts are now used for a second purpose—to provide a representation that can be searched by computer. Unfortunately, these two purposes are not fully compatible. For retrieval purposes, redundancy is desirable. That is, a topic is best represented in more than one way. For example, including the synonyms "triangular wings" and "delta wings" in some abstract increases the probability that the item will be retrieved—one searcher may use "triangular" while another may think of "delta." For the human reader, on the other hand, consistency rather than redundancy is desirable. Indeed, a user may be very confused if ideas are described in a number of different ways within an abstract.

For retrieval purposes, the longer the abstract the better. At least, the longer the abstract the more access points it provides, and the more access points the greater the potential for high recall in retrieval. At the same time, it must be recognized that precision is likely to deteriorate: the longer the abstract the more the "minor" aspects of the document will be brought in and the greater the potential for false associations (as discussed in Chapters 6, 11, and 13). For the human reader, of course, brevity is desirable. It is also desirable for the subscribers to printed tools since longer abstracts lead to more expensive publications.

For the human reader, negative references are valuable: "but excludes cost considerations" tells the reader what not to expect in the document. Inclusion of the word "cost" in the abstract, of course, will cause it to be retrieved in searches in which cost is an important facet—exactly the situation in which it should not be retrieved.

For retrieval purposes, too, certain words are best avoided. The common word "aids" will create problems in many databases for it will cause retrieval of items on the disease AIDS, while "to lead" will cause retrieval of items in a search on the metal lead. For more effective retrieval, then, abstractors should avoid terms known to create problems of this type.

Even the conventions of punctuation and syntax that make sense to the human reader may create problems for the computer. Consider, for example, a sentence ending with the word "acid" and followed immediately by one beginning with "precipitation." In many systems this item will be retrieved in a search on "acid precipitation" although it may have nothing at all to do with this subject.

The mini-abstracts of Lunin (1967) (see preceding chapter), unlike the conventional abstract, are designed primarily to facilitate searching by computer. While they can be interpreted by intelligent users, they are definitely more difficult to read and understand, and it is not known how a stylized statement of this kind would be accepted by the users of a retrieval system.

All of this points to the fact that an abstract "optimum" for the human reader may not be optimum for searching by computer. Within the foreseeable future, however, abstracts will continue to serve both purposes. Even if the importance of printed services declines (see Chapter 15), abstracts will still be needed as an intermediate output in computer-based searches. One implication of this is that the publishers of secondary services need to revise their instructions so that abstractors are led to create abstracts that, as far as possible, are effective surrogates for searching as well as for reading.

Fidel (1986) has done a great service by analyzing the abstracting instructions prepared by 36 producers of databases. Her summary of instructions that appear relevant to the retrievability characteristics of abstracts is reproduced as Exhibit 45. More than anything else, her summary reveals some polarities of opinion: use author language, do not use author language, use language identical with the language of assigned index terms, use language that complements the assigned terms, and so on. The most sensible rule is probably the one that specifies that the abstract should include relevant terms that are missing from the descriptors and from the title. Frequently these will be terms more specific than the controlled vocabulary terms.

The In-House Bulletin

The fact that bibliographic databases are available in virtually all fields of endeavor, and that for some fields several competing databases exist, does not necessarily eliminate the need for an in-house abstracting bulletin. The information center of a company, or other organization having a strong research program, may want to produce its own bulletin because:

1. Published abstracting journals may not be sufficiently current in covering the core material of greatest interest to the organization.
2. No single database, in printed or electronic form, is likely to embrace all the material of interest to the organization. Indeed, many databases may be relevant to organizational interests when diversity of subject matter and of documentary forms are taken into account.
3. No external database will cover certain materials of importance, most obviously the organization's own internal reports, manufacturers' literature, advertising material of competitors, and so on.

In order to optimize the procedures used to produce the in-house bulletin it will be necessary to identify those materials that should be abstracted directly. These would presumably include the company's own internal reports and external material judged of particular importance. For example, one member of the center's staff might review all new patents and prepare abstracts for those of possible interest to the company—an art in itself. Using the methods discussed in the next chapter, a "core" of journals that are expected to be unusually productive in terms of the interests of the organization can be identified. These too will be abstracted directly.

It is possible that the sources regularly scanned in this way will yield, say, 80 to 90 percent of the literature that should be included in the internal bulletin. To push this coverage well above the 90 percent level will require the use of more general published sources. The team members who scan the core journals for articles of interest should also scan appropriate indexing/abstracting services in printed form. This should reveal other relevant items—e.g., from sources not subscribed to directly. A comprehensive science source such as *Chemical Abstracts* is particularly

The Content of Abstracts

General statements
Use 'important' concepts and terms (e.g., those which will enhance free-text retrieval, those for which a document gives enough information, or key words).
Index terms
Co-ordinate concepts used in abstracts with assigned descriptors.
   (a) Assign concepts in abstracts that are identical to descriptors.
   (b) Assign concepts in abstracts that complement descriptors (e.g., relevant terms that are missed in descriptor indexing and in titles, terms that are more specific than descriptors, or a particular type of term that is important to the subject area, such as geographic names).
   (c) Assign concepts in abstracts that both complement and are identical to descriptors.
Enhance indexing independent of any index language used.

Check lists
Follow a list of retrieval-related elements that should be included in abstracts.
Forms of check lists:
   (a) Categories that should be included in abstracts (e.g. materials, properties and processes) and the conditions under which they should be included (e.g. only when they are discussed elaborately, or whenever mentioned).
   (b) Specific and particular guidelines (e.g. 'whenever dealing with a new product, mention the company name').

The Language of Abstracts

Use of author language
Use author language.
Do not use author language.
   (a) Use standardised and concrete terms specific to a subject area.
Use both author language and synonyms.

Relationship to index language used
Co-ordinate terms in abstracts with descriptors.
Complement descriptors with terms in abstracts (e.g. use synonyms or more specific terms).
Use specific and well-accepted terms for particular categories (such as materials, processes and products).

Practices to avoid
Do not use the negative (e.g. use *sick* instead of *not healthy*).
Do not list terms which have a common last word as a series (such as 'upper, middle, and working class').

Word forms
Follow local language practices (e.g. change American spelling for British database).
Always spell out terms in certain categories (such as processes, materials, products).
When a term and a descriptor are the same, record the term in the form used by the descriptor.
Express terms both in their abbreviated form and in their complete form.

Exhibit 45
Rules for abstractors that relate to retrievability characteristics of abstracts
Reproduced from Fidel (1986) by permission of Aslib

useful in the location of more obscure items of potential interest.

The question may be raised as to why, in the 1990s, one would scan secondary services in printed form rather than performing regular online searches in the appropriate databases. This would be the preferred mode of operation for an organization whose interests are clearly circumscribed and can be expressed rather comprehensively in a search strategy. But some organizations may have such a diversity of heterogeneous concerns that it becomes very difficult to locate items of potential interest except by the browsing of broad sections of published sources. Moreover, serendipity can play an important role here: a good information specialist can identify items of relevance to a company that may fall outside of its interest profile—e.g., a potential new application for a company product.

Anyway, the in-house bulletin should be compiled by the scanning of both primary and secondary sources, the latter complementing the coverage of the former. In a large information center, the team responsible for scanning the literature might include some individuals whose main task is to scan foreign materials, prepare English abstracts, and undertake complete translations when items are judged of sufficient importance.

As to abstracting itself, the individuals responsible can save a lot of time by marking up the text of the item so that input can be made directly from the publication. In some cases it will be possible to use author abstracts directly, or the author abstract may require some alteration—editing or augmentation. In other cases, a perfectly good "abstract" can be prepared by extracting portions of the text—perhaps from the summary or conclusions section. Of course, there will always be some items for which original abstracts must be prepared—because no good abstract exists, extraction is inadequate, or some aspect of great interest to the company, but of minor interest to the author, needs to be given emphasis.

Abstracts prepared for internal use can be disseminated in one of two ways. Most obviously, a duplicated bulletin can be issued on a regular basis. Since this can be considered an intelligence tool of major importance to the company, it should be issued weekly if at all possible. The abstracts should be organized into sections that remain more or less the same from week to week to facilitate scanning. An analytical contents page, showing section and subsection breakdown, should be included. A bulletin of this type might contain in the range of 80 to 150 abstracts. Each abstract should be given a unique number for identification and ordering purposes. Included in the bulletin should be a form to allow recipients to place orders for items abstracted.

The abstracts bulletin will go out on a distribution list. For certain key individuals in the organization the information center may go one step further, attaching a memorandum to the front of the bulletin to draw attention to items that may be particularly relevant to each recipient's interests. The standard form can be worded somewhat as follows: "If you have time to look at only a few items, the following will probably be of particular interest."

An alternative to the bulletin per se, of course, is to disseminate the abstracts as discrete items. This implies that the disseminators have a clear and comprehensive picture of individual interests—so that each individual receives only items likely to be pertinent—or that some computer program is used to match characteristics of the abstracts with individual interest profiles.

The distribution of separate abstracts is not really recommended. It requires a lot more work on the part of the information center and eliminates the possibility of browsing. A well-organized bulletin is a more effective dissemination tool. The highlighting of selected items in the bulletin to save the time of key individuals is an effective substitute for the dissemination of separate abstracts.

In creating an in-house bulletin, of course, the information center is building a database. Moreover, it is a database that should be of great potential value to the organization. It should be accessible online within the company in a form amenable to effective searching. Each abstract can be indexed (by the same individuals who prepare the abstracts), the text of the abstracts can be searchable, or the retrieval system can operate on a combination of index terms and text expressions.

Subject Slanting

Subject slanting was referred to in the previous chapter. Where an abstracting publication is designed for use by a group of individuals with clearly defined and specialized interests (as would be true for an in-house bulletin), it is clearly desirable that each abstract be tailored to the precise interests of the group. This was recognized in the modular content analyses project (Lancaster et al., 1965) as described in Chapter 7. To make these analyses of maximum use to a diverse group of secondary services it was proposed that they should incorporate "subject modules." A content analysis would include a "basic" abstract plus supplementary paragraphs, each of these tailored to the interests of a particular group. The index entries supplied would also reflect this diversity of interests. Appendix 2 illustrates the approach: the basic abstract on flame impingement is supplemented by paragraphs relating the work to interests in physiology and medicine, the plastics industry, the rubber industry, and the protective clothing and aircraft industries.

9

Evaluation Aspects

The subject of evaluation is treated in several chapters of this book. For example, Chapter 1 touches upon criteria for evaluating the results of searches performed in a database while Chapter 6 deals with the quality of indexing and the criteria by which quality may be judged.

Indexing and abstracting are not activities that should be looked upon as ends in themselves. It is the results of these activities that should be evaluated and this can only be done within the context of a particular database, whether in printed or machine-readable form. In this context, the indexing can be judged successful if it allows searchers to locate items they want without having to look at many they do not want. Abstracts are successful if they correctly predict which documents will be useful to a searcher and which will not.

A bibliographic database cannot be evaluated in isolation but only in terms of its value in responding to various information needs. In relation to a particular information need, a database can be evaluated according to four principal criteria:

1. *Coverage.* How much of the literature on a topic, published within a particular time period, is included in the database?
2. *Retrievability.* How much of the literature on the topic, included in the database, can be found using "reasonable" search strategies?
3. *Predictability.* Using information in the database, how well can a user judge which items will be useful and which not?
4. *Timeliness.* Are recently published items retrievable or do indexing/ abstracting delays lead to a situation in which items retrieved represent "old" rather than "new" research results?

Coverage

Evaluating the *coverage* of a database is very similar to evaluating the completeness of the collection of a library on some topic. Indeed, the collection of books in a library is itself a database, as is the catalog of the library—one a database of artifacts and the other of representations of these artifacts.

116

One way to evaluate the coverage of a library's collection on some subject is to find reliable bibliographies on the subject and to check these against the collection. This technique can also be used to evaluate the coverage of indexing/abstracting services. Martyn (1967) and Martyn and Slater (1964) have illustrated the use of this method. Suppose, for example, that you want to evaluate the coverage of *Index Medicus* on the subject of feline leukemia. If you are lucky, you might find a bibliography that looks or claims to be comprehensive on this subject for some period. In this case, the task is easy: entries in the bibliography are checked against the author index to *Index Medicus* to determine which items are included and which are not. As a result of this, one might conclude that *Index Medicus* covers, say, 84 percent or so of the literature on this subject. Of course, one needs to know something about the policies of the database being evaluated—e.g., that *Index Medicus* is devoted almost exclusively to periodical articles and includes no monographs.

This technique is not without its problems. In the first place, comprehensive bibliographies are not that easy to find. Moreover, one may know nothing about how a bibliography was compiled. If the feline leukemia bibliography was compiled primarily from the use of *Index Medicus* (or its machine-readable equivalent) it would be of very little use in evaluating this tool.

The fact is, of course, that we do not really need a comprehensive bibliography in order to estimate the coverage of a database on some subject; all we need is a representative sample of items. One way of obtaining such a sample is to use one database as a source of items through which to evaluate the coverage of another. For example, suppose one wanted to know how complete is the coverage of the *Engineering Index* on the subject of superconductors. One might go to *Physics Abstracts* to identify, say, 200 items that this service has indexed under "superconductors" or "superconductivity" and use this set to estimate the coverage of the *Engineering Index*. After checking these against the author indexes of *Engineering Index,* one might find that 142/200 are included there, giving us a coverage estimate of 71 percent. The fact that the 200 items are not all the items published on superconductors is not important; it is, in some sense, a "representative" set of superconductor items and may be a perfectly legitimate sample to use in the estimation of coverage.

Clearly, it would be possible to go in the reverse direction, using items drawn from the *Engineering Index* to assess the coverage of *Physics Abstracts.* In this way one can also determine overlap and uniqueness in two (or more) services, as in the following example:

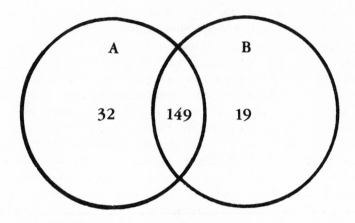

These results might be achieved by drawing a random sample of superconductor items from *A* and checking them against *B* and drawing a random sample of superconductor items from *B* and checking them against *A*. Such samples would allow us to estimate *A*'s coverage (181/200 or about 90 percent in the above hypothesized example), *B*'s coverage (168/200 or about 84 percent), the overlap between the services (149/200 or about 75 percent), and the uniqueness (about 16 percent of the items included by *A*, that is 32/200, appear in that service only while the comparable figure for *B* is a little below 10 percent [19/200]). The same kind of results could be achieved, and in some ways more easily, if we could draw a sample from a third source, *C*, to estimate the coverage, overlap, and uniqueness of *A* and *B*.

In the above discussion, the evaluation of a database in printed form was assumed. The procedures would not differ significantly were they applied to one in electronic form—accessible online or as CD-ROM. It is tedious, of course, to enter perhaps hundreds of author names in order to determine the coverage of some online source. The solution to this problem is to first perform a broad subject search (needed anyway if one wants to determine retrievability—see later discussion) and then do supplementary searches by author. Using the same example, one could draw a sample of items indexed under SUPERCONDUCTORS or SUPERCONDUCTIVITY from the INSPEC database in order to evaluate the coverage of this topic in COMPENDEX. The first step would be to search COMPENDEX on the superconductor terms to see how many of the sample items were retrieved. The next step would be to perform author searches to determine whether or not the other sample items appear in COMPENDEX and, if they do, discover how they were indexed.

There is a possible problem associated with drawing a sample of items from one database to evaluate the coverage of another. In some cases a database in printed form will index items only under the terms considered "most important." This is true for *Index Medicus,* for example, so items indexed under the term FELINE LEUKEMIA VIRUS will only be those dealing centrally with the subject and not those dealing with it peripherally. In using a sample drawn from *Index Medicus* to evaluate some other service, then, we must recognize that the estimate of coverage for this service relates only to coverage of journal articles dealing "centrally" with the topic. However, if we draw our sample from the MEDLINE database (essentially the electronic equivalent of *Index Medicus*), this problem will not arise since an index term such as FELINE LEUKEMIA VIRUS may be used there to refer to this subject when treated peripherally as well as when treated centrally. In certain printed indexes, too, no distinction is made between "major" and "minor" terms. For example, a subject sample could be drawn from one of the *Excerpta Medica* indexes with a reasonable expectation that the items chosen would include some in which the subject is dealt with less than centrally.

Obviously, in drawing samples from one indexing/abstracting service to evaluate another, one must take into account publication dates. For instance, one might draw a sample of items included in *Excerpta Medica* in the year 1987. If using this to evaluate the coverage of *Index Medicus,* one would presumably check the author indexes for 1987 first. Any items not found there should be checked against 1988 (and even perhaps later) or 1986 (and even, in some cases, earlier) to account for the fact that the two publishers will not necessarily have indexed things in the same time frame. In doing this, of course, one might get some idea of the relative timeliness of the two tools. The topic of timeliness is discussed later in this chapter.

There is another source that can be used to assess the coverage of a database: the bibliographic references that appear in journal articles. To return to the example already used, suppose that we can identify a number of recently published articles, appearing in scholarly journals, that deal with feline leukemia. The bibliographic references included in these papers can be used to form a bibliography that could be applied to assess the coverage of *Index Medicus* or one of the *Excerpta Medica* indexes.

There is one obvious difference between using items from bibliog-raphies on feline leukemia (or items indexed under this term in some bibliographic tool) and using bibliographic references from journal articles: the former, presumably, are items dealing with feline leukemia per se while the latter are the sources needed by researchers working in the area of feline leukemia. The latter sources can be expected to extend well beyond the specific subject and, indeed, may encompass a broad area of the biological sciences and perhaps even other fields. The evaluator may choose to exclude any items that seem peripheral to the topic of the evaluation or may include them on the grounds that a bibliographic tool useful to the investigator on this subject should provide access to all related materials needed to support his research.

In the evaluation of a database that restricts itself almost completely to journal articles (as is the case with *Index Medicus*) one could take an obvious shortcut to arriving at an estimate of coverage. Having drawn a sample from some other source or sources, one could identify the journal articles and then simply check to see if these journals are routinely covered in *Index Medicus*. In all probability this would give an acceptable estimate of coverage. If one wanted to be more precise, however, the sample items (or at least a subset picked at random) should be checked by author to account for the fact that some journals may be indexed only selectively and that some articles (and perhaps even complete issues of some journals) that should have been indexed were not indexed for some reason.* The journal title shortcut is of less use in evaluating the coverage of a database that includes published items of all types and of no use at all in the case of a highly specialized database that attempts to include everything on some topic, from whatever source, and does not restrict itself to a particular set of journals.

There are several possible reasons why an evaluation of coverage might be performed. For example, some information center may want to know if a particular database, say that of *Chemical Abstracts,* covers the center's area of specialization comprehensively or if it would need to draw upon several databases for more complete coverage. The producer of a database, too, may be interested in knowing how well it covers a particular subject area. In this case, it would be important to determine which types of publications are covered well and which less well. To do this one would need to categorize the items covered, and those not covered, by such

---

*For example, Thorpe (1974), studying the rheumatology literature, got a somewhat different coverage estimate for *Index Medicus* on the basis of journal titles than he did on the basis of journal articles. Brittain and Roberts (1980) also present evidence on the need to study coverage and overlap at the article level.

characteristics as document type, language, place of publication, and journal title. From these data one could determine how the coverage might be improved in the most cost-effective manner.

In considering the coverage of databases it is important to be aware of the phenomenon of *scatter*. This phenomenon works against the highly specialized database, and the highly specialized library or information center, and favors the more general database, library, or center. Consider, for example, a specialized information center on AIDS (acquired immunodeficiency syndrome) that wants to collect the literature on this subject completely and thus create a comprehensive database. The dimensions of this problem are illustrated in Exhibits 46-50 based on searches performed in the MEDLINE database in 1988. Exhibit 46 shows that only 24 journal articles had been published on AIDS up to the end of 1982; by 1987 this literature had grown to 8,510 items. In 1982 all of the AIDS literature was embraced by three languages, but by 1987 there were 25 languages involved and 54 countries contributing to the literature (Exhibits 47 and 48). Most telling is Exhibit 49 which shows that the entire AIDS literature could be found in only 14 journals in 1982, but by 1987 almost 1,200 journals had contributed!

All of these exhibits demonstrate the phenomenon of *scatter*. As the literature on some subject grows, it becomes increasingly scattered (more countries involved, more languages involved, more journals involved, more document types involved) and thus more difficult to identify, collect, and organize.

Year	Number of items published	Cumulative number of publications
1982	24	24
1983	641	665
1984	1,158	1,823
1985	1,707	3,530
1986	2,117	5,647
1987	2,863	8,510

Exhibit 46
Growth of the science literature on AIDS
(Source: MEDLINE)

The most dramatic aspect of scatter relates to the dispersion of journal articles over journal titles. It was Bradford who first observed this phenomenon in 1934, and the phenomenon is now referred to as Bradford's Law of Scattering. It is demonstrated clearly in Exhibit 50 which shows the scatter of periodical articles on AIDS for the period 1982-1987. The top journal on the list contributed 550 papers in a six-year period, the second contributed 351 papers, and the third 307 papers. Note that 2 journals each contributed 67 papers, 2 contributed 47 each, and so on

	1982	1983	1984	1985	1986	1987
Number of languages	3	14	21	21	20	23
Cumulative number of languages	3	14	22	25	25	25

Exhibit 47
AIDS literature: coverage by language, 1982-1987
(Source: MEDLINE)

	1982	1983	1984	1985	1986	1987
Number of contributing countries	5	30	38	43	39	42
Cumulation of contributing countries	5	30	39	48	52	54

Exhibit 48
AIDS literature: coverage by country, 1982-1987
(Source: MEDLINE)

Year	Number of journals	Cumulative number of journals
1982	14	14
1983	228	234
1984	257	464
1985	492	719
1986	582	952
1987	676	1,170

Exhibit 49
Number of journals that published articles on AIDS, 1982-1987
(Source: MEDLINE)

down to the bottom of the list where we have 452 journals each of which contributed only a single paper to the AIDS literature in six years. Rather more than one-third of the literature is concentrated in as few as 15 journals. To get the next third, however, one needs to add a further 123 journals, while the final third is scattered over more than a thousand additional journals. This distribution provides a dramatic demonstration of the law of diminishing returns. This is revealed even more clearly in Exhibit 51 which plots the percentage of articles against the percentage of journals contributing. Note that, as one moves up the curve, the scatter of articles over titles increases at an approximately geometric rate: the first third of the articles from 15 journals, the second from 123 journals (15 x 8.2), and the final third from 1,008 journals (very roughly 15 x 8.2^2). Such a distribution is typically Bradfordian.

It is clear that an information center establishing a database on the subject of AIDS could not form such a resource on the basis of direct subscriptions to all contributing journals. However, the ranked list of journals contributing (Exhibit 50) can be used to identify some core of journals that should be worth purchasing and scanning on a regular basis. Exhibit 52 shows what the top of this list would look like based on data from 1982 to 1987. How far down the ranked list the information center can afford to go will partly depend upon its financial resources. However, even with unlimited resources, the center could not acquire all the journals that publish on AIDS. As one goes down the ranked list, the predictability of the journal titles diminishes. Thus the top ten titles for 1982-1987 may be the top ten for the next five years. Even this is not certain. In the case of AIDS, for example, new journals devoted exclusively to this subject now exist and would presumably appear in the top ten for the period 1987 onward, perhaps even in the first position. Nevertheless, it is quite likely that all of the journals in Exhibit 52 will continue to be among the most productive journals on AIDS for some time to come. The journals in the middle of the distribution (i.e., around the middle of the table in Exhibit 50) are much less predictable—they may continue to publish AIDS-related articles or they may not. Those titles at the bottom of the table are quite unpredictable: a journal that has contributed only one paper on AIDS in five or six years may never contribute another on the subject.

In trying to build a specialized database on AIDS, then, the information center must cover some of this literature by direct subscription—perhaps 100 or so journals—and identify the other AIDS-related items by regular searches in other databases of wider scope: MEDLINE, BIOSIS, and so on.

Martyn (1967) and Martyn and Slater (1964) have performed the "classic" studies of the coverage of indexing/abstracting services, but many other studies of coverage or overlap exist in the literature. For example, Goode et al. (1970) compared the coverage of *Epilepsy Abstracts,* a product of Excerpta Medica, with that of *Index Medicus,* while Wilkinson and Hollander (1973) compared the coverage of *Index Medicus* and the *Drug Literature Index.*

Two studies have compared the coverage of *Biological Abstracts, Chemical Abstracts,* and *Engineering Index* and their machine-readable equivalents: Wood et al. (1972) compared the coverage of the three tools in terms of journal titles while Wood et al. (1973) compared them in terms of journal articles selected for coverage.

No. of journals	No. of articles	Cumulative no. of journals	Cumulative no. of articles	No. of journals	No. of articles	Cumulative no. of journals	Cumulative no. of articles
1	550	1	550	2	29	42	3,954
1	351	2	901	3	28	45	4,038
1	307	3	1,208	5	27	50	4,173
1	303	4	1,511	2	26	52	4,225
1	289	5	1,800	7	25	59	4,400
1	217	6	2,017	3	24	62	4,472
1	200	7	2,217	3	23	65	4,541
1	104	8	2,321	3	22	68	4,607
1	98	9	2,419	2	21	70	4,649
1	97	10	2,516	5	20	75	4,749
1	83	11	2,599	4	19	79	4,825
1	78	12	2,677	7	18	86	4,951
1	70	13	2,747	7	17	93	5,070
2	67	15	2,881	4	16	97	5,134
1	60	16	2,941	7	15	104	5,239
1	59	17	3,000	8	14	112	5,351
1	54	18	3,054	14	13	126	5,533
1	52	19	3,106	12	12	138	5,677
1	49	20	3,155	13	11	151	5,820
1	48	21	3,203	11	10	162	5,930
2	47	23	3,297	15	9	177	6,065
2	46	25	3,389	14	8	194	6,101
2	40	27	3,469	40	7	234	6,481
1	39	28	3,508	42	6	276	6,733
1	36	29	3,544	50	5	326	6,983
2	34	31	3,612	87	4	413	7,331
4	33	35	3,744	117	3	530	7,682
1	32	36	3,776	188	2	718	8,058
4	30	40	3,896	452	1	1,170	8,510

Exhibit 50
Scatter of the journal literature on AIDS
(Source: MEDLINE)

Probably the largest of overlap studies was one reported by Bearman and Kunberger (1977); it examined 14 different services and almost 26,000 journals indexed by them and considered overlap and uniqueness of coverage.

While *Index Medicus* may have been looked at more often than any other tool, the *Bibliography of Agriculture* has been the subject of the most intensive coverage study. In two related reports, Bourne (1969a,

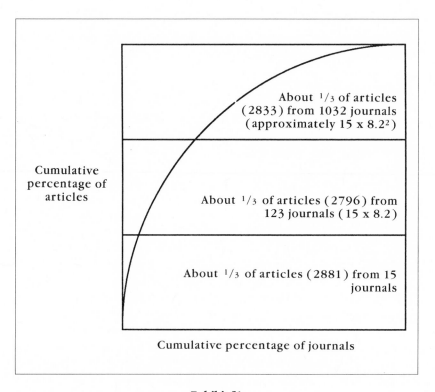

Exhibit 51
Plot of the scatter of the AIDS literature

Rank	Title	Yield
1	*Lancet*	550
2	*Journal of the American Medical Association*	351
3	*New England Journal of Medicine*	307
4	*Annals of Internal Medicine*	303
5	*Nature*	289
6	*Science*	217
7	*British Medical Journal*	200
8	*MMWR*	104
9	*American Journal of Medicine*	98
10	*Journal of Infectious Diseases*	97

Exhibit 52
Science journals that published the most papers on AIDS, 1982-1987
(Source: MEDLINE)

1969b) compared the coverage of this tool with that of 15 other services and estimated its coverage on specific topics using bibliographies accompanying chapters in annual reviews.

Montgomery (1973) studied the coverage of the literature of toxicology in *Chemical Abstracts, Biological Abstracts, Index Medicus, Excerpta Medica, Chemical Biological Activities,* and the *Science Citation Index.* This study was unusual in that it assembled a set of 1,873 references to the toxicology literature (1960-1969) from 221 members of the Society of Toxicology and used these as the basis for a comparison of the various tools.

O'Connor and Meadows (1968) studied the coverage of astronomy in *Physics Abstracts,* Gilchrist (1966) the coverage of the literature of documentation (specifically items on the evaluation of information systems) in six services, and Fridman and Popova (1972) the coverage of experimental primatology in the *Referativnyi Zhurnal.* Brittain and Roberts (1980) focus on overlap in the field of criminology, and Robinson and Hu (1981) compare the coverage of databases in the field of energy. Edwards (1976) included coverage as one aspect of his study of indexes in library and information science. La Borie et al. (1985) studied the overlap of four secondary services in library/information science, based on journal titles, and compared the titles covered by these services with those covered by six services in the sciences and the social sciences. Other investigators have looked at the coverage of particular types of publications (e.g., Hanson and Janes [1961] investigated the coverage of conference papers in several services and Oppenheim [1974] looked at the *Chemical Abstracts* coverage of patents), or at the coverage of a highly specific topic (e.g., Smalley's [1980] comparison of two databases in their coverage of the literature on operant conditioning).

Studies of coverage or overlap are not necessarily mere intellectual exercises. Some are performed with definite goals in mind, most obviously how to improve the coverage of some service. Another purpose might be to identify a "core" of journals in some field, identified by the fact that they are all judged to be worth indexing by several different services. One example of a study of this type is reported by Sekerak (1986), who was able to identify a core list of 45 journals in the field of psychology from a study of overlap among five services in the psychology/health care area.

Retrievability

For someone seeking information on a particular subject, the coverage of a database on that subject will be important, especially if a comprehensive search is required. Also important, of course, is retrievability; given that a database includes n items on a subject (which can be established through a study of coverage), how many of these is it possible to retrieve when searching the database?

This can be tested by a study that is supplementary to an investigation of coverage. Suppose we want to study coverage and retrievability in a variety of subject areas falling within the scope of the AGRICOLA database. For each of ten topics, we have a set of bibliographic items (established by one of the methods described earlier) and, for each set, know which items are included in AGRICOLA and which are not. For each topic we could have a search performed by an information specialist familiar with AGRICOLA and can judge retrievability on the basis of the proportion of the known items that the searcher is able to retrieve. For example, in the first search, on insects hazardous to soybeans, we know of 80 items on this topic that are included in AGRICOLA. The searcher, however, was able to find only 60 of these, a *recall* (see Chapter 1) of only 75 percent.

Of course, this type of study is testing more than the database and its indexing; it is also testing the ability of a particular searcher. The effect of this variable can be reduced by having the same search performed independently by several information specialists to determine what results can be expected in a search on this subject *on the average*. The results could also be considered as probabilities—e.g., 50/80 were found by all three searchers (probability of retrieval 1.00), 6/80 by two of the three searchers (probability of retrieval .66), 4/80 by only one of the searchers (probability of retrieval .33), and 20/80 by none of them (probability of retrieval zero).

Note that retrievability (recall) is judged only on the basis of the items known in advance to be relevant to the search topic and to be included in the database. The search on insect pests affecting soybeans may retrieve a total of 200 items, of which, say, 150 seem relevant. If only 60 of the 80 "known relevant" items are retrieved, the recall estimate is .75 implying that the 150 items retrieved represent roughly 75 percent of the total relevant items in the database.

Of course, the recall ratio relates to only one dimension of the search. To establish a *precision ratio* (see Chapter 1), one would need to have all items retrieved judged for relevance in some way (e.g., by a group of subject specialists). An alternative would be to measure cost-effectiveness by determining the cost per relevant item retrieved. For example, the total cost of an online search (including time of the searcher) might be $75. If 150 relevant items are retrieved, the cost per relevant item is $0.50.

There is an alternate way of studying the retrievability of items from a database; it involves a type of simulation. Suppose we are aware of 80 items relevant to topic X that are included in a database, and that we can retrieve and print out records to show how these items were indexed. We can then, as it were, simulate a search by recording the number of items retrievable under various terms or term combinations. A hypothetical example of this is shown in Exhibit 53. In this case, 38/80 items known to be relevant to the subject of superconductors appear under the term SUPERCONDUCTORS while a further 12 can be found under SUPERCONDUCTIVITY. Additional items cannot be found under these two terms but

Term	Number of items retrievable
Superconductors	38
Superconductivity	12
A	7
B	5
C	3
D	3
E	3
F	2
G	2
H	2
I	2
J	1
Total	80

Exhibit 53
Hypothetical example of distribution of "superconductor"
items under terms in a printed index

Term	No. of items retrievable	Cumulative no. of items retrievable
LYMPHOCYTES	23	23
B-LYMPHOCYTES	7	30
THYMUS GLAND	6	36
CELL MEMBRANE	2	38
SWINE	2	40
ANTIGENS	1	41
ANTIBODY FORMATION	1	42
HISTOCOMPATIBILITY	1	43
GENES	1	44
ANTILYMPHOCYTE SERUM	1	45

Exhibit 54
Distribution of items on cellular immunology
in the pig under terms in *Index Medicus*
From Albright (1979) by permission of the author

only under terms *A-J*. One might conclude from an analysis of this type that 50/80 items are easily retrievable and that 62/80 should be found by an intelligent searcher because terms *A* and *B* are either closely related to "superconductors" or are explicitly linked to the term SUPERCONDUCTORS by cross references in the database. One might further conclude that 18/80 would probably not be retrieved because they appear only under terms not directly related to "superconductors" (e.g., they may represent applications of the principle of superconductivity).

Albright (1979) undertook a detailed study of this type using *Index Medicus*. Simulated searches, performed for ten different topics, revealed that, on the average, 44 different terms would have to be consulted to retrieve all items known to be relevant to a particular topic. While some of these were linked, through the hierarchical or cross-reference structure of the system vocabulary, many were not so linked, and it would be unlikely that even a persistent and ingenious searcher would consult them. Exhibit 54 shows one example from Albright's work. It would indeed be a very knowledgeable and persistent searcher who would achieve high recall in a search on this topic in *Index Medicus*.

Just as journal articles are scattered over journal titles, items on a topic included in a database may be scattered over many different terms. This is represented diagrammatically in Exhibit 55. It may be that, for any particular topic, a relatively high percentage of the relevant items can be found under a small number of "obvious" terms (e.g., SUPERCONDUCTORS or SUPERCONDUCTIVITY for a search on superconductors). By adding other closely related terms, perhaps linked to these terms in the structure of the vocabulary of the database, recall might be pushed up to, say, 80-90 percent. There remains, in this hypothetical case, an elusive 10 to 20 percent of the covered items that the searcher would be unlikely to find.

This discussion on simulations has been deliberately simplified in that it has mostly assumed that a search will have only a single facet or, at least, it will be a search performed in a printed index where only one term at a time can be consulted. The simulation of a search in an online database, which will usually involve more than one facet, will be a little more complicated. For example, in a search on insect pests affecting soybeans, one would have to assume that an item would be retrieved only if it had been indexed under an "insect" term as well as a term indicating "soybeans."

Albright (1979) has performed the most complete study of retrievability but using only a single tool, *Index Medicus*. Martyn (1967) and Martyn and Slater (1964) looked at the scatter of relevant material under index terms for several printed services, and Bourne (1969a, 1969b) also looked at scatter in his studies of the *Bibliography of Agriculture*. Carroll (1969) looked at the scatter of the literature of virology in *Biological Abstracts* and found papers on this subject dispersed over 20 sections of this tool beyond those dealing directly with virology. O'Connor and Meadows (1968) found similar scatter of the astronomy literature in *Physics Abstracts*.

Davison and Matthews (1969) looked at retrievability of items on computers in mass spectrometry in 11 services, as well as coverage of these services on this subject. Thorpe (1974) estimated recall and precision for searches on rheumatology in *Index Medicus*, and Virgo (1970) used the subject of ophthalmology to compare retrieval from the MEDLARS database with that from its printed product, *Index Medicus*. Jahoda and Stursa (1969) compared the retrieval capabilities of a "single entry" subject index with an index based on keywords in titles, Yerkey (1973) compared the retrieval capabilities of a KWIC index with the *Engineering Index* and the *Business Periodicals Index*, and Farradane and Yates-Mercer (1973) evaluated the *Metals Abstracts Index* by means of simulated searches.

The most thorough studies of retrieval performance in printed indexes have been reported by Keen (1976) using the subject of library and information science. Searches were performed by students and the results were evaluated in terms of recall, precision, and search time. Keen (1977b) has also presented an analysis of search strategy as applied to printed indexes.

Conaway (1974) has developed a single figure of merit for a printed index, the Coefficient of Index Usability (CIU), which reflects how long it takes for a searcher to locate the full bibliographic details for a particular item. A subject search was judged successful if a searcher was able to find an item known in advance to be "relevant" to a given topic. If the item was located, the time taken to find the full bibliographic data was recorded. Using Conaway's methods, numerical scores can be given to different indexes by averaging the results achieved on a number of topics by several searchers. The CIU is essentially a measure of cost-effectiveness. However, it is a very weak one since effectiveness is determined solely on the basis of whether or not a single known item is retrieved. A much better cost-effectiveness measure is the unit cost (in dollars or in user time) *per relevant item retrieved.*

Predictability

The discussion on evaluation of retrievability made a major assumption: that it is possible to recognize a "relevant" item from the information on that item contained in a database. This information may comprise:

1. The title of the item
2. Title plus a list of index terms
3. Title plus an abstract
4. Title plus terms plus abstract

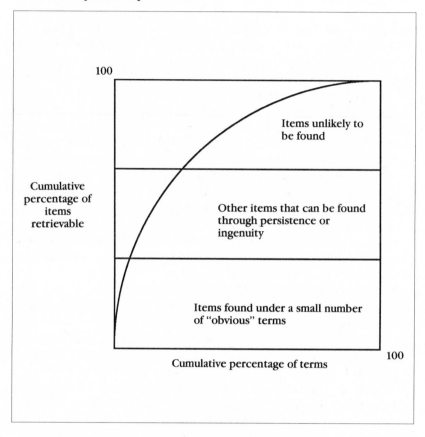

Exhibit 55
Scatter of items under index terms

In general, the longer the representation the more clues it provides as to whether an item will be of interest to a user or not. The least information provided by a database would be the title of the item. How well the title reflects the subject matter is very largely dependent on the type of publication involved. In general, articles from scholarly journals tend to have quite descriptive titles while, at the other extreme, newspaper articles may have titles that are cute or eye-catching but not very descriptive of their contents. Technical or trade publications also tend toward the cute title: the *Journal of Metals* may have very descriptive titles while *Iron Age* is less likely to.

Titles are not provided in isolation, of course. In a printed index, for example, the title may be considered within the context of the index term under which the title appears. The title "A Rare Complication of Tuberculosis" tells us little about the contents of an article even if it appears under the heading TUBERCULOSIS, PULMONARY. If this title appears under the subject heading AMYLOIDOSIS, however, one has a much better idea of what it deals with. In some cases, too, a clue to the subject matter may be provided by the title of the journal (or book) in which an article appears. Thus an article entitled "Effects on the Presentation of Information" has little meaning on its own. Within a book entitled *Electronic Publishing*, on the other hand, the title is much more predictive of its content.

It is somewhat rare for a printed index to include a complete list of the index terms associated with an item (although the *Excerpta Medica* indexes do so), but it is usually possible to generate such a list in a printout from an online database in which human indexing has been employed. The combination of title and index terms may be quite powerful in indicating what a publication is about.

Abstracts, of course, should be the best indicators of content. How well they perform as predictors is the major criterion by which their quality can be judged.

To test the value of various forms of document surrogate as indicators of content requires that one present to users of a retrieval system (or to individuals substituting for such users under experimental conditions) various document representations of increasing length. For example, suppose a search in a database has retrieved 30 records. Representations of these items could be submitted to the requester of the search in a sequence of increasing length of record with the following results:

Record presented	No. of items presented	No. of items judged clearly irrelevant	No. of items judged relevant or possibly relevant
Title of article	30	12	18
Title of article plus title of journal	30	13	17
Title of article (and journal) plus list of index terms	30	15	15
Title of article (and journal) plus abstract	30	18	12
Title of article (and journal) plus abstract and index terms	30	18	12
Full text of articles	30	16	14

In this hypothetical situation, the requester, on viewing the full text of the journal articles, judges 14 to be relevant and 16 not. His predictions of relevance got better as the length of the document representation increased, although the addition of index terms to abstract did not differ from use of the abstract alone. Even the best surrogate (title plus abstract) was not perfect; it underrepresented the relevant items and overrepresented the irrelevant ones.

Investigations of effect of document surrogates on relevance predictability have been performed by several investigators including Rath et al. (1961a), Resnick (1961), Kent et al. (1967), Dym (1967), Shirey and Kurfeerst (1967), Saracevic (1969), Marcus et al. (1971), and Keen (1976). Marcus et al. showed clearly that the "indicativity" of a document surrogate is directly related to its length in number of words. On the other hand, there may well be an optimum length beyond which it is uneconomical to go, at least for purposes of predictability. Hagerty (1967), for example, found that, while the length of an abstract improved relevance predictions, the effect of increasing the length was surprisingly slight.

Investigations of the value of abstracts in predicting the relevance of documents generally assume that the abstract is separate from the document, appearing in a printed abstracting service, or in the output of a retrieval operation. Thompson (1973), however, looked at the use and value of abstracts accompanying documents (at the head of journal articles or at the beginning of technical reports). He gathered data on disposition decisions made by engineers and scientists at three military laboratories for documents crossing their desks in the normal course of events over a four week period. He was not able to confirm that disposition decisions for documents having abstracts were made more rapidly than decisions made for those without abstracts. Moreover, when the subjects of the experiment were given copies of the document again, at a later time, for "deliberate re-examination," their earlier relevance decisions for documents having abstracts were no more likely to agree with the later more deliberate decisions than was true for the documents without abstracts. These results do not cast doubt on the value of abstracts per se, or even on the value of abstracts accompanying articles or reports (since these are frequently adopted or modified by secondary services), but they do suggest that abstracts may have limited use in initial screening decisions. Many recipients of publications may prefer to judge their relevance to current interests by glancing through the text, looking at tables or figures, or even checking the bibliographic references (e.g., to see if they themselves have been cited!).

The quality of abstracts per se is discussed in Chapter 8 while the subject of automatic abstracting is dealt with in Chapter 14.

Timeliness

Timeliness or "currency" is a measure of the speed with which new publications are listed in an indexing/abstracting service. It is a criterion that is immediately visible to users, because the date of publication of a printed index is known and the date (or at least the year) of first publication of each item included is part of the bibliographic reference for that item. Timeliness is less apparent to users of online systems but is still perceptible.

This visibility is unfortunate because it usually leads to invalid conclusions. One human tendency is to note exceptional cases, and another tendency is to give expectations undue weight in making a judgment. A user of a printed volume of abstracts may scan a number of references. On observing that some of them refer to material published perhaps two or three years earlier, the user may unjustifiably conclude that the service is generally very slow in identifying and processing new items.

There are many reasons why entry of a reference into a file may be delayed. The interval between publication of a journal and its receipt by the secondary service may be long for geographical or economic reasons; for example, a U.S. service may receive U.S. journals through the mails a day or so after publication, but foreign journals may take six or seven weeks to arrive. Some classes of material, such as conference proceedings, are difficult to locate and once located may be hard to acquire. Documents in difficult languages may require longer than average processing times because of a shortage of qualified translators. "Fringe" material, which usually means material published in journals or other publications not routinely scanned by the service, takes longer to locate than core material, because it is often identified by scanning other secondary services and therefore suffers a double set of processing delays. Some services have faster processing systems than others, and some delays are attributable to system inefficiency. When an indexing/abstracting service is used for current awareness, a user's judgment may be influenced by the number of items in the latest issue of which he is already aware. The presence of some known items tends to promote confidence in the reliability of the service but too many erode confidence in its timeliness.

From the evaluator's point of view, timeliness has great charm as a criterion of effectiveness. Timeliness is relatively easy to measure and is incontrovertible when measured, because it does not depend on subjective judgments. The only influence the evaluator exerts on the measure is in the choice of which dates to use. For printed databases, date of appearance of the reference is normally taken as the date of publication of the service. For an online service, the date should be that on which the reference is entered into the file, but this date cannot always be ascertained retrospectively. A possible solution is to determine from the publisher the interval between release of the update for the machine-readable file and its equivalent printed version, and to adjust the measurements accordingly. For date of appearance of the primary publication to which the secondary service refers, the evaluator can choose between the date of actual publication and the date of availability.

Actual publication date presents some problems, because it is seldom given exactly in secondary services. One may have to refer to a copy of the publication, and, in most cases, the date is given only to the nearest month. The actual day of publication may be found only by asking the publisher. Unfortunately, the date on a journal cover is not always reliable, some journals being published in the month preceding the nominal month of issue, most appearing later than the nominal date of issue.

The availability date is, in some countries, a trouble-free alternative. Although the availability date does not truly measure timeliness of a service, it provides a measure of the effective timeliness from the viewpoint of users in the country in which availability dates are taken. Journal availability dates in the United States could be taken as the dates of receipt at the Library of Congress or one of the other national libraries. These dates may be stamped on the journal covers or would likely be available in some check-in record maintained by the library. The lag between availability of a journal in the United States and notification of its existence by some secondary service can thus be measured. Strictly, the availability date of the secondary service should be taken rather than its publication date, but there is seldom a large difference. The update of the machine-readable database will usually occur before the printed index to which it relates.

Data collection entails drawing a random sample of items from the latest issue of some secondary service, noting the date of publication (or update) of the service, and adding to this, usually from a different source, the original publication or availability data. If, as is often desirable, breakdowns by language, country of origin, and form of publication (e.g., journal article, thesis, or monograph) are required, sample sizes will have to be larger than would be true if only an overall estimate of timeliness is desired.

Timeliness is probably the most easily measured characteristic of a secondary service. It is also probably the least important. Publishers may be concerned with timeliness as a measure of the effectiveness of their activities, but users, although often expressing a desire for speed in service, may be less affected. When the interval between the performance of a piece of research and its first publication is taken into consideration, the additional delay of using a secondary service to locate the research is relatively small.

Other Evaluation Aspects

Various other approaches have been employed to look at the performance and use of printed indexes. For example, Torr et al. (1966) describe four methods that can be used to "observe" index users: (1) have the user keep a written record of his thought processes and strategy in performing a search, (2) have the searcher use a tape recorder for the same purpose,* (3) have an observer accompany the searcher, and (4) use a combination of human observation and a camera to study index use. These investigators found it difficult to get "real users" to cooperate in such studies, which was also the experience of Hall (1972a, 1972b).

Other investigators have used interviews or questionnaires to solicit the opinions of users concerning various indexing/abstracting services, including Hall (1972a, 1972b), Keen (1976), Drage (1969), and Cluley (1968).

In considering retrievability, this chapter has focused more on printed indexing and abstracting services than on retrieval from electronic databases. This partly reflects the focus of the present book: indexing and abstracting rather than other aspects of information retrieval. Clearly, methods used to study coverage, predictability, and timeliness are relevant to all types of databases, printed or electronic. Coverage studies and timeliness studies are completely objective, predictability studies somewhat less so. Studies of retrievability are inherently subjective in that they are dependent on human decisions regarding which items are relevant (or pertinent) ** and which are not. In studying retrieval effectiveness, one needs to use a measure reflecting the proportion of the relevant items that are retrieved in a search (recall ratio) as well as some measure of the *cost* of retrieving this much of the relevant literature. The precision ratio is commonly used as an indirect measure of the cost since it reflects the number of items that a user must somehow look at in order to identify n useful ones. Another indirect measure of cost is the *expected search*

---

*Keen (1977b) has also used this technique.

**The relevance/pertinence issue has been discussed by many writers. See, for example, Lancaster (1979), Wilson (1973), and Swanson (1986).

length as described by Cooper (1968). Of course, cost can be measured in a more direct way by taking all costs of a search, including the time of the searcher and costs of database access, into account (see, for example, Elchesen [1978]). The cost of the search can then be related to the number of relevant (or pertinent or useful or "new") items retrieved; the "cost per relevant reference retrieved" is a good measure of the cost-effectiveness of a search.

Effectiveness measures such as recall and precision (or others as described, for example, by Robertson [1969]) are applicable to studies of retrieval from any type of database, whether in printed or machine-readable form. However, when we study retrieval effectiveness it is quite difficult to isolate the effects of indexing/abstracting from other factors such as the vocabulary of the database, the search strategies used, and the user/system interaction. This was touched upon in Chapter 6. A detailed account of evaluation methodology (measurement of precision, estimation of recall, diagnostic analysis to determine the precise causes of recall and precision failures) is outside the scope of this book. The subject is fully treated in another book by this author (Lancaster, 1979).

Azgaldov (1969) has identified a number of criteria that can be used for assessing the quality of printed indexes. These are: *adequacy* (which covers a whole host of properties including coverage, characteristics of the vocabulary used in indexing, and such indexing factors as exhaustivity and consistency), *generality* (which relates primarily to the diversity of searches that can be performed), *ergonomicity* (ease of use), *currency* (how up-to-date the tool is), and *cost*. He points out, quite correctly, that:

> The most efficient printed index will be a failure with the users if its convenience parameter [ergonomicity and currency] is low, and vice versa, an index that is simple and easy to use will gain wide popularity even if its retrieval performance is not very high. (Page 281)

This quotation provides a good lead-in to Chapter 10 which looks at the characteristics of various indexing and abstracting services.

10

APPROACHES USED IN INDEXING AND ABSTRACTING SERVICES

THE PURPOSE OF THIS CHAPTER is to illustrate various approaches to the implementation of indexing and abstracting services in printed form. In particular, it looks at printed databases in terms of their properties as tools for information retrieval.

Basically, two major approaches to the organization of such tools can be identified. In one approach, entries appear under relatively specific subject headings or descriptors arranged in alphabetical order. Entries may be duplicated under more than one heading and/or cross references can be used to link related headings. In this approach no subject index is needed but other types of index, most obviously author indexes, will be required. In the other major approach, some form of classification is used: entries can be arranged under highly specific class numbers or grouped under relatively broad subject categories (possibly with subcategories). In either case, subject indexes are needed to allow alternative approaches or more specific access to the subject matter.

Alphabetico-Specific Indexes

One example of this approach is the monthly *Index Medicus* and its cumulation, *Cumulated Index Medicus* (Exhibit 56). Various characteristics of this index are worth attention:

1. Note how subheadings are used to give greater specificity.
2. No abstracts are provided so that it is feasible to duplicate the bibliographic reference under more than one heading. For example, the ninth entry under LEUKAPHERESIS (Exhibit 56) would presumably be duplicated under MULTIPLE SCLEROSIS.
3. The combination of heading, subheading, and article title usually gives a fairly clear picture of what an item deals with. For example, one can infer that the item titled "Alternate dosage regimens..." in Exhibit 56 has some relevance to methods of leukapheresis even though this is not explicit from the title.
4. Two types of cross-reference appear in the printed index to refer from headings not used to those preferred in their place: *see* is used to link terms considered synonymous or almost synonymous and *see under* to refer from an unused specific term to the appropriate more general term.

No attempt is made in this printed index to link related terms. Indeed, to get a complete picture of the network of associations among the terms used it is necessary to consult two other tools: *Medical Subject Headings* (MeSH) and the *MeSH Tree Structures*. Exhibit 57 shows a sample page from *MeSH*. Note how *MeSH* displays *see* and *see under* references (and their reciprocals *x* and *xu*) as well as a few *see related* references (reciprocal *XR*) used to link two semantically related terms, usually from different hierarchies. More importantly, perhaps, each heading in *MeSH* is given one or more class numbers to indicate where it appears in the hierarchical tree structures (Exhibit 58). Thus, while the vocabulary used by the National Library of Medicine is quite rich in associations, *Index Medicus* is not self-contained in that the associations are not displayed there. Consequently, it is a useful tool in relatively specific searches but difficult to use in broader searches that would require the consultation of many different headings.

Exhibit 59 shows sample entries from the author index of *Cumulated Index Medicus*. Note that this is completely self-contained in that it is not an index to the subject section. Indeed, for any particular item found in the author index it is frequently quite difficult to determine what subject headings it appears under. Note also that the author index, unlike the subject section, lists all authors of each article and gives the title of the article in its original language (at least for those in the Roman alphabet), not in translation.

The many printed indexes produced by the H. W. Wilson Co. (of which the *Readers' Guide to Periodical Literature* and *Library Literature* are good examples) are similar in many ways to *Index Medicus* in that they use specific headings with subheadings and incorporate *see* references. They differ from *Index Medicus* by using *see also* references to link semantically related terms, making it somewhat easier to perform broad searches that might involve several different headings. For example (see Exhibit 60) a user consulting the term Magnetohydrodynamics (in the *Applied Science and Technology Index*) is told to look also under Plasma, Plasma waves, and Synchrotron radiation.

The *Engineering Index* also arranges entries under specific headings and subheadings (see Exhibit 61) and includes both *see* and *see also* references, although these are not very extensive. The major difference between this index and the ones previously illustrated, of course, is that it includes abstracts. Each abstract is given a unique identifying number. The author index, then, is a true index to the subject arrangement, leading from the name of an author to the numbers of the abstracts with which his name is associated (Exhibit 62).

LEUCOVORIN see CITROVORUM FACTOR

LEUCYL–BETA–NAPHTHYLAMIDASE see under
LEUCINE AMINOPEPTIDASE

LEUCYL T RNA SYNTHETASE see under AMINO ACYL
T RNA SYNTHETASES

LEUKAPHERESIS

Leukapheresis for control of chronic myelogenous leukemia
during pregnancy. Fitzgerald D, et al. **Am J Hematol** 1986
Jun;22(2):213–8
Leukapheresis for treatment of psoriasis: is therapeutical
benefit related to reduced activities of neutral proteinases
of polymorphonuclear leukocytes? Gliński W, et al.
Arch Dermatol Res 1985;278(1):6–12
Natural killer (NK) activity in normal donors undergoing
leukapheresis. Frydecka I, et al.
Arch Immunol Ther Exp (Warsz) 1985;33(5):659–63
Leukapheresis in the treatment of cutaneous T–cell
lymphomas. Belter SV, et al. **Br J Dermatol** 1986 Aug;
115(2):159–66
Lymphocytapheresis—a feasible treatment for rheumatoid
arthritis. Emery P, et al. **Br J Rheumatol** 1986 Feb;
25(1):40–3
Effect of heparin and aspirin on platelet and clotting
activation during leukapheresis. **Eur J Clin Invest** 1985 Aug;15(4):188–91
Long–term lymphocytapheresis therapy in multiple sclerosis.
Preliminary observations. Maida E, et al. **Eur Neurol** 1986;
25(3):225–32
Monoclonal antibody CO17–1A and leukapheresis in
immunotherapy of pancreatic cancer. Tempero MA, et al.
Hybridoma 1986 Jul;5 Suppl 1:S133–8
Effect of lymphocytapheresis plus cyclophosphamide on the
course of a chronic progressive form of multiple sclerosis.
Ferla S, et al. **Ital J Neurol Sci** 1985 Sep;6(3):283–6
Lymphocytoplasmapheresis in multiple sclerosis: one–year
results in 6 patients. Ghezzi A, et al. **Ital J Neurol Sci**
1986 Feb;7(1):119–23
Use of lymphoplasmapheresis or plasmapheresis in the
management of acute renal allograft rejection. Kleinman
S, et al. **J Clin Apheresis** 1982;1(1):14–7
Method for processing leukocyte– and platelet–poor red cells
in closed bags. Shimizu T, et al. **Vox Sang** 1986;50(4):203–7
[Lymphoplasmapheresis in the treatment of rheumatoid
arthritis] Di Matteo L, et al. **Boll Soc Ital Biol Sper** 1985
Jun 30;61(6):883–90 (Eng. Abstr.)   (Ita)
[Lymphocytapheresis therapy. 3. Systemic lupus
erythematosus] Hashimoto H, et al. **Rinsho Ketsueki** 1985
Nov;26(11):1892–7   (Jpn)
[Lymphocytapheresis therapy. 1. Chronic lymphocytic
leukemia and hairy cell leukemia] Taniguchi N, et al.
Rinsho Ketsueki 1985 Nov;26(11):1876–84   (Jpn)
[Lymphocytapheresis therapy. 2. Adult T–cell leukemia]
Tsubaki K, et al. **Rinsho Ketsueki** 1985 Nov;26(11):1885–91
                                                     (Jpn)
[Anemia in rheumatoid arthritis. II. Morphofunctional
characteristics of the erythron during
lymphocytoplasmapheresis] Alnadzhian AO, et al.
Revmatologiia (Moskva) 1985 Jul–Sep;(3):14–6 (Eng.
Abstr.)   (Rus)
[Lymphocytoplasmapheresis in various rheumatic diseases]

Gembitskil EV, et al. **Ter Arkh** 1985;57(8):23–7   (Rus)
[Therapeutic leukapheresis in chronic granulocytic leukemia
and term twin pregnancy] Morales Polanco MR, et al.
Ginecol Obstet Mex 1985 Oct;53:287–90 (Eng. Abstr.)
                                                     (Spa)

ADVERSE EFFECTS

The effect of acute and chronic leukapheresis on the natural
killer (NK) cell function of normal human volunteers.
Stevenson HC, et al. **Am J Hematol** 1986 Jun;22(2):123–32

INSTRUMENTATION

[Use of the Fenwal CS–3000 automatic blood cell separator
for cytopheresis (review)] Fiala J. **Vnitr Lek** 1986 Feb;
32(2):173–9 (Eng. Abstr.)   (Cze)

METHODS

Continuous–flow centrifugation hemapheresis in the horse.
Gordon BJ, et al. **Am J Vet Res** 1986 Feb;47(2):342–5
Depletion lymphocytapheresis in chronic lymphocytic
leukemias: criteria for predicting which patients will
respond to treatment. Rossi PL, et al.
Int J Artif Organs 1986 Jan;9(1):59–62
Alternate dosage regimens for high molecular weight
hydroxyethyl starch. Rock G, et al. **J Clin Apheresis** 1985;
2(4):375–7
Alternate dosage regimens for high–molecular–weight
hydroxyethyl starch. Rock G, et al. **Transfusion** 1985
Sep–Oct;25(5):417–9
Effects on immunity of multiple leukapheresis using a rapidly
excreted analog of hydroxyethyl starch. Strauss RG, et
al. **Transfusion** 1986 May–Jun;26(3):265–8
A multicenter trial to document the efficacy and safety of
a rapidly excreted analog of hydroxyethyl starch for
leukapheresis with a note on steroid stimulation of
granulocyte donors. Strauss RG, et al. **Transfusion** 1986
May–Jun;26(3):258–64
[Leukapheresis therapy. 4. Rheumatoid arthritis] Ito K, et
al. **Rinsho Ketsueki** 1985 Nov;26(11):1898–902   (Jpn)
[Obtaining leukocytes by the method of filtration
leukapheresis] Matkovits I. **Gematol Transfuziol** 1985 Jul;
30(7):60–3   (Rus)

STANDARDS

Centrifugal leukocytapheresis and thrombocytapheresis:
recommendations concerning donor safety, quality control
of the prepared concentrate, and use of equipment.
J Clin Apheresis 1983;1(3):117–195

VETERINARY

Evaluation of leukapheresis and thrombocytapheresis in the
horse. Gordon BJ, et al. **Am J Vet Res** 1986 May;
47(5):997–1001

LEUKEMIA

Chronic leukemias: oncogenes, chromosomes, and advances
in therapy [clinical conference] Champlin R, et al.
Ann Intern Med 1986 May;104(5):671–88 (191 ref.)
Effects of
3'–deamino–3'–(3–cyano–4–morpholinyl)doxorubicin and
doxorubicin on the survival, DNA integrity, and nucleolar
morphology of human leukemia cells in vitro. Wassermann
K, et al. **Cancer Res** 1986 Aug;46(8):4041–6
Advances in therapy and classification of the acute leukemias.
Miller KB. **Compr Ther** 1986 Aug;12(8):48–53

Exhibit 56
Example of entries from *Cumulated Index Medicus*
Reproduced by permission of the National Library of Medicine

LEUCONOSTOC
B3.525.800.511

LEUCOTOMY see PSYCHOSURGERY

LEUCOVORIN see CITROVORUM FACTOR

LEUCYL-BETA-NAPHTHYLAMIDASE see under LEUCINE AMINOPEPTIDASE

LEUCYL T RNA SYNTHETASE see under AMINO ACYL T RNA SYNTHETASES

LEUKAPHERESIS
E2.110.570   E5.909.262.363.570
79; was see PLASMAPHERESIS 1978
X   LEUKOCYTAPHERESIS
X   LEUKOPHERESIS
X   LYMPHAPHERESIS
X   LYMPHOCYTAPHERESIS

LEUKEMIA
C4.557.337+
XR MYELOPROLIFERATIVE DISORDERS

LESCH-NYHAN SYNDROME
C10.228.140.163.551   C10.496.509
C18.452.648.798.594   F3.709.346.508
73
see related
HYPOXANTHINE PHOSPHORIBOSYLTRANSFERASE
XR HYPOXANTHINE PHOSPHORIBOSYLTRANSFERASE

LET see ENERGY TRANSFER

LETHAL DOSE 50
G12.602
76; was see under TOXICOLOGY 1975
X   LD50

LETHAL MIDLINE GRANULOMA see GRANULOMA, LETHAL MIDLINE

LETHARGY see SLEEP STAGES

LETS PROTEINS see FIBRONECTINS

LETTERER-SIWE DISEASE
C15.604.667.490.570

LEUCENINE see MIMOSINE

LEUCENOL see MIMOSINE

LEUCINE
D12.125.142.441   D12.125.70.637

LEUCINE AMINOPEPTIDASE
D8.586.277.656.81.511+
65
XU LEUCYL-BETA-NAPHTHYLAMIDASE

LEUCINE ENKEPHALIN see ENKEPHALIN, LEUCINE

LEUCOGENENOL see under SPIRO COMPOUNDS

LEUCOHARMINE see HARMINE

LEUCOKININ see TUFTSIN

LEUCOMYCINS
D9.203.408.51.485   D20.85.461
81; was KITASAMYCINS see under ANTIBIOTICS 1976-80;
CARBOMYCINS & SPIRAMYCINS were CARBOMYCIN &
SPIRAMYCIN, respectively, 1963-80; JOSAMYCINS was JOSAMYCIN see
under ANTIBIOTICS 1975-80; TYLOSINS was TYLOSIN (with
DEHYDRORELOMYCIN as see ref to it) see under ANTIBIOTICS 1975-80;
MARIDOMYCINS was see under ANTIBIOTICS 1978-80, was
MARIDOMYCIN II see under ANTIBIOTICS 1975-77; ROSAMICINS (with
JUVENIMYCINS & ROSARAMICINS as see refs to it 1979-80) was see
under ANTIBIOTICS 1979-80
X   CARBOMYCINS
X   DEHYDRORELOMYCINS
X   DELTAMYCINS
X   JOSAMYCINS
X   JUVENIMYCINS
X   KITASAMYCINS
X   MARIDOMYCINS
X   ROSAMICINS
X   ROSAMYCINS
X   ROSARAMICINS
X   SPIRAMYCINS
X   TYLOSINS

LEUKEMIA, ALEUKEMIC see LEUKEMIA, SUBLEUKEMIC

LEUKEMIA, EXPERIMENTAL
C4.557.337.372+   C4.619.531+
XU LEUKEMIA L5178
XU LEUKEMIA P388

LEUKEMIA, GRANULOCYTIC see LEUKEMIA, MYELOCYTIC

LEUKEMIA, HAIRY CELL
C4.557.337.415   C15.604.515.553
C20.683.515.517
78
X   HAIRY CELL LEUKEMIA
X   LEUKEMIC RETICULOENDOTHELIOSIS
X   RETICULOENDOTHELIOSIS, LEUKEMIC

LEUKEMIA L1210
C4.557.337.372.594   C4.619.531.594

LEUKEMIA L5178 see under LEUKEMIA, EXPERIMENTAL
X   LYMPHOMA L5178

LEUKEMIA, LYMPHOBLASTIC
C4.557.337.428.511   C15.604.515.560.568
C20.683.515.528.511
67
X   LEUKEMIA, LYMPHOCYTIC, ACUTE
XR LYMPHATIC DISEASES

LEUKEMIA, LYMPHOCYTIC
C4.557.337.428+   C15.604.515.560+
C20.683.515.528+
X   LEUKEMIA, LYMPHOCYTIC, CHRONIC
XR LYMPHATIC DISEASES

LEUKEMIA, LYMPHOCYTIC, ACUTE see LEUKEMIA, LYMPHOBLASTIC

LEUKEMIA, LYMPHOCYTIC, CHRONIC see LEUKEMIA, LYMPHOCYTIC

LEUKEMIA, MEGAKARYOCYTIC see THROMBOCYTHEMIA, HEMORRHAGIC

LEUKEMIA, MONOBLASTIC
C4.557.337.484.512   C20.683.515.584.512
67
X   LEUKEMIA, MONOCYTIC, ACUTE

LEUKEMIA, MONOCYTIC
C4.557.337.484+   C20.683.515.584+
X   LEUKEMIA, MONOCYTIC, CHRONIC
X   LEUKEMIA, SCHILLING TYPE

LEUKEMIA, MONOCYTIC, ACUTE see LEUKEMIA, MONOBLASTIC

LEUKEMIA, MONOCYTIC, CHRONIC see LEUKEMIA, MONOCYTIC

LEUKEMIA, MYELOBLASTIC
C4.557.337.539.512   C20.683.515.639.612
67
X   LEUKEMIA, MYELOCYTIC, ACUTE

Exhibit 57
Example of entries from *Medical Subject Headings*
Reproduced by permission of the National Library of Medicine

LEUKEMIA	**C4.557.337**
LEUKEMIA, EXPERIMENTAL	**C4.557.337.372**
AVIAN LEUKOSIS	**C4.557.337.372.216**
LEUKEMIA L1210	**C4.557.337.372.594**
LEUKEMIA L5178 ·	**C4.557.337.372.602**
LEUKEMIA P388 ·	**C4.557.337.372.782**
LEUKEMIA, HAIRY CELL	**C4.557.337.415**
LEUKEMIA, LYMPHOCYTIC	**C4.557.337.428**
LEUKEMIA, LYMPHOBLASTIC	**C4.557.337.428.511**
LEUKEMIA, MAST CELL	**C4.557.337.440**
LEUKEMIA, MEGAKARYOBLASTIC	**C4.557.337.450**
LEUKEMIA, MONOCYTIC	**C4.557.337.484**
LEUKEMIA, MONOBLASTIC	**C4.557.337.484.512**
LEUKEMIA, MYELOCYTIC	**C4.557.337.539**
LEUKEMIA, MYELOBLASTIC	**C4.557.337.539.512**
LEUKEMIA, PLASMACYTIC	**C4.557.337.595**
LEUKEMIA, RADIATION–INDUCED	**C4.557.337.650**
LEUKEMIA, SUBLEUKEMIC	**C4.557.337.706**
LEUKOSARCOMA	**C4.557.337.801**
LYMPHOMA	**C4.557.386**
HISTIOCYTOSIS, MALIGNANT	**C4.557.386.345**
HODGKIN'S DISEASE	**C4.557.386.355**
IMMUNOPROLIFERATIVE SMALL	
INTESTINAL DISEASE	**C4.557.386.390**
LYMPHOMA, NON–HODGKIN'S	**C4.557.386.480**
BURKITT'S LYMPHOMA	**C4.557.386.480.165**
LYMPHOMA, GIANT FOLLICULAR	**C4.557.386.480.455**
LYMPHOMA, HISTIOCYTIC	**C4.557.386.480.460**
LYMPHOMA, LYMPHOCYTIC	**C4.557.386.480.465**
LYMPHOMA, MIXED	**C4.557.386.480.470**
LYMPHOMA, UNDIFFERENTIATED	**C4.557.386.480.475**
MAREK'S DISEASE	**C4.557.386.480.545**
MYCOSIS FUNGOIDES	**C4.557.386.480.620**
PLASMACYTOMA	**C4.557.386.720**
MULTIPLE MYELOMA	**C4.557.386.720.550**
RETICULOENDOTHELIOSIS	**C4.557.386.802**

Exhibit 58
Examples from *Medical Subject Headings* Tree Structures
Reproduced by permission of the National Library of Medicine

A

A/Gadir H see Haroun EM

A-Ghany YS see Rida SM

Aabakken L, Osnes M: Endoscopic choledochoduodenostomy (ECDT) as palliative treatment of malignant periampullary obstructions of the common bile duct: a follow-up study. Gastrointest Endosc 1986 Feb; 32(1):41-2

Aabakken L, Kåresen R, Serck-Hanssen A, Osnes M: Transpapillary biopsies and brush cytology from the common bile duct. Endoscopy 1986 Mar;18(2):49-51

Aabech J, Caldara A, Durhuus H: Reduktionsmammoplastik a.m. Pers—Bretteville-Jensen på almen kirurgisk afdeling. En efterundersøgelse af patienter opereret for hypertrophia mammae i almenkirurgisk regie. Ugeskr Laeger 1986 Jun 9;148(24):1468-9 (Eng. Abstr.)   **(Dan)**

Aabech J, Caldara A, Waaben B: Vaerdien af rutinemaessig røntgenundersøgelse af colon hos haemoroidektomerede patienter. Ugeskr Laeger 1986 Jan 27;148(5):252-3 (Eng. Abstr.)   **(Dan)**

Aaberg TM: The changing epidemiologic variables involving follow-up data for ophthalmologic studies [editorial] Am J Ophthalmol 1986 Jun 15;101(6):733-4

Aaberg TM see Caya JG

Aabo K, Pedersen H, Kjaer M: Carcinoembryonic antigen (CEA) and alkaline phosphatase in progressive colorectal cancer with special reference to patient survival. Eur J Cancer Clin Oncol 1986 Feb;22(2):211-7

Aabo K: Patienters evne til at opfatte og huske information. Ugeskr Laeger 1985 Dec 2;147(49):4041-3 (Eng. Abstr.)   **(Dan)**

Aabo K, Walbom-Jørgensen S: Central nervous system complications by malignant lymphomas: radiation schedule and treatment results. Int J Radiat Oncol Biol Phys 1986 Feb;12(2):197-202

Aabo K see Hansen SW

Aabo K see Mortensen SA

Aaboe T see Toft B

Aaby P, Bukh J, Hoff G, Leerhøy J, Lisse IM, Mordhorst CH, Pedersen IR: High measles mortality in infancy related to intensity of exposure. J Pediatr 1986 Jul;109(1):40-4

Aaby P, Bukh J, Hoff G, Lisse IM, Smits AJ: Cross-sex transmission of infection and increased mortality due to measles. Rev Infect Dis 1986 Jan-Feb;8(1):138-43

Aaby P, Bukh J, Lisse IM, Smits AJ: Severe measles in Sunderland, 1885: a European-African comparison of causes of severe infection. Int J Epidemiol 1986 Mar; 15(1):101-7

Exhibit 59
Sample entries from author index to *Cumulated Index Medicus*
Reproduced by permission of the National Library of Medicine

Magnetohydrodynamics
  See also
  Plasma (Physics)
  Plasma waves
  Synchrotron radiation
Alpha-torque forces. P. Graneau. bibl il diags *Electron Wirel World* 95:556-9 Je '89; Discussion. 95:875-6 S '89
Drop-on-demand operation of continuous jets using EHD techniques. D. W. Hrdina and J. M. Crowley. bibl flow chart diags *IEEE Trans Ind Appl* 25:705-10 Jl/Ag '89
Hydrodynamics of double-charged ions in a plane low-pressure discharge. D. A. Shapiro. bibl *J Phys D* 22:1107-13 Ag 14 '89
Iodine laser creates plasma X-rays. B. Dance. *Laser Focus World* 25:26+ Je '89
The magnetohydrodynamical instability of a current sheet created by plasma flow. A. I. Podgorny. bibl diags *Plasma Phys Control Fusion* 31:1271-9 Jl '89
A personal-computer-based package for interactive assessment of magnetohydrodynamic equilibrium and poloidal field coil design in axisymmetric toroidal geometry. W. P. Kelleher and D. Steiner. bibl diag *Fusion Technol* 15:1507-19 Jl '89
Why Extrap? B. Lehnert. bibl(p38-43) il diags *Fusion Technol* 16:7-43 Ag '89
      Mathematical models
Induction electrohydrodynamic pump in a vertical configuration. J. Seyed-Yagoobi and others. bibl diags *J Heat Transf* 111:664-74 Ag '89
Mass transport and the bootstrap current from Ohm's law in steady-state tokamaks. J.-S. Kim and J. M. Greene. bibl *Plasma Phys Control Fusion* 31 no7:1069-94 Je '89
Reduction of thermal expansion in Z-pinches by electron beam assisted magnetic field generation. J. A. Heikkinen and S. J. Karttunen. bibl *Plasma Phys Control Fusion* 31 no7:1035-48 Je '89
Magnetometers
Scanner can detect brain damage. il *Engineer* 269:49 Ag 31-S 7 '89
      Design
Electronic balancing of multichannel SQUID magnetometers. H. J. M. ter Brake and others. bibl diags *J Phys E* 22:560-4 Ag '89

Exhibit 60
Sample entries from the *Applied Science and Technology Index,* 1986
Copyright © 1986 by the H. W. Wilson Co.
Material reproduced by permission of the publisher

ELECTRIC DRIVE

Control

128527   Digitale Drehzahl- und Lageregelung eines Synchron-Servoantriebs mit selbsteinstellender Zustandsregelung. [Digital speed and position control of a synchronous servo drive with a self-tuning state feedback control]. Because of their low moment of inertia synchronous servo drives have an excellent dynamic performance. The high acceleration torque will often cause oscillations of the mechanical system. In order to avoid these oscillations a state variable controller and a state observer were implemented on a signal processor system. The design of a state feedback control is difficult and requires a good knowledge of the plant. Therefore, tuning of the state control was done automatically by the signal processor. The mechanical system was approximated by an elastically coupled two mass system. The parameters of this model will be identified from the step response of the drive. The automatic tuning of the controller and the observer is done by means of a searching strategy. The advantage of the state control is demonstrated by experimental tests with a machine tool. (Author abstract) 3 Refs. In German.

Loebe, Wolfram (Univ Erlangen-Nuernberg, Erlangen, West Ger). *ETZ Arch* v 11 n 4 Apr 1989 p 131-135.

Mathematical Models

128528   Zeitdiskrete Modellbildung und Entwurf optimaler Regler am Beispiel eines spannungszwischenkreisumrichtergespeisten Gleichstromantriebs. [Time discrete modelling and optimal control design illustrated by a voltage-source converter fed dc drive]. In this paper a new method for modelling voltage-source converter fed electrical drives is presented. The method which describes the control system consisting of converter and drive motor as a nonlinear sampling system underlies the design of optimal current and speed controllers. It is shown that the non-linearities can be ignored if the sampling time was appropriately chosen. Hence usual linear sampling methods like z-transformation and state space design procedures can be applied to the optimization of the controllers. The procedure is illustrated in detail by the example of a transistor pulse-converter fed dc drive. (Author abstract) 6 Refs. In German.

Nuss, Uwe (Univ Karlsruhe, Karlsruhe, West Ger). *ETZ Arch* v 11 n 3 Mar 1989 p 75-82.

Stresses

128529   Beanspruchungen in Frequenzumrichtern mit ungesteuerter Einspeiseschaltung im stationaeren Betrieb und beim Auftreten impulsfoermiger Netzueberspannungen. [Stress in line-side converters and dc-link circuits of pwm controlled ac drives in the presence of line overvoltages]. Power electronic equipment may fail due to overvoltages in the ac supply line. The German Standard DIN VDE 0160 defines specific overvoltage waveforms which such equipment should withstand without being damaged. Different circuit topologies for the line-side converter are analyzed. The parameters for limited internal voltage stress are determined. The steady-state rms currents in the dc link capacitor and the fuses are calculated. (Author abstract) 7 Refs. In German.

Holtz, Joachim (Univ Wuppertal, Wuppertal, West Ger); Krah, Jens Onno; Stadtfeld, Siegfried. *ETZ Arch* v 11 n 6 Jun 1989 p 169-178.

Transients

128530   Transiente Vorgaenge im Antriebssystem mit Beruecksichtigung von Kupplungselastizitaeten. [Transients in driving system when including elasticity of coupling]. Any driving system may be represented by series of lumped masses linked by elastic couplings. In the paper, transients during starting of a driving system for different properties of the coupling have been analyzed. A moment of an asynchronous motor was taken as a driven one. The calculations of the transient moment for a two-element system have been compared with investigations. (Author abstract) 4 Refs. In German.

Karolewski, Boguslaw (Politechniki Wroclawskiej, Wroclaw, Pol); Pytel, Jan. *ETZ Arch* v 11 n 6 Jun 1989 p 199-203.

Variable Speed

128531   Design for a digital communications link for AC adjustable frequency drive controllers. The design of a simple, rugged digital communication system for AC adjustable-frequency drives is presented. The system is composed of a microprocessor-based local controller circuit located at the drive controller proper and an RS-422 connection to a programmable logic controller. The microprocessor-based system features remote control, status monitoring, and network capability. A natural outgrowth of the microprocessor implementation is the ability to do distributed closed-loop control functions at the drive controller. This ability allows the use of high-level commands, which reduces the work load at the programmable logic controller. 2 Refs.

Innes, Mark E. (Square D Co, Columbia, SC, USA); Liptak, J. Michael. *Conf Proc IEEE SOUTHEASTCON* v 2 (of 3), Energy and Information Technologies in the Southeast, Columbia, SC, USA, Apr 9-12 1989. Publ by IEEE, IEEE Service Center, Piscataway, NJ, USA, 1989 Available from IEEE Service Cent, (cat n 89CH2672-4), Piscataway, NJ, USA, p 449-454.

128532   Gate-turn-off thyristor: a breakthrough for the retrofit of existing induction motors from fixed to adjustable speed. Gate-turn-off (GTO) technology, application considerations, and new inverter design features are presented, and an example of drive economics is provided. Motor stresses for a retrofitted induction motor such as thermal heating, voltage stress, electrical resonance, and torsional problems are discussed. Drive control, diagnostic capability, and fiberoptic gate control are given as examples of drive equipment features. One of the major advantages of GTO technology is a nearly sinusoidal output waveform for the motor. Since this new product is directed for use with existing induction motors, downtime and expense for conversion on-site to adjustable speed can be greatly reduced. 9 Refs.

Hickok, Herbert N.; Wickiser, Michael R. *IEEE Trans Ind Appl* v 25 n 3 May-Jun 1989 p 523-532.

Exhibit 61

Sample from the *Engineering Index Monthly* (October 1986)
Copyright © 1986 by Engineering Information Inc.
Reprinted by permission of Engineering Information Inc.

```
Golgovskikh, A.V., 131057
Golikova, O.A., 133994
Golledge, S.L., 134465
Golluh, J.P., 135297
Golodets, G.I., 126538, 132138
Gololobov, E.M., 135072
Goloskokov, K.P., 133099
Golosman, E.Z., 125687, 126575
Golovicher, L.E., 127155
Golovin, A.A., 130968
Golovin, O.L., 134691
Golson, Steve, 128211
Golub, Morton A., 129448, 129449
Golub, T.P., 129742
Golubchikov, O.A., 127960
Golubeva, N.D., 126625
Golubicic, Z., 132195
Golubov, A.D., 135125
Gomalevskii, A.G., 130268
Goman, V.G., 129610
Gombani, Andrea, 127903
Gombar, A., 134255
Gombeer, P., 133434
Gomes De Azevedo, E.J.S., 130978
Gomes, V.M.S., 134033
Gomez, J., 126656
Gomez, Louis M., 130246
Gomez-Pina, Gregorio, 132860
Gomez-Ribelles, J.L., 132722
```

Exhibit 62
Sample entries from author index to the *Engineering Index*
Copyright © 1986 by Engineering Information Inc.
Reprinted by permission of Engineering Information Inc.

Many (but by no means all) of the printed indexes are based on some form of controlled vocabulary—a thesaurus or list of subject headings. The vocabulary used in the *Engineering Index* is known as *Subject Headings for Engineering*. Such controlled vocabularies can be of great value to someone searching the printed index, especially in cases where the index itself includes little or no cross-reference structure, as is true of *Index Medicus*.

Classified Indexes

There are basically two types of classified index. In one, entries appear under highly specific class numbers derived from a general or special-purpose classification scheme. One example is *Library and Information Science Abstracts* (LISA). In LISA, entries are arranged according to a faceted classification scheme devoted to the special field of library and information science. Exhibit 63 shows some sample entries relating to CD-ROM. Note how the notation relating to databases in CD-ROM form *(Zjjc)* is subdivided by notations from elsewhere in the classification *(Rn, Vtic)* to give greater specificity, and how an alphabetical label is used to explain each specific notation. Exhibit 64 shows specimen entries from the alphabetical subject index including some entries relating to the items shown in Exhibit 63.

ZjjcRnNak—CD-ROMs. Data bases. Information services.
 Economic aspects   88/5339
     The CD-ROM marketplace: a producer's perspective. Christopher Pooley. *Wilson Library Bulletin*, 62 (4) Dec 87, 24-26.
     Contribution to a special issue devoted in part to CD-ROM. When laser disc technology was first introduced to libraries, librarians recognised the great possibilities of the medium, especially its vast storage capacity. Examines the major differences between print, on-line and CD-ROM versions of the same data base which fall in 3 key areas: content, currency or update frequency, and pricing. Discusses competition in the marketplace and emphasises that the future for CD-ROM in libraries is excellent with more products, more new products offering combinations of data bases, better software and networking systems available to stimulate the growing use of CD-ROM products. (A.G.)

ZjjcRnNko—CD-ROMs. Data bases. Information services.
 Cost-benefit analysis. PsycLIT   88/5340
     Justifying CD-ROM. Ralph Alberico. *Small Computers in Libraries*, 7 (2) Feb 87, 18-20.
     Considers data bases on CD-ROM in terms of costs and benefits, by examining PsycLIT, an abbreviated CD-ROM version of the PsycINFO data base. PsycLIT was one of the first CD-ROM data bases and is one of the best and one of the most expensive. Compares the CD-ROM version to print and on-line products and stresses that as the number of users grow prices will decrease. (P.B.)

ZjjcVtic—CD-ROMs. User-System interface   88/5341
     Entering unchartered territory: putting CD-ROM in place. Nancy Crane, Tamara Durfee. *Wilson Library Bulletin*, 62 (4) Dec 87, 28-30. illus.
     Contribution to a special issue devoted in part to CD-ROM. Discusses considerations that need to be raised before implementing end-user CD-ROM

and offers some proposals as to how solutions may be found. These include: assessing the environment; choice of a CD-ROM system; components needed in setting up a workstation; vendor services; placement; user constraints; training for searching; statistics and ongoing assessment; effects on staff; and desired features of CD-ROM services. The rationale for end-user CD-ROM is presented. (A.G.)

Exhibit 63
Sample entries from *Library and Information Science Abstracts*
Reproduced by permission of the editor

Note how the terms used as alphabetical labels in Exhibit 63 become entry points in the subject index. The principle followed is that of chain indexing (see Chapter 4); each step in the hierarchical chain is indexed from the most specific up to the most general:

> Cost-benefit analysis, Information services, Databases, CD-ROMs, Computerized information storage and retrieval
> Information services, Databases, CD-ROMs, Computerized information storage and retrieval
> Databases, CD-ROMs, Computerized information storage and retrieval
> Computerized information storage and retrieval (this most general entry does not appear in Exhibit 64)

CD-ROMs
Computerised cataloguing 387
Computerised information storage and retrieval
422−441, 978−983, 1540−1542,
2088−2091, 2093, 2612−2617, 3155−3165,
3669−3674, 4222−4226, 4699−4710,
5319−5341, 6241−6260
Computerised information storage and retrieval:
Comparison with On-line information
retrieval 1570, 4702, 4704, 5321−5322,
6244−6245
Computerised information storage and retrieval:
Comparison with On-line information retrieval
and Printed information services 5323
Computerised union catalogues 5292
Computers 491−494, 1052, 1591, 2653,
3206−3207, 3765, 4292, 4831−4833, 6434
Computers: Library equipment 205, 1837,
2391−2392, 3451−3452, 4499, 5067, 5799
Document delivery: On-line information
retrieval 4825

Cost benefit analysis
Computerised acquisitions 1968
Computerised information work 3025
Information services: Data bases: CD-ROMs:
Computerised information storage and
retrieval 5340
Of Business information: Information services:
Data bases: On-line information retrieval 471
Reference work 2471

Data bases
See also Computerised bibliographic records
CD-ROMs: Computerised information storage
and retrieval 428−440, 979−983, 1542,
2089−2091, 2613−2616, 3157−3165,
3672−3673, 4222−4226, 4703−4710,
5327−5340, 5344−5345, 6248−6259
CD-ROMs: Computerised information storage
and retrieval: *Comparison with* On-line
information retrieval 1570, 4702, 4704,
5321−5322, 6244−6245
CD-ROMs *and* Videodiscs: Computerised
information storage and retrieval 2093
Command languages: User-system interface:
On-line information retrieval 1585
Computerised information storage and retrieval
419, 2606
Concepts: Computerised subject indexing 5313
Free text searching: On-line information
retrieval 2136

Full text searching: On-line information
retrieval 480, 1038, 2640, 3748, 3750−3751
Gateway facilities: On-line information
retrieval 3704−3705
Hypertext: On-line information retrieval 6417
In-house systems: On-line information retrieval
6262
Laser optical discs: Computerised information
storage and retrieval 977, 5318
Laser optical discs: *Use for* Periodicals: Subject
indexing 2061
Multiple data base searches: On-line
information retrieval 2643
On-line information retrieval 460−479,
1019−1036, 1558−1580, 2108−2128, 2623,
2626−2638, 3182−3195, 3727−3746,
4256−4279, 4766−4809, 5344, 5357−5370,
6321−6382

Information services
Data bases: CD-ROMs: *Comparison with*
On-line information retrieval 4704
Data bases: CD-ROMs: Computerised
information storage and retrieval 428−440,
980−983, 1542, 2089−2091, 2613−2616,
3157−3165, 3672−3673, 4223−4226,
4703−4710, 5327−5340, 5344−5345,
6248−6258
Data bases: CD-ROMs *and* Videodiscs:
Computerised information storage and
retrieval 2093
Data bases: Command languages: Man-machine
interface: On-line information retrieval 1585
Data bases: Computerised information storage
and retrieval 419, 2606
Data bases: Computerised subject indexing
5313
Data bases: Free text searching: On-line
information retrieval 2136
Data bases: Full text searching: On-line
information retrieval 480, 1038, 2640, 3748,
3750−3751
Data bases: Gateway facilities: On-line
information retrieval 3704−3705
Data bases: Laser optical discs: Computerised
information storage and retrieval 977, 5318
Data bases: Laser optical discs: *Use for*
Periodicals: Subject indexing 2061
Data bases: Multiple data base searches:
On-line information retrieval 2643
Data bases: On-line information retrieval
460−479, 1019−1036, 1558−1580,
2108−2128, 2626−2638, 3182−3195,
3727−3746, 4256−4279, 4766−4809, 5344,
5357−5370, 6321−6382

Exhibit 64
Sample entries from the subject index to
Library and Information Science Abstracts
Reproduced by permission of the editor

PsycLIT (the name of a database) is not a bona fide index term in LISA and thus does not generate an entry in the subject index, although it does generate one in the separate name index.

While LISA employs a special-purpose classification scheme, other printed indexes are based on general schemes, the one most commonly used being the *Universal Decimal Classification* (UDC).

In the other classified approach to the organization of a printed database, entries are grouped under relatively broad subject categories and more specific subject access is provided by means of indexes. One example is *Biological Abstracts.* Exhibit 65 shows the broad subject categories under which abstracts are organized and Exhibit 66 shows some sample entries. Note that subheadings are used in this tool also, and that extensive cross-referencing is employed. The subject index to *Biological Abstracts* is a KWIC index (Exhibit 67) so the quality of the specific subject access will depend to some extent on how well the titles of the items included actually reflect what they deal with. However, some titles are enhanced by the addition of further keywords, thus providing more access points and clarifying otherwise imperfect titles. *Biological Abstracts* includes other types of index—a "generic" index (by genus or genus-species names) and a "biosystematic" index (organized according to a taxonomic classification).

Chemical Abstracts resembles *Biological Abstracts* in that entries are organized under subject categories and subcategories. However, the subject index is quite different, based on the principle of articulation (see Chapter 4): strings of terms assigned by human indexers are manipulated in a standard way to provide a group of consistent access points for each item (Exhibit 68). While this articulated subject index appears only in the cumulations of *Chemical Abstracts,* a keyword index appears in each weekly issue (see Exhibit 69). *Chemical Abstracts* also includes an index by chemical formula (see Exhibit 70).

Other Indexes

Most of the other indexing/abstracting services in printed form are variations on the types already illustrated. The *Sociology of Education Abstracts,* unlike *Biological Abstracts* and *Chemical Abstracts,* simply lists abstracts in numerical order without grouping under broad subject categories. The subject index, described as a "modified keyword index," indexes the abstracts under keywords or phrases appearing in the title or the abstract itself. Proper names are also indexed. Exhibit 71 shows two sample abstracts and Exhibit 72 shows sample index entries, including some (e.g., black dropouts, class cutting, compulsory education) relating to the abstracts of Exhibit 71.

	Page
Aerospace and Underwater Biological Effects	AB-1
Agronomy	AB-1
Allergy	AB-22
Anatomy and Histology, General and Comparative	AB-29
Animal Production (includes Fur-Bearing Animals)	AB-30
Bacteriology, General and Systematic	AB-49
Behavioral Biology	AB-50
Biochemistry	AB-54
Biophysics	AB-77
Blood, Blood-Forming Organs and Body Fluids	AB-85
Bones, Joints, Fasciae, Connective and Adipose Tissue	AB-107
Botany, General and Systematic	AB-124
Cardiovascular System	AB-139
Chemotherapy	AB-203
Chordata, General and Systematic Zoology	AB-222
Circadian Rhythm and Other Periodic Cycles	AB-232
Cytology and Cytochemistry	AB-233
Dental and Oral Biology	AB-245
Developmental Biology-Embryology	AB-252
Digestive System	AB-264
Disinfection, Disinfectants and Sterilization	AB-290
Ecology (Environmental Biology)	AB-291
Economic Botany	AB-351
Economic Entomology (includes Chelicerata)	AB-351
Endocrine System	AB-366
Enzymes	AB-401
Evolution	AB-411
Food and Industrial Microbiology	AB-411
Food Technology (non-toxic studies)	AB-421
Forestry and Forest Products	AB-437
General Biology	AB-448
Genetics of Bacteria and Viruses	AB-450
Genetics and Cytogenetics	AB-459
Gerontology	AB-508
Horticulture	AB-509
Immunology (Immunochemistry)	AB-525
Immunology, Parasitological	AB-568
Integumentary System	AB-574
Invertebrata, Comparative and Experimental Studies	AB-578
Invertebrata, General and Systematic Zoology	AB-598
Laboratory Animals	AB-620*
Mathematical Biology and Statistical Methods	AB-620
Medical and Clinical Microbiology (includes Veterinary)	AB-620
Metabolism	AB-645
Methods, Materials and Apparatus, General	AB-650
Microbiological Apparatus, Methods and Media	AB-651
Microorganisms, General (includes Protista)	AB-651
Morphology and Anatomy of Plants (includes Embryology)	AB-652
Morphology and Cytology of Bacteria	AB-652
Muscle	AB-653
Neoplasms and Neoplastic Agents	AB-660
Nervous System (excludes Sense Organs)	AB-766
Nutrition	AB-814
Paleobiology	AB-826
Paleobotany	AB-827
Paleozoology	AB-828
Palynology	AB-829
Parasitology (includes Ecto- and Endoparasites)	AB-829
Pathology, General and Miscellaneous	AB-838
Pediatrics	AB-840
Pest Control, General (includes Plants and Animals); Pesticides; Herbicides	AB-840
Pharmacognosy and Pharmaceutical Botany	AB-841
Pharmacology	AB-844
Physical Anthropology: Ethnobiology	AB-954
Physiology and Biochemistry of Bacteria	AB-956
Physiology, General and Miscellaneous	AB-964
Phytopathology	AB-969
Plant Physiology, Biochemistry and Biophysics	AB-990
Poultry Production	AB-1018
Psychiatry	AB-1023
Public Health	AB-1053
Radiation Biology	AB-1102
Reproductive System	AB-1107
Respiratory System	AB-1129
Sense Organs, Associated Structures and Functions	AB-1144
Social Biology (includes Human Ecology)	AB-1165
Soil Microbiology	AB-1167
Soil Science	AB-1168
Temperature: Its Measurement, Effects and Regulation	AB-1171
Tissue Culture: Apparatus, Methods and Media	AB-1174
Toxicology	AB-1175
Urinary System and External Secretions	AB-1226
Veterinary Science	AB-1240
Virology, General	AB-1241

*There are no references to this concept in this issue. See page listed for instructions on locating related topics.

Exhibit 65

Subject categories used by *Biological Abstracts*

Copyright © Biological Abstracts Inc. (BIOSIS)
Reproduced with permission

CYTOLOGY AND CYTOCHEMISTRY

See **also:** *Anatomy and Histology, General and Comparative –
Micro– and Ultramicroscopic Anatomy • Biophysics • Genetics
and Cytogenetics • Methods, Materials and Apparatus, General
– Cytology and Cytochemistry • Morphology and Cytology of
Bacteria • Neoplasms and Neoplastic Agents – Neoplastic Cell
Lines • Organ System Headings, especially Blood,
Blood–Forming Organs and Body Fluids – Blood Cell Studies;
Reproductive System • Tissue Culture, Apparatus, Methods and
Media*

See: *Specific systematic sections for cyto–taxonomic studies*

ANIMAL

2001. VEOMETT, GEORGE E. (Sch. Biol. Sci., 348 Manter Hall Life Sci.,
Univ. Nebr.-Lincoln, Lincoln, Nebr. 68588–0118.) J INTERFERON RES 8(2):
217-226. 1988. **Effect of interferon on secretion of proteins by various murine
cell lines.**—The interferons (IFNs) have been shown to be antagonistic to the
growth stimulatory effects of mitogens on cultured cells. A report of the interactions of IFN–β and platelet–derived growth factor on BALB/c-3T3 mouse cells
established that IFN itself induced the secretion of a limited number of proteins
from this cell line. The present work was undertaken to determine if other
murine cell lines treated with homologous IFN–β also secreted new or
additional protein(s) in response to this agent and if this response correlated with
other phenotypic properties of the cells. The cell lines examined included L929
cells and two derivatives of this line (GM347 and WDIFN), CAK-TK⁻,
Swiss-3T3, and BALB/c-3T3. Each line was exposed to [^{35}S]methionine in the
absence and in the presence of IFN–β, the supernatant fluids collected, and the
radioactive, secreted proteins examined by fluorography after electrophoresis
through SDS–containing polyacrylamide gels. Two cell lines (GM347 and
Swiss-3T3) did not appear to secrete new or additional proteins after IFN
treatment. However, four lines (L929, WDIFN, CAK-TK⁻, and BALB/c-3T3)
did secrete new or additional proteins in response to IFN. Thus IFN–induced
secretion of protein appeared to be a common but not universal phenomenon. In
addition, although the number and apparent size(s) of the IFN–induced, secreted
proteins were different in these various lines, one protein (M_r = 89–90,000)
appeared to be secreted by each of them. In this respect it was unique. Moreover
the IFN–induced secretion of protein did not appear to correlate with the
antiviral or antiproliferative effects of IFN.

2002. CARMO-FONSECA, MARIA, ANTONIO J. CIDADAO and
JOSE F. DAVID-FERREIRA*. (Dep. Biol. Cell., Inst. Gulbenkian Ciencia,
Apartado 14, P-2781 Oeiras Codex/Portugal.) EUR J CELL BIOL 45(2):
282-290. 1987(1988). **Filamentous cross–bridges link intermediate filaments to
the nuclear pore complexes.**—Intermediate filament–nuclear matrix interactions
were studied in cultured rat ventral prostate cells and isolated rat uterine
epithelial cells. Cytokeratin filaments were identified by immunoelectron
microscopy. In addition to conventional thin section of Triton X-100 treated
cells, subcellular residues composed of intermediate filaments and nuclear matrix
were critical-point dried and platinum–carbon replicated. The results
demonstrate the presence of a previously unrecognized type of filamentous
cross–bridges that link intermediate filaments to the nulcear pore complexes.

Exhibit 66
Sample entries from *Biological Abstracts*
Copyright © Biological Abstracts Inc. (BIOSIS)
Reproduced with permission

UISM STUDY DNA SUGAR	**PUCKER** /CONVERSIONS OF POLY-2-AMIN	43705
MENT SUCTION MACULAR	MEMBRANE ENGAGEMENT HYDR	19169
AL MEMBRANE MACULAR	PHOTORECEPTOR LAYER ATROP	92091
AL VASCULITIS MACULAR	RETINAL HAMARTOMA DIAGNOSI	102765
CONFORMATION/ RIBOSE	**PUCKERING** STRUCTURE DYNAMICS ENER	13648
NING VECTOR BASED ON	**PUC9** BACTERIA DNA FRAGMENTS DRUG	107108
CEREALS WHEAT BREAD	**PUDDING** GRAIN PRODUCTS FOOD PROCE	106932
FOOD ADDITIVES VANILLA	LEGUMES GELATINIZATION VIS	13304
S FOOD DAIRY INDUSTRY	**PUDDINGS** YOGURTS/ DETERMINATION O	85404
MOUS CELL CARCINOMA/	**PUDENDAL** CANCER WHICH HAS SPECIFIC	15865
MAN SKIN SHORTAGE/ A	FASCIOCUTANEOUS FLAP ITS	38774
EURONAL RESPONSES TO	NERVE INPUT RAT ELECTROP	120781
RMAL SUBJECTS HUMAN	NERVE VISCERAL AFFERENTS/	57012
L TRANSECTIONS ON THE	NERVE-EVOKED RESPONSE IN	71854
FLEX HYPEREXCITABILITY	NUCLEUS BULBOCAVERNOSU	59688
VATIONS ON THE HUMAN	**PUDENDO-ANAL** REFLEX FECAL INCONTIN	67422
STASIS PROGNOSIS PENIS	**PUDENDUM** SURGERY ELECTRON BEAM B	35719
AL FLUID PROTEIN LEVEL	**PUDENZ-HEYER** VALVE HAKIM-CORDIS VA	77704
LAKES IN THE STATE OF	**PUEBLA** MEXICO ANGIOSPERMS SPECIES	84478
AT AMALUCAN STATE OF	MEXICO HUMAN DRAINAGE IRRIG	102833
E FROM SOUTHWESTERN	MEXICO STEGNOSPERMA-SANCH	72563
STUDY APACHE NAVAJO	**PUEBLO** INDIAN CULTURAL GROUP DEMO	49531
STARCH FACTORY JAPAN	**PUERARIAE** DIADZIN DAIDZEIN PUERARIN	17275
CH AND ISOFLAVONES IN	RADIX PUERARIA-LOBATA PU	47309
RADIX PUERARIA-LOBATA	**PUERARIN** DIADZIN DAIDZEIN NATURAL P	47309
S BLOCKING EFFECT OF	ON BETA-ADRENOCEPTOR OF I	36921
ARIAE DIADZIN DAIDZEIN	PHARMACOLOGICALLY ACTIVE	17275
GNANTS NEWBORNS AND	**PUERPERAE** HUMAN FERROUS SULFATE V	745
IENCY IN A WOMAN WITH	**PUERPERAL** ALACTOGENESIS HUMAN MIL	85066
O COWS WITH POTENTIAL	DISORDERS ON TENTH DAY F	93179
IRTH UTERINE PROLAPSE	ENDOMETRITIS FUNCTIONAL	93179
ETENTIO SECUNDINARUM	ENDOMETRITIS LABORED DE	61192
CTION· AN OUTBREAK OF	FEVER CAUSED BY GROUP G	112475
BREECH PRESENTATION	FEVER GESTATIONAL AGE M	8728
MA URINARY RETENTION	FEVER UTERINE ATONY FETA	123525
ITY BRAZIL 1980 HUMAN	INFECTION HYPERTENSION N	38567
INETICS PREVENTION OF	LACTATION WITH PARLODEL	7361
TOMATIC BACTERIURIA IN	PATIENTS HUMAN LABOR IN	34786
IAN VEIN INVOLVEMENT/	PELVIC THROMBOPHLEBITIS	41021
RTUM HEMORRHAGE ON	PITUITARY FUNCTION HUMA	102418
AL TRAUMA TREATMENT/	URINARY RETENTION HUMA	103513
UMAN HEALING PYREXIA	**PUERPERIAL** COMPLICATIONS/ CLINICAL	49029
S CYCLE GESTATION AND	**PUERPERIUM** /CONCENTRATIONS OF EST	20221
LLICLE CYST PREGNANCY	ENDOMETRIAL CYST NUCLE	8730
NG PREGNANCY AND THE	HUMAN ANTICONVULSANT-	47431
CITIS IN PREGNANCY AND	HUMAN DIAGNOSIS SURGE	95071
BLOOD PRESSURE IN THE	HUMAN DIURNAL VARIATIO	11310
DITIS OCCURRING IN THE	HUMAN EDEMA/ TRANSIEN	51663
CLIN IN PREGNANCY AND	HUMAN RAT 6 KETOPROST	49859
DURING PREGNANCY AND	IN STREPTOZOTOCIN-INDU	32818
EBIASINIDAE FROM NEAR	**PUERTO** AYACUCHO RIO ORINOCO DRAIN	115752
ION AND CLIMATE IN THE	BLANCO MOUNTAINS SOUTHWES	78236
GAMMA LACTONE FROM	RICAN LYNGBYA-MAJUSCULA/ S-	69158
UNDERSTORY BIRDS IN A	RICAN RAINFOREST DACRYODES-	106052
CRIPTIONS OF LARVAE OF	RICAN SPECIES OF ANTILLISCARI	76331
EMATURE THELARCHE IN	RICO A SEARCH FOR ENVIRONME	124252
LIDA POLYCHAETA FROM	RICO AND FLORIDA USA AND A N	65988
HECATE HYDROIDS FROM	RICO AND THE VIRGIN ISLANDS	76427
ILED HAWK NEST SITES IN	RICO BUTEO-JAMAICENSIS VEGE	63160
OL OF AEDES-AEGYPTI IN	RICO DISEASE VECTOR INSECTIC	69817
EZUELA BOLIVIA GUYANA	RICO DISTRIBUTION AROMATIC S	115136

Exhibit 67

Sample entries from subject index to *Biological Abstracts*
Copyright © Biological Abstracts Inc. (BIOSIS)
Reproduced with permission

Mandarin orange
amino acids of, of Australia, 153016z
ascorbic acid and dehydroascorbic acid detn. in, by
dichlorophenolindophenol titrn. and
fluorometry, 22364p
canned, nickel of, of Germany, 56322p
carotenoids and vitamin A activity of, of Finland,
211229j
Clementine, compn. of, Wenzhou Honey orange oil
in relation to, 230387a
desulfurizing agents contg., for hydrogen sulfide
removal from gases, P 138523u
eastern dodder control on, with glyphosate, 187753c
fertilizer expt. with, with zinc, 230615y
fruit thining in, 90511j
juice, limonin detn. in, by HPLC, 211054y
nitrification in krasnozem soil under, nitrogen
fertilizer form effect on, 191706g
Satsuma
antioxidative activity and tocopherols in flavedo
of, rind spot effect on, 72661d
ascorbic acid and sugars in peel of, in growth and
development, 21199b
satsuma, disease, rind spot, antioxidative activity
and tocopherols of flavedo in relation to,
72661d
Satsuma
ethylene formation by, during fruit development,
cyanide metab. in relation to, 21201w
fertilizer expt. with, with potassium rates,
38196w
flavonoid glycosides and adenosine of peels of,
hypotensive effect and structure of, 69120w
flavonoid glycosides of peel of, isolation and
structure and hypotensive effect of, 189403n
glycosides from leaves of, citrosides A and B as,
189387k
juice, ascorbic acid and sugars in peel and, in
growth and development, 21199b
juice, potassium fertilizer effect on yield and
compn. of, 38196w
naringinase of waste of, treated with brewers'
yeast, 6335z
Penicillium digitatum inhibition on,
thiabendazole effect enhancement by
carbohydrate fatty acid esters in, 6616s
pollen fertility induction in, by nitrosoethylurea,
189619n
terpenoids and terpenoid glycosides from, 54482s
vitamin B_{12} detn. in, by *Alteromonas
thalassomethanolica* bioassay, 171865e
tangerine
aroma, energy food contg. leucine and isoleucine
and valine and, P 211346v
canned, tin detn. in, by oscillog. polarog. titrn.,
56109z
juice, carotenoids detn. in concs. of, by HPLC,
orange juice adulteration in relation to,
56052a
juice, glucose and sucrose of, 211250j
pectins of, extn. of, with use of microwave, P
175439s
preservation of, ethylene–decompg. compns. in, P
56330q
puree conc., provitamin A carotenoids detn. in by
HPLC, 73937k
tissue culture of, essential oil manuf. with, P
55999c
volatile acids detn. in, by distn. and titrn.,
133781s
wastewater from processing of, treatment of,
Penicillium janthinellum and activated sludge
process in, 44290p

Exhibit 68
Sample entries from subject index to *Chemical Abstracts*
Reprinted by permission of Chemical Abstracts Service

Thermolytic
    dissocn water hydrogen oxygen
        P 136408h
Thermolyzed
    chalk polymn filling 134413g
Thermomagnetic
    material iron rhodium manuf 137011k
Thermomech
    analysis coating characterization
        135519h
    chem pulp tissue 135751c
    property polyamide fiber 135343w
    pulp mech property 135752d
    pulp storage latency 135761f
    pulp thiol bleaching 135763h
    strengthening copper alloy 138017d
    treatment aluminum alloy aging
        138016c
    treatment austenite transformation review
        137609m
    treatment austenitized maraging steel
        137685h
    treatment steel silicon structure
        137688m
Thermometer
    automated helium 3 melting 140908p
    electronic silicon transistor sensor
        136035j
    NMR samarium acetate hydrate
        144753g
    noise ceramic resistor 144278f
Thermometric
    titrn anionic surfactant 135953v
Thermometry
    noise thermocouple high temp 140909q
Thermonuclear
    neutron scattering plasma 141608c
Thermooptical
    liq crystal display P 143716k
    time resolved spectrochem analysis
        145099k
Thermoperlite
    bending strength metal oxide P 138826s
Thermophoresis
    sol gel coating 138577m
Thermophys
    property data bank 140925s
    property data center London 140926t
    property fabric 135346z
    property process simulation 140762m
    property study China review 140860s
Thermopiezic
    analysis absorption desorption 140310n
Thermoplastic
    elec conductive blend P 134864e
    electromagnetic interference shielding
        P 144516g
    polyester blend adhesive sheet
        P 135111u
    polyester elastomer blend molding
        P 135276b
    resin film manuf P 135110t
    resin magnetic fluid recording
        P 143692z
    resin polyolefin electrophotog toner
        P 143539e
    surface treatment flame 135013p

Exhibit 69
Sample entries from keyword index to *Chemical Abstracts*
Reprinted by permission of Chemical Abstracts Service

$C_{52}H_{44}N_3O_2P_2Tc$
Technetium, [1,3-bis(4-methylphenyl)-1-=
triazenato-N^1,N^3]dicarbonylbis=
(triphenylphosphine)-
$(OC-6-14)-$ [99354-95-7], 14057b

$C_{52}H_{44}N_4O_6P_2$
Phosphonic acid, (3,3',4,4',6,6'-hexaphenyl[6,6'-=
bi-6H-pyrrolo[1,2-b]pyrazole]-2,2'-diyl)bis-
tetramethyl ester, $(R*,S*)-$ [100418-78-8],
88671u
tetramethyl ester, $(R*,S*)-$, compd. with
trichloromethane (1:1), monohydrate
[100418-79-9], 88671u

$C_{52}H_{44}N_6OZn$
Zinc, [4-(diethylamino)-N-[2-(10,15,20-=
triphenyl-21H,23H-porphin-5-yl)phenyl]=
butanamidato(2-)-$N^{21},N^{22},N^{23},N^{24}$]-
$(SP-4-2)-$ [102497-59-6], 224763e

$C_{52}H_{44}N_6O_4$
2-Naphthalenecarboxamide, 4,4'-[(3,3',5,5'-=
tetramethyl[1,1'-biphenyl]-4,4'-diyl)bis=
(azo)]bis[3-hydroxy-N-(4-methylphenyl)-
[81287-27-6], P 196932p

$C_{52}H_{44}N_6O_6$
2-Naphthalenecarboxamide, 4,4'-[(3,3',5,5'-=
tetramethyl[1,1'-biphenyl]-4,4'-diyl)bis=
(azo)]bis[3-hydroxy-N-(2-methoxyphenyl)-
[81287-28-7], P 196932p

$C_{52}H_{44}N_8O_4$
2-Naphthalenecarboxamide, 4,4'-[1,4-piperazine=
diylbis(4,1-phenyleneazo)]bis[3-hydroxy-=
N-(4-methylphenyl)- [101701-09-1], P
196932p

$C_{52}H_{44}N_8O_6$
2-Naphthalenecarboxamide, 4,4'-[1,4-piperazine=
diylbis(4,1-phenyleneazo)]bis[3-hydroxy-=
N-(3-methoxyphenyl)- [101701-10-4], P
196932p

$C_{52}H_{44}O_5Sb_2$
Antimony, bis(benzeneacetato-O)-μ-=
oxohexaphenyldi-
stereoisomer [99825-05-5], 50926t

$C_{52}H_{44}P_2Rh$
Rhodium(1+), [[1,1'-binaphthalene]-2,2'-=
diylbis[diphenylphosphine]-P,P][(1,2,5,6-=
η)-1,5-cyclooctadeiene]-
chloride, stereoisomer [101627-26-3], 168628a
——, [[1,1'-binaphthalene]-2,2'-diylbis=
[diphenylphosphine]-P,P][(1,2,5,6-η)-1,5-=
cyclooctadiene]-
stereoisomer, perchlorate [82822-45-5], 168628a

$C_{52}H_{45}CoN_4O_3S$
Cobalt, (1-butanol)(ethyl mercaptoacetato-S)[5,=
10,15,20-tetraphenyl-21H,23H-porphinato=
(2-)-$N^{21},N^{22},N^{23},N^{24}$]-
$(OC-6-23)-$ [100203-75-6], 64759c

Exhibit 70
Sample entries from the formula index to *Chemical Abstracts*
Reprinted by permission of Chemical Abstracts Service

88S/037 **Compulsory education and home schooling: truancy or prophecy?**
M. A. PITMAN, *Education and Urban Society,* 19(3), 1987, pp 280—289.

Starting from the premise that American schooling is experiencing a crisis of meaning, the author looks at the increased incidence of in-school truancy or class cutting, and the increase in home schooling. Approximately 25 percent of the school population are educated at home, though at least another 9 percent are persistent truants, and up to 20 percent in-school truants. A variety of research is cited throughout the article. Home schoolers are defined as falling into three main categories: religious; progressive; and academic. Religious concerns centre upon the poor quality of public schooling, the moral education of the children and a desire for closer parent-child relationships. The author has carried out a survey of a New Age or Progressive community in the northeastern United States, where the emphasis is on Green politics and alternative lifestyles and approaches. For these people, home schooling makes sense as it allows for unorthodox views and treatment to be provided. The academic home-schoolers are concerned about the academic quality (or lack of it) in public schools. Surveys do show that home-schooled children do perform on average better than public school educated children, though the parents themselves tend to be more highly educated than the population at large. Legally, the laws concerning schooling do not compel education; rather they compel attendance, so home-schoolers tend to receive a disproportionate amount of school superintendent time and activity. In the history of society, the emphasis on compulsory attendance is very recent, and is occurring at the precise time when parents are questioning the quality and nature of public education provided.   —*NM*

88S/038 **A comparative study of black dropouts and black high school graduates in an urban public school system.** S. B. WILLIAMS, *Education and Urban Society,* 19(3), 1987, pp 311—319.

A sample of 50 black male and female dropouts from an urban southeast Texan school district in 1985–86 is compared with 50 black male and female graduates from the same school in the same year to ascertain significant differences between them. Data was collected from records, tests and home visits. All the students lived in the attendance zone for the school, which provided a homogeneous socioeconomic background. The researcher was a participant observer, having been a resident in the community for 30 years. Church attendance was found to be a significant factor, with 72 percent of the graduates and 14 percent of the dropouts attending. Graduate status, however, did not help the students in gaining social security assistance. There was a higher incidence of detentions and grade retentions (being kept down a year) for the dropouts than for the graduates, and a lower attendance at vocational educational programmes. Though there was no significant difference in the occupational levels of parents, the parents of the graduates were more highly educated. Similar sibling attainment, and the friendship of other graduates were also significant factors in the background of the graduates. The graduates also had more positive views towards the school than the dropouts, who felt alienated and on the periphery of school and community life. The dropout experiences pervasive feelings of isolation, disconnectedness and rejection, and these must be addressed if the dropout is to be rehabilitated to schooling.   —*NM*

Exhibit 71
Sample abstracts from *Sociology of Education Abstracts*
Reproduced by permission of Carfax Publishing Company

ability grouping, 109, 112, 127
ability grouping research, 111
Aboriginal schooling, 024
academic achievement, 035, 081, 101
academic marketplace, 113
academic performance, 120
academic women, 148
achievement, 046, 084, 108, 121
adolescence, 060, 079
adolescents, 047
adult claimants, 139
adult education, 002, 003, 140
Afro-Caribbean students, 138
Alabama, 042
Alaska, 080
amalgamation, 019
America, 080
American school policy, 144
American society, 118
anti-social behaviour, 030
appraisal, 145
apprenticeships, 023
Arab-Israeli students, 125
art, 044
Asian students, 138
assistant professors, 133
Atlanta, 007
Australia, 015, 019, 105
Austria, 045

best-evidence synthesis, 109, 111
biology, 072
black adults, 085
black children, 007, 081, 083, 084
black dropouts, 038
black males, 030
black school politics, 007
black students, 051, 120
black youths, 086
Botswana, 035
Brazil, 062
Brazilian education, 062
British universities, 075
building design, 145
business schools, 029

Canada, 025, 026, 027, 028
Canadian census figures, 028
career opportunities, 118
careers advice, 141
careers guidance, 018
Caribbean, 033
Caribbean homes, 043
Catania, 090
chemistry, 072
childbirth, 133
church, 086
civic education, 067
class cutting, 037
classroom advice, 142
classroom instruction, 111

classroom interactions, 072
classroom research, 014
classroom teaching, 105
classrooms, 046, 055
college opportunities, 117
college quality, 077
Commonwealth Caribbean, 069
community education, 089
community educators, 089
competency testing, 005
comprehensive schools, 060
compulsory education, 037
computing, 018
continuing education, 140
corporal punishment, 115
counselling, 017
creativity, 101
Cuba, 064
cultural diversity, 044
cultural influences, 065
culture, 011
curriculum, 057, 057, 070, 075, 096, 105, 145
curriculum changes, 116
curriculum development, 015

decision making, 042, 094
design education, 044
developing countries, 068

Exhibit 72
Sample of subject index entries from *Sociology of Education Abstracts*
Reproduced by permission of Carfax Publishing Company

haloperidol, aminophylline, amphetamine, anticonvulsive agent, arecoline, bicuculline, cocaine, convulsant agent, kindling, n methyl dextro aspartic acid, neurotransmitter, tetracaine, mouse, 989
- behavior disorder, carbamazepine, fluphenazine decanoate, phenytoin, schizophrenia, adult, blood level, drug therapy, 1110
- central nervous system, electroencephalogram, evoked visual response, lithium, myoclonus, neuroleptic agent, neurotoxicity, side effect, 969

head injury, central nervous system, computer assisted tomography, epidural hematoma, epilepsy, incidence, skull fracture, subdural hematoma, complication, 1001
- electrocardiography, emergency medicine, glucose blood level, hematocrit, migraine, orthostatic hypotension, seizure, syncope, childhood, epidemiology, etiology, morbidity, 1086

heart arrhythmia, asystole, electrocardiogram, electroencephalogram, epilepsy, seizure, adult, etiology, pacemaker, 1108

heart graft, convulsion, cyclosporin a, risk assessment, adult, drug therapy, etiology, 994

heart infarction, acidosis, bleeding tendency, brain disease, coma, convulsion, diarrhea, hemorrhagic shock, hypovolemic shock, syndrome, diagnosis, infant, kidney function, liver function, pathogenesis, 1087

heart rate, amygdaloid nucleus, convulsion, epileptogenesis, hippocampus, respiration control, single unit activity, adult, diagnosis, etiology, 1040
- blood pressure, convulsion, timolol, aged, animal model, cat, drug therapy, 939

heat shock protein, brain region, epileptic state, kainic acid, seizure, histochemistry, rat, 904

hematocrit, electrocardiography, emergency medicine, glucose blood level, head injury, migraine, orthostatic hypotension, seizure, syncope, childhood, epidemiology, etiology, morbidity, 1086

hemiparesis, anosognosia, epilepsy, seizure, transient ischemic attack, adult, aged, diagnosis, etiology, 1010
- behavior disorder, brain abscess, mental deficiency, neurologic disease, seizure, age, child, complication, electroencephalograpphy, follow up, infant, sex difference, surgery, 1084

Exhibit 73
Sample entries from the subject index to *Epilepsy Abstracts*
Reprinted by permission of Elsevier Science Publishers
This index is typical of the subject indexes produced in the Excerpta Medica series

The many abstracts bulletins produced in the Excerpta Medica Series (Elsevier Science Publishers) also group items under broad subject categories. The subject indexes are highly specific. All of the terms assigned (from a thesaurus) by indexers appear in an index entry. Most of the terms become entry points in the index, the other terms being carried as modifiers. The modifiers are arranged in alphabetical order in two sequences: terms that will themselves become entry points precede the terms that are modifiers only and will not be entry points. Exhibit 73 provides an example. Note how the string of terms acts as a kind of mini-abstract, providing a clear indication (in most cases) of what each item is about. The Excerpta Medica subject indexes are discussed more completely in Chapter 4.

BTI Heading STEEL : Production : Furnaces, Arc : Ladles

References LADLES : Arc furnaces : Steel production.
See STEEL : Production : Furnaces,
Arc : Ladles
ARC FURNACES : Steel production. See
STEEL : Production : Furnaces, Arc
FURNACES, Arc : Steel production. See
STEEL : Production : Furnaces, Arc

CTI Heading STEEL : Production : Furnaces, Arc : Ladles

References LADLES
See
Steel : Production : Furnaces, Arc : Ladles
ARC FURNACES
See
Furnaces, Arc
FURNACES, Arc
See
Steel : Production : Furnaces, Arc

Exhibit 74
Differences in presentation of references between *British Technology Index* (BTI) and *Current Technology Index* (CTI) for an item on ladles for arc furnaces producing steel. The author is grateful to Tom Edwards, editor of the *Current Technology Index,* for this example

Most alphabetico-specific indexes arrange bibliographic references under subject headings, perhaps with subheadings, and duplicate entries under two or more such headings (as in *Index Medicus*), or they organize abstracts under subject headings/subheadings and use some form of cross-referencing to provide alternative subject access approaches (as in the *Engineering Index*). Some variations on this alphabetico-specific approach exist. For example, the former *British Technology Index* (BTI), as described in Chapter 4, used index entries consisting of a string of controlled terms in a "systematic order." Exhibit 19 provides an example. A bibliographic reference appeared in only one place in the index, this being determined by the sequence in which terms were combined. Other approaches were provided by systematic cross-referencing based on chain indexing principles. For example, *see* references were used to provide alternative access points for the "fabrics" items illustrated in Exhibit 19 (from such terms as "finishing," "dyeing," and "laminating"). Note also how this index links terms judged to be semantically related ("related headings"). While the principles underlying the indexing have remained the same, the current version of this publication, known as the *Current Technology Index* (CTI), uses a somewhat different approach to the presentation of the references. This change was made to save space and to avoid the rather densely packed page that was characteristic of the BTI. The differences between the BTI and CTI layouts are illustrated in Exhibit 74.

A number of printed indexes have made use of PRECIS (the Preserved Context Index System). One example is the *British Education Index*. Some sample entries are shown in Exhibit 75. A bibliographic reference will appear under all of the "significant" terms appearing in a subject statement, each one being "shunted" to the entry position as described in Chapter 4. For example, the second entry appearing in Exhibit 75 will be duplicated under "Pupils" and under "Primary schools." Since 1986, PRECIS is no longer used as the basis of indexing in the *British Education Index*.

Citation Indexes

The Institute for Scientific Information (ISI) now publishes three citation indexes: the *Science Citation Index,* the *Social Sciences Citation Index,* and the *Arts and Humanities Citation Index*. Since these are quite different from the other printed indexes described in this chapter, they deserve some attention in their own right.

The primary use of a citation index is to find, for a particular bibliographic item known to the searcher, later items that have cited it. Exhibit 76 shows some sample entries from the *Social Sciences Citation Index* (the other citation indexes observe the same principles). Suppose we know that an article by W. E. Lambert, beginning on page 44 of the *Journal of Abnormal and Social Psychology,* volume 60, 1960, is highly relevant to a current research interest. By entering the SSCI under the name of the author (Exhibit 76) we can locate this article and find later ones that have cited it. In this example the article is cited by two other items published in 1989 (by Hogg and by Spears) and brief bibliographic details of these are given.

Exhibit 76 is taken from the Citation Index section of the *Social Sciences Citation Index*. Note that, under the name of each author, entries appear in order of publication date. Only brief bibliographic details are given for the citing items. To get more complete bibliographic data we must go to another section of the SSCI, the *Source Index*. For example, the citing item by Spears appears in the *European Journal of Social Psychology,* volume

19, 1989, and begins on page 101. To get more complete bibliographic details (title and full page numbers) we must look under his name in the *Source Index*.

AGGRESSION
See also
  Violence
AGGRESSION. Children
Coping by adults
  Coping with physical violence : some suggestions / John Jamieson.
  — *Mal. Ther. Educ.*, Vol.2, no.2 : Autumn 84. — p39-45
  Bibliography: p45

AGGRESSION. Pupils. Primary schools
Identification
  Identification of aggressive behaviour tendencies in junior age
  children : first stage in a study of aggression / C. Gilmore ... [et
  al.]. — *Educ. Rev.*, Vol.37, no.1 : Feb 85. — p53-63
  Bibliography: p63

AGRICULTURAL COLLEGES
Curriculum. Innovation — Australasia — Case studies
  Learning to be a capable systems agriculturist / Richard Bawden
  and Ian Valentine. — *Program. Learn. Educ. Technol.*, Vol.21,
  no.4 : Nov 84. — p273-287
  Education for Capability. — Bibliography: p286-287

AGRICULTURAL COLLEGES
Management (curriculum subject). Courses. Development — Nigeria
  Development of management courses for the agriculture sector in
  Nigeria / A.E. Shears. — *Program. Learn. Educ. Technol.*,
  Vol.21, no.2 : May 84. — p88-94
  Dissemination and Diffusion. — Bibliography: p94

AGRICULTURAL COLLEGES
Teaching aids: Microcomputer systems — Case studies
  Computers in agricultural education / by Andrew Todd. —
  Comput. Educ., No.48 : Nov 84. — p24

AGRICULTURAL LECTURERS
Lecture notes. Inclusion of new material — Case studies
  Sources of new materials included in lectures by lecturers in
  agriculture / J.T. Smith, B.W. Rockett
  Bibliography: p299
  Pt 2: An analysis of published sources used. — *High. Educ.*,
  Vol.13, no.3 : Jun 84. — p289-299

Exhibit 75
Sample PRECIS entries from the *British Education Index*
Reproduced by permission of the British Library

The source indexes to the *Social Sciences Citation Index* and to the *Arts and Humanities Citation Index* (but not to the *Science Citation Index*) provide, for each item included, a list of the bibliographic references appearing at the end of the article (see Exhibit 77 for an example).

In the citation indexes, a novel form of keyword index provides a subject approach to the citing (source) items. Known as the Permuterm Subject Index, it is based on keywords occurring in the titles of citing items. Exhibit 78 shows a sample entry under terms beginning with the

LAMBERT RA VOL PG YR
KWALL RR TEX LAW REV 67 685 89
LAMBERT RD
71 SEX ROLE IMAGERY CHI
BURKE PJ SOC PSYCH Q 52 159 89
79 CANADIAN REV SOCIOLO 16 47
GUIMOND S CAN R SOC A 26 193 89
86 TRANSFORMATION INDIA
DRIVER ED CONT SOCIOL B 18 366 89
86 1984 CANADIAN NATION
CURTIS JE CAN J SOC 14 143 89
87 CANADIAN REV SOCIOLO 24 529
BRUCE PG IND RELAT 28 115 89
LAMBERT RS
87 S CAROLINA LOYALISTS
POTTER J AM HIST REV B 94 513 89
LAMBERT RW
82 SOC NEUR ABSTR 8 318
GABRIEL M EXP BRAIN R 76 441 89
88 PATIENT EVALUATION C
HALEY SM T EAR CHILD 9 106 89
LAMBERT S
86 CD ROM NEW PAPYRUS
COOPER LKD INF PR MAN 25 161 89
87 ASPECTS PRINTING 160
LAMBERT S PAST PRESEN 36 89
87 CDI INTERACTIVE VIDE
HUGHES H FOREIGN LAN 22 283 89
LAMBERT VA
85 J NURSING SCHOLARSHI 17 50
REVENSON TA J CONS CLIN 57 344 89
LAMBERT W
68 READINGS SOCIOLOGY L
HORNBERG NH APPL LING 10 214 89
LAMBERT WE
59 AM J PSYCHOL 72 77
LEMMON CR APPL PSYCH 10 133 89
60 J PERS 28 350
KOHN PM J RES PERS 23 214 89
60 J ABNORMAL SOCIAL PS 60 44
HOGG MA GENET SOC G 115 153 89
SPEARS R EUR J SOC P 19 101 89
67 CHILDRENS VIEWS FORE
SILVERST B AM PSYCHOL R 44 903 89
69 SUBSTANCE STRUCTURE
NELDE PH J MULTILING 10 73 89
72 BILINGUAL ED CHILDRE
LEAVER BL FOREIGN LAN 22 269 89
WAGNER DA APPL PSYCH 10 31 89
72 BILINGUAL EDUCATION
SNOW MA TESOL QUART 23 201 89
72 LANGUAGE PSYCHOL CUL
WATTS RJ J PRAGMATIC 13 203 89
74 CULTURAL FACTORS LEA
HOGG MA GENET SOC G 115 153 89
75 ED IMMIGRANT STUDENT
CUMMINS J J MULTILING 10 17 89
75 INT J SOCIOL LANG 4 127
HOGG MA GENET SOC G 115 153 89
76 TU VOUS USTED
BROWN R LANG SOC 18 159 89
77 BILINGUALISM PSYCHOL 15
MIONI AM J PRAGMATIC B 13 467 89
79 CHILD REARING VALUES
EDWARDS CP YOUNG CHILD 44 15 89
ROSENTHA DA INT J BEHAV 12 207 89
79 LANGUAGE SOCIAL PSYC 186
HOGG MA GENET SOC G 115 153 89
80 PATTERNS BILINGUALIS 3
OKSAAR E J MULTILING 10 33 89
86 CAN J BEHAV SCI 18 35
87 ETHNICTY LANGUAGE 58
MOGHADDA FM CAN J BEH S 21 160 89

Exhibit 76
Sample entries from the *Social Sciences Citation Index*
Reprinted with permission from the *Social Sciences Citation Index*
Copyright © 1988 by the Institute for Scientific Information®, Philadelphia, PA, USA

JARADAT D
RELIABILITY VALIDITY AND GRADING
EDUC PSYC M 48(3) 627-635 88 9R Q3592
YARMOUK UNIV IRBID JORDAN
ABUSAYF FK 79 ED TECHNOLOGY 19 5
COLLET LS 71 J ED MEASUREMENT 8 209
[illegible] 53 ED PSYCHOL MEASUREME 13 309
DRESSEL PL 53 13 574
FELDT LS 80 PSYCHOMETRIKA 45 99
FRARY RB 88 APPLIED PSYCHOL MEAS 4 79
GIBBONS JD 79 PSYCHOMETRIKA 44 259
JARADAT D 86 J EDUC MEAS 23 169
[illegible] 61 [illegible] TESTS M
JARADIAZ SR
MULTIOUTPUT ANALYSIS OF TRUCKING OPERATIONS USING SPATIALLY DISSAGGREGATED FLOWS
TRANSP R B 22(3) 159-171 88 16R P0196
UNIV CHILE DEPT CIVIL ENGN CASILLA 228-3 SANTIAGO CHILE
BAILEY EE 81 AM ECON REV 71 178
BAUMOL WJ 82 CONTESTABLE MARKETS
BRAEUTIGAM RR 80 ESTIMATION HYBRID CO
[illegible] 83 4 LAT AM C EC SOC SA
HARMATUCK DJ 79 LOGISTICS TRANSP REV 15 277
. 81 J TRANSPORT EC POLIC 15 135
HASENKAMP G 76 J ECONOMETRICS 4 253
JARADIAZ SR 81 THESIS MIT
. 81 8TH EARIE C BASL
. 82 T REV 2 257
. 82 TRANSPORT SCI 16 522
KEELER TE 74 REV EC STATISTICS 56 201
PANZAR JC 75 33 BELL LAB EC DISC
SPADY R 79 ECONOMETRIC ESTIMATI
SPADY RH 70 BELL J EC 9 159
TAUCHEN H 83 J TRANSP ECON POLICY 17 25
FARAH M—VALUATION OF USERS BENEFITS IN TRANSPORT-SYSTEMS
TRANSP REV 8(3) 197-218 88 32R P3529
UNIV CHILE DEPT INGN CIVIL CASILLA 228-3 SANTIAGO CHILE
AGNELLO RJ 77 TRANSPORTATION RES 11 365
ANAS A 83 TRANSPORTATION RES B 17 13
CARLTON DW 79 AM EC REV 69 688
DIAMOND PA 74 J PUBLIC EC 3 3
DOMENCICH TA 75 URBAN TRAVEL DEMAND
HAU TDK 83 EC LETT 11 203
HAUSMAN JA 81 AM EC REV 71 662
HICKS JR 56 REVISION DEMAND THEO
HOTELLING H 38 ECONOMETRICA 6 242
JACOBSEN SE 79 AM EC REV 69 423
JARADIAZ SR 82 TRANSPORTATION RES B 16 57
. 86 J REGIONAL SCI 26 379
. 86 4 ACT C PAR ING TRAN 411
. 87 TRANSPORTATION RES B 21 165
. 87 5TH INT C TRAV BEH A
LANCASTER KJ 66 J POLITICAL EC 74 132
MALINVAUD E 69 LECONS THEORIE MICRO
MARSHALL A 20 PRINCIPLES EC
MISHAN EJ 76 COST BENEFIT ANAL
MOHRING H 76 TRANSPORTATION EC
MOREY ER 84 AM EC REV 74 163
NEUBERGER HLI 71 J TRANSPORT EC POLIC 5 52
SASAKI K 82 ENV PLANNING A 14 169
SMALL KA 81 ECONOMETRICA 49 105
THOMSON JM 74 MODERN TRANSPORT EC
TURVEY R 71 EC ANAL PUBLIC ENTER
VARIAN HR 78 MICROECONOMIC ANAL
WILLIAMS HCW 76 J REGIONAL SCI 16 147
. 77 ENV PLANNING A 9 285
WILLIG RD 76 AM EC REV 66 589
WILSON AG 67 TRANSPORTATION RES 1 253
. 69 J TRANSPORT EC POLIC 3 108

Exhibit 77
Sample entry from the source index to the *Social Sciences Citation Index*
Reprinted with permission from the *Social Sciences Citation Index*
Copyright © 1988 by the Institute for Scientific Information®, Philadelphia, PA, USA

DEBT

DEBT (CONT)
RELIEVING - - GRUNEWAL D
REPUTATION - DIAMOND DW
RESPONSE - - UNDERWOO J
RESTRUCTUR - BUCHHEIT LC@
- ROGERS CA
RICARDIAN - - PASINETT LL
RISKY - - - - - CHOI JJ
- - - - - TITMAN S
ROLE - - - - - OTANI I
- - - - - YEAGER LB •
SAVINGS - - - TRUDEAU RH •
SECURITIZA - TIGERT RR
SEWARD - - - GRUNEWAL D
SIMPLIFIED - - DATTATRE RE
SOCIAL-POL - GOTTLIEB N •
SOVEREIGN - - BUCHHEIT LC@
- - CHAMBERL M
SPENDING - - BARTH JR
STABILIZAT - BENNETT KM
STRATEGY - - MISTRY PS •
STRUCTURAL - EDWARDS S
SUB-SAHARAN DITTUS P
SWAPS - - - - TIGERT RR
TAXATION - - - PASINETT LL
TAXES - - - - DEMACEDO JB
TECHNIQUES - BUCHHEIT LC
THEORY - - - - PASINETT LL
THIRD-WORLD ◆ECON POLIT■
LISSAKER K
TIGERT RR
WEBB SB •
TIME - - - - - WALLER NG
TRADE - - - - EDWARDS S
TRANSFERS - - LOPEZGAR MA
TRINIDAD-A - BENNETT KM
UNITED-STA - COX WM
- TABELLIN G
VALUATION - - POITRAS G
VALUE - - - -
- - - - WALLER NG
VALUING - - - DATTATRE RE
VOLUNTARY - LAMDANY R
- LOPEZGAR MA
WORLD - - - - ABBOTT GC •
- - - - BIRD G •
- - - - FRANK AG
WORLD-BANK - UNDERWOO J
WORSE - - - - BIRD G •
- - - - CLAIRMON FF •
- - - - HAYNES J •
- - - - SINGER HW •
3RD-WORLD - - BIRD G •

DEBT-EQUITY
ANALYTICS - ◆HELPMAN E
SIMPLE - - - - "
SWAPS - - - - "

DEBT-FINANCED
IMPROVEMEN ◆J TAXATION■
PARTNERS - - "■
TAX-EXEMPT - "■

DEBT-FOR-EQUITY
ASSOCIATED ◆CORNETT MM
DEBT - - - - ◆TIGERT RR
EFFECTS - - - CORNETT MM
EQUILIBRIUM ◆ERRUNZA VR
EQUITY-FOR - CORNETT MM
EXCHANGE - - "
INFORMATION "
OFFERS - - - - "
PERSPECTIV - TIGERT RR
RATIONAL-E - ERRUNZA VR
RECENT - - - - TIGERT RR
REGULATORY - "
SECURITIZA - "
SWAPS - - - - ERRUNZA VR
- - - - TIGERT RR
THIRD-WORLD "

DEBTOR
PROCEDURAL ◆LAWLESS RM
RELIEF - - - - "

DEBTORS
CHAPTER-11 ◆ZAYED RJ
CONSUMER - - "
ELIGIBLE - - - "
INDIVIDUAL - - "
RELIEF - - - - "

DEBTS
ACKNOWLEDGE ◆GARFIELD E
AMERICAS - ◆ROBINSON M
DEFICITS - - ◆EDWARDS S •
- - - ROBINSON M
DOLLARS - - - EDWARDS S •
INTELLECTU - GARFIELD E
INTERNATIO ◆BARTA V
INTRODUCTI - GARFIELD E
INVESTIGAT ◆GIGUERE A •
KOCHEN,MAN - GARFIELD E
NOT-SO-TRO - ROBINSON M
THIRD-WORLD GIGUERE A •
WELL - - - - - GARFIELD E

Exhibit 78
Sample entry from the Permuterm Subject Index to the *Social Sciences Citation Index*
Reprinted with permission from the *Social Sciences Citation Index*
Copyright © 1988 by the Institute for Scientific Information®, Philadelphia, PA, USA

(CC666)

**Applied and
Environmental Microbiology**
Articles and Abstracts in English

Amer. Soc
Microbiol

VOL. 55 NO. 12 DECEMBER 1989 (L,A)

CONTINUED

86   ©1990 by ISI® CURRENT CONTENTS ®

Exhibit 79
Sample page from *Current Contents*
Reprinted with permission from *Current Contents*®, Copyright ©1986
by the Institute for Scientific Information®, Philadelphia, PA, USA

CC Pg	J Pg		CC Pg	J Pg		CC Pg	J Pg		CC Pg	J Pg
GLUCOSE			**GLUCOSE-UTILIZING**			**GLUTAMATE-IMMUNOREAC-TIVITY**			**GLUTEAL**	
41	1421		79	6808		262	118		211	875
"	1507		**GLUCOSE-1,6-BISPHOSPHATE**			**GLUTAMATE-PYRUVATE**			"	884
45	9447		68	1229		55	1420		**GLUTEN-SENSITIVE**	
48	20910		**GLUCOSE-6-PHOSPHATASE**			**GLUTAMATERGIC**			23	1093
55	1240		189	692		288	516		**GLYBURIDE**	
59	263		**GLUCOSE-6-PHOSPHATE-DEHYDROGE-NASE**			**GLUTAMINE-RICH**			39	1741
"	331		75	429		77	827		**GLYCATED**	
86	3214		**GLUCOSIDE-PHOSPHATI-DYLCHOLINE**			**GLUTAMINE-SYNTHETASE**			45	9464
"	3234		51	225		29	2623		**GLYCATION**	
89	467		**GLUCOSIDES**			270	223		48	20947
105	3661		297	3361		**GLUTARALDEHY-DE**			**GLYCEMIC**	
172	1370		**GLUCOSINOLATE**			136	205		55	1415
181	683		41	1507		**GLUTATHIONE**			"	1474
186	465		**GLUCOSYLCERA-MIDE**			32	1371		223	665
215	J-24		89	573		43	437		"	694
223	725		**GLUCURONIDES**			"	613		**GLYCERALDE-HYDE-3-PHOSPHATE**	
235	998		57	1673		52	203		79	6696
252	638		**GLUTAMATE**			65	353		**GLYCERALDE-HYDE-3P-DEHYDROGE-NASE**	
271	361		51	150		67	449		134	2065
284	881		79	6776		"	455		**GLYCEROL**	
GLUCOSE-H-2			113	1213		105	3653		193	371
224	253		262	5		"	3697		"	393
"	254		263	293		"	3807		290	987
GLUCOSE-HOMEOSTASIS			277	363		108	4291		**GLYCERYL**	
223	709		290	1039		"	4307		113	1296
GLUCOSE-INDUCED			291	1143		112	1025		**GLYCINE**	
48	20910		294	397		121	209		51	257
GLUCOSE-TRANSPORT						159	6917		86	3119
43	389					"	7020		97	39
GLUCOSE-UPTAKE						**GLUTATHIONE-S-TRANSFERASES**				
79	6808					64	113			
266	1302									
GLUCOSE-UTILIZATION										
110	69									

Exhibit 80
Sample entries from the keyword index to *Current Contents*
Reprinted with permission from *Current Contents*®, Copyright ©1986
by the Institute for Scientific Information® Philadelphia, PA, USA

root "debt" as they appear in the titles of several citing items. Note that a few compounds (e.g., debt-financed) are used as well as single words. Each entry shows, in alphabetical order, other keywords that have co-occurred with it in the titles of citing items. Thus, one item under DEBTS (by Giguere) deals with Third World debts, one (by Garfield) with intellectual debts, and so on. Note that entries will be repeated under each significant keyword in a title (e.g., one entry under the keyword "Third World" will be modified by the term "debts"). Of course, the effectiveness of this type of subject index is entirely dependent on the descriptive quality of the titles used to generate it and on the ingenuity of the searcher since no form of vocabulary control is used.

The various sections make such citation indexes quite powerful searching tools. Several different search approaches are possible. A search can begin with the bibliographic reference to an item known to be of interest or it can begin with a keyword. Keywords can lead to other possible keywords and the titles of citing items can also suggest further keywords that might be useful in the search. To take a hypothetical example, a keyword search of the SSCI for 1985 might yield a highly relevant item that can be followed up to find later items that have cited it. These might then suggest further keywords that could lead to other papers that can also be followed for later citations, and so on in a series of iterations. For those citation indexes in which the source index includes the bibliographic references (see Exhibit 77), other forms of iteration are possible. For example, a search on an item known to be highly relevant can lead to a highly relevant citing item. Some of the references in the citing item can then be followed up to locate other items that cite them, and so on.

As with most of the indexes mentioned in this chapter, the printed citation indexes have equivalent databases in electronic form—as CD-ROM or accessible online. The citation principle—one bibliographic item citing (referring to) an earlier one—can also be used to link publications in other ways—by bibliographic coupling or co-citation (see Chapter 14).

Another well-known product of the Institute for Scientific Information is *Current Contents,* a weekly, published in various subject-related sections, that reproduces the contents pages of a wide range of journals. Exhibit 79 shows a sample page. Each issue of *Current Contents* includes a very simple keyword index, as illustrated in Exhibit 80; one of the terms in this exhibit *(glucose)* relates to one of the items in Exhibit 79. Note that the index includes some phrases and names as well as single keywords. Each entry leads to a page in *Current Contents* and to a page number in the journal represented there. For example, two entries under *glucose* refer to page 86 of CC (Exhibit 79) and specifically to the items beginning on pages 3,214 and 3,234 of the December 1989 issue of *Applied and Environmental Microbiology.* This simple index can be used in one of two ways. Obviously, one can simply follow up all references to a particular keyword. However, a more sophisticated searcher, looking for more specific information, might choose to combine keywords. For example, if one were looking for articles on glucose in the context of yeasts, one could compare the numbers appearing under the term *glucose* with those appearing under *yeast* and *yeasts* to see if any numbers appear under both terms. If they do, they presumably refer to items that deal precisely with the topic of the search, including one of the articles appearing in Exhibit 79. This is essentially a variant of the Uniterm system (or at least the physical implementation of that system), as referred to in Chapter 2. The Uniterm system was a very early form of post-coordinate retrieval system.

Conclusion

Several different approaches to the implementation of an indexing/ abstracting service in printed form have been illustrated in this chapter. While some individuals will prefer one approach and others another, no one approach is ipso facto better than the rest. It very much depends on how the tool is to be used.

For current awareness purposes, those tools that use some form of classified approach will usually be superior to the alphabetico-specific indexes, at least to the extent that the classification scheme corresponds to the interests of a particular user. For example, someone interested in keeping current with new developments in parasitology in general would probably find *Biological Abstracts,* which devotes a section to this topic (see Exhibit 65), more useful than *Index Medicus* where references to the subject are likely to be scattered over a wide variety of subject headings. Nevertheless, for someone whose current awareness interests are highly specific, the alphabetico-specific approach might actually be more convenient. For example, *Index Medicus* would probably be a very useful tool for keeping up with the literature of, say, pulmonary fibrosis.

In considering these various tools as search and retrieval devices, of course, all of the performance factors discussed elsewhere in this book will come into play. That is, the effectiveness of a printed index as a search tool will depend on the number of access points provided, the specificity of the vocabulary used to index, the quality and consistency of the indexing, and the extent to which the tool offers positive help to the searcher (e.g., by linking of semantically related terms). Because the *Excerpta Medica* indexes provide more subject access points per item than *Index Medicus,* they are likely to give better recall. On the other hand, *Index Medicus,* since it indexes each item under only the "most important" terms, may well give greater precision.

Printed tools that include abstracts are superior to those that do not in that they provide more information to help the user decide whether or not a particular item is really likely to be useful. This is especially valuable in the case of hard to find items or those in languages unfamiliar to the searcher. Nevertheless, abstracts are not always essential. For example, the combination of the title of an item, together with the subject heading and subheading under which it appears, as in the *Index Medicus* example, is often enough to indicate its potential relevance.

Finally, it is obvious that indexes based only on title words offer a rather limited approach to retrieval. However, even these have their advantages. For example, a highly specific search involving, say, a name, might actually be more successful in a title word index than in one based on a broader controlled vocabulary. Moreover, when items are retrieved on keyword-in-title searches, providing the keyword is highly specific, there is a very good chance that they will be "relevant."

ENHANCING THE INDEXING

THROUGHOUT THIS BOOK it has generally been assumed that the end result of indexing a particular document is a simple list of terms, perhaps selected from some controlled vocabulary, that collectively describe the subject matter discussed. Frequently, all terms in the list are considered equal (i.e., the indexer does not specify that some are more important than others) and, usually, no explicit relationships among the terms are specified. But indexing can be a bit more sophisticated than this: terms can be weighted to reflect the indexer's perception of their importance and/or an attempt can be made to add some "syntax" to the terms so that their interrelationships become more clear.

Weighted Indexing

Much subject indexing entails a simple binary decision: a term is either assigned to a document or it is not. While this simplifies the process of indexing, it does create some problems for the user of a database who cannot devise a search strategy that will distinguish items in which a topic receives substantial treatment from those in which it is dealt with in a very minor way.

In weighted indexing, an indexer can assign to a term a numerical value that reflects his opinion on how important that term is in indicating what a particular document is about. Usually, the more central the subject matter, or the more detail that is given on this subject, the higher will be the weight. Consider, as an example, a numerical scale having five points with five being the highest score. Applied to the item illustrated in Exhibit 3, the terms *public opinion, telephone surveys, attitudes,* and *Middle East* might be given a weight of five, *United States* a weight of four, *Israel* and *Egypt* a weight of three, and so on. Clearly, this is subjective and different indexers will arrive at different weights. Nevertheless, most could be expected to give *Middle East* a high weight but *political leaders* or *foreign aid* a low one.

Weighted indexing of this type can be used in two ways in retrieval from a database. One way is simply to allow a searcher to specify that only items indexed under a term carrying a particular weight should be retrieved. Thus, someone interested in articles directly on the subject of Middle Eastern leaders might require that both terms, *Middle East* and *Political Leaders,* carry at least a weight of four. This would prevent retrieval of the item illustrated in Exhibit 3, which deals with political leaders in only a very minor way, and presumably many others like it.

The alternative application is to use the weights to rank the items retrieved in a search. Thus, in a search requiring the co-occurrence of *Middle East* and *political leaders,* items in which both terms carry a weight of five (total weight of ten) would be printed out or displayed first, with items scoring nine appearing second, and so on down to items scoring only two.

The assignment of numerical weights to terms has long been advocated by Maron (Maron & Kuhns, 1960; Maron et al., 1959; Maron, 1988), who refers to this type of indexing as "probabilistic." Despite this advocacy, I know of no conventional retrieval systems (i.e., based on human indexing) that employ numerical weights in quite this way, although the weighting of terms is implicit in certain automatic or semi-automatic retrieval systems such as SMART (see Chapter 14).

Nevertheless, some databases do incorporate a simple weighting technique by distinguishing between "major" and "minor" descriptors, which is tantamount to adopting a numerical scale having two values. This practice may be tied to the production of a printed index, the major descriptors being those under which an item appears in the printed index and the minor descriptors those that are associated only with the database in machine-readable form. This is the practice, for example, at the National Library of Medicine (*Index Medicus* and the MEDLARS or MEDLINE database), the National Technical Information Service (NTIS), and the Educational Resources Information Center (ERIC). Even this simple weighting method allows some of the flexibility in searching alluded to earlier. A searcher can specify that items should be retrieved only when a term (or terms) appears as a major descriptor. Alternatively, a crude ranking of output can be achieved, as in the example:

M * M
M * m
m * m

That is, items in which two terms, used by a searcher in an *and* relationship, are both major *(M)* descriptors appear first, followed by those in which only one of the two is a major descriptor, and then by those in which both are minor *(m)* descriptors only.

Some information services go a little beyond a two point weighting scale. At BIOSIS, for example, Concept Headings can be assigned at any of three "levels of emphasis": primary (the item appears under this heading in printed indexes), secondary (a comparatively strong emphasis), and tertiary—a minor emphasis (Vleduts-Stokolov, 1987).

Note that weighted indexing, in effect, gives the searcher the ability to vary the exhaustivity of the indexing. Returning to Exhibit 3, it is possible that the first five terms listed would all be considered major descriptors, while the remaining nine terms are considered minor. This being so, a search strategy that specifies major descriptors only would, in effect, be equivalent to searching on a less exhaustive level of indexing.

It is important to recognize the distinction between *weighted indexing,* of the type described, and *weighted term searching.* The latter need have nothing to do with weighted indexing. Instead, it refers to the construction of a search strategy the logic of which is governed by numerical weights rather than Boolean algebra. For example, the search strategy might take the following form:

Term	Weight	
A	10	
B	10	
C	2	Threshold = 20
D	2	
E	1	
F	1	

The lowest acceptable weight is 20, which means that terms *A* and *B* must both be present in a record before it will be retrieved. However, a record may exceed the minimum weight (threshold) so that, conceivably, some records might score 26 (if all six terms were present), some 25, and so on, and these high scoring items would appear first in a printout. In this way a ranked output can be achieved even though no weighting of index terms is employed. This approach to the searching of databases was quite common in batch processing systems, especially those applied to Selective Dissemination of Information (SDI), but is much less appropriate to searching in the online mode.

The ideal approach to weighting might involve a team approach to indexing (see Chapter 5) with the terms that all indexers agree on given highest weight and those that only one indexer would assign given the lowest weight. Such an ideal can rarely be implemented because of the costs involved.

Linking of Terms

A further examination of Exhibit 3 will reveal that the document represented could be retrieved in a number of searches for which it is not really an appropriate response. Some of these can be avoided by the use of weighted indexing or by reducing the exhaustivity of the indexing. For example, either approach could avoid the retrieval of this document in a search for information on political leaders in general, for which this item could be considered of only very marginal value.

Other unwanted retrievals could be caused by *false associations,* cases in which the terms that cause an item to be retrieved are really quite unrelated in the document. One example of this is the combination *United States* and *political leaders.* Clearly, this document does not discuss United States political leaders although it is likely to be retrieved in a search on this subject. As previously noted, the probability that false associations of this type will occur increases with the length of the record (i.e., with the number of access points provided or with the exhaustivity of the indexing).

One way of avoiding false associations is by the linking of index terms. That is, the document is, in a sense, partitioned into several subdocuments, each dealing with a separate, although possibly closely related, subject. The document illustrated in the exhibit might be divided into such links as:

Middle East, Arab Nations, Political Leaders, Israel, Egypt, Palestine Liberation Organization
Public Opinion, Telephone Surveys, United States, Attitudes, Middle East
United States, Foreign Aid, Egypt, Israel
Peace Conferences, Middle East, Palestine Liberation Organization

and so on.

Note that all terms in each link are directly related and that some terms may appear in several of the links. Each link is identified by some alphanumeric character that is carried in the database itself. In an online retrieval system this would be associated with the document number within the inverted file. Thus, document 12024 may be partitioned into 12024/1, 12024/2, 12024/3, and so on. This gives the searcher the opportunity to specify that two terms should co-occur not only in the document record but in a particular link within that record, thereby avoiding many of the false associations of the *United States/political leaders* type.

Role Indicators

While links can be effective in avoiding certain unwanted retrievals, they will not solve all problems. Some terms may be directly related in a document, and thus appear in the same link, but not be related in the way the searcher wants them to be related. Exhibit 3 provides an excellent illustration: the item in question could well be retrieved in a search on Middle East attitudes toward the United States, whereas it is exactly the opposite relationship that is dealt with.

To avoid this type of problem (an *incorrect term relationship*) it is necessary to introduce some syntax into the indexing in order to disambiguate. The "traditional" method is to use *role indicators* (or *relational indicators*)—codes that make term relationships explicit. To disambiguate the *United States/Attitudes/Middle East* situation, only two role indicators would be needed. These would be directional indicators. For example, one might use the letter *A* to stand for the idea of "recipient, target, or patient" and *B* to represent "sender, giver, source." In this case, one would associate the *role A* with *Middle East* and *B* with *United States* since the former is the target of the attitudes while the latter is their source.

Obviously, not all ambiguity problems can be solved through the use of only two roles. If they are kept relatively basic, however, a rather small number of role indicators can solve most problems.

Links and roles were introduced into retrieval systems, at the same time, in the early 1960s, when post-coordinate systems were still relatively young and computer-based retrieval was in its infancy. For a while it was very fashionable to index using both links and roles due largely to the influence of the Engineers Joint Council (EJC), which introduced a set of role indicators (see Exhibit 81) that was quite widely adopted. This type of highly structured indexing did not remain in favor for very long. Not only was it very expensive because indexers needed much more time to accomplish it, but it proved to be extremely difficult to apply the role indicators consistently. It is difficult enough (see Chapter 5) to achieve consistency in relatively simple approaches to indexing, but the difficulty increases dramatically the more explicit the indexer must be in expressing term relationships. The problems are not so great as long as one thinks only of two or three terms at a time. However, it is frequently very difficult to determine all the relationships that apply to a larger group of terms. Moreover, the addition of a further term to a group may change the relationships somewhat, necessitating a change in the role indicators or, at the very least, increasing the number of roles that apply to each term. In the case of the EJC role indicators, the problems were compounded by the fact that role 8 was not a relational indicator at all but, rather, a means of weighting the most important term. Searchers found it so difficult to decide what roles an indexer might have applied to a term that they frequently omitted the roles entirely, which is equivalent to requiring that

8 8
The primary topic of consideration is; the principal subject of discussion is; the subject reported is; the major topic under discussion is; there is a description of

1 1
Input; raw material; material of construction; reactant; base metal (for alloys); components to be combined; constituents to be combined; ingredients to be combined; material to be shaped; material to be formed; ore to be refined; sub-assemblies to be assembled; energy input (only in an energy conversion); data and types of data (only when inputs to mathematical processings); a material being corroded

2 2
output; product, by-product, co-product; outcome, resultant; intermediate products; alloy produced; resulting material; resulting mixture or formulation; material manufactured; mixture manufactured; device shaped or formed; metal or substance refined; device, equipment, or appraratus made, assembled, built, fabricated, constructed, created; energy output (only in an energy conversion); data and types of data (only as mathematical processing outputs)

3 3
Undesirable component; waste; scrap; rejects (manufactured devices); contaminant; impurity, pollutant, adulterant, or poison in inputs, environments, and materials passively receiving actions; undesirable material present; unnecessary material present; undesirable product, by-product, co-product

4 4
Indicated, possible, intended present or later uses or applications. The use or application to which the term has been, is now, or will later be put. To be used as, in, on, for, or with; for use as, in, on, for, or with; used as, in, on, for, or with; for later use as, in, on, for, or with

5 5
Environment; medium; atmosphere; solvent; carrier (material); support (in a process or operation); vehicle (material); host; absorbent, adsorbent

6 6
Cause; independent or controlled variable; influencing factor; "X" as a factor affecting or influencing "Y"; the "X" in "Y is a function of X"

7 7
Effect; dependent variable; influenced factor; "Y" as a factor affected or influenced by "X"; the "Y" in "Y is a function of X"

9 9
Passively receiving an operation or process with no change in identity, composition, configuration, molecular structure, physical state, or physical form; possession such as when preceded by the preposition *of, in,* or *on* meaning possession; location such as when preceded by the prepositions *in, on, at, to,* or *from* meaning location; used with months and years when they locate information (not bibliographic data) on a time continuum

10 10
Means to accomplish primary topic of consideration or other objective

0 0
Bibliographic data, personal names of authors, corporate authors and sources, type of documents, dates of publication, names of journals and other publications, other source-identifying data, and adjectives

Exhibit 81
The EJC system of role indicators
Reproduced by permission of the American Association of Engineering Societies

a term appear in any role and completely negates the value of the device. The problems involved in the use of links/role indicators in retrieval systems have been discussed in considerable detail elsewhere (Lancaster, 1964; Montague, 1965; Mullison et al., 1969; Sinnett, 1964; Van Oot et al., 1966).

Even more elaborate than the EJC method of indexing using links and roles was the "semantic code" approach to retrieval introduced by the Center for Documentation and Communication Research at Western Reserve University (Perry & Kent, 1958; Vickery, 1959). The semantic code was applied to a computer-based retrieval system in the field of metals, designed and operated by Western Reserve for the American Society for Metals.

The document surrogate was a "telegraphic abstract." Telegraphic abstracts were prepared in standardized format, according to a set of rules, to eliminate variations and complexities of English sentence structure. Subject analysis forms were specially designed to assist the indexer in recording important aspects of subject matter in the form of telegraphic abstracts. The terms in the telegraphic abstracts were encoded by means of a "semantic code dictionary." The basis of the semantic code was a semantic "stem." The stems (there were about 250 in the system) represent relatively broad concepts. Each stem was given a four-digit code consisting of three characters with a space for interpolation of a fourth character, as in the following examples:

C-TL   Catalyst
C-TR   Container
C-TT   Cutting and drilling
D-DD   Damage
D-FL   Deflection

Individual terms were built up by inserting a one-letter "infix" into the semantic stem and possibly by appending a numerical suffix. For example, DADD represented both "wound" and "decay," where *D-DD* is the semantic stem for "damage" and the infix *A* merely stands for "is a." In other words, a "wound" is a type of damage. A numerical suffix is added merely to distinguish terms having identical stems and infix structure; the suffix in itself has no semantic significance.

The full list of infixes is presented in Exhibit 82. The use of infixes with a stem allows the expression of various shades of meaning. For example, "bag" and "barrel" were both represented by *CATR*, where the infix *A* indicates that these are *types of* container. "Side wall," on the other hand, was represented by *CITR*, where the infix *I* indicates *part* of container. An individual complex concept may be built up from several "semantic factors." For example, the topic "telephone" may be expressed by

DWCM.LQCT.MACH.TURN.001

where

D-CM	represents Information
L-CT	represents Electricity
M-CH	represents Device
T-RN	represents Transmission

and 001 is the unique suffix that distinguishes this term from others (e.g., telegraph) having the same semantic factors. A maximum of four semantic codes could be combined to form a code for a specific concept.

A	is a
E	is made of
I	is part of
O	is made up of several
Q	makes use of, is produced, by means of
U	is used for, produces (frequently used for verbs ending in *ing*)
V	acts upon
W	brings about, affected by, is acted upon by (frequently used for verbs ending in *ed*)
X	is characterized by the absence of
Y	is connected with, characterized by, characteristically
Z	resembles, but is not
P	is characterized by an increase of
M	is characterized by a decrease of

Exhibit 82
Semantic infixes in the Western Reserve System
Source: Aitchison and Cleverdon (1963)

Terms in a telegraphic abstract are syntactically related by means of role indicators. A list of these as used in indexing the literature of metallurgy is given in Exhibit 83. An example of the application of roles is:

KOV.KEJ	crystal
,KOV.KEJ.KUJ.	metal
,KOV.KEJ.KUJ.	alloy
,KOV.KEJ.KUJ.	beryllium
,KWV	hexagonal close packed
,KWV	elastic

which indicates that metal alloy crystals, specifically beryllium, are being processed in some way, and that they have the properties of being "hexagonal close packed" and "elastic." Note the use of "companion roles" in this system. *KOV* and *KWV* are companion or paired roles. When one of these is assigned to a particular term we expect to find the companion assigned to a second term, to tie the terms together and indicate their exact relationship. Thus, "crystal," by the role *KOV,* is shown to have a property given for it. These given properties are "elastic" and "hexagonal close packed" as indicated by the role *KWV.*

KEJ	material processed
KUJ	major component
KIJ	minor component
KOV	property given for
KWV	property given
KAM	process
KQJ	means of process
KAH	condition of process
KUP	property affected or determined by process
KAP	property affected by KAL
KAL	factor influencing KAP
KWJ	product

Exhibit 83
Role indicators of the Western Reserve System
as used in indexing the literature of metallurgy
Source: Aitchison and Cleverdon (1963)

In addition to role indicators, the system used a highly elaborate method of linking terms (and roles) in the telegraphic abstracts. This linking was achieved by various levels of "punctuation":

1. *Subphrase.* A term with one or more role indicators attached.
2. *Phrase.* A set of closely related terms in a particular relationship. A finite number of phrase patterns is recognized. For example:
    KAM   (process)
    KQJ   (means of process)
    KAH   (condition of process)
3. *Sentence.* This is comprised of phrases and is also built up in standard patterns. For example, a sentence may cover a product and its manufacture or a material tested and the properties determined for it.
4. *Paragraph.* This is a set of sentences, and it may be co-extensive with the abstract itself. It can also be used to distinguish completely different topics within a single telegraphic abstract. A complete telegraphic abstract as it would be recorded on some electronic medium, and showing punctuation, roles, and semantic factors, is illustrated in Exhibit 84.

In conducting a search in this system, the request statement was converted to a strategy comprised of semantic factors and role indicators. Various "levels," corresponding to the punctuation of the telegraphic abstracts, were used to restrict criteria to terms occurring within certain units. For example, search level four asks merely that a particular term be associated with a particular role indicator. This corresponds to the subphrase in punctuation of the telegraphic abstract.

```
KOV.KEJ.CARS.009.,KOV.KEJ.CARS.006.,KUJ.KEJ.KOV.MATL.
4.□BQE.,-KAM.CUNG.MWTL.PASS.RQHT.003.,KAM.MAPR.
032.,KAH.DACT.001.*,KAH.LAMN.037.,KAH.DACT.001.*,KAH.
LAMN.024.,KAH.DYFL.6X.PAPR.002.*,KAH.PAPR.PYSH.2X.
001.,-KUP.RANG.009.*,KUP.RAPR.225.,KUP.DASM.006.*,KUP.
PYPR.004.,KUP.DYFL.MATN.002.*,KUP.PYPR.004.,KUP.KAP.
PAPR.017.,KUP.KAP.PAPR.010.,KAL.PAPR.004.,KAL.RANG.
009.*,KAL.MAPR.041.,KUP.PAPR.45X.PWSH.2X.TYRM.001.
,KUP.KAP.PAPR.001.*,KUP.KAP.PAPR.PYSH.2X.001.,KUP.
KAL.MAPR.114.,KUP.KAL.MAPR.087.*,KUP.KAL.MAPR.041.
,KUP.KAL.RANG.009.*,KUP.KAL.MAPR.041.,KUP.KAP.MAPR.
032.*,KUP.KAP.PAPR.PYSH.2X.001.,KAL.DYFL.6X.PAPR.002.
*,KAL.PAPR.PYSH.2X.001.,KAL.RANG.009.*,KAL.PAPR.058.
*,KAL.BYSS.3X.RAPR.002.
```

Exhibit 84
Telegraphic abstract as recorded on tape
Source: Perry and Kent (1958), *Tools for Machine Literature
Searching*. Copyright © 1958, John Wiley & Sons, Inc.
Reprinted by permission of John Wiley & Sons Inc.

The Western Reserve system was highly ingenious and was capable of expressing very fine shades of meaning. It had great flexibility. One could search with great precision using punctuation, roles, and specific semantic factors. Alternatively, one could search with relative broadness (for high recall) by ignoring these devices and by using the structure of the semantic codes as a means of generalization (e.g., using the general concept *D-DD* for "damage" wherever it occurs as a component in a complex code).

Unfortunately the system was too ingenious for the intended application. It was complicated to apply, and both indexing and search formulation were time-consuming and expensive operations. Subsequent experience has taught us that, in most retrieval applications, one does not need the level of sophistication built into the Western Reserve system. The system was too complex and expensive to be economically viable, and it was eventually abandoned by the American Society for Metals in favor of a simpler, more cost-effective approach.

Subheadings

The highly structured approach to indexing, exemplified by the use of links and roles or by the semantic code, was prevalent in the early 1960s when computer-based systems were still in a very early state of development. Then it was considered necessary to get very precise retrieval results—to avoid at any cost retrieving irrelevant items. The wild illustration frequently given was the need to distinguish between Venetian blinds and blind Venetians! The absurdity of this example should be obvious to anyone: what is the likelihood that articles on both subjects would appear in the same database and how much literature exists on blind Venetians anyway? Nowadays one recognizes and accepts the fact that unwanted retrievals, due to false or spurious associations, will occur. However, their occurrence is usually considered to be within acceptable limits. In the MEDLARS evaluation reported by Lancaster (1968), about 18 percent of the approximately 3,000 precision failures occurring in 302 searches were due to such ambiguous relationships among terms. It is usually considered better to accept some failures of this kind than to try to avoid them through the use of more elaborate and costly indexing methods.

The problems of false or ambiguous associations are now less severe than they were 25 years ago because a higher level of pre-coordination exists in most systems. These problems are most prevalent in systems based on single word indexing (Uniterms) or in natural language systems (see Chapter 13). As thesauri have incorporated a higher level of pre-coordination, the probability of false or ambiguous associations declines. To take one simple illustration, the terms COMPUTERS and DESIGN, applied to a document, are ambiguous: are computers being designed or are they being applied to the design of something else? On the other hand, the more pre-coordinate combination

    COMPUTERS
    AIRCRAFT DESIGN

is much less ambiguous, and the combination

    AIRCRAFT DESIGN
    COMPUTER-AIDED DESIGN

seems completely unambiguous.

One way of achieving some pre-coordination, without greatly increasing the size of a controlled vocabulary, is through the use of subheadings. In a post-coordinate system, subheadings can be applied in much the same way that they are in the traditional subject catalogs of libraries. The best candidates for subheadings are those terms that might potentially apply to many of the other terms in the vocabulary. Thus a vocabulary of 5,000 descriptors plus 20 subheadings in theory yields 100,000 (5,000 x 20) unique terms. In practice, however, each subheading may be applicable to only a particular category of term so the number of possible combinations would not be so great.

To return to the earlier example, the term DESIGN might be a good candidate to be a subheading in certain databases. Thus, COMPUTERS/ DESIGN is much less ambiguous than the combination DESIGN and COMPUTERS. Obviously, the addition of a subheading to a main heading (descriptor) is a rather simple form of linking. In effect, however, subheadings can virtually act as links and simple roles at the same time. For example, consider the combination:

AIRCRAFT/DESIGN
COMPUTERS

Not only is the term DESIGN linked explicitly to AIRCRAFT but its use as a subheading actually implies the relationship most likely between the term AIRCRAFT and the term COMPUTERS (i.e., that the computers are used as tools in the design of aircraft).

In MEDLARS/MEDLINE, the National Library of Medicine has been very successful in using subheadings in just this way. In some cases, subheadings complement each other. Thus, the combination

DISEASE X/CHEMICALLY INDUCED
DRUG Y/ADVERSE EFFECTS

implies that disease X was caused by drug Y, whereas the combination

DISEASE X/DRUG THERAPY
DRUG Y/THERAPEUTIC USE

expresses a completely different relationship between X and Y.

While the main justification for subheadings in MEDLARS was to facilitate use of the printed *Index Medicus,* they have proven to be effective in reducing ambiguities in the searching of the machine-readable database. Although indexing with main heading/subheading combinations will undoubtedly be less consistent than indexing with main headings alone (Lancaster, 1968), subheadings present fewer problems than role indicators do and, unlike role indicators, are immediately understandable by users.

Index Language Devices

Such devices as weighting, links, and role indicators are considered *precision devices* because they allow the possibility of increased precision in searching a database. Other devices, such as synonym control, on the other hand, are referred to as *recall devices* because they tend to improve recall. The complete array of such devices is sometimes referred to as *index language devices* (Lancaster, 1972; Raitt, 1980). This is a little misleading: some of them, such as subheadings and synonym control, are indeed integral components of an index language, while others, such as linking or weighting, are quite independent of the index language. That is, they are operations applied to terms in indexing rather than components of a controlled vocabulary. One could, in fact, separate *index language devices* from *indexing devices* but this might be considered hair splitting.

The indexing devices discussed in this chapter are all precision devices with the exception of certain components of the semantic code. A precision device essentially increases the size of the vocabulary used to index while a recall device reduces its size. For example, a five point weighting scale virtually increases the size of the vocabulary by a factor of five. Instead of having a single term, POLITICAL LEADERS, for example, one now has five terms—POLITICAL LEADERS 5, POLITICAL LEADERS 4, and so on. Links and role indicators have a similar effect.

Another way of looking at this is in terms of class size: precision devices create a greater number of smaller classes while recall devices create a smaller number of larger ones (Exhibit 85).

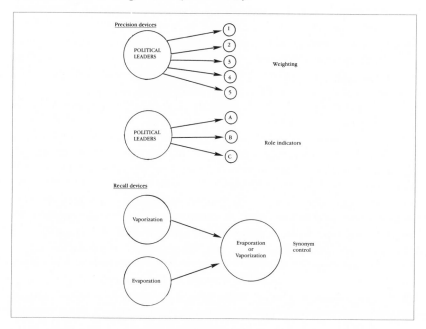

Exhibit 85
Precision devices create smaller classes; recall devices build larger ones

12

ON THE INDEXING AND ABSTRACTING OF IMAGINATIVE WORKS

Subject indexing has a very long history, vast experience has been accumulated, and a considerable body of literature on the subject now exists. However, one important application has been rather neglected, at least until very recently: the indexing of imaginative works such as fiction and feature films. The purpose of this chapter is to consider to what extent the indexing and abstracting of an imaginative work presents problems similar to those involved in dealing with "substantive" works such as textbooks, periodical articles, or documentary films.

As we have seen earlier in the book, subject indexing involves two steps—"conceptual analysis" and "translation"—that are quite distinct intellectual processes even though they may seem to be performed as one operation. The conceptual analysis step determines what a document is "about." The subject of "aboutness" as it relates to indexing has been discussed elsewhere, e.g., Maron (1977), Hutchins (1978), and Swift et al. (1978)—while Pejtersen (1979) has specifically dealt with the "aboutness" of fiction. Various aspects of the aboutness of texts in general are discussed by Eco (1979) and by Troitskii (1979, 1981).

These authors raise several theoretical or philosophical issues on the meaning of aboutness which I will not attempt to repeat here. For present purposes, I will use the word *about* as equivalent to "capable of informing on." That is, if certain people can learn something about farming through reading a book or seeing a film I would say that the book (film) is "about" farming.

Indexing a documentary film that deals with some technique of farming is essentially no different from the indexing of a book, periodical article, or technical report on farming. By our definition, all can be considered about farming. But can a feature film that happens to be set on a farm be considered to be about farming, especially if farming is completely incidental to the plot of the film? Can a film that depicts farming in passing be considered about farming? If the hero of a film happens to be a farmer, does this make the film about farming? Does it even make it about farmers?

The indexing of any type of imaginative work—whether a play, a novel or a film—does present problems that are somewhat different from the

182

problems of indexing substantive works. The two types are created for different purposes: the former primarily to entertain or inspire, the latter primarily to convey information. That the former may convey some substantive information is incidental to the major purpose of the medium. That the latter may occasionally entertain is equally incidental to the major purpose of that medium.

If we assign the term FARMING to a documentary film or to a periodical article on this subject, we imply that these items can convey certain information on farming and that users of an index will approach items through this term because they want to learn something about this particular subject.

On the other hand, if someone looks under the term FARMING in an index to imaginative works—say films—it is certainly not to find information about farming. Why, then, would one look under such a term? A number of possibilities exist:

1. to find out which films have a farming setting,
2. to count how many such films have been made in order to study trends in film-making over particular periods of time, or
3. to identify the title of a particular film when all one can remember is that it is set on a farm or in a farming community.

The second of these implies some scholarly use. The first suggests some form of "production" use (i.e., film or television producers seeking to discover how some event, locale, person, activity, or profession has been represented by others). The third type of question represents a more popular use. It is, however, the type of question that one might expect to receive in the reference department of a public library. Insofar as questions of these types do arise, some subject indexing of feature films seems entirely justified, even if the films cannot really be considered "about" the subject matter implied by the index terms. Exactly the same argument can be put forward for some "subject approach" to fiction. "20,000 Leagues Under the Sea" contributes little, if anything, to our knowledge of submarines. It is doubtful if one could reasonably consider the novel "about" submarines. Nevertheless, subject indexing of fiction does have value. A person might legitimately want to know "What novels have been set in submarines?, How many novels have been set in submarines?, What was the first novel to be set in a submarine? or What was that early classic that predicted the development of submarines?

This is not to imply that films and novels have no substance, no aboutness. The film "Patton" is clearly about General Patton. It would be about Patton even if it possessed little historical accuracy. Most viewers would agree that the film illustrates Patton's ambition. Whether this makes the film about ambition, or justifies indexing it under the term AMBITION, is entirely another matter. The film also illustrates tank warfare. Does this mean it is about tank warfare? Is it about generals, about generalship, about military strategy? Can it be considered about England or about France just because parts of the film may be set in these two countries?

In practical application, of course, what we are discussing is really a relationship between a work and index terms assigned to represent that work. When we assign an index term to a book or journal article we imply, in almost all cases, that the work conveys some information on the topic represented by that term. In the case of an imaginative work, on the other hand, an index term may be assigned to it for different reasons, most obviously to represent:

1. Its central theme or themes.
2. What it may illustrate, perhaps incidentally.
3. Its environmental setting.

In point of fact, of course, the first two of these are not significantly different. At least, the only difference relates to the extent to which the subject is treated.

The environment of the film may have space, time, and "character" dimensions. The space dimension may be quite precise—Pigalle, Paris, or France—or imprecise—a jungle, a river, a farming community. The time dimension, likewise, can be precise—e.g., the French Revolution—or ill-defined (e.g., the nineteenth century or "before Christ"). The "character" dimension relates to the environment provided by the types of characters depicted. The fact that a leading character in a film or novel happens to be a nurse does not necessarily make the film about nursing or even about nurses. In the film "Doctor Zhivago," Lara appears at various times as a university student, a nurse, and a librarian. Nevertheless, the film is not really about these various roles since it can hardly be considered to convey information on them. On the other hand, in some sense, "The Browning Version" can be regarded as about teachers and teaching since teacher-student relationships are central to the plot of the work. Teaching is not merely a "dressing" or environmental constraint.

From a pragmatic point of view none of this is really important. The central question is not whether a work is about nursing, illustrates nursing, or uses nursing as its setting, but whether the index term NURSING should be applied to it.

One major difference between the indexing of imaginative works and the indexing of other types is that the former is likely to be more subjective and interpretative than the latter. Studies of indexing consistency have shown that different indexers are unlikely to agree completely on which terms should be assigned to a particular item, even when the subject matter dealt with is reasonably concrete. In the case of imaginative works, the chance that agreement would exist is likely to be much less. This would be particularly true in the case in which the imaginative work deals primarily with some emotion or quality—jealousy, ambition, or greed, for example.

Imaginative works have another important characteristic that complicates subject indexing: their scope is essentially open-ended. That is, there are no real limits to what they can depict. In this sense, the indexing of imaginative works has something in common with subject cataloging for a large general library or the indexing of a general newspaper. At least it has more in common with this situation than it does with a more restricted subject environment such as indexing a collection of items in agriculture or in education. The vocabulary used in indexing must also be open-ended since films and novels are constantly being produced that deal with personalities, events, and locations not previously dealt with in these media.

Two major considerations relating to subject indexing include:

1. who is to do the indexing, and
2. what policies the indexers are to follow.

In the indexing of substantive works in a limited subject field, it is clear that some level of subject knowledge may be necessary. How much subject knowledge is needed will depend largely on how esoteric is the subject matter and its terminology. One feels intuitively that indexing in mathematics or applied mechanics may require greater subject expertise than indexing in, say, transportation, where the terminology is more likely to be familiar to the general public. A good indexer does not necessarily have to be a subject expert; conversely, a subject expert will not necessarily make a good indexer.

Since the content of imaginative works is not restricted by subject matter, subject expertise, in the conventional sense, is irrelevant to the situation. Moreover, what is depicted can be considered to fall in the "general knowledge" category, and it has nothing directly to do with the techniques involved in producing imaginative works. One has no reason to suppose, for example, that the indexing of films need be done by scholars of the cinema (although such people could provide valuable input on the types of terms that would be useful, at least to them) or even that it requires any particular knowledge of film-making techniques.

Two characteristics of an index that will have a significant impact on its performance are:

1. the exhaustivity of the indexing, and
2. the specificity of the terms used.

As discussed earlier in the book, *exhaustivity* refers to the extent to which the contents of a work are covered by the terms used in indexing. Exhaustivity relates to breadth of coverage. In this context, the opposite of "exhaustive" is "selective." In general, exhaustivity equates to the number of index terms used. If the film "Geronimo" appeared only under the terms GERONIMO and APACHE INDIANS in some index, such indexing would be quite selective. In the subject index to the first edition of the *American Film Institute Catalog,* however, this film was indexed under 17 different terms; the indexing is rather exhaustive.

There are pros and cons associated with high exhaustivity. In theory, exhaustive indexing makes things easier to find: the ability to find an item can be expected to increase as the number of access points (i.e., entries) provided increases. This is true, however, only up to a certain point. Indexing can be overly exhaustive, causing a dilution in the effectiveness of the index—the less significant obscuring the more significant and making the latter harder to find. To take an extreme example, it would be rather difficult to identify films or novels that deal at a significant level with dogs if the index term DOGS were assigned to every work in which a dog appears, however briefly. The problem, of course, is that subject indexing usually involves a simple binary decision (a term either is or is not applied) rather than a weighted decision (a term applies with a certain weight). Consequently, for some index uses the chaff may obscure the wheat.

While exhaustivity relates to the breadth of coverage, *specificity* relates to depth of treatment of content. Exhaustivity is established as an indexing policy decision, whereas specificity is a property of the vocabulary used to index. In general, it is good indexing practice to use the most specific term available to describe some feature of a document. This principle, however, needs to be tempered with common sense. In designing an index one should try to arrive at a level of specificity appropriate to the needs of the users of that index. Lassie is presumably a collie. It would be technically correct to index Lassie movies under COLLIES. However, one feels intuitively that users of a film catalog are unlikely to want, or look under, anything more specific than DOGS. On the other hand, one would want to index much more specifically than DOGS in an encyclopedia of pets. Clearly, the more specific the terms used, the fewer the entries per term on the average. This makes it easier to find something highly specific but more difficult to perform more general searches.

Sapp (1986) and Baker and Shepherd (1987) discuss the classification of fiction on the shelves of libraries and the limitations of existing bibliographic classification schemes or lists of subject headings, which make little provision for topical access to imaginative works. Baker (1988) describes the results of experiments on the classification of fiction in public libraries. Sapp (1986) also discusses approaches used in such printed tools as the *Short Story Index*, the *Cumulated Fiction Index*, and the *Fiction Catalog*. While these publications do index stories under more than one heading, they suffer from the disadvantages of printed indexes in general— i.e., not allowing the user to combine headings in a search. Thus, it might be possible to identify detective stories and stories set in China but it will be much more difficult to identify detective stories with a Chinese setting.

The most sophisticated approach to the indexing of fiction is that described by Pejtersen (e.g., 1979, 1984) and Pejtersen and Austin (1983, 1984). Based on an analysis of how the users of public libraries characterize the contents of books, Pejtersen identified four major "dimensions" of a fictional work: subject matter, frame (time, place, social environment, profession), author's intention or attitude, and accessibility. Building on this, she devised an indexing scheme involving the following dimensions and categories:

    1. Subject matter
       a. action and course of events
       b. psychological development and description
       c. social relations
    2. Frame
       a. time: past, present, future
       b. place: geographical, social environment, profession
    3. Author's intention
       a. emotional experience
       b. cognition and information
    4. Accessibility
       a. readability
       b. physical characteristics
       c. literary form

This scheme is used in indexing several online databases at the Danmarks Biblioteksskole. Searches can be performed using bibliographical data, controlled keywords, classification terms, and words/phrases in a natural language annotation. The overall structure of the scheme is illustrated in Exhibit 86 and its application in Exhibit 87.

One major advantage of such a highly structured approach to the indexing of fiction is that it will allow searches to be performed in a kind of "pattern matching" mode, catering to the many readers who want books "similar" to one they recently read. The criteria by which imaginative works are sought by library users may be more personal and idiosyncratic than the criteria and characteristics usually associated with subject searches in bibliographic databases covering, say, journal articles. While this presents

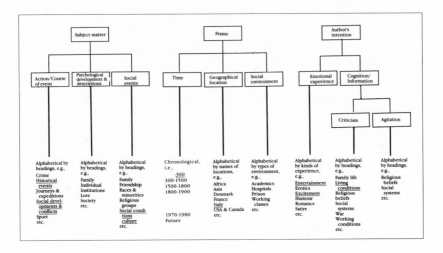

Exhibit 86
Structure of the Pejtersen scheme for the indexing of fiction
Terms underlined are those used to index the novel Spartacus. Reprinted from Pejtersen
and Austin (1983) by permission of Aslib

BRANNER, H. C. *Barnet leger ved stranden*
Psychological description: After a failed marriage, a man isolates himself
in a holiday cottage and lives through a deep crisis. He meets two people,
who exercise influence on him. *Time:* 1930s. *Place:* Denmark, a holiday
cottage near the sea. *Social environment:* Middle classes. *Cognition/
information:* the relationship between the experiences of childhood and
the fears and marriage failures of adult life. Psychoanalytical perspective.
Readability: Difficult. *Typography:* Large. *Form:* Diary. *Bibliog. data:*
Copenhagen: Povl Branner, 1937.—379 p.

Access points: 1930-1939
                  Diaries
                  Depression
                  Fear
                  Guilt
                  Psychological descriptions
                  Identity problems
                  Psychological problems
                  Repression

Exhibit 87
Example of a novel indexed using the Pejtersen approach
Reprinted from Pejtersen and Austin (1983) by permission of Aslib

significant challenges to the designer of retrieval systems, it also suggests innovative approaches to the retrieval problem. One could visualize a public library database that stores information on the fictional works borrowed by each patron. Programs could then be designed to look for groups (perhaps pairs) of patrons who have many books in common. This information could then be used to generate suggested reading lists for library users. For example, if User *A* has borrowed items *a, b, c, d, e* and User *B* has borrowed *a, d, e,* and *f,* perhaps *A* might like to know about *f* and *B* about *b* and *c*.

It is likely that imaginative works present greater difficulties for the indexer than other types of publications. Consistency is likely to be even lower, unless a very small controlled vocabulary of broad terms is used, especially if the indexer is required to express the "viewpoint" of the author. The indexing of fiction (for example) seems inherently more subjective than the indexing of scholarly journals or books about fiction. Another problem is that the skimming of fiction for indexing purposes is not at all easy and the indexer is not aided by the topical headings and subheadings one expects to find in many other types of publication (Jonak, 1978). To make the indexing of fiction or feature films really practicable, some form of accurate synopses must be available.

Abstracting

Imaginative works require summarization just as much as other types of publication, but the characteristics of such *summaries* or *synopses* are quite different from the characteristics of abstracts of scholarly publications as discussed earlier in this book. A good summary should give the essentials of the plot or action, indicating the setting (geographic, chronological) and the emotions depicted where appropriate. The synopsis can be structured as in the example presented in Exhibit 87 or it can be in simple narrative form as in the example of Exhibit 88. While the characteristics of the synopsis

---

A rabbit enters a garden to eat vegetables. The farmer sees him and gives chase. The rabbit escapes.

Peter Rabbit, freed from restraints, enters a garden patch to eat the vegetables. Mr. McGregor, the owner, sees him and attempts to rid his garden of the pest. After a harrowing chase, Peter succeeds in escaping and returning home.

Exhibit 88
Two possible synopses for *The Story of Peter Rabbit* by Beatrix Potter
Modified from Krieger (1981) by permission of the author

---

differ significantly from those of the abstract, the major purpose is similar— to indicate to a reader whether or not he wants to read or view the item

A BLOODSMOOR ROMANCE

Author: Joyce Carol Oates (1938-   )
Type of plot: Historical romance fantasy
Time of plot: 1879-1900
Locale: Bloodsmoor, a valley in Eastern Pennsylvania
First published: 1982

> *Principal characters:*
> JOHN QUINCEY ZINN, a gentleman-inventor and the father of
>   a large family
> PRUDENCE KIDDEMASTER ZINN, his wife, mother of the Zinn
>   daughters
> CONSTANCE PHILIPPA, their oldest daughter who later
>   becomes a son
> MALVINIA, another daughter, later a famous actress
> OCTAVIA, another daughter, later a wife and mother
> SAMANTHA, another daughter who serves as her father's lab-
>   oratory assistant
> DEIRDRE, an adopted daughter and spiritualist

The Novel

Joyce Carol Oates's book *A Bloodsmoor Romance* is not a kind of fiction
that is easily named, although it is not hard to recognize. The work combines both realism and fantasy in a display of authorial skill: Oates uses several techniques to achieve this effect. First, she sets her romance in a past
that closely resembles the historical past; in that setting one finds both fictional characters and characters who bear the names of figures from history.
In addition, the characters of the work are interested in many of the things
that interested the real nineteenth century: spiritualism, the theater, the
westward movement, experimental science, abnormal psychology, female
sexuality, and the nature of marriage.

It is Oates's second technique that sets the work apart from historical romances per se: She freely manipulates the order of historical events and
even adds events that could not possibly occur. John Quincey Zinn demonstrates both of these intrusions of fantasy: He invents the ballpoint pen and
solar heating but dismisses them as useless. He invents an operating time
machine, but he destroys it after he uses it to misplace one of his pupils.
Similarly, Zinn's daughter Constance combines fantasy with history. Reared
for marriage, Constance spends her early life accumulating household lin-
ens, but when the wedding night comes, she panics, and placing in her
groom's bed the dress form used to fit her trousseau, she runs away.
Disguising herself as a man, she heads west and tries her hand at being a

Exhibit 89
Example of an entry from *Masterplots II*
Reproduced from *Masterplots II: American Fiction Series,* volume 1,
pages 186-187. By permission of the publisher, Salem Press Inc.
Copyright 1986, Frank N. Magill

cowboy, an outlaw, a deputy sheriff, and a gambler. During her masquerade, she turns physically into a man as well, and when she returns to the family home at Bloodsmoor, she poses as Philippe Fox, Constance's agent. Eventually, "he" apparently elopes with a childhood girlfriend.

The plot of the book unfolds by following the lives of the daughters as they grow up. In their adventures, the reader meets several characters drawn from history. For example, Deirdre, the Zinns' adopted daughter, is kidnaped by a mysterious stranger in a black balloon who deposits her on the lawn of a character named Madame Elena Blavatsky. This Madame Blavatsky shares the quirks of the historical Madame Blavatsky, cofounder of the American Theosophical Society. Recognizing Deirdre's talents, Oates's Blavatsky teaches Deirdre to become a medium, contacting spirits beyond the grave, and takes her on a world tour. The reader meets other fictional characters with real counterparts as well: Mark Twain, for one.

As may be inferred from the events recounted above, *A Bloodsmoor Romance* is an often hilariously comic work, yet one that at the same time attempts to capture some of the boundless enthusiasm of the late nineteenth century, an enthusiasm that was often as undiscriminating as it was energetic.

Exhibit 89 (cont.)
Example of an entry from *Masterplots II*
Reproduced from *Masterplots II: American Fiction Series,* volume 1,
pages 186-187. By permission of the publisher, Salem Press Inc.
Copyright 1986, Frank N. Magill

described. Moreover, basic principles governing the writing of abstracts—accuracy, brevity, clarity—apply just as much to the summarization of imaginative works.

Guidelines on the preparation of synopses for fiction are few and far between. The publishers of Masterplots (Magill, 1976) do give some guidance but in very general form:

> Designed primarily for reference, the format of MASTERPLOTS is styled and standardized to afford maximum information in the quickest time. Each of the digests is preceded by carefully checked, concisely stated reference data which furnish at a glance the type of work, authorship, type of plot, time of plot, locale, and first publication date. Following this will be found a list of principal characters and their relationship, often a highly useful feature. Next is the *Critique,* a short, incisive critical analysis of the original book. Then follows the plot summary, given as a well-rounded story and devoid of quotations from the original work. (Page v)

In *Masterplots II* (Magill, 1986) a somewhat different format was adopted:

> along with a summarization of plot, narrative devices are often explored and characterization studied in more depth than before—an aspect useful for younger students. In addition, the major themes of the novel at hand are identified and analyzed, and the overall success of the author's effort is usually discussed in an interpretive summary. (Pages vii-viii)

Exhibit 89 presents an example from *Masterplots II.*

13

Natural Language in Information Retrieval *

FOR ALMOST THIRTY YEARS the literature of information science has included a liberal sprinkling of discussions on the relative merits of natural language and controlled vocabularies in the operation of information retrieval systems. This literature is of variable quality: some balanced discussions, some opinion pieces having no experimental or experiential evidence to back them up, some controlled comparisons, some comparisons with virtually no controls whatever, and some contributions that are quite trivial and probably should not have been published.

Definitions

The term *natural language* can be considered synonymous with "ordinary discourse"—i.e., the language commonly used in writing and conversation and the opposite of "controlled vocabulary." In the information retrieval context, the term usually refers to the words occurring in printed text and, thus, "free text" can be considered to be a synonym. Free text can consist of:

1. the title,
2. an abstract,
3. an extract, or
4. the full text of a publication.

The ability to store a complete text in machine-readable form and to search for words or word combinations by computer is usually referred to as "full text search capability." While "free text" usually refers to some intact portion of a text, it can also be used to refer to words or phrases extracted from the text by a human indexer (or by computer program) and included in a bibliographic record representing the text. In some cases these extracted terms are added to the titles of items indexed and thus form "expanded" or "enriched" titles.

*This chapter first appeared as the keynote chapter in *Perspectives in Information Management* 1; ed. by C. Oppenheim et al. London, Butterworths, 1989.

Some History

"Modern" approaches to the use of natural language in information retrieval can be traced back to the Uniterm system described by Taube in 1951. The principles of the Uniterm system had immediate appeal: the subject matter of documents could be adequately represented by single words (uniterms) extracted from the text of documents by indexers of a relatively low level of expertise. By writing or typing, document numbers were "posted" to specially designed cards, each card representing a single term, and searches were performed by comparing the numbers on two or more cards (in much the same way that a modern online system compares lists of numbers associated with terms).

Taube had considerable influence on the development of information retrieval systems in the 1950s. Unfortunately, however, the Uniterm system proved less attractive than it seemed at first sight. It suffered from all of the problems that controlled vocabularies were set up to solve. Closely related subject matter appeared under several different uniterms, and a comprehensive search on a topic would require that the searcher think of all of the ways that this topic might be represented in text—not always an easy task. These problems led to a return to controlled vocabularies and the development of the information retrieval thesaurus (Holm & Rasmussen, 1961).

Besides the terminological problems, the Uniterm system suffered from mechanical limitations. A human searcher can readily compare numbers on only two cards at a time. Thus, a search on A related to B, where A might be represented by four uniterms and B by ten, would require 4×10 separate card comparisons. While possible, this would be a tedious and time-consuming task. Moreover, while the Boolean *and* relationship (involving comparison of numbers) is easy to achieve through the manipulation of Uniterm (or peek-a-boo) cards, it is very difficult in manual systems of this kind to perform a Boolean *or* search (involving the amalgamation of lists) and especially to combine *(and)* sets of terms in an *or* relationship. Such term manipulations, of course, are trivial in computer-based systems. The computer, then, solves the "mechanical" problems involved in manipulating large numbers of uncontrolled terms but does not in itself solve the intellectual problems created by lack of vocabulary control.

Nevertheless, when computers were first applied to information retrieval at a significant level in the late 1950s and early 1960s, it was recognized that text searching, and even full text searching, had become an attractive possibility. In tracing the history of computer-based systems for information retrieval, two principal lines of development can be recognized. One stems from the large systems, developed by such agencies as the National Library of Medicine (NLM), the Department of Defense (DOD), and the National Aeronautics and Space Administration (NASA), that operated on the basis of index terms drawn from a controlled vocabulary and assigned to documents by human indexers. The other line of development began in the field of law and involved putting complete text (e.g., of statutes) into machine-readable form and using a computer to search for words or word combinations in this text. Work of this nature actually predated the development of thesauri and the emergence of the large systems based on human indexing. Full text legal retrieval can be traced back to the work of Horty and his colleagues at the Health Law Center of the University of Pittsburgh (Horty, 1960, 1962; Kehl et al., 1961). It was in the legal field that modern techniques for the searching of free text were first developed, and the early work at Pittsburgh laid the foundations for the contemporary legal retrieval systems exemplified by LEXIS and WESTLAW. Myers (1973) has presented a very useful review of the state of the art in the searching of legal text by computer.

The distinction between those systems based primarily on controlled vocabularies and indexing records created by humans (often misleadingly referred to as "bibliographic" systems) and those based on the searching of text has become increasingly blurred over the years. Gradually, the "bibliographic" systems allowed the searching of words occurring in titles and, later, in abstracts, while some of the full text systems added humanly assigned index terms to improve access and some databases (e.g., INSPEC) were designed from the beginning to include both controlled terms and uncontrolled "keywords." As more and more text has become available in machine-readable form as a byproduct of publishing or dissemination activities, text searching of abstracts has become commonplace, and full text searching now extends well beyond law: newspapers, popular magazines, scholarly journals, encyclopedias, and other sources are now accessible in full text form. In fact, it would probably be correct to say that more searches are now performed on text words than on controlled terms, but it is difficult to get accurate data on this.

Text searching can be achieved in two ways. In the first approach, nontrivial words are entered into "inverted" files showing, for each word, which document it appears in (and frequently its exact position in that document). Searching is performed in these indexes (which in the original implementation at Pittsburgh were referred to as a "concordance") rather than in the text itself. The other alternative is to search the text sequentially, word by word, with no use of indexes. This was the technique commonly used to provide Selective Dissemination of Information (SDI) services from machine-readable databases before online systems were widespread. That is, stored profiles of user interests were matched against periodic updates of the database (words in titles or abstracts). This "streaming" approach to the searching of text was more attractive for SDI applications than for retrospective searching because the amount of text to be scanned at any one time is much less in SDI. Today, however, special-purpose computers can search text so rapidly that streaming searches of even very large databases are quite feasible. For example, the Fast Data Finder (Yu et al., 1987) can search text at the rate of 12.5 million characters per second. This is equivalent to about 12.5 500-page novels every second.

While the "streaming" approach is no different conceptually from the inverted index approach, it does have improved capabilities. For example, it is much easier to search on word "fragments," especially strings of characters occurring in the middle or end of a word.

Searching Aids

Even in the very early days of natural language searching, various aids were developed to assist the searcher. The most primitive is the alphabetic display (or printout) of the "significant" words occurring in the database, with an indication of how frequently each one occurs. Some type of word-distance indicator (metric operator) is also common. The ability to specify how close two words must be is particularly useful in the searching of full text databases where words occurring in different paragraphs may not be directly related at all.

Perhaps the most powerful aid to natural-language searching is the ability to search on parts of words—that is, to truncate or perform word-fragment searching. The value of word-fragment searching has been described by Williams (1972). The most flexible software allows searching on any fragment: right truncation (e.g., all words beginning with "condens"), left truncation (all words ending with "mycin"), "infix" truncation (the beginning and end of a word are specified but the middle is not), or any possible combination of these (e.g., all words including the character string "magnet," wherever it appears). Although potentially useful in all fields, word-fragment searching seems most valuable in science and technology, where the language tends to be more predictable. In a sense, this capability allows one to compensate for lack of a controlled vocabulary by building useful classes of words into a strategy. Thus, searching on the stem "condens" will presumably allow retrieval of a group of documents having something to do with condensers and condensation; searching on the suffix "mycin" will produce documents dealing with antibiotics; and searching on "tri...cobaltate" (infix unspecified) will retrieve a related family of chemical compounds.

Word-fragment searching achieves some of the capabilities of the conventional thesaurus but does so at the time of output rather than imposing control at the input stage. For example, the ability to search on the suffixes "biotics or illin or mycin or cycline or myxin" goes a long way toward equivalency with a conventional thesaurus entry "antibiotics" that leads to a list of narrower antibiotics terms. The conventional thesaurus is a pre-controlled vocabulary, whereas the building of word or word-fragment classes into a search strategy is a kind of "post-controlling" process.

Natural Language Versus Controlled Vocabulary: Some General Considerations

Some major factors influencing the performance of information retrieval systems can be illustrated by further reference to Exhibit 3. On the left are three free-text representations of a document (a title and two abstracts of varying length), while two sets of index terms (selective and exhaustive coverage of the subject matter) appear on the right. The terms are drawn from the *UNBIS Thesaurus* (United Nations, Dag Hammarskjold Library, 1985). One major factor influencing the performance of information retrieval systems is the number of access points provided. Clearly, the expanded abstract provides more than the brief abstract which, in turn, provides more than the title. Likewise, the exhaustive indexing provides almost three times the number of access points provided by the selective indexing.

A text search on the title alone is likely to allow this item to be retrieved only in a search for the central subject matter of the document. As one adds more text, the item becomes retrievable in searches on other aspects. The brief abstract could allow retrieval in searches on: U.S. aid, the PLO, the Palestinian State, Israel, U.S. aid to Israel, and peace conferences, while the expanded abstract adds further access points, such as peace efforts and Middle East leaders. Of course, the same is true of the comparison between the selective indexing and the exhaustive indexing. The selective indexing mirrors only the title of the item and provides no more access points than the title, while exhaustive indexing is more or less equivalent in breadth to the expanded abstract.

In considering the retrievability of the item depicted, it is the length of the record, rather than type of vocabulary, that is of most importance. The selective indexing is equivalent in this respect to the title, while the exhaustive indexing falls somewhere between the two abstracts in the extent to which it covers the subject matter of the item. Because the brief abstract provides more access points than title or selective indexing, the item it represents will be more retrievable. Likewise, the exhaustive indexing may make this item more retrievable than it would be in a search on the brief abstract but less retrievable than it would be in a search on the expanded abstract.

A database consisting of thousands of items indexed exhaustively, as in the example of Exhibit 3, is likely to allow a much higher recall than one providing access through titles only. Similarly, a database consisting of "expanded" abstracts is likely to allow higher recall than one based on selective indexing or even, perhaps, exhaustive indexing. This has nothing to do per se with the comparison of natural language versus controlled vocabularies in information retrieval, but relates only to the length of the searchable record.

Unfortunately, several investigators have failed to control for the length of the record in comparing retrieval based on free text with retrieval based on indexing. That exhaustive indexing gives higher recall than titles is hardly surprising and does not prove that human indexing is superior to free text. That a lengthy abstract gives higher recall than selective indexing is hardly surprising and does not prove that free text is superior to human indexing.

Nevertheless, abstracts will frequently provide more access points than will a set of descriptors assigned by an indexer, and the full text of a document will certainly do so, so one would expect that free text databases will generally allow greater recall than those based on human indexing.

Another important factor affecting the performance of a retrieval system is the specificity with which the subject matter of a document can be described. The *UNBIS Thesaurus* terms are quite specific in describing most aspects of the subject matter of the item depicted in Exhibit 3. Nevertheless, the free text does provide greater specificity in that it allows retrieval on the names of Middle East leaders, while the indexing allows only a search at the "political leaders" level.

The more access points provided for retrieval, the higher the recall possible but the lower is likely to be the precision. One reason is simply the fact that the more access points provided, the more likely it is that some of these will relate to rather minor aspects of a document. Thus a requester receiving the Exhibit 3 item in a search relating to Arafat might judge it to be of no use because it deals with Arafat too briefly and tangentially.

The more access points provided, also, the greater the possibility that some spurious relationships will exist. As discussed in Chapter 11, these are of two types: (1) false associations (2) incorrect term relationships. Many possibilities can be seen in Exhibit 3. For example, the expanded abstract might cause this item to be retrieved in a search on telephone interviews with Middle East leaders (or any of the individual leaders mentioned), and the exhaustive indexing might cause it to be retrieved in a search on political leaders of the United States. These are false associations in that the terms that caused retrieval are essentially unrelated in the document (*telephone interviews* is not directly related to *leaders* and *United States* is not directly related to *political leaders*).

A more subtle type of spurious relationship is illustrated in the selective indexing or even in the title. Either might cause this item to be retrieved in a search on Middle East attitudes toward the United States. In this case the terms *Middle East, attitudes,* and *United States* are directly related, but the relationship is ambiguous.

The longer the record, the greater the chance that spurious relationships will occur. Spurious relationships, of course, cause lower precision.

Some further lessons on the differences between controlled vocabulary and natural language can be learned from Exhibit 90. In this case the *UNBIS Thesaurus* does a poor job of indexing this item. The abstract is much more specific than the controlled terms: no term exists in the thesaurus for "peer tutoring" or even for "tutoring." This exhibit also illustrates the fact that natural language will tend to be more redundant than controlled indexing terms. For example, the abstract contains the term *programmed learning* as well as the term *programmed instruction* so the item could be retrieved on whichever of these terms a searcher happens to use. The full text of a document is likely to provide considerable redundancy, increasing the chance that it will include an expression used by a searcher and thus improving recall.

Human indexing, of course, is a subjective intellectual process, and indexers may not always include a topic that should be included, represent a topic with the best possible term, or make explicit some relationship of potential interest to certain users. The completeness and redundancy of full text avoid this type of problem. Horty (1962), the real pioneer of full text searching, recognized this more than 20 years ago:

> When the full text of documents is used as the basis for a retrieval system an inquiry is not bound by the way in which the documents have been indexed. Almost inevitably an indexer is unaware of certain subjects to which the statutory section is applicable or might be applicable in the future. Yet research, by its very nature, dictates that the researcher is looking for novel relationships between a number of subjects;

relationships which may not have been anticipated by an indexer. By completely dispensing with an index and going to the original text for each search, such novel relationships can be found. (Page 59)

THE USE OF PEER TUTORING AND PROGRAMMED RADIO INSTRUCTION; VIABLE ALTERNATIVES IN EDUCATION
Hannum, W. H.; Morgan, R. M.
1974, 38p.

Florida State University
College of Education
Center for Educational Technology
Tallahassee, Florida 32306

Educational radio*
Programmed instruction*
Developing countries
Nonformal education
Teaching personnel

Educators in developing countries are likely to achieve more by applying the principles rather than the things of educational technology. The principles of program learning have been shown to be effective in promoting learning in a wide variety of circumstances. The most effective instructional materials can be developed through use of the principles of programmed instruction and mastery learning. Radio, when combined with the use of peer tutors, can be an effective educational tool in developing countries. The concepts of programmed learning and mastery learning can be incorporated in the design of educational radio programs. Such programs, accompanied by peer tutors, can accomplish the total educational effort within the resources of many developing countries. This type of educational system is a viable alternative to traditional formal education. Such a system should be tried in several developing countries to explore its full potential.

Exhibit 90
Comparison of abstract and indexing using a controlled vocabulary
The abstract is reproduced from *A.I.D. Research & Development Abstracts* by permission of the Center for Development Information and Evaluation, United States Agency for International Development
The terms marked * are those the indexer considered most important for this item

On the other hand, of course, this very redundancy creates great problems when the text of many documents is combined to form a large database—there are many ways in which a topic can be expressed in full text and, in some cases, the topic is represented implicitly rather than explicitly (O'Connor, 1965), making high recall difficult to achieve. A controlled vocabulary reduces this diversity of terminology. Moreover, by linking semantically related terms, it helps the user to identify all the terms that would be needed to achieve a complete search.

Another factor to be considered is "recency." New terms will enter titles or abstracts long before they appear in a controlled vocabulary. For new topics, then, natural language is likely to win hands down. Precision will be better because the controlled vocabulary will not allow a specific search. Recall is also likely to be better because the searcher will not need to guess what terms to use. Finally, use of the controlled vocabulary will tend to favor the information specialist, who can become fully familiar with the policies and protocols behind it, while natural language may favor the subject specialist user.

So far we have identified several characteristics of free text and also of human indexing with controlled terms and have related these to their probable effects on recall and precision. These relationships are summarized in Exhibit 91. It is obvious from this that the situation is a complex one in that some factors favor controlled terms and some favor free text. The specificity of text words tends to improve precision but to make it more difficult to achieve high recall, at least in broad "conceptual" searches, while the length of text tends to improve recall but to reduce precision. Whether one is to be preferred to another in a particular situation is very much influenced by the type of search being conducted: a broad conceptual search will favor controlled terms, a highly specific search (particularly one involving named individuals, organizations, and so on) will favor free text, a really comprehensive search on a topic (e.g., every possible reference to some drug) will favor full text, while a highly selective search (only the more important items) is likely to favor controlled term indexing.

In general, other authors have come to similar conclusions. For example, Fugmann (1985) points out that natural language searching may yield good results in the case of "individual concepts" but not for "general concepts"; Dubois (1987) claims that one of the advantages of free text is "no delay in incorporating new terms"; and Perez (1982) states that "a controlled vocabulary may result in a loss of precision" while free text has "no loss of specificity." Knapp (1982) mentions "specific topics," "hot topics," and "new terminology" as examples of cases in which natural language is likely to be more useful.

Of course, cost aspects must also be taken into account in a natural language/controlled vocabulary comparison. The cost of human intellectual processing continues to rise rapidly relative to the cost of machine processing, and indexing with a controlled vocabulary is a labor-intensive, costly proposition. Construction and maintenance of a controlled vocabulary can also be expensive. As more and more text becomes available cheaply in machine-readable form, as a byproduct of publishing or dissemination activities, it is natural that the managers of information services should look carefully at the situation to decide whether the advantages of controlled

Factors favoring recall	Effect of type of representation
Length of record (number of access points)	Most free text representations (except for titles only) will be longer than a set of assigned index terms. This will tend to improve recall but reduce precision (cases of "slight mention" and spurious relationships both increase)
Redundancy	Will usually be greater in free text, improving the chance that a particular item will be found. Nevertheless, the great variety of ways in which a topic may be represented in a large text database makes it difficult to achieve high recall.
Presence of broad "concept" terms	Much more likely to appear in a controlled vocabulary representation. May be implicit rather than explicit in text.
Linkage of semantically related terms	Clearly favors the well-constructed controlled vocabulary.
Factors favoring precision	
Specificity	Free text will usually be more specific, favoring precision. The diversity of the way concepts are represented, however, makes it very difficult to achieve a high recall in broad "conceptual" searches. In searches of this kind the relatively broader controlled terms will be much preferable.
Factors affecting both	
Currency	Free text representations will always be more current. To find a brand new topic in a controlled vocabulary system may require the searcher to experiment with several terms (reducing precision) and he still may not find everything on the topic (reducing recall).
Familiarity	Information specialists, fully familiar with a controlled vocabulary, will use it more effectively than others. The "end user" may do better with the natural language occurring in documents in his subject field.

Exhibit 91
The pros and cons of free text versus controlled vocabulary

vocabulary indexing really justify the additional costs.

From the standpoint of cost-effectiveness one can look at the comparison as a tradeoff between input and output. By abandoning human indexing and controlled vocabularies, one is very likely reducing input costs. However, this is achieved at the expense of greater output costs in the sense that an increased intellectual burden is placed upon the user of the database. Among factors that might influence a decision involving this input/output tradeoff are the volumes of documents and searches involved, indexer and searcher costs, and the degree of importance attributable to the results of a search.

Review of Related Studies: Before 1980

Early writings on the experience with full text searching in the legal field were imbued with great enthusiasm for this new capability. However, these writers undertook no experiments to compare full text searching with controlled vocabulary indexing.

Swanson (1960) built a small test collection of 100 articles in nuclear physics and determined which of these were relevant to each of 50 questions. The collection was also indexed using subject headings "designed especially for the field of nuclear physics." The full text searches, which were aided by the use of a "thesaurus-like collection of word and phrase groups," produced, according to Swanson, results superior to those achieved by the searches on subject headings.

The "Cranfield" investigation on the characteristics and performance of index languages seems to have had a profound influence in persuading many information professionals of the advantages of natural language for information retrieval. As reported by Cleverdon et al. (1966), this was a controlled experimental study. A test collection of 1,400 research papers, mostly dealing with aerodynamics, was indexed in three different ways: (1) concepts discussed were recorded (e.g., "cascade losses"), (2) concepts were broken into component words in singular form ("cascade," "loss"), and (3) related concepts were grouped together to form "links" or "themes" (e.g., axial flow compressor/cascade loss). The items were indexed exhaustively: 30 to 50 "concepts" per item were not uncommon.

A group of 221 test questions was compiled. These questions were devised by subject experts and were based upon actual research papers that they themselves had authored. The test collection was sifted by postgraduate students at the College of Aeronautics (Cranfield, England), and items of any conceivable "relevance" were sent to the originator of the question to be judged on a five-point scale (of which one category was "not relevant at all"). As a result, it was known which items in the collection were relevant to each test question (at least in the eyes of the author of that question) and which were not.

The entire study was performed as a type of simulation. Different types of vocabularies were "assembled," ranging from the simplest (single words with no controls whatever, singular/plural conflation, word form control [word stem search], simple synonym control) to the complex (grouping of terms into hierarchies as they would appear in a true hierarchical classification). Each question was posed against the test collection 33 times, where each application tested a different vocabulary (33 in all), allowing a comparison of the results achieved by the various vocabularies. When recall and precision measures were combined into a single measure of performance (referred to as "normalized recall"), vocabularies consisting of single-word natural language terms (with word forms controlled, with synonyms controlled, or with no controls whatever) outperformed all others.

The Cranfield study was very controversial and has generated great criticism over the years. However, much of this criticism arises from a lack of understanding of what was actually done in the study. For example, Soergel (1985) has suggested that both the indexing and the index language were of doubtful quality. Since the present author was one of these indexers, he can attest to the great care that went into the indexing—much more care than is likely in a normal production setting—and that the indexers had very considerable previous experience. Even today the criticisms still surface. Some writers have tried to discredit the Cranfield results on the grounds that, since questions were based on real documents, this would create a bias in favor of natural language. It is hard to understand this criticism in view of the fact that items considered relevant by authors of questions were not the items on which they had based the questions.

In any case, it is not my intention here to defend the Cranfield studies but merely to point out that, flawed or not, they brought many people to the belief that, under certain circumstances at least, natural language systems might do as well as or better than those based on controlled vocabularies. In some of his writings following the Cranfield tests, Cleverdon implied that a natural language system, if properly implemented, would always outperform one based on vocabulary control. Somewhat later, Klingbiel (1970) used the Cranfield results, together with his own experience at the Defense Documentation Center, to claim that "highly structured controlled vocabularies are obsolete for indexing and retrieval" and that "the natural language of scientific prose is fully adequate for indexing and retrieval." A little later, Bhattacharyya (1974) was to state that:

> The findings of various experiments on the testing and evaluation of indexing languages, carried out during the last decade, have demonstrated again and again the strength of the natural language, with minimal or no control, as optimally the best indexing language (that is, taking both

retrieval effectiveness and efficiency into account). (Page 235)

Following the Cranfield studies, and influenced by them, a number of other investigators came to similar conclusions on the merits of natural language in information retrieval. For example, Aitchison et al. (1970) undertook some tests to derive data to aid decisions concerning the indexing of the INSPEC database. Results were compared for searches on: (1) title, (2) titles plus abstracts, (3) index terms used in the printed *Science Abstracts,* (4) "free language" human indexing, and (5) controlled terms drawn from a draft thesaurus compiled by the INSPEC staff. The test environment consisted of 542 articles in electronics and 97 questions supplied by researchers. Assessments were made to determine which articles were relevant to which questions. Care was taken to establish some level of "equivalence" among the strategies used in the various search modes. It was found that retrieval based on the draft thesaurus gave better results than any of the other modes of searching. Nevertheless, it was recommended that the assignment of free language terms by human indexers, which ranked second in performance, should be the method adopted. As it happens, the INSPEC database now incorporates both thesaurus terms and free text terms.

In a major study, Keen and Digger (1972) compared the performance of various types of vocabularies in the field of information science. The major characteristics of the test may be summarized as follows:

1. Five different index languages were used: UL, an uncontrolled postcoordinate language formed by indexers selecting words from the documents themselves; CT, a postcoordinate "compressed term" language of fewer than 300 terms with thesaurus structure imposed; Pre-HS, a precoordinate hierarchically structured language in the form of a faceted classification scheme; HS, a hierarchically structured language (the classification scheme is modified to allow it to be used in a postcoordinate fashion); Pre-RI, a precoordinate language in which terms from the hierarchical classification are combined into indexing phrases ("analets") using the relational operators of Farradane.
2. A test collection of 800 documents on library and information science was indexed by the two investigators using each of the five vocabularies.
3. The physical indexes set up were entirely manual, the postcoordinate one on optical coincidence cards.
4. Sixty-three search requests, gathered from librarians and other information specialists, were processed against these indexes.
5. Searches were conducted by 19 students of library and information science using a Latin square experimental design.
6. Twenty instructors in the subject made relevance judgments for the test requests in relation to each document in the collection.
7. The tests were conducted with different "versions" of the five indexes. These versions reflected changes made to the index language or to indexing

policy. The major variables thus examined were the effect of the exhaustivity of indexing (that is, the number of terms assigned per document), the specificity of the vocabulary, differing methods of coordinating terms at the time of search, the degree to which terms are linked (by cross-reference or hierarchical structure) in a vocabulary; linking related terms together at the time of indexing (that is, "partitioning"), the use of the relational operators, and the provision of "context" in the search file (the searcher in an optical coincidence index is led by document number to a "context file" where an alphabetical chain index entry represents the specific subject matter discussed in the document, this being roughly equivalent to the context provided in a precoordinate index).

The different languages were employed in different comparisons (that is, not all comparisons are relevant to all languages), and for some comparisons a subset of 241 documents and 60 search requests was used. The results of the various comparisons are mostly presented in the form of recall ratios and absolute numbers of nonrelevant items retrieved.

Perhaps not too unexpectedly, this investigation produced results that tend to corroborate findings of earlier studies:

> The Uncontrolled languages tested performed overall just as well as the Controlled languages by providing a consistently good retrieval effectiveness and efficiency performance that was never as bad as the worst controlled language, nor as good as the best, and in no case were these differences statistically significant. (Volume 1, pp. 166-167)

The investigators further claim that:

> the prescription for the best index language is clearly one of the highest specificity possible without the use of precision devices more sophisticated than simple coordination (and with little or no pre-coordination of terms) And it does seem that natural language English single words comes close to providing this optimum level of specificity. (Volume 1, p. 169)

Keen and Digger went on to suggest that the case against controlled vocabularies was now well proven, going so far as to say that "this should be the last time that traditional controlled index languages are humiliated by being demonstrated to offer no advantage" (Volume 1, p. 170).

Lancaster et al. (1972) performed a study of online searching by biomedical researchers in the Epilepsy Abstracts Retrieval System (EARS). The objective was to determine how well these investigators could search the text of abstracts in the field of epilepsy, and some free text/controlled term comparisons were undertaken. It was found that, over 47 searches, use of the index terms assigned by Excerpta Medica gave about half the recall that searches on abstracts achieved. Note, however, that the abstracts generally provided many more access points so the comparison was more one of record length than a true comparison of free text versus controlled term searching. The investigators concluded that the text search gave better recall because of: (a) number of access points, (b) greater redundancy, (c) better match between user terms and text words, (d) errors and inconsistencies in the human indexing, and (e) overlap among index terms. It was hypothesized that performance might be greatly improved if some type of "search thesaurus" were added to the system.

Using documents and questions assembled by Lancaster (1968) in his evaluation of MEDLARS, Salton (1972) produced results suggesting that his SMART system could outperform the costly indexing and vocabulary control activities associated with MEDLARS. This comparison is somewhat different from the conventional comparison of searching in natural language and controlled vocabulary databases. SMART operates not on the basis of Boolean algebra but through a type of "pattern matching," the text of abstracts being matched against the text of natural language requests, with the user being given a set of search options of varying levels of sophistication. In Salton's studies, SMART seemed to outperform MEDLARS only when some user feedback was employed. That is, users evaluated preliminary search results and the search was re-run on the basis of relevance feedback from the user. This raises the obvious question of how well MEDLARS would have done with relevance feedback. SMART is described in Chapter 14.

A major study undertaken in this period is one frequently overlooked. Cleverdon (1977) compared natural language and controlled term searching in a subset of the NASA database consisting of 44,000 items. Online searches were performed at four centers with ten searches conducted at each. Each search was conducted in one mode by one individual and in a different mode by a second individual. The two individuals who searched on the same topic, each in a different mode, first discussed the requirement to get some agreement on what the requester wanted. The modes were: (a) controlled terms only, (b) natural language of titles and abstracts, (c) controlled terms and natural language combined, and (d) natural language search aided by use of a list of "associated concepts." It was found that the natural language searches gave a significantly higher recall and differed little in precision from the controlled term searches. Cleverdon concluded, and rightly so, that it was the length of the abstract that was largely responsible.

Unfortunately, Cleverdon's study is marred by inadequate reporting. For example, those searches in which both controlled terms and natural language were used performed less well on both recall and precision than

the searches involving natural language alone. This is quite the opposite
of what one would expect and is difficult to explain, especially since these
"joint mode" searches retrieved twice as many items as the natural language
searches did. Cleverdon fails to explain this anomaly. Another anomaly is
that natural language searches aided by the "associated concept file" also
performed less well than those conducted using natural language alone.
This too is not clearly explained and it is difficult for readers of Cleverdon's
report to come to their own conclusions since the "associated concepts
file" itself is not fully described. All one can surmise from Cleverdon's
description is that it was derived from the co-occurrence of terms in the
titles of documents in the collection.

A later paper by Martin (1980) offers some clarification but adds further
mystery of its own. He makes clear that the natural language component
of the database consisted of single words extracted from titles and abstracts
by computer but later edited by humans to remove "stopwords" and to
normalize the vocabulary by eliminating variant spellings and word forms.
The associated concept file was a file of the keywords extracted from titles
only showing, for each, which keywords co-occurred most frequently in
titles. Martin summarizes the results as follows:

	Recall (%)	Precision (%)
Controlled terms	56	74
Natural language	78	63
Natural language plus controlled terms	71	45

He then goes on to state that "for every relevant document retrieved by
controlled language, natural language alone retrieved 1.4, natural language
plus controlled language 1.6...," which is quite incompatible with the recall/
precision values given. Martin also makes clear that the "natural language
plus controlled term" searches include some that involved controlled terms
alone (where the searcher saw no need to augment with natural language)
so "they did not represent the full potential of CL plus NL." The
inconsistencies in the results and statements about them, as well as concerns
regarding the instructions given to the searchers, cast some doubt on the
validity of this comparison.

Only one study performed in this period claims to have found superior
results for human indexing with a controlled vocabulary. Hersey et al. (1971)
used a subset of the Smithsonian Science Information Exchange (SIE)
database, consisting of 4,655 project descriptions, in their comparison of

free text versus "scientist indexing." The indexing involved the use of subject codes, assigned by subject specialists, and drawn from a specially prepared classification scheme. For 27 searches performed at SIE itself, the following results were derived:

	Recall (%)	*Precision (%)*
Text of project descriptions	66	81
Subject indexing	95	95

Again, poor reporting makes it very difficult for the reader to understand exactly what was done. The questions used were some that had been "previously asked," but it is not clear whether the results for subject indexing were derived when the searches were originally performed for customers or were derived later, at the time the free text searches were performed. The following points are also unclear: on what basis the relevance assessments were made (they were apparently made by SIE staff rather than original requesters), in what form the request was given to the person doing the free text search (online in the Data Central system), and whether or not any controls were imposed on the searchers to achieve some level of equivalence in search approach between text search and index term search.

Each of these factors could exert a profound influence on the results of the study. For example, if the request used as the basis for the free text search was not in the requester's original words, but had been "compromised" as a result of interaction with SIE personnel, the results of the comparison might well be biased toward the subject codes. The fact that the recall/precision results of this study were very much higher than those achieved in other investigations, and much higher than those achieved in the day-to-day operation of retrieval systems (Lancaster, 1968), coupled with the rather imprecise reporting, raises serious questions concerning the validity of the comparison. The unusually high precision scores, however, are partly explained by the fact that the test file of project descriptions was really an amalgamation of four separate test files in completely different subject areas.

A supplementary study on this database was performed by the Biological Sciences Communication Project of George Washington University using 12 SIE questions. Searches on the subject codes retrieved 91 projects of which 74 were judged relevant (precision of 81 percent), while text searches retrieved 70 of which 43 were judged relevant (precision of 61 percent). By combining the results for free text and subject code searching, one can conclude that recall was about 50 percent for text and 90 percent for subject indexing, but some unique items were retrieved by each search mode.

Byrne (1975) used 50 SDI profiles on the COMPENDEX database and compared results when searches were performed on titles, abstracts, and subject headings, and various combinations of these. The results for one search mode were compared with the combined results for all modes. Using this standard, subject headings alone retrieved 21 percent of the items, abstracts alone 61 percent, titles plus abstracts 75 percent, and titles plus subject terms 41 percent. Not surprisingly, then, the longer representations seemed to give much better recall. However, no real relevance assessments were made in this study: everything retrieved was ipso facto considered an appropriate response.

Review of Related Studies: Since 1980

By and large, the comparisons of free text and controlled vocabulary searching performed in the 1960s and 1970s showed that free text could do as well as, if not better than, controlled terms. However, these studies were performed on rather small files, and sometimes trivially small. They were mostly experimental studies rather than involving real information services operating under actual working conditions. Since 1980 some studies have been done with databases of greater size and/or involving real operating services.

Markey et al. (1980) undertook an analysis of controlled vocabulary and free text search statements in online searches of the ERIC database. They also performed "online searching tests" comparing free and controlled vocabulary but only using six topics. They concluded that free text gave higher recall and controlled terms gave higher precision. As in many other studies, reporting of the test is woefully inadequate. No details are given on how the relevance assessments were made and none on how the searches were performed, so the reader does not know if any attempt was made to "control" the search strategies to avoid favoring either search mode. The uncharacteristically high scores (93 percent recall and 71 percent precision for free text, 76 percent recall and 95 percent precision for the controlled terms) cast doubt on the validity of the study.

A number of studies have been undertaken in the field of law. Coco (1984) used a database of circuit court cases (1960-1969) and 50 actual "research problems" taken from a 1977 Federal Judicial Center study to compare retrieval in the WESTLAW and LEXIS systems. LEXIS includes only the text of the opinions associated with these cases, while WESTLAW adds "editorial components" to the text of the opinions, including various forms of synopses. The stated objective of this study was to compare the results of searches based on the text alone with those achieved with text plus editorial additions. Since the searches on WESTLAW were performed with and without the editorial additions, the comparison with LEXIS was quite unnecessary and only served to confuse the reader. In any event, the comparison of LEXIS and WESTLAW could not be considered completely valid because the databases were not exactly comparable. As Coco says, "the systems contained *approximately* [italics added] the same number of cases for this period." Moreover, no real systematic attempt was made to determine whether or not the cases retrieved were in any sense relevant to the research problems.

If the one example provided by Coco is representative of all items in the database, the augmented text in WESTLAW is almost twice the length of the opinion text alone. It is hardly surprising, then, that it retrieved more cases (913 versus 728, although we do not know how many were "relevant"). In fact, one might reasonably expect that a doubling of the text would yield more than a 20 percent increase in the number of cases retrieved. That it did not must in part be attributable to term overlap between the text and the editorial additions. The results of this study were completely predictable from the outset and we hardly needed such an investigation to tell us that doubling the text will increase the number of items retrieved.

Blair and Maron (1985) have undertaken a study of the full-text searching of documents relevant to a large corporate lawsuit using the STAIRS system (about 350,000 pages of text, or 40,000 documents, and 40 information requests). Paralegals performed extensive iterative searches online and only stopped searching when attorneys for whom they were working were satisfied that at least 75 percent of the relevant references had been retrieved. By sampling, however, the investigators estimated that no more than 20 percent recall had been achieved. They conclude that their results cast serious doubt on the efficacy of full text searching and, on the basis of some very dubious cost analyses, that full text searching is much more costly than alternative approaches. They completely overlook the fact that large controlled vocabulary systems may not perform any better. For example, a study of 535 MEDLINE searches, performed by 191 different searchers, is said to have produced an average recall of only 23 percent at a precision of 67 percent (Wanger et al., 1980). Although based largely on Blair and Maron's results, Dabney (1986a) gives an excellent discussion of the problems of full-text retrieval in the legal field. Responses to Dabney by McDermott (1986) and by Runde and Lindberg (1986), as well as a follow-up comment by Dabney (1986b), are also worth examination.

One of the better studies, comparing full text with abstracts and controlled indexing, was completed by Tenopir (1984). Using the *Harvard Business Review* online, Tenopir achieved the following results, averaged over 31 searches.

	Full text	Abstracts	Controlled terms
Number of documents retrieved (mean)	17.8	2.4	3.1
Relevant documents retrieved (mean)	3.5	1.0	1.2
Recall (relative to union of all methods)	73.9	19.3	28.0
Precision	18.0	35.6	34.0
Cost per search	$20.57	$4.95	$5.32
Cost per relevant item retrieved	$7.86	$3.89	$3.54

Tenopir's cost figures cannot be taken too seriously since she included the costs of obtaining full copies of documents for achieving relevance judgments, whereas in real life this would rarely occur (i.e., users would judge on the basis of titles and/or abstracts viewed online). Perhaps the most significant result of Tenopir's research is her finding that the controlled term searches retrieved some items not retrieved by full text, and vice versa, arguing for the need for both.

More recently Ro (1988) performed a follow-up study on the *Harvard Business Review* database that yielded similar results to those achieved by Tenopir.

The improvements in recall that are possible by using text terms in addition to controlled terms have been demonstrated by several investigators, including McCain et al. (1987), who compared the results of searches in five databases for 11 topics in the medical behavioral sciences.

Various other studies have reported the results of searches on full or partial text but without comparisons with searches on controlled terms. Some of these studies have involved systems (similar in some ways to SMART) that use probabilistic and/or linguistic methods to rank documents, or paragraphs from them, on the basis of their similarity to request statements or search strategies. For example, Bernstein and Williamson (1984) evaluate such procedures applied to the Hepatitis Knowledge Base, and Tong et al. (1985) evaluate artificial intelligence techniques applied to full text retrieval in a database of news items.

The review of the literature included here has focused on studies comparing the performance of free text databases with that of databases indexed by means of controlled vocabularies when searching is performed on Boolean combinations of terms. While some other types of study have been mentioned, no attempt has been made to review all of the literature dealing with the searching of text using non-Boolean approaches.

It is evident from the review that the early extravagant enthusiasm for natural language searching has been toned down over the years as the problems involved have been more clearly identified. Some of the early studies were based on experimental databases that were trivially small. Because one can tolerate very low precision when only a handful of items are retrieved, it is possible to achieve an acceptable level of recall. This situation changes dramatically when one moves to databases containing hundreds of thousands of items. Low levels of precision are no longer acceptable because of the number of items retrieved ("output overload") and it is correspondingly difficult to achieve high recall at an acceptable level of precision. However, some evidence exists (Wanger et al., 1980) that this is also true of large systems based on controlled vocabularies and not just a peculiarity of free text searching.

It is important to recognize the distinction between the terms *free text* and *full text*. Conclusions reached as a result of studies on full text databases are not automatically transferable to databases containing less than full text (e.g., abstracts). In full text databases the problem of scale is compounded. That is, with a very large database of full text it will be even more difficult to achieve acceptable recall at tolerable precision. Full text should give greater recall but lower precision than a database of less than full text. This was demonstrated clearly by Tenopir (1984).

It is an unfortunate fact that most of the studies that purport to compare the retrieval performance of free text with that of a set of index terms selected from a controlled vocabulary do no such thing. Rather, they compare the retrieval performance of records of varying length. A valid comparison of controlled terms versus free text per se would have to hold constant the length of the records (e.g., all of the topics mentioned in an abstract would have to be translated, insofar as possible, into equivalent controlled terms) and also the search strategy (i.e., a "conceptual" strategy would have to be created and then translated exactly into: [a] text expressions, and [b] terms selected from the controlled vocabulary). This has never been done as far as I am aware, at least not since the Cranfield studies. Tenopir controlled her search strategies but, since she was using an existing database, could not control for record length. Consequently, her conclusions relate much more to length of record than they do to the natural language/controlled vocabulary controversy.

Also unfortunate is the fact that the literature still contains wild claims, based on anecdotal evidence, from proponents of one or other camp who refuse to accept the fact that natural language and controlled vocabularies each have their own advantages. See Fugmann (1987) for a good example.

A careful examination of the literature included in this review gives the author no reason to change his original views on the pros and cons of the two approaches, as summarized in Exhibit 91. The fact is that each has advantages and disadvantages. Free text records tend to be longer and thus provide more access points, will frequently include some terms more specific or more current than those in any controlled vocabulary, and will usually provide greater redundancy. The controlled vocabulary, on the other hand, imposes consistency in the representation of subject matter among documents, provides the broad "concept" terms that are frequently lacking in text, and, by means of hierarchical and cross-reference structure, give the user positive aid in identifying appropriate search terms.

Hybrid Systems

Virtually every writer on free text searching, including Henzler (1978) and Perez (1982), as well as most of the authors already cited, have come to the unsurprising conclusion that the ideal retrieval system will include some controlled terms as well as some free text. The advantages of such hybrid systems are obvious, and they were described and illustrated many years ago by Uhlmann (1967), Holst (1966), and Lancaster (1972). The value of the hybrid approach is supported by the fact that, in most of the studies performed, free text searches retrieved some relevant items not found by controlled vocabulary searches, and vice versa.

The term *hybrid* can be used to refer to any system operating on a combination of controlled terms and natural language, including those in which both sets of terms are assigned by human indexers and those in which a database can be searched on a combination of humanly assigned controlled terms and words occurring in titles, abstracts, or full text.

Consider, for example, a system based on three separate vocabulary components:

1. a small vocabulary of broad subject codes, perhaps 300 codes in all;
2. a list of codes representing geographic areas; and
3. keywords or phrases occurring in the titles or texts of documents.

Indexing with such vocabulary elements might represent a significant economy over indexing that uses a large carefully controlled vocabulary for two reasons:

1. The subject codes would be broad enough to be assigned without much difficulty by an indexer not having a high level of education or subject expertise.
2. The number of codes (subject and geographic) is small enough that the indexer can retain most in memory and avoid having to constantly look them up in a vocabulary listing.

Although any one of the vocabulary elements on its own is relatively crude, the joint use of a keyword (to give specificity) and a subject or geographic code (to give context) is an extremely powerful device. For example, the keyword *plants* may mean something entirely different when combined with a subject code relating to agriculture than when combined with a subject code relating to some industry. Likewise, the keyword *strike* associated with the geographic code for Lebanon may indicate a military operation; when it is coordinated with the geographic code for England, on the other hand, it is more likely to signify a labor dispute. Moreover, the joint use of broad subject codes, geographic codes, and keywords is extremely effective in illustrating relationships, even when these relationships are not explicitly specified. Many of the databases that are now accessible through online networks can be searched on combinations of controlled terms and keywords or phrases occurring in titles or abstracts, the latter permitting greater specificity.

The Post-Controlled Vocabulary

Several authors have pointed out that natural language searching can be considerably improved through the construction and use of various forms of searching aid. Piternick (1984) has described some possible tools of this kind. The most obvious aid would be a "search thesaurus" or "post-controlled vocabulary" as envisioned by Lancaster (1972), Lancaster et al. (1972), and, in more detail, by Lancaster (1986).

The earliest system developed to search large bodies of legal text (at Pittsburgh) used a kind of thesaurus to aid the search process. This was merely a compilation of words with similar meanings, resembling *Roget's Thesaurus* more than the thesaurus structure commonly used in information retrieval. Even without any significant degree of "structure," such a thesaurus could be an extremely valuable searching aid; words with similar meanings are potentially substitutable in a search, and such a tool relieves individual searchers from having to think of all the words that might express a particular idea. Investing in the construction of such a searching aid allows significant economies in a system in which large numbers of searches are performed. This simple type of thesaurus is a kind of controlled vocabulary, with the control applied at output rather than input. It is a post-controlled vocabulary.

The properties of the post-controlled vocabulary can be further illustrated with an example. Consider a public affairs database that is indexed with a thesaurus. The thesaurus includes the term *airlines,* so it is possible to perform a broad search on this subject. It is not possible, however, to limit a search to a particular airline since specific names do not appear in the thesaurus. Thus, it would be impossible to restrict a search to "financial conditions of Varig"; the best one might do is to retrieve everything on the financial conditions of airlines. The general search tends to be easy in the pre-controlled vocabulary situation, but certain highly specific searches may be virtually impossible.

In contrast, consider an alternative public affairs database that dispenses with indexing but allows searches on titles and abstracts. Retrieving items on Varig or Swissair will likely be easy. More difficult would be the general search on airlines. To perform a comprehensive search, one would need to go far beyond the use of the word *airlines* and would need such synonyms as *air carriers* and names of individual companies. The search strategy might look like *"airlines* or *air carriers* or *Varig* or *Swissair* or *Lufthansa* or..." — perhaps a very long list. What the searcher is doing is creating part of a post-controlled thesaurus. Regrettably, in present information services, such thesaurus entries are rarely retained and stored once they have been created and used. Within a large network, much duplication of effort takes place. *Airlines* may appear as a facet of many searches performed during a year, and the work of building the search strategies of varying degrees of completeness will be repeated time and time again. How much more sensible to store it in retrievable form for future use.

A true post-controlled vocabulary consists of tables with names and identifying numbers that can be called up and consulted by users of natural-language databases within some online network. Thus, the searcher could retrieve the "airlines" entry, the "financial affairs" entry, and so on. The tables can be viewed online and terms selected from them. Alternatively, the entire table can be incorporated into a search strategy by its identifying numbers. Such tables need not be restricted to words but may incorporate word fragments. Thus, a surgery table might look like "surg..., operat..., section..., ...section, ...otomy, ...ectomy, ...plasty," and so on. The vocabulary can also be given some minimal structure by cross-referencing of related tables.

A post-controlled vocabulary system can offer all the advantages of natural language with many of the attributes of the pre-controlled vocabulary. Such a system might perform better than one based on a pre-controlled vocabulary. To return to an earlier example, one could search for individual airlines with ease or use the "airlines" table to form the class defined by "airlines" in the conventional thesaurus. One of the advantages of natural language is that it is database independent. Thus, an "airlines" table would be equally applicable to all databases in the English language. One could visualize a natural-language thesaurus that would be applicable to several hundred databases.

The closest tool to the post-controlled vocabulary was the TERM database implemented by Bibliographic Retrieval Services (BRS) and described by Knapp (1983). TERM was a database of tables, representing concepts, that include both controlled terms and free-text terms needed to perform searches in a variety of databases in the social and behavioral sciences. A sample table is displayed in Exhibit 92.

```
TI  POVERTY AREAS
ER  POVERTY-AREAS+/
ME  POVERTY-AREAS*.
PS  POVERTY-AREAS. CONSIDER ALSO: GHETTOS.
SO  CONSIDER: SLUM. GHETTO, APPALACHIA.
EN  SLUMS.
FT  POVERTY AREAS. SKID ROW. BOWERY. SLUM. INNER CITY. POOR
    NEIGHBORHOODS. MILIEU OF POVERTY. DEPRESSED AREAS. SLUMS.
    GHETTOS. GHETTO. GHETTOES. APPALACHIA. LOW INCOME AREAS.
    GHETTOIZATION. STREET CORNER DISTRICT. ETHNIC NEIGHBOR-
    HOOD. BLACK NEIGHBORHOOD. BLACK COMMUNITY. SEGREGATED
    NEIGHBORHOOD. DISADVANTAGED AREA. BLACK SCHOOL DISTRICTS.
    MINORITY NEIGHBORHOOD. REDLINED AREAS. REDLINING.
```

Exhibit 92
Example of entry in the TERM database
Reproduced by permission of Maxwell Online Inc.

The title (TI) of the table is POVERTY AREAS. This term is used to retrieve items on this topic in ERIC (ER), in databases indexed by *Medical Subject Headings* (ME), and in the PsycINFO (PS) database (in which a related term is GHETTOS). In *Sociological Abstracts* (SO), possible terms are SLUM, GHETTO, and APPALACHIA, whereas a narrower ERIC term (EN) is SLUMS. Finally, a detailed list of related free text (FT) terms, useful for a search on this subject in any English-language database, is given. A strategy could be developed on the TERM database and saved and executed on the bibliographic databases at a later time. Unfortunately, this database is no longer maintained.

A post-controlled vocabulary in a particular subject field can be built by human intellectual effort in much the same way as a conventional thesaurus. The task might be simplified considerably by machine manipulation of the words occurring in relevant databases so that various levels of "statistical association" are derived. Perhaps it would be more sensible, however, to collect and edit the "search fragments" actually entered by users of some online systems (any list of terms entered in an OR relationship would be a candidate), thus producing a kind of "growing thesaurus" as visualized by Reisner (1966), but with some editorial control imposed later.

Conclusions

Systems that dispense with conventional vocabulary control and human indexing can work and have been proven to do so over a period of some 30 years. Nevertheless, they do present problems when broad "conceptual" searches must be performed. While there are definite advantages to natural language, it is clear that appropriate enhancements (limited use of indexing and/or development of searching aids) are likely to improve the effectiveness of natural language systems. Moreover, as databases get larger, and more full text is accessible for searching, it may become increasingly necessary to implement systems that will rank retrieved items by "probable relevance" rather than simply dividing the database into "retrieved" and "not retrieved" (Maron, 1988).

14

AUTOMATIC INDEXING, AUTOMATIC ABSTRACTING AND RELATED PROCEDURES

A RATHER SIMPLISTIC picture of the information retrieval problem was presented in Exhibit 1. A more sophisticated version is given in Exhibit 93. In essence, the problem is that of matching information needs against messages. This can only be done in a rather indirect way. Most messages (what authors want to convey) appear as texts (some are in pictorial, audio, or other nontextual form) while the information needs are presented as requests made to some type of information service. The information service creates representations of the texts, stores these in a database, and provides some device that allows these representations to be searched. The database can be stored in paper, microimage, or electronic form, and the "device" allowing it to be searched can be as simple as the arrangement of entries in a card catalog or printed index or as sophisticated as a computer and a set of computer programs. The information service also creates representations of the requests (search statements of some type) and processes these against the database, retrieving those text representations that match or best match the request representations.

Representations of texts will consist of the full text itself (e.g., an exact electronic "reproduction" of words printed somewhere on paper), parts of the text, or some other form of representation humanly or automatically constructed. Representations of requests will consist of terms, terms presented in logical relationships, textual statements, or "items" (e.g., a system may allow a searcher to enter details of an item already known to be relevant and will then look for others that resemble it in some way).

To aid the construction of representations (of texts or requests), various intellectual aids may be made available. The most obvious is the conventional controlled vocabulary, but other aids, such as the post-controlled vocabulary referred to in Chapter 13, could also be used.

Of course, many variations on the basic theme of Exhibit 93 are possible. For example, in many situations the information service creating the text representations (i.e., building the database) will not be the same as the services that search it. Moreover, the seeker of information may not delegate the search to an information specialist but may conduct it himself. While many such variations exist, they are not important for the purposes of the present discussion.

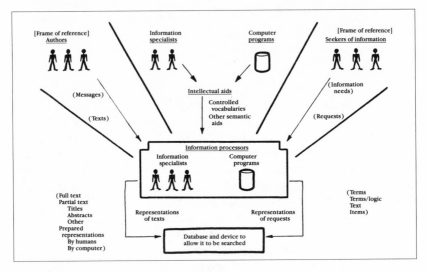

Exhibit 93
The essential problems of information retrieval

The problems of information retrieval should be obvious from the diagram. Texts may not be perfect representations of messages (while this is a definite communication problem it is not usually considered an information retrieval problem) and, as we have seen from the earlier chapters, the representations of texts may also be imperfect. By the same token, requests are rarely perfect representations of information needs and search statements may not be perfect representations of requests. Moreover, the frame of reference ("schemata") of a requester may not coincide with the frame of reference of an information specialist or, indeed, the frame of reference of authors. The information retrieval problem, then, can be considered essentially one of trying to match approximations of information needs with approximations of messages. Small wonder that the results are not always completely satisfactory.

As Bates (1986) has pointed out, the information retrieval problem is more complex than it appears on the surface; she refers to it as "indeterminate" and "probabilistic." It now seems fashionable to concentrate more on the output side of the activity (information need—request—representation) than on the input side (message—text—

representation), the implicit assumption being that the output side is more "complex." In fact, Belkin (1980) and Belkin et al. (1982) refer to matching the "anomalous state of knowledge" of a requester with the more "coherent" state of knowledge of authors. As pointed out as early as Chapter 2, the indexer's role—predicting the types of requests for which a particular document is likely to be a useful response—is not necessarily simpler than that of the search intermediary—understanding what types of documents might satisfy some requester at a given time.

Be that as it may, Exhibit 93 is presented at this point primarily to illustrate the fact that algorithmic processes can be used in various information retrieval activities as a substitute for human intellectual processing. Computers can be applied in automatic indexing and automatic abstracting, as well as in other operations involving the formation of classes of documents and of terms, in the development of searching strategies, and in establishing networks of associations among terms. As the diagram implies, computers can, to some extent, substitute for humans in virtually all of the activities illustrated. At present they do not independently generate messages or information needs unless specifically programmed to do so by humans, but perhaps some day they may. Since indexing and abstracting are the focal activities of this book, it will be the application of computers to these tasks that will be given most attention in this chapter.

Automatic Extraction Indexing

Early in the book a distinction was made between assignment indexing and indexing by extraction. Most human indexing is assignment indexing, involving the representation of subject matter by means of terms selected from some form of controlled vocabulary. In extraction indexing, words or phrases appearing in a text are extracted and used to represent the content of the text as a whole. Human indexers will try to select textual expressions that appear to be good indicators of what a document is about. Presumably they will be swayed by the frequency with which a term appears in a document and perhaps by where it appears—in title, in summary, in captions to illustrations, and so on—and by its context.

Given that the text exists in machine-readable form, it is obvious that a computer can be programmed to perform extraction indexing using these same frequency, positional, and contextual criteria. Automatic indexing based on word frequency can be traced back to the 1950s and the work of Luhn (1957) and Baxendale (1958). Simple programs can be written to count the occurrences of words in a text, once the text has been compared with a "stoplist" to remove nonsubstantive words (articles, prepositions, conjunctions, and suchlike) from consideration, and then to rank the words by frequency of occurrence. It is the words at the top of the list, of course, that are selected to be the "index terms" for the document. The cutoff point established can observe any of several possible criteria: an absolute number of words, a number related to the length of the text, or words occurring with a frequency above some threshold. A slightly more complicated program can extract phrases occurring significantly often in the text. Thus a document can be represented by a combination of words and phrases, the frequency criterion for the selection of the phrases being less stringent than the one on which significant words are selected.

Rather than selecting words and phrases, the programs can instead be written to select word roots. Thus, the root *heat* might be selected and stored in place of the variants *heat, heating,* and *heated.* Programs for automatic stemming can be used to remove only selected word endings (e.g., "ed", "ing"). Of course, words, phrases, or roots can all be given weights reflecting the frequency with which they occur in the document. For example, the root *heat* can be given a numerical weight associated with the fact that it appears in the text, say, 12 times.

Frequency criteria can be supplemented by other criteria. For example, Baxendale (1958) proposed that only the first and last sentences of every paragraph be processed because one of her studies had shown that the first sentence was the "topic sentence" 85 percent of the time and the last sentence was in another 7 percent of the cases. The "topic sentence" was the one judged to be that providing the most information concerning the content. In the early days of automatic indexing, various other methods for identifying "information rich" segments of text were proposed or tested; computer programs would look for such elements as: prepositional phrases, text following "clue words" like *conclusions* and *summary,* and parts of the text that include the most initial occurrences of nouns.

One obvious disadvantage of using simple word or phrase frequency in the selection of terms is that, even after use of a stoplist, some of the words that occur frequently in a document may not be good discriminators— serving to distinguish this document from others in the database—because they also occur frequently in the database as a whole. To take an obvious example, the words *library* and *information* would not be very good discriminators of individual items within a collection on library and information science. Thus, in a particular document the word *library* may occur 12 times while the word *asbestos* occurs only four times. Nevertheless, the latter is much the better discriminator because it is a term that rarely occurs in the literature of library science. It would be a highly significant term in a collection on this subject even if it occurred only once in a document. *

The frequency with which a word occurs in a document is not the only frequency to be concerned with in the computer processing of text. The frequency with which a word occurs in the database as a whole is even more significant. That is, words that are the best discriminators are those that are unexpected and rare in a collection—e.g., *asbestos* in library science, *library* in the database of an asbestos company. In actual fact, it is not necessary to compute the frequency with which a word occurs in a complete database of text but only the frequency with which it occurs in the inverted file used to search the text (i.e., the number of occurrences of a word related to the number of occurrences of all words in the file).

Rather than the absolute frequency with which a word occurs in a document, then, a relative frequency approach to the selection of terms can be used (Oswald et al., 1959). With this approach, words or phrases are selected when they occur in a document more frequently than their rate of occurrence in the database as a whole. This is a bit more complicated than the absolute frequency approach since it requires that a count be maintained of how frequently each word occurs in the database (relative to the total number of word occurrences in the database) and a comparison of this occurrence rate with the rate of occurrence of a word in a particular document.

A list of words or phrases extracted from a document on the basis of relative frequency will be different from a list derived on the basis of absolute frequency but not radically so. Many of the terms will remain the same. The few new terms will be those that occur infrequently in a particular document, perhaps only once, but even more infrequently in the database as a whole—a single occurrence among the 5,000 words of a journal article is highly significant if that word has occurred only five times so far in a database of 10 million words! The terms that disappear, obviously, will be those that, while they may occur frequently in a document, occur frequently in the database as a whole.

Of course, terms selected on the basis of relative frequency should *not* be radically different from those selected on the basis of absolute frequency. For effective information retrieval one wants terms that are good discriminators of documents but also terms that form effective classes of documents. It is useful to be able to zero in on the very rare item—the only document in the database perhaps that discusses the hazards of asbestos

*This discussion is somewhat oversimplified. Very rare terms will be good for retrieving items on very rare topics but the inclusion of many such terms will make it difficult to get high recall on searches on more general topics (e.g., "insulation" rather than "asbestos").

in library ceilings—but one also wants to retrieve groups of related documents. Words such as *hazards* or *dangers* may not be quite as rare in a library science database as *asbestos* but they will be useful in retrieving a certain class of document that may interest some users. For effective information retrieval one usually wants classes that consist of more than a single item.

Criteria for the extraction of terms from documents, then, include absolute frequency, relative frequency, or a combination of the two, as well as positional or syntactic criteria. * If a relative approach to the selection of words is used, of course, stoplists are not really necessary: prepositions, conjunctions, and articles will occur frequently in individual items, but they will also occur frequently throughout the database and thus will be rejected, along with the substantive but commonly occurring words (such as *library* in library science).

Terms can also be extracted from text when they match some type of stored dictionary of "acceptable" terms. This was the basis of the important work on machine-aided indexing performed in the 1970s at the Defense Documentation Center (see, for example, Klingbiel [1971]). In essence, word strings occurring in titles and abstracts were matched against a Natural Language Data Base (NLDB). Word strings that matched became candidate index terms. Klingbiel and Rinker (1976) compared the results of the machine-aided indexing with the results of human indexing. As a result of three case studies, they concluded that unedited machine-aided indexing (MAI) can achieve recall levels comparable to those achieved by human indexing and that the precision achieved by the MAI is at least as good as that achieved by the human indexing. Edited machine indexing achieved comparable recall results and better precision than the human indexing. It is important to note, however, that the MAI procedures assigned natural language expressions to documents, not the descriptors assigned by the human indexers, so the studies reported by Klingbiel and Rinker are not "pure" comparisons of human indexing versus machine-aided indexing but are more comparisons of natural language indexing versus controlled vocabulary indexing.

Automatic Assignment Indexing

The extraction of words and/or phrases from documents is a task that computers can accomplish rather well. Automatic extraction has one clear

*For a complete discussion of various criteria for the selection of terms on the basis of frequency of occurrence see Salton and McGill (1983).

advantage over human extraction: it is completely consistent. However, most human indexing is not extraction indexing but assignment indexing and performing this task by computer is altogether more difficult. The obvious way to perform assignment indexing by computer is to develop, for each term to be assigned, a "profile" of words or phrases that tend to occur frequently in documents to which a human indexer would assign that term. This type of profile for the term *acid rain* might include such phrases as acid rain, acid precipitation, air pollution, sulfur dioxide, and so on.

If every term in a controlled vocabulary had such a profile associated with it, computer programs could be used to match the significant phrases in a document (essentially those that would be extracted by the frequency criteria mentioned earlier) with this collection of profiles, assigning a term to the document when the document profile matches the term profile above some threshold.

This sounds relatively straightforward. In practice, however, it is not that easy. In the first place, the matching criteria would have to be somewhat sophisticated. If *acid rain* occurs ten times in a journal article, the index term ACID RAIN should almost certainly be assigned. Suppose, on the other hand, that *acid rain* occurs only twice in the document, but *atmosphere, sulfur dioxide,* and *sulfuric acid* all occur rather frequently. Should the term ACID RAIN be assigned? It is clear that many different combinations of words or phrases could signal the fact that a particular index term should be a candidate for assignment. Moreover, the significance of each combination, as a predictor that a particular term should be assigned, would involve the use of different co-occurrence values. For example, if the words *heat, lake,* and *pollution* all occur a few times in a document, this might be enough to cause the term THERMAL POLLUTION, as well as WATER POLLUTION, to be assigned. But *heat* and *lake* without the appearance of *pollution* would have to occur together in a document many times before THERMAL POLLUTION would be a good bet for assignment.

The phrase *acid rain* is very likely to occur frequently in a document dealing with this subject so the correct assignment of the index term ACID RAIN may not be as difficult as the above discussion might suggest. The term THERMAL POLLUTION is more of a problem since it is less likely that most of the "thermal pollution" items will include frequent occurrences of this phrase. Some other terms that a human indexer can assign rather easily almost defy assignment by computer. O'Connor (1965) has discussed some of the problems. One good example is the term TOXICITY. A human indexer may legitimately assign such a term on encountering a construction such as "Two days after the substance was ingested several symptoms developed" but it is rather difficult to build all such predictors (that the term TOXICITY should be assigned) into a computer program even if they could all be pre-identified.

Because of such problems, early attempts to assign terms automatically were not very successful, even when very small vocabularies of index terms were involved (for example, Borko and Bernick [1963]). In the past 25 years, however, better procedures have been developed, and it is now possible to perform assignment indexing with greater success.

A comparison of automatic assignment indexing with manual indexing is reported by Van der Meulen and Janssen (1977). In this case the human indexing used by INSPEC was compared with a scheme for automatic indexing that replaces expressions occurring in abstracts with "concept numbers" drawn from a stored "thesaurus." Although the authors claim that the automatic indexing produced results as good as those achieved by the human indexing, this conclusion was arrived at on the basis of results from only two searches.

One of the most sophisticated programs for automatic assignment indexing, in place at BIOSIS, is discussed by Vleduts-Stokolov (1987). Words appearing in the titles of journal articles are matched against a Semantic Vocabulary, consisting of about 15,000 biological terms, and these in turn are mapped to a vocabulary of 600 Concept Headings (i.e., relatively broad subject headings). Thus, Concept Headings can be assigned by computer on the basis of words/phrases occurring in titles. Vleduts-Stokolov reports that about 61 percent of the Concept Headings assigned by humans could be assigned by computer based on titles alone. If only primary and secondary assignments are considered (BIOSIS uses a three level term weighting scheme—primary, secondary, and tertiary), about 75 percent of the assignments could be performed automatically. In fact, however, the existing programs do not achieve such a high performance level. They achieve about 80-90 percent success in primary and secondary assignments (i.e., assign 80-90 percent of the 75 percent that could theoretically be assigned based on titles) and almost that level of success in all assignments (i.e., around 80 percent, or a little better, of the 61 percent of assignments that could occur based on titles only). In other words, some *underassignment* occurs; that is, the programs fail to assign some terms that should be assigned and would be assigned by humans. At the same time some *overassignment* also occurs: some terms are assigned that should not be. This is in the same range as the underassignment: between 80 and 90 percent of the term assignments made by computer are correct in the sense that human indexers would also have made them.

A somewhat similar approach, described by Trubkin (1979), was used to automatically index the abstracts in ABI/INFORM (a database in the field of business) for the period 1971-77. A "bridge vocabulary" of almost 19,000 terms was developed to lead from text expressions to the terms of a controlled vocabulary. Since a single occurrence of a term in a title or abstract was enough to cause a controlled term to be assigned, the automatic indexing procedures tended to assign more terms to an item than human indexing would (average of 16 per item as opposed to 8-12). Although Trubkin considers the automatic indexing procedures to have been successful, it is noteworthy that they were used only to index the back file of ABI/INFORM. Since 1978 the indexing has been performed by humans.

Again similar to the work at BIOSIS are the procedures for machine-aided indexing implemented by the American Petroleum Institute (Brenner et al., 1984). The goal is to develop methods that will allow the computer to assign the controlled terms of the API thesaurus on the basis of the text of abstracts. Brenner et al. report that an early version of the system assigned only about 40 percent of the terms that human indexers would assign and also assigned many unwanted terms. By learning from this experience, however, they were optimistic that the machine procedures could assign about 80 percent of the terms that should be assigned and that this would be accompanied by a significant reduction in unwanted assignments. In fact, considerable improvements have occurred since the first tests. Martinez et al. (1987) discuss the improvements and also describe the problems encountered in mapping from text expressions to thesaurus terms.

A more sophisticated method for mapping text expressions to descriptors has been developed at the Technische Hochschule Darmstadt. The most complete description, by Knorz (1983), is now somewhat out of date and needs to be supplemented by later references (e.g., Fuhr, 1989). The Darmstadt method is a weighted approach that estimates the probability that a descriptor should be assigned to an item given that a particular text expression occurs in title or abstract.

While automatic assignment indexing has improved considerably in the last 25 years, we have not yet reached a point at which terms from a large vocabulary (say 10,000 descriptors in a thesaurus) could be assigned completely automatically without human intervention.

In point of fact, automatic assignment indexing has little real interest today except in the production of printed indexes. Twenty five years ago it was of more general concern. Because it was then very costly to store and process large quantities of text by computer, any method that reduced the text to something shorter was justifiable. Now, of course, if the full text of an item exists in machine-readable form, or if an adequate abstract exists, it makes little sense to contemplate indexing it unless some form of printed index is to be generated from the database.

A special form of printed index is the "back of the book" index. Work on producing this type of index by computer also goes back more than 25 years. Artandi (1963) produced book indexes by computer in the field of chemistry. For each index entry ("expression term"), she derived a list of associated phrases ("detection terms") the occurrence of any one of which, in a page of text, would cause one of the index entries to be selected for that page. Artandi claimed that an index produced in this way was comparable in quality to a humanly prepared index but much more expensive. However, a large part of the cost was that of putting the text into machine-readable form. Since virtually all printing is now done from machine-readable input, the cost factors would no longer favor the human intellectual effort. Nevertheless, the problems of producing indexes to books automatically are more difficult than Artandi's work implies. Even in a restricted subject field a very large vocabulary of expression terms would be needed and, for each, the number of possible detection terms could also be very large. Moreover, both vocabularies would have to be kept up-to-date to reflect new developments and changing terminology in the field.

Of course, Artandi was attempting assignment indexing. Extracting phrases from the text of a book that are suitable for use as index entries is an easier proposition. Earl (1970) describes a method of producing book indexes by computer that involves the extraction of noun phrases. She claims that: "There is every indication that satisfactory back-of-the-book indexes could be produced automatically, with post-editing to delete superfluous terms." More recently, Salton (1989) describes how syntactic analysis procedures can be used to generate phrases suitable for use in indexes to books.

Most automatic indexing systems are not really "automatic," in the sense of substituting computers for humans, but are intended to assist the human indexer. A better term for them is "machine-aided." In general, two major approaches to machine-aided indexing can be identified:

1. The computer is used to provide various types of online display and prompts to aid the indexer. Errors made by the indexer (e.g., use of nonstandard terms or invalid main heading/subheading combinations) may be recognized in real time and the indexer immediately notified.
2. Computer programs are used to read text (perhaps only titles and/or abstracts) and to select index terms by extraction or assignment

procedures. The terms thus selected may be checked by a human indexer who may add further access points that the programs were unable to assign and/or delete terms erroneously assigned by them.

Procedures for machine-aided indexing were reviewed by Fangmeyer (1974) and procedures for machine-aided indexing and for fully automatic indexing by Sparck-Jones (1974) and Stevens (1970), but these reviews are now badly out of date.

Other Forms of Classification

As discussed in Chapter 2, indexing is a form of classification: the assignment of a term to an item places that item in a class along with others to which that term has been assigned. Other types of classification are possible when various data on bibliographic items exist in machine-readable form. It is possible to use automatic procedures to generate classes of documents or classes of terms.

In "conventional" retrieval systems, the conduct of a search is aided by the associations among terms made by a human mind, aided perhaps by relationships provided by a thesaurus or some other controlled vocabulary. In a more automatic approach to retrieval—for example, one based on the matching of natural language queries against the full text of items, against abstracts, or against document representations created by computer—it is also desirable to incorporate automatic procedures for developing relationships among terms in order to improve the effectiveness of searches. The obvious relationship to be exploited by computer is co-occurrence. The more frequently two terms occur together (in the text of documents or in lists of terms assigned to documents), the more likely it is that they deal with similar subject matter. To carry this to its logical conclusion, if term A never occurs without B and term B never occurs without A (which would be a very rare situation), the two terms are totally interdependent and would be completely interchangeable in searching. Besides the direct association (X and Y tend to occur together), indirect associations among terms can also be derived on the basis of co-occurrence data. Suppose, for example, that term D almost never occurs in a particular database without W and that term T also tends not to occur without W, yet D and T never co-occur in documents. One concludes that some relationship exists between D and T: they are related by the fact that each one co-occurs strongly with W. In all probability D and T are exactly synonymous in this context: synonyms tend not to occur with each other yet the terms they co-occur with will be very similar. In this hypothetical example D might be "delta," T "triangular," and W "wing."

In fact, the degree of association between two terms should be calculated not on simple frequency of co-occurrence but on the co-occurrence frequency related to the occurrence frequency of each term. For example, if terms A and B co-occur 20 times in a database, while A occurs 10,000 times, and B 50,000 times, the "association factor" between A and B will be a weak one. On the other hand, suppose A occurs 50 times, B occurs 25 times, and they co-occur 20 times. The association factor in this case will be great because B is very unlikely to occur without A and almost half the occurrences of A coincide with occurrences of B. Therefore, the relatedness (R) of two terms is usually defined by the simple equation

$$R = \frac{a \ and \ b}{a \ or \ b}$$

When R exceeds some pre-established threshold, the two terms are assumed to be related.

Co-occurrence data can be used in two ways within an "automatic" retrieval system: (1) a network of associations among terms can be developed and stored, or (2) discrete classes of terms can be identified and stored based on associations derived from the network. In the first case, the terms input by a searcher, in the form of a list or within a statement in phrase or sentence form, can be elaborated on automatically to produce an expanded list of search terms. In the method developed by Stiles (Stiles [1961], Salisbury & Stiles [1969]), the terms thus added to a search strategy are those closely related to all of the original search terms on the basis of co-occurrence frequency. For example, A, B, and C occur in the original strategy, and X and Y are added because these tend to co-occur with all three of the starting terms. The process could be continued further to bring in, say, term P because it is found to be associated with A, B, C, X, and Y. Items in the database can be given a numerical weight, reflecting the number of terms that match between item and search strategy and the strengths of association that exist among these terms (based on co-occurrence), and items can be retrieved in order of weight. It is thus possible that some items appearing high in the ranking may not contain any of the terms that the searcher began with.

In the second application, any word occurring in a search statement can be replaced by the class of words to which it belongs. This substitution can be automatic or under the searcher's control. The types of word classes that can be derived from co-occurrence data have been clearly identified by Salton and McGill (1983). In one type, referred to as a *clique*, all words in the group are associated with all other words in the group above some chosen threshold. In a *single-link* group, on the other hand, each word need be linked only to one other word in the group above the established threshold.

The classes formed by statistical procedures will be much less pure than those of a conventional thesaurus. A group of words that strongly co-occur may include genus/species, part/whole, and other relationships, as in the following example:

WING	AERODYNAMICS
AIRFOIL	FLOW
DELTA	
TAIL	
FLUTTER	

The purity of the class is not the main issue. What is important is whether the class is potentially useful in retrieval. For example, is it likely that the hypothetical class of words identified above, if automatically substituted for any one of its members, would improve search results? Depending on the particular query, it seems likely that this type of substitution might improve recall. At the same time, it might cause a severe decline in precision, especially if the class (as in the example) is a very heterogeneous ensemble of terms.

Salton and McGill (1983) give examples of thesaurus entries automatically derived from a document collection in engineering (Exhibit 94). With such a thesaurus, the query "cryogenic properties of x" could be expanded to "x in relation to concept 415." As a result, items on the superconductivity (i.e., containing the stem "superconduct") of x might be retrieved.

This discussion has so far considered only methods by which classes of terms may be formed on the basis of the documents in which they occur. The data that permit this classification are derived from a matrix showing which terms occur in which documents (term/document matrix). It is clear that the reverse operation can also be performed through use of these data. That is, classes of documents can be formed on the basis of the terms they contain. Salton (1975) and Salton and McGill (1983) have identified various types of such classes:

1. The clique

in which all the items *A-E* are strongly connected with each other.

2. The star

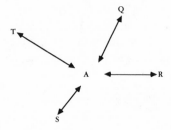

in which a class *AQRST* is defined by the fact that *Q, R, S,* and *T* are all closely linked with *A* in some way.

3. The string

A <—> B <—> C <—> D <—> E

in which *B* is closely connected with *A, C* with *B,* and so on up to *E,* which is not closely connected to any other item except *D.*

4. The clump

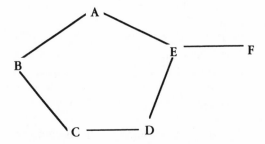

which can be formed on the basis of any of several criteria. In general, however, each member is associated with the other members of the group at a value above some given threshold.

Stars, strings, and clumps are all examples of single-link groups as defined earlier.

Classes of documents can also be formed on the basis of nonterminological characteristics, especially various forms of citation linkage. The possibilities are illustrated in Exhibit 95. Here *X, Y,* and *Z* are recently published documents that cite the earlier items *A, B,* and *C.* A very simple class would consist of a document and the later ones that cite it; e.g., *A, X,* and *Y.* Since *X* and *Y* both cite *A,* a good possibility exists that all three have some subject matter in common. This, of course, is the basis of citation indexing. By entering a citation index under *A* the searcher can find *X* and *Y,* the later items that cite *A.* If *A* is an item highly relevant to the searcher's current interests, X and Y may also be relevant. If so, the searcher has met with some success without the use of conventional subject indexing.

408	DISLOCATION	413	CAPACITANCE
	JUNCTION		IMPEDANCE-MATCHING
	MINORITY-CARRIER		IMPEDANCE
	N-P-N		INDUCTANCE
	P-N-P		MUTUAL-IMPEDANCE
	POINT-CONTACT		MUTUAL-INDUCTANCE
	RECOMBINE		MUTUAL
	TRANSITION		NEGATIVE-RESISTANCE
	UNIJUNCTION		POSITIVE-GAP
409	BLAST-COOLED		REACTANCE
	HEAT-FLOW		RESIST
	HEAT-TRANSFER		SELF-IMPEDANCE
410	ANNEAL		SELF-INDUCTANCE
	STRAIN		SELF
411	COERCIVE	414	ANTENNA
	DEMAGNETIZE		KLYSTRON
	FLUX-LEAKAGE		PULSES-PER—BEAM
	HYSTERESIS		RECEIVER
	INDUCT		SIGNAL-TO-RECEIVER
	INSENSITIVE		TRANSMITTER
	MAGNETORESISTANCE		WAVEGUIDE
	SQUARE-LOOP	415	CRYOGENIC
	THRESHOLD		CRYOTRON
412	LONGITUDINAL		PERSISTENT-CURRENT
	TRANSVERSE		SUPERCONDUCT
			SUPER-CONDUCT
		416	RELAY

Exhibit 94
Example of thesaurus entries derived by automatic methods
Reprinted from Salton and McGill, *Introduction to Modern Information Retrieval*, 1983, by permission of McGraw-Hill Publishing Company

Other classes can be identified in the simple relationships shown in Exhibit 95. For example, X and Y can be considered to form a class because they both cite A and B. This is the principle of *bibliographic coupling* (Kessler, 1962, 1963, 1965). The more bibliographic references two (or more) items have in common, the more strongly they are coupled. X and Y are strongly coupled because they both cite A, B, and C. Z is less strongly coupled to *X* and *Y* because it has only two references in common with these items. Another way of saying this is that *X* and *Y* form a strong class (strength of 3), while *X* and *Z* and *Y* and *Z* are weaker classes (strength of 2). It is clear that the more alike are the lists of references included in two publications the more likely they are to deal with the same subject. Thus, if *Q* cites *F, G, H,* and *I* only, and paper *R* also cites only these four items, *Q* and *R* almost certainly deal with the same subject. If the two papers have these four references in common but each includes, say, ten references that the other does not include, there is less chance that *Q* and *R* deal with the same subject although the relationship between *Q* and *R* can still be considered fairly close.

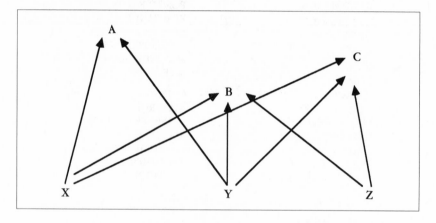

Exhibit 95
Citation/reference linkages

A final relationship depicted in Exhibit 95 is that of *co-citation* (Small, 1973). Items *A, B,* and *C* can be considered to form a class because they are cited together (co-cited) by *X* and *Y.* As with bibliographic coupling, co-citation can occur with varying strength. In Exhibit 95, items *A, B,* and *C* are weakly related since only two items cite them together. The more items that co-cite them the more strongly related they are assumed to be.

Classes formed on the basis of citation linkages have some advantages over classes formed through conventional subject indexing. Most obviously, they are independent of language and changing terminology. The name of a disease may change more than once over the course of time but this is no impediment to performing a search on this disease in a citation index, especially if the first paper to identify the disease is known to the searcher and is still frequently cited. The principle of bibliographic coupling, of course, can be used to link papers in completely different languages; for example, identifying papers in, say, Russian and Chinese that are strongly coupled to an English language paper. Likewise, a class of co-cited papers could include items in several languages. More importantly, of course, the classes formed by co-citation change with time as new interrelationships among research results are seen by later investigators. Returning to Exhibit 95, the authors of X and Y see some relationship among the items A, B, and C, but this relationship may have remained unobserved for very many years. A, B, and C form a class of items for the first time in, say, 1989 because it was in 1989 that X and Y were both published, but A may have been published in the 1930s, C in the 1950s, and B in the 1970s.

Studies that have compared the classes formed by conventional subject indexing with those formed on the basis of citation linkages can be traced back for 25 years (Kessler, 1965) and they still continue to appear (e.g., Pao [1988]; Pao and Worthen [1989]). A search based on citation linkages (direct citation, bibliographic coupling, or co-citation) may well uncover useful items not found through conventional subject searches in printed indexes or online databases, but the conventional approach is also likely to find useful items that the citation links fail to disclose. The two approaches are complementary rather than competitive.

Kwok (1985a, 1985b) refers to the fact that reference/citation linkages can be used in information retrieval to form an "augmented collection" of retrieved items. That is, when a search strategy is applied to a database in the normal way, using text words or controlled terms, the set of items thus retrieved can be augmented by those items linked to them through bibliographic citations. He suggests that the set of terms associated with the items originally retrieved might be augmented by the addition of terms drawn from the items that they cite. These new terms could be index terms assigned to the cited items or they could be text expressions drawn from abstracts or titles. He suggests that augmentation by drawing terms from the titles of cited items is most practicable. Salton and Zhang (1986) have tested the value of augmenting the set of terms associated with retrieved items by adding title words drawn from "bibliographically related" items. Title words were drawn from (a) items cited by the retrieved items, (b) items citing the retrieved items, and (c) co-cited items. They conclude that, while many "useful" content words can be extracted in this way, many terms of doubtful value will also be extracted, and that the procedure is not sufficiently reliable to warrant inclusion in operating retrieval systems.

Nevertheless, in 1990 this principle was adopted by the Institute for Scientific Information for the searching of *Current Contents* on diskette (Key Words Plus).

Automatic Abstracting

If computers can be programmed to select terms from documents according to frequency criteria, they can also be programmed to select sentences from documents. This is the basis of what is usually called "automatic abstracting" although it is more accurately referred to as "automatic extracting." Luhn (1958), the originator of the operation, observed the following procedures:

1. A stoplist eliminates all the nonsubstantive words from further processing.
2. Occurrences of all remaining words are counted and the words ranked by frequency of occurrence (in place of words, roots [stems] can be used).
3. All words occurring more than x times are defined as "high frequency" or "significant" words.
4. Sentences containing concentrations of these high frequency words are located. Two words are considered related within a sentence if there are no more than four intervening words.
5. A "significance factor" for each sentence is calculated, as follows:
   a) the number of "clusters" in the sentence is determined (a cluster is the longest group of words bounded by significant words in which the significant words are not separated by more than four intervening words);
   b) the number of significant words in the cluster is determined and the square of this number is divided by the total number of words within the cluster;
   c) the significance factor for the sentence can be defined either as the value of the highest cluster or the sum of the values of all the clusters in the sentence.

This sounds more complicated than it is in practice and is easily explained through an example. Consider the sentence

A B C D* E F* G* H I J* K L M N O P Q R

where each letter represents a word and the asterisked words are those judged "significant." The cluster formed by the words *D-J* contains four significant words so the significance factor for the cluster is $4^2/7$ or 2.3. This is also the significance factor for the sentence since it contains only one cluster.

According to Luhn's procedures, the sentences having the highest significance factors are selected and printed out, in the sequence in which they occur in the text, to form the "abstract." A cutoff point can be established to control the number of sentences selected. This can be based on a fixed number of sentences or on the number of sentences needed to equal a certain percentage of the total document text. Exhibit 96 is an example of an "auto-abstract" produced by Luhn's procedures.

When dealing with very long documents it may be desirable to have the programs select and print out significant sentences for each section of the publication. Since abstracts should emphasize the particular significance of an item to the organization for which the abstract is prepared, an additional weighting could be given to a certain category or list of words to ensure that sentences containing one or more occurrences of these words will be selected for inclusion in the abstract.

Source: The Scientific American, Vol. 196, No. 2, 86-94, February, 1957

Title: Messengers of the Nervous System

Author: Amodeo S. Marrazzi

Editor's Sub-heading: The internal communication of the body is mediated by chemicals as well as by nerve impulses. Study of their interaction has developed important leads to the understanding and therapy of mental illness.

Auto-Abstract*

It seems reasonable to credit the single-celled organisms also with a system of chemical communication by diffusion of stimulating substances through the cell, and these correspond to the chemical messengers (e.g., hormones) that carry stimuli from cell to cell in the more complex organisms. (7.0)†

Finally, in the vertebrate animals there are special glands (e.g., the adrenals) for producing chemical messengers, and the nervous and chemical communication systems are intertwined: for instance, release of adrenalin by the adrenal gland is subject to control both by nerve impulses and by chemicals brought to the gland by the blood. (6.4)

The experiments clearly demonstrated that acetylcholine (and related substances) and adrenalin (and its relatives) exert opposing actions which maintain a balanced regulation of the transmission of nerve impulses. (6.3)

It is reasonable to suppose that the tranquilizing drugs counteract the inhibitory effect of excessive adrenalin or serotonin or some related inhibitor in the human nervous system. (7.3)

*Sentences selected by means of statistical analysis as having a degree of significance of 6 and over.
†Significance factor is given at the end of each sentence.

Exhibit 96
Example of a Luhn auto-abstract (Luhn 1958)
Copyright © 1958 by International Business Machines Incorporated;
reprinted with permission

It is clear that an abstract formed in this way will not look much like a humanly prepared abstract. Since some sentences may come from the first paragraph, some from the last, and several others perhaps from the middle of the work, the extract may seem quite disconnected. In point of fact, this is not terribly important as long as the chosen sentences collectively give an accurate picture of what the document deals with. Some investigators, however, disagree with this and insist that automatically-derived extracts should have more continuity (Rush et al., 1971, Mathis et al., 1973).

While Luhn (1959) and Oswald et al. (1959) used word or phrase frequency in the selection of sentences, other investigators have proposed or used alternative criteria. Edmundson (1969) identified four possible methods:

1. *Key method.* This was similar to the word frequency criterion used by Luhn. Sentences are given a weight that is the sum of the weights of the component words.
2. *Cue method.* The presence of certain words in a sentence signals the fact that it is likely to be one that is a good indicator of content. A "cue dictionary" includes a list of words that receive a positive weight and a list of words with a negative weight. The significance value of a sentence is the sum of the weights of the component words.
3. *Title method.* The assumption underlying this method is that words occurring in titles and subheads are good indicators of content. Sentences are given a significance value based on the number of title and subhead words they contain.
4. *Location method.* In this method weights are given to sentences on the basis of where they appear in a document. Sentences appearing in certain sections (first and last sentences of paragraphs, first and last paragraphs, text preceded by headings such as Introduction or Conclusions) are assumed to be more indicative of content than others.

It was discovered that the cue, title, and location methods were more likely to agree on sentences to be selected than any combination of methods involving the key procedure, leading Edmundson to conclude that the key procedure, based on frequency criteria only, was inferior to the other methods.

Rush et al. (1971) make the point that any useful approach to extracting should include criteria for the rejection of sentences as well as their selection. Their method for evaluating sentences takes into account "contextual influence"—a word or word string, and its surrounding context, offers clues as to whether a sentence should be accepted or rejected. The extracting method they describe is based on the matching of text against a Word Control List (WCL) which includes a list of expressions that, if present in a sentence, would cause it to be rejected and a much smaller list of expressions that would cause it to be selected. Rejection expressions include indicators that the sentence deals with background material rather than the objectives, methods, and results of the present work. Selection expressions are those (such as "this paper," "this study," or "present work") that will almost always signify that the sentence deals with the main thrust of the article. Sentences containing significant words from the title of the item may also be selected. Frequency criteria are not overlooked, but they are used only to modify the weights associated with the positive and negative cues in the WCL. The extracting methods developed by Rush et al. offered several advances over earlier procedures, including the ability to modify extracted sentences (e.g., by deleting parenthetical expressions).

Another feature was "intersentence reference": when a sentence was selected for inclusion in an extract, it was tested to determine if its meaning was dependent on immediately preceding sentences (e.g., because it includes such expressions as "hence" or "for this reason"). If the meaning was so dependent, the preceding sentences, up to a maximum of three, were included in the abstract even if they did not satisfy other acceptance criteria. This approach to extracting, then, has the potential for creating extracts that have better continuity than those derived by less sophisticated procedures. An example of an extract produced by the Rush et al. procedures (the ADAM automatic abstracting system) is given in Exhibit 97.

THE CLAVICHORD AND HOW TO PLAY IT. #MARGERY HALFORD, CLAVIER 9(2), 36-41 (1970).# ESSENTIALLY, THE CLAVICHORD IS A SHALLOW RECTANGULAR BOX WHOSE FRAGILE STRINGS, UNDER LIGHT TENSION, ARE STRUNG HORIZONTALLY FROM A SINGLE BRIDGE OVER A THIN SOUNDBOARD. THE KEYS ARE SIMPLE LEVERS WITH A BRASS BLADE CALLED A TANGENT MOUNTED VERTICALLY ON THE FAR END. THE SOUND PRODUCED IS EXTRAORDINARILY RICH IN OVERTONES. THE TONE OF THE CLAVICHORD DOES NOT EXIST READY-MADE AS IT DOES ON THE PIANO AND HARPSICHORD; IT IS FORMED AND SHAPED BY THE FINGER, AS ON A BOWED STRINGED INSTRUMENT, WITH THE RESULT BEING A GENUINE, DIRECT, LIVING "FEEL OF THE STRINGS". AS LONG AS HIS FINGER REMAINS IN CONTACT WITH THE KEY, THE PLAYER RETAINS CONTROL OF THE SOUND. THE CLAVICHORD IS THE LEAST MECHANIZED AND THE MOST RESPONSIVE OF ALL KEYBOARD INSTRUMENTS IN THAT IT MEETS THE PLAYER HALFWAY IN ITS INSTANT AND FAITHFUL TRANSMISSION OF HIS SLIGHTEST MUSICAL INTENTIONS. EMBELLISHMENTS CAN BE PLAYED CRISPLY AND BRILLIANTLY. SHAKES, SNAPS, APPOGGIATURAS, TRILLS, TURNS, MORDENTS, AND SLIDES—ALL SO CHARACTERISTIC OF THE PERIOD WHEN THE CLAVICHORD ENJOYED ITS GREATEST POPULARITY—ARE IDEALLY SUITED TO THE INSTRUMENT'S EXQUISITE CLARITY AND RICHNESS OF TONE. THE ACTION IS SHALLOW AND VIRTUALLY WEIGHTLESS. IT IS A PHENOMENON OF THE DOUBLE—ENDED LEVER THAT THE TONE PRODUCED BY A STRIKING FORCE WILL SOUND BETTER, SWEETER, AND RICHER AT MAXIMUM LEVER LENGTH. FOR THIS REASON, THE KEYS OF THE CLAVICHORD ARE PLAYED AS NEAR TO THE FRONT EDGES AS POSSIBLE. EXCEPT FOR THE PLAYING OF OCTAVES, THE THUMB IS NEVER USED ON A RAISED KEY; DISPLAY PIECES OF A VIRTUOSO CHARACTER ARE GENERALLY UNSUITED TO THE PERSONAL QUALITIES OF THE CLAVICHORD. CRAMER SAYS THAT THE ESPECIALLY REMARKABLE FEATURES OF CLAVICHORD MUSIC ARE FLUIDITY, SUSTAINED MELODY DIFFUSED WITH EVER-VARYING LIGHT AND SHADOW, THE USE OF CERTAIN MUSICAL SHADING AND ALMOST COMPLETE ABSTINENCE FROM PASSAGES WITH ARPEGGIOS, LEAPS, AND BROKEN CHORDS;

Exhibit 97
Example of an extract produced by the ADAM automatic abstracting system
Reproduced from Mathis (1972) by permission of the Department of Computer and Information Science, Ohio State University

Mathis et al. (1973) introduce improvements on the extracting methods described by Rush et al. The improvements relate primarily to the sentence modification and intersentence reference features of the earlier procedures and are designed to produce representations that are more "readable."

Earl (1970) performed experiments to determine whether or not significant sentences could be identified by syntactic analysis. The assumption was that sentences having certain syntactic structures might be more indicative of content than others. The results were unpromising, due largely to the very great number of sentence types that could be identified. A more promising procedure involved the use of both syntactic and statistical criteria: noun phrases in a text are identified, the substantive words in the phrases are identified, word counts are made, and sentences are selected on the basis of the number of high frequency words they contain.

Paice (1981) has described automatic extracting procedures based on the identification of sentences likely to be good indicators of what a document is about (e.g., containing such expressions as "the principal aim," or "a method is described").

Fum et al. (1982) have described an approach to automatic abstracting in which, they claim, parsing and weighting procedures identify the most important information conveyed in a text, eliminate nonessential elements, and restructure the remainder into a condensed and meaningful summary. They give the example of the sentence.

> The need to generate enormous additional amounts of electric power while at the same time protecting the environment is one of the major social and technological problems that our society must solve in the next (sic!) future

being reduced to

> The society must solve in the future the problem of the need to generate power while protecting the environment.

While this is impressive at the sentence level, they fail to demonstrate that the procedures they describe will produce a meaningful and useful summarization of an entire article.

Hahn and Reimer (1984) describe work proceeding on the development of an "expert system" approach to text condensation based on the use of a frame knowledge base applied to the parsing of text. They prefer the term *text condensation* to *abstracting* because the methods can, in principle, be used to generate condensations at various levels of length and detail.

Of course, the more formal and consistent the texts of documents, the more successful extracting procedures are likely to be. For example, Borkowski and Martin (1975) claim better than 90 percent success in the automatic extraction of case summaries and case dispositions from the text of legal decisons.

"Automatic" Retrieval Operations

Since indexing and abstracting are the central topics of discussion in this book, automatic indexing and automatic abstracting are the foci of attention in this chapter. Nevertheless, certain other automatic approaches to information retrieval are sufficiently related to warrant some consideration here, if only briefly.

Over the years a major objective of several investigators has been the development of procedures that would allow a request phrased as natural language text to be matched against the text of documents—full text, partial text, or some form of representation. This can be regarded as a kind of pattern matching: the texts in the database can be given some type of score, reflecting the degree to which they match the text of a request, thus allowing them to be presented to the searcher in the form of a ranked output.

Various types and levels of match are possible. For example, consider the request

> Pathology, physiology, radiography and therapy of radiation pneumonitis
> or radiation pulmonary fibrosis

and assume that the database consists of the text of abstracts. The simplest method of scoring a match would be one that merely takes into account how many words of the request occur in an abstract. Thus an abstract might receive a high score if it contained the words "pathology," "physiology," "radiography," "radiation," and "therapy" (i.e., five of the eight significant word occurrences of the request) although, clearly, it is unlikely to be relevant since it contains none of the words of the request that are most discriminating.

Many refinements of this crude level of matching are possible. One is to give each word a score that reflects the number of times it appears in the database as a whole. Thus, "fibrosis" and "pneumonitis" might receive quite high scores since they are likely to be less common in a medical database than the other, more general, terms of the request. Consequently, an abstract that contains these two words could receive a high score, even if none of the other request words are present.

The number of occurrences of a word in a request and abstract could also be taken into account in the ranking of documents. By this criterion, an abstract that contains the word *radiation* several times is likely to receive a high score because this word is the only one occurring more than once in the request. In the case of a database containing the full text of items, the length of the items needs to be taken into account. Otherwise very long documents will always have a proportionally greater probability of being retrieved.

Matching can be based on word roots rather than complete words. By this criterion an abstract that includes the words *radiating* and *radiates*, as well as *radiation*, might get a high score in relation to the sample request.

If a machine-generated thesaurus exists in the system it would be possible to substitute for one or more of the request words the thesaurus group (see Exhibit 94) to which that word belongs. If such a substitution occurred for the request words *radiation* and *pulmonary*, the weights of abstracts containing the words *lung* and *ray* might increase considerably because *lung* and *pulmonary* should belong in the same thesaurus group (along, perhaps, with the root *pneum*), as should *radiography, radiation,* and *ray.*

Of course, matching will be more precise if based on phrases rather than single words, so the capability of searching on phrases should definitely exist in any system that matches the text of a request against the text of documents. Abstracts containing the phrase "radiation pneumonitis" should receive a high score in relation to the hypothetical request, as should those containing "radiation pulmonary fibrosis." Abstracts containing the phrase "pulmonary fibrosis" might also receive a high score although they are less likely to be relevant unless the "radiation" aspect is also present.

From this discussion it is obvious that different criteria can be used in assigning a score to a piece of text to reflect the degree to which it matches the text of a request, and that the score assigned can be based on more than one of the criteria discussed (e.g., it could take into account the number of word or phrase matches as well as the rate of occurrence of these words or phrases in the database as a whole). Ideally, then, an "automatic" system should incorporate several possible matching criteria and should allow the user to choose among them.

The most sophisticated system of this general type is the SMART system of Salton, which has been developed and refined over a period of more than 25 years. A considerable literature on SMART exists but a good summary can be found in Salton and McGill (1983). SMART is designed to assign numerical weights to items, to reflect the extent to which they match request statements, and to present these items to the user in a ranked order, those with highest weights displayed first. SMART incorporates several different matching criteria, including the weighting of terms to reflect their rate of occurrence in a database, phrase matching, and matching on word roots. It also allows for the incorporation of a thesaurus that is arrived at by a combination of computer and human processing. Another essential element in SMART is "relevance feedback." If, in a preliminary output, the user can indicate which items are relevant and which irrelevant, the system can recalculate the weight of the items in the database. This is done by reducing the weights associated with the characteristics of the nonrelevant items and increasing the weights of the characteristics associated with the relevant ones. Recently Salton (1989) has described how the syntactic analysis of the text of book chapters, followed by phrase generation procedures, can be used to generate back-of-the-book indexes.

While SMART is an "experimental" system in the sense that it is not in regular use by any major information center, some "operational" systems do allow a user to enter a request in the form of a textual statement. A notable example is the CITE system developed by Doszkocs (1983), which also incorporates relevance feedback. CITE (Computerized Information Transfer in English) has been used as a natural-language interface to the National Library of Medicine's MEDLINE and CATLINE databases. CITE can operate on a database of records consisting of index terms (which is what MEDLINE is) or on one involving free text (e.g., abstracts). The system can stem words automatically (i.e., reduce words to their root forms), assign weights to query terms automatically (the weights reflect the rarity of the term—terms that occur infrequently in the database get the highest weight) and display possible terms for the user's approval or rejection. As in SMART, items in the database are given a numerical score reflecting the degree to which they match the request statement.

In CITE, terms related to those used in a query are identified only when the query has been processed against the database. The raw material worked with is the set of words (terms) associated with the documents retrieved. Thus, in items retrieved on terms *A, B,* and *C,* terms *R* and *T* may also occur frequently and may be useful in the expansion of the search. Terms *R* and *T* are not considered significant, however, unless they occur in the retrieved set more frequently than expected. Thus, frequency of occurrence of a term in the database as a whole is also taken into account. For example, a library science database may yield 85 abstracts on the simple query "collection evaluation" (which is interpreted as "collection" *and* "evaluation"). The word "library" occurs in 59 of these but is not considered significant because its rate of occurrence in the retrieved set (59/85) does not exceed its occurrence rate in the database as a whole. On the other hand, the word "delivery" might be judged to be significantly associated with "collection" and "evaluation"—even though it occurs in only 8 of the 85 abstracts, its rate of occurrence (8/85) greatly exceeds its rate of occurrence in the database as a whole.

A major advantage of the Doszkocs approach is that it does not require the a priori calculation of term associations, a daunting proposition for a very large database. The ability to derive useful term associations a posteriori (after the query has been processed against the database), which requires much less machine processing, makes automatic search optimization procedures viable within very large operating information systems.

Systems based on natural language searching and the ranking of retrieved items are now commercially available. A notable example is Personal Librarian®, one application of which has recently been described by Seloff (1990).

An interesting natural language interface, described by Clemencin (1988), allows a subscriber to query the "yellow pages" in France's online telephone directory using problem statements such as "I would like to repair an old camera," "I want to find a private chauffeur," "My windshield wipers are broken," or "I wrenched my ankle." In response to such a statement the interface will retrieve details on relevant businesses or professionals in the directory (approximately 6 million entries under 2,500 headings).

A somewhat different approach is used in the system known as Grateful Med (Snow et al., 1986; Bonham & Nelson, 1988). A formatted online display prompts the user into the formulation of a search strategy. The system will also suggest additional search terms to the user (derived from relevant items already retrieved); a help screen offers suggestions for modifying a search strategy when this has failed to retrieve any items.

Although much progress has been made in the last several years in the processing of natural language by computer, it must be recognized that computer "understanding" of text is still very limited. That is, morphologic, syntactic, and semantic aids can be built to help a computer to interpret text, but this is still far removed from what occurs when a human reads a text and understands what the author means.

Artificial Intelligence

It is now very fashionable in the field of information retrieval to use the term *artificial intelligence* to refer to any operation in which computers undertake tasks previously performed by humans. Frequently the term is completely misused because no intelligence of any kind is exhibited in the operations referred to (e.g., the computer programs do not learn from mistakes made and modify the procedures used accordingly). In fact, some people use the term to refer to very simple word frequency approaches as implemented by Luhn some 30 years ago. It is doubtful that any of the procedures now being applied to information retrieval activities can legitimately be considered as involving artificial intelligence.

Kuhlen (1984) suggests that we do not know enough about the intellectual processes involved in abstracting (and, by analogy, indexing) to develop programs whereby these activities could be simulated by computer:

> Abstracting...is an intellectual art and as such not directly transferable to automatic procedures. Cognitive psychology and artificial intelligence have, so far, not provided us with sufficient knowledge about the processes really going on in abstracters' minds when they understand texts and condense them. Thus the direct imitation of an intellectual procedure such as abstracting seems to be out of reach. (Page 98)

Other terms in vogue, and frequently used in association with *artificial intelligence,* are *expert system* or *knowledge-based system.* These terms are more acceptable since they imply the development of a database reflecting human knowledge or experience in some area. A prime example is a system designed for medical diagnosis in which the knowledge base is a compilation of the signs and symptoms that physicians have learned to associate with various disease states. In indexing it is also possible to develop a knowledge base reflecting indexing rules and certain decisions previously made by human indexers. Consequently, a lot of experimentation is now proceeding toward the development of interactive, knowledge-based indexing systems. One of these, known as MedIndEx, being developed for the National Library of Medicine, is designed to interact with MEDLINE indexers by prompting them to enter *MeSH (Medical Subject Headings)* terms into indexing "frames" displayed online. In response to subject headings entered by an indexer, the system is able to suggest other headings or subheadings that may be applicable (see Humphrey & Miller, 1987; Humphrey & Kapoor, 1988; Humphrey & Chien, 1990). Certain other machine-aided indexing systems also claim to be "rule-based expert systems" (e.g., Martinez et al., 1987) although they are based only on the matching of the text of a document with some database of text fragments that lead to terms in a thesaurus or other form of controlled vocabulary. It is doubtful that systems of this kind can be regarded as true expert systems.

An example of an expert system approach to text condensation (abstracting and other forms of summarization), based on "heuristic text parsing," is described by Hahn and Reimer (1984).

15

THE FUTURE OF INDEXING AND ABSTRACTING SERVICES *

BEFORE LOOKING FORWARD to possible future developments affecting indexing and abstracting services, it makes sense to look backwards at some of the events that have affected these services during the past 40 years. The secondary services cannot be considered in isolation but must be viewed in conjunction with other institutions that they affect and are affected by. The most obvious interactions are those with the primary literature and with libraries.

Since the end of World War II, the secondary services have been the object of both negative and positive influences. On the negative side, rapid growth of the primary literature plus escalating costs on all fronts—human intellectual processing, paper, printing, mailing—have meant that the cost to the subscriber of these services has increased at rates that are completely out of line with inflation in the economy as a whole. The subscription costs of some indexing and abstracting services have jumped as much as 850 percent in a decade, which makes price increases in energy and health care seem moderate. An obvious concomitant of this is that, unless the income of subscribers increases at approximately the same pace, the accessibility of these services is reduced. Personal income has not grown at anything like these rates, and even the budgets of large academic libraries—which may double in about a seven-year period—are unable to accommodate the rapidly increasing costs of the primary as well as the secondary literature.

It seems reasonable to assume that some, at least, of the secondary services were originally conceived as going directly to individual subscribers. But most priced themselves out of the individual subscriber market some years ago and became accessible only through institutions. Later, some priced themselves out of the reach of the smaller institutions or out of the reach of institutions to which a particular service was of less than central relevance. Moreover, even the large institutions have found it

---

*This chapter is an update of a paper co-authored with Julie M. Neway that appeared in the *Journal of the American Society for Information Science,* May 1982, pp. 183-189. Copyright © 1982 by John Wiley & Sons Inc. Reproduced by permission of John Wiley & Sons Inc.

necessary to reduce the number of their subscriptions. Thus, a large academic library that may once have had four or five subscriptions to some service, distributed among several departmental collections, may now find itself with one or two.

It is clear that the disappearance of the individual subscriber, coupled with fewer copies within the library community, reduces the accessibility of these important resources. Moreover, increased resource sharing among libraries, which serves to compensate for reduced numbers of subscriptions to primary journals, has no equivalent value as far as the secondary literature is concerned. This literature is intended primarily to serve current awareness and literature searching needs, needs that are difficult, if not impossible, to satisfy if a copy of the publication is not immediately accessible.

Computer Processing

The major positive force affecting abstracting and indexing (A&I) services has obviously been the use of computer technology to generate machine-readable databases from which printed publications could be produced through a photocomposition interface. While this development may have kept the cost of the printed product from rising even more rapidly than it has, it has produced an even greater benefit: the ability to use the same database to provide other information services—group and personalized SDI and retrospective searching on demand—and to generate more specialized publications (as, for example, the recurring bibliography series of the National Library of Medicine).

The existence of machine-readable databases, coupled with the ability to access these resources online, has created a virtual revolution in information services. Online systems have offered several dramatic benefits to libraries. First and foremost, they have allowed libraries that formerly had no strong traditions in literature searching to offer literature searching services of a high quality. Academic libraries, hospital libraries, small libraries in general, and, more recently, public libraries have all benefited in this way. Even industrial libraries, which have always tended to offer strength in literature searching, have been able to improve their productivity very markedly. For example, Hawkins (1980), referring to the Bell Laboratories Network, has mentioned that three information scientists performed 100 searches a year in a predominantly manual search mode in 1972 and three information scientists performed over 1500 online searches in the year 1979.

One can also assume that online access to databases significantly improves the quality of literature searching since these databases tend to provide many more access points, searches of greater complexity (e.g., involving large numbers of terms) are possible, and much greater flexibility in search approaches is provided (e.g., ability to search on words in titles or abstracts, to use truncations, or to use access points that printed tools are unlikely to provide). Moreover, online searching has been shown to be more cost effective than the use of printed tools for literature searching (Elchesen, 1978; Lancaster, 1981).

The ability to access databases online has had other benefits and impacts. First and foremost, it makes a much wider range of information resources available to most libraries. Thus, a small industrial library that little more than a decade ago subscribed to only four or five secondary services, and had to rely almost entirely on these to support literature searching activities, now finds itself with several hundred databases readily accessible. To subscribe to all of these in printed form (assuming all existed in this form) would be out of the question. In the online environment, a database needed once a year is no less accessible than one needed once a week. This is quite untrue of the print-on-paper situation, where subscription to a publication (and, therefore, access to it) can only be justified if a reasonable volume of use can be anticipated.

Online access, in fact, completely changes the economics of information services. In the print-on-paper environment, the only way to make a publication readily accessible is to subscribe to it. A library subscription to a secondary service buys one thing only: access to that service. The subscription cost, plus perhaps as much as an additional 15-20 percent for handling and storing the publication, is consumed even if the item is never used. In other words, libraries can achieve convenient access only through an investment in ownership.

In the online situation, however, the investment is made in equipment capable of providing access to a wide variety of information sources. Cost of the access itself is only incurred when the information need arises. The obvious result of this is that many librarians have come to recognize that they should be more concerned with *access* than with *ownership.*

One important effect of the decline in significance of ownership is the process of increasing "leveling" as far as geographic location is concerned. It is becoming less and less necessary to think of a great research library in terms of a large collection of resources in print-on-paper form. Consequently, in ability to access information resources, it is beginning to matter less and less where a researcher happens to be located or with what institution he or she is affiliated. Electronic technology leads to a kind of "geographic democratization" in access to information. While this process is now most evident in North America and in Western Europe, the spread of value-added telecommunications networks is making the phenomenon increasingly international.

The growth of machine-readable databases, both bibliographic and nonbibliographic, as well as the increasing use of these resources, has been reported elsewhere and need not be repeated here. For many of the databases accessible online there exist print-on-paper publications that are more or less directly equivalent. Such publications can be referred to as dual-mode publications since they are available in both forms. In some cases, however, a resource exists only in machine-readable form. Such resources, which include A&I services as well as files of physical, chemical, and other types of data, can be considered as early forms of true electronic publications. They are examples of "reference books" that happened to emerge in the age of electronics rather than the age of paper. In some cases, at least, it is extremely unlikely that the publication would ever have appeared if print on paper were the only distribution option available.

Electronic technology, then, improves access to information resources in several ways: by making the dual-mode publications more accessible, by allowing the production of new services that might not otherwise exist, and by providing a much greater level of access to the individual items recorded in a database. In fact, as important information resources have become less and less accessible in print-on-paper form, they have become more and more accessible in electronic form. At the same time, over the past 20 years, the cost of making these resources accessible in electronic form has declined rapidly while the cost of making them accessible as print on paper has increased rapidly.

More recently, of course, many databases have become available in CD-ROM form. Databases in this form resemble online databases in that they can be searched by computer, accessed through a terminal, and interrogated by means of Boolean logic. On the other hand, they resemble paper databases in that they are *distributed* rather than made *accessible* through some network. At present it probably makes sense for a library to acquire on CD-ROM a database used very frequently but not those used less often.

The Migration from Print on Paper

It is well known that the number of subscribers to many secondary services in paper form is declining while use of these services in online or CD-ROM form is increasing at a rapid rate. In the case of the *Engineering Index,* for example, Creps (1979) reported that revenue from sales of printed products was still growing in 1979, but very slowly, while revenue from sales of magnetic tapes was growing "erratically." Online royalty income was said to be "growing rapidly." Use of the database online was increasing at the rate of about 23 percent per year. In the same year, *Chemical Abstracts* reported that printed products still accounted for 80 percent of revenue. The number of subscribers to the printed service was declining but revenue from print on paper was increasing at 10 percent a year, revenue from online use charges was growing at 25 percent a year (about $1.8 million in online revenue in 1979).

Neufeld (1982), executive director of the National Federation of Abstracting and Information Services, reported that, in 1982, some 50-85 percent of revenues of major secondary services was still coming from sales of printed products. Revenues from print had not fallen because prices had been raised to compensate for the declining number of subscribers.

Williams (1981, 1982), after analyzing 14 years of financial data from one major database producer, comes to different conclusions. She points out that such an organization faces a major problem in maintaining a balanced financial status given growing income from electronic products, declining income from print on paper, and overall increases in the cost of operation. The decrease in subscription income must be compensated for by increased revenues from online use. Somewhat later (Williams, 1984) she claimed that by 1984 some publishers were already approaching or had even passed the point at which one half of revenue was earned by electronic products.

More recently, Pemberton (1988) addressed the issue as follows:

> It has been long in coming but we are finally seeing overt acknowledgment that the days of printed indexes as the primary mainstays of database revenue are nearly over....The actual production of printed indexes may linger for a long period. But they will never again be the principal pillars of database economics. (Page 8)

It seems obvious from these figures that some libraries began more than a decade ago to discontinue subscriptions to some services in favor of online access on demand. This phenomenon, which has been referred to as the "migration" from paper to electronics, has been discussed by Stanley (1979), Trubkin (1980), Timour (1979), Pfaffenberger and Echt (1980), Lancaster and Goldhor (1981), Herring (1983), Hitchingham et al. (1984), and Caren and Somerville (1986).

Lancaster and Goldhor used a questionnaire, sent to 200 libraries in government, industry, and academia, to assess the extent of this migration. They discovered a significant level of cancellation of subscriptions to A&I services, although much of this activity was attributed more to general decline in purchasing power than to online accessibility per se. They also discovered that several libraries that had not yet cancelled any subscriptions were then (1980) reconsidering their policies vis-a-vis ownership versus access. Perhaps the most interesting finding, however, was that the more recently established libraries tended to move directly into online access without ever going through a transitional print-on-paper phase.

Librarians responding to the survey were able to identify the major barriers to further migration at that time. An obvious barrier is the fact that existing systems are not perceived to be "user cordial," necessitating delegation of the search to an information specialist, whereas searches of paper sources are frequently performed in a nondelegated mode. A second barrier is that many academic and public libraries have not had the resources to completely subsidize online searching. They are unwilling to discontinue printed subscriptions on the grounds that, if online access alone is available, the library will be discriminating against those who can least afford the costs. A final barrier is the fact that many librarians are simply reluctant to discontinue a subscription that may have existed for years.

These barriers are gradually being lifted; "user friendly" interfaces are now commonplace and many libraries are now providing free access to at least those databases that are available in CD-ROM form. It is likely, then, that migration from print on paper to electronic forms will accelerate in the near future. A more recent survey, by Hitchingham et al. (1984), found a higher level of migration than that by Lancaster and Goldhor.

The Future: Some Forecasts

The literature contains many predictions relating to the future of A&I services. One focus of many such forecasts is the integration of primary and secondary publishing. The opportunities for such integration already exist. When journals are photocomposed, the machine-readable text can be reused in other ways including input to secondary services. The "heads" of journal articles, consisting of titles, author information, abstracts, and other elements, can be used to produce journal indexes and other inputs required by secondary services (Lerner, 1980).

As the full text of journals becomes available online, the traditional lines between primary and secondary publishing become increasingly blurred (Goldhar, 1979). Burchinal (1977) predicted in the 1970s that by the 1990s secondary services ("accessing services") would be derived automatically from electronic-based primary materials and be available simultaneously with the publication of the primary literature. Users would be able to move from these accessing tools to the full text of documents from the same online terminal.

Winter et al. (1977) predict that publishing of primary sources in electronic form will reduce browsability and therefore increase dependence on secondary services. Secondary services should act as a kind of "Michelin Guide" to the primary journals. Such a guide would weight journals or articles on a "star" scale in much the same way that restaurants and hotels are evaluated.

Many advantages have been claimed for the integration process. Authors will assume greater responsibility for indexing and abstracting their own articles online, and the need for other indexers will thus decrease. This will improve the cost effectiveness of access and will reduce delays in the production of secondary databases (Drott et al., 1977). Cuadra (1981) refers to the advantages and disadvantages of a rather different dimension of integration: the producer of the database serving also as the provider of online access.

Other writers have spoken of the need for "one-stop" information centers and indicated that such centers will depend on cooperation between primary and secondary publishers (Bearman, 1978, Rowlett et al., 1970). A coordinated effort must be made by these services to take advantage of opportunities permitting or promoting the creation of machine-readable material (Drott et al., 1977). Standardization of bibliographic data elements must occur first in the primary sources and then eventually across all secondary services. Agreement on ownership and copyright privileges must also occur (Lerner, 1980).

Integration of primary and secondary publishing might occur more rapidly and effectively through the medium of the editorial processing center (EPC). An EPC would apply the benefits of centralized operations to computer-based journal publishing and would also be involved in the subsequent use of machine-readable byproducts in secondary publishing. Drott et al. (1977) have considered a variety of policy alternatives relating to the operation of EPCs in this way.

Integration was implemented successfully by the American Institute of Physics (AIP). Under a grant from the National Science Foundation, the AIP integrated various facets of primary and secondary source production through a single keyboarding operation and a single processing of several of the bibliographic elements (Alt et al., 1974; Lerner et al., 1976; Metzner, 1973).

Other projects having some relevance to integration have also been performed. The American Chemical Society conducted experiments to determine the best strategy for online searching of the full text of papers and the cost effectiveness of such searching (Baker, 1981). The All Union Institute for Scientific and Technical Information in the USSR (VINITI) has developed an integrated information system in which each document—journal article, report, patent, or whatever—is processed only once and the results are put into the computer for subsequent repeated and multiple use (Borko and Bernier, 1975). The potential for secondary services delivered into the home via viewdata has also been considered (Barlow, 1976).

The future of A&I services depends on their ability to deal with several problems they currently face. The continuing growth of the primary literature and the concurrent declining market for secondary services in paper form, it is claimed, can both be solved if the services are willing to adapt to the forces of technological change (Barlow, 1978; Williams & Brandhorst, 1979). Secondary services must cooperate first with the primary producers and then coordinate activities among themselves. Greater use of computer manipulation and a reduction of human intellectual processing will improve cost effectiveness (Conrad, 1976). Future integrated information systems should be "friendly" online systems which automatically provide necessary adjustments to cue or lead the user easily to appropriate alternatives, to improved browsing, and to retrieving relevant information (Baker, 1978).

A Personal View: The Near Future

In the near future we can expect existing trends to continue and some at a greatly accelerated pace. More new databases will emerge. Since the broad disciplinary areas of science and technology are already well covered, it seems likely that this growth will occur more in the social sciences and the humanities, although new databases in interdisciplinary areas, increasingly specialized databases, and databases of "general interest" (e.g., of appeal to public libraries and their users), as well as increasing numbers of nonbibliographic files, can also be expected. Use will continue to grow with the spread of microcomputers and user-friendly interfaces and as more databases become readily accessible in CD-ROM form. The penetration of online access into the less developed countries seems likely to lead to new national and international services. Countries such as India and Brazil, for example, are already acutely aware that their researchers have much better access to the foreign literature than they do to their domestic literature. While the literature of the developed countries is usually perceived to be of higher quality, the national literature is perceived to be more directly "relevant," at least in those areas (e.g., agriculture, family planning, rural sociology, environmental factors) where local conditions profoundly affect research and practice. Furthermore, improving the quality of national journals is likely to become a deliberate goal of many developing countries. To quote one example, Brazilian scientists prefer to publish in English rather than in Portuguese because English language journals are considered more prestigious and because many of these scientists studied outside Brazil. This creates a somewhat anomalous situation in which the results of Brazilian research are more accessible abroad than they are at home. Strengthening of the national journals, coupled with a rise in quality of higher education, particularly at the doctoral level (leading to more postgraduate education at home and less abroad) can be expected to produce an increase in publication in the national journals and a decrease of publication elsewhere.

It seems reasonable to expect, then, a gradual improvement in the quality of the primary literature produced in several of the developing countries. As this occurs, databases providing access to this literature can be expected to emerge. It remains to be seen whether these databases will be purely "national" in character or will be produced cooperatively by several of the developing countries, possibly within the framework of some United Nations agency (after the INIS/AGRIS model). This international perspective is introduced simply to illustrate the fact that the growth of databases, and of the use of such resources through online networks, will not be a phenomenon restricted to the developed world.

The migration from paper to electronics can be expected to accelerate over the next few years. There are several reasons for such expectations. Most obviously, it is inevitable that costs of distributing secondary services in printed form will increase much faster than costs of making these resources available electronically. At the same time, there will be other incentives: gradual recognition that institutional funds are as legitimately spent on electronic access as they are on ownership, a movement toward nondelegated searching brought about the rapid spread of inexpensive terminals and greatly improved "cordiality" in the user/system interface, and a pervasive movement to more paper-free activities throughout society.

A Longer-Term View

It seems reasonable to suppose that electronic technology applied to the primary literature will more or less parallel its application to the secondary literature, lagging these developments by some years. In fact, we can already see signs of this: Most primary journals are now photocomposed and we already have some online access to the full text of primary journals. No new "electronic only" journals yet exist (apart from some rather informal examples existing within computer conferencing and other networks), although some experimentation with such journals has been performed and at least one such journal is in the planning stage. Given this assumption, one could hypothesize some logical steps occurring to effect an evolution from a predominantly paper-based publishing environment to one that is predominantly electronics-based. These steps are as follows:

1. Dual-mode publication applied to the secondary services (i.e., electronic databases existing side by side with their paper equivalents).
2. New secondary services emerging in electronic form only.
3. Dual-mode publication applied to the primary literature.
4. New primary literature emerging in electronic form only.
5. Disappearance of printed secondary services with total reliance on distribution of databases in electronic form.
6. Disappearance of the printed journal.
7. Disappearance of secondary databases as we now know them.

This seems a logical evolutionary sequence. Phase 1 began almost 30 years ago and the second phase is of almost the same vintage. The third phase has been in effect for some time in the sense that machine-readable text of primary literature has existed, although little use has been made of the machine-readable data once these are used to generate print on paper. Online access to full text of primary literature is already a reality. The fourth phase has not quite been reached but we are now on the threshold of it.

The remaining phases are purely speculative although they do seem logical extensions of what has already taken place. The time scale is also in doubt. However, one thing seems clear: the developments of the next 30 years are likely to occur much more rapidly than those of the last 30.

Ironically, although secondary services have been the leaders in electronic publishing, changes in the primary literature are likely to be more rapid and more dramatic. It seems certain that, in terms of capabilities, electronic publishing will develop through two phases. In the first, the electronic publication is little more than a print-on-paper publication presented electronically (as existing online catalogs are little more than card catalogs in electronic form). An encyclopedia designed for print on paper but accessible through a terminal cannot really be considered an electronic encyclopedia. Neither can an existing journal accessible online be looked upon as a true electronic journal. In this phase, then, the electronic version is little more than a direct analog of the printed page, offering some advantages over print on paper but also having some notable disadvantages. True electronic publications will only emerge in the second phase, a phase in which new publications will be designed *ab initio* for electronic distribution only. In this phase the real capabilities of electronics will be exploited and the new publications will divest themselves completely from the inherent limitations of print on paper, i.e., a static, essentially linear mode of presenting information.

A detailed discussion of what true electronic publications may look like is beyond the scope of this chapter. Suffice it to say that they will be dynamic and multidimensional rather than static and one dimensional. Narrative description could be presented as a hypertext, reorganizable under the control of the user. Many static illustrations will be replaced by animation or by electronic analog models (e.g., of physical phenomena, the operation of equipment, the conduct of an experiment). Supplementation of text and illustration by audio output could also occur if certain forms of electronic distribution are adopted.

The most important point to be made is that the entire character of primary publications is likely to change rather drastically and that electronic capabilities will have a radical effect on the way that information is presented, perhaps leading to a situation in which much narrative text is replaced by alternative modes of presentation and publications become "interactive," the user being able to manipulate and interact with the data presented. In other words, future electronic publications may look less like present publications than like the more sophisticated programs now existing within systems for computer-aided instruction or, to use a more extreme analogy, like the electronic game. A wide variety of publications will be affected, the scholarly journal as well as the popular journal, the textbook as well as the encyclopedia. The secondary services, then, may find that the primary literature with which they deal may become something significantly different from the primary literature dealt with in the past.

The fifth phase in the evolution—the disappearance of printed secondary services—will occur, first and foremost, because subscribers to the printed services will continue to decline while users of the machine-readable equivalents will grow steadily. The migration will accelerate as increasing numbers of primary journals become accessible online. It will then make little sense to use a paper product as entry to a vast array of primary resources in electronic form. Further impetus will be given by the increase in interfacing of databases of various types. For example, it is already possible to perform an online search in a secondary database, locate a few useful items, switch to another database to see which libraries own these items, and make a request for them, with all of these activities achieved through electronic networking. This type of integrated processing will grow rapidly, causing greatly reduced dependence on paper products of all kinds.

The sixth phase will occur, some years later, for the same reasons that the printed secondary services will disappear, but with one important additional migration factor: the electronic sources will be so much more powerful, as means of presenting information, than those in print-on-paper form.

The final phase of the evolution may be the complete disappearance of most, if not all, secondary services, at least the disappearance of such services as we know them today. The justification for this assertion can be illustrated by a hypothetical and somewhat simplified example. Suppose some secondary service, established several years ago, deals with a highly specialized subject area, such that only 50 journals are covered. When first established, the service was writing abstracts for most articles in each journal and was indexing each article by use of a controlled vocabulary. As the years went on, however, it was preparing fewer and fewer abstracts; since most of the journals were already carrying acceptable abstracts, it was content to accept these intact. The service then moved into the dual-mode phase and began to issue a machine-readable database. By this time, all of the 50 periodicals included acceptable abstracts. The task of "abstracting," then, involved nothing more than putting the author abstracts into machine-readable form. After the database had been used for some time, it was recognized that the indexing activity was becoming redundant, since perfectly acceptable searches could be done on the text of titles plus abstracts. The human indexing was retained solely to produce a usable printed tool. As the years went by, however, subscriptions to this printed tool declined to the point at which online income was actually subsidizing the printed product. The printed tool was then abandoned. When this occurred, the role of the secondary service, vis-a-vis the 50 periodicals, consisted solely of putting bibliographic references plus abstracts into machine-readable form. By this time, however, many of the 50 periodicals were already accessible in full text form through online networks. A few years later all 50 became so accessible. It was then recognized that the secondary service served no useful purpose. All 50 periodicals were stored in a single online service center and this center, as well as providing access to full text, was able to build a searchable database of abstracts. The secondary services was thus replaced by the online service center.

This fairy tale is oversimplified in a number of respects. First, it assumes that all journals carry acceptable abstracts, which is not true at present but could well be true in the future since it could be made a condition for an online service center accepting the journal and making it accessible. Second, it takes no account of the language problem. This need not necessarily be a problem in the future since improvements in machine translation make it possible to reduce all abstracts automatically to a common language.

The biggest oversimplification is one of scale. To talk of 50 journals is one thing, to talk of 100,000 is quite another. Nevertheless, in principle, given that the journals exist in machine-readable form and include abstracts, there is no reason why acceptable "accessing databases" could not be built directly from the primary literature. A series of filters (really subject profiles) would be necessary to form major discipline-oriented and mission-oriented databases from all items newly added to all databases (i.e., not restricted to a particular set of journals). More refined filters would form more specialized databases from the first level databases. User interest profiles could then be applied to the second-level databases. An individual user, then, could log on to some system and be informed that X items, matching his profile of interest, have been published since last he used the system. The user may then view abstracts and, if required, get online access to the complete item. Rather than "subscribing" to any one electronic journal, the filters would keep him informed of everything matching his interest wherever published. At various levels, databases of abstracts would be available for searching when specific information needs arise.

The situation envisioned is illustrated in Exhibit 98. The diagram does not imply any particular number of databases or the use of any particular technology. Nor does it imply any particular institutional configuration. Those organizations that now produce secondary services might still play an important role in the total system (e.g., in building and maintaining subject profiles) but it will be a somewhat different role from that now played. What the diagram does imply is that, given that primary sources in print-on-paper form will eventually be replaced by equivalent sources in machine-readable form, the need for organizations to abstract and index the literature disappears. Instead, the equivalent organizations of the future will be concerned with building the various levels of filters and searching aids (synonym tables, text-based "thesauri") that will be needed to provide effective current awareness and literature searching services at the user level. This topic was dealt with in greater detail in Chapter 13.

Price (1983) also takes it for granted that at some future date "a substantial portion of scholarly material will be published only—or at least primarily—in electronic form." He points to one possible danger of such a development as it affects abstracting. In a "pay for each use" situation, publishers may be tempted to use the abstract to make a paper sound

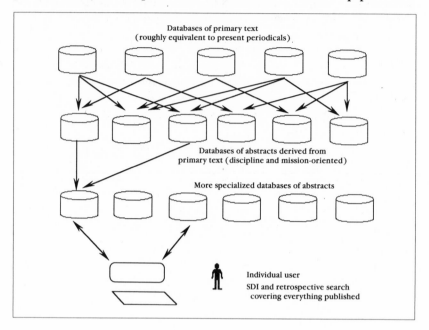

Exhibit 98
Filtering levels in a paperless publishing environment

more interesting or important than it really is. Moreover, since data on how frequently each article is read could be made easily available, at least in the case of electronic journals accessible through some network, authors too might want abstracts to promote interest in their work, especially if volume of use were one criterion used in promotion/tenure decisions. Although Price does not specifically mention it, abstracts could grow increasingly long since the length of the abstract would be one important factor affecting frequency of retrieval. Kuhlen (1984) suggests that abstracts will continue to play an important role as a filtering mechanism in computerized retrieval and dissemination systems. Indeed, while printed abstracting publications may disappear, the value of abstracts may actually increase.

16

INDEXING EXERCISES

PRACTICE MAKES PERFECT in indexing and abstracting as in other activities. The last two chapters of this book contain some exercises in indexing and abstracting. Clearly, the few exercises that can be included in a book of this kind are far from enough to produce accomplished indexers and abstractors. Nevertheless, they are presented in the hope that they will at least provide some concrete illustrations of major points made in the earlier chapters.

On the next few pages appear several abstracts of reports or journal articles. Some are actual abstracts of real publications. Others are abstracts of "hypothetical" articles, although they are based on actual publications.

You are to index each of these items using terms from the *UNBIS Thesaurus* (New York, United Nations, Dag Hammarskjold Library, 1985). If you wish, you may first write down words or phrases representing your conceptual analysis of each item and then attempt to translate each of these statements into a term or terms from the thesaurus. In any case, divide up your descriptors into major and minor descriptors, the former being terms that you consider most important in representing the subject matter.

Following the abstracts you will find suggested indexing for each item so that you can check your indexing against that of the author. Remember, however, that indexing is a somewhat subjective process. While the author believes in his indexing, there is no claim that it is "correct" in any absolute sense. Explanations of why indexing was done in a particular way are included.

Items 6-13 first appeared in the January 1977 issue of *A.I.D. Research and Development Abstracts* and are reproduced with the permission of the Center for Development Information and Evaluation, United States Agency for International Development.

Items to be Indexed

1. *Alcohol fuel today.* (Based on an article appearing in *Smithsonian,* March 1981, pp. 44-53)

Describes the various sources from which ethanol can be distilled, including crops of various types, agricultural waste products, municipal wastes and industrial sludge. Compares production costs of ethanol with those of gasoline and discusses problems involved in converting from pilot plant production of ethanol to full-scale commercial production. Discusses the advantages and disadvantages of gasohol, a blend of gasoline and alcohol fuel, and explores the problems that must be solved before alcohol-powered cars become practical.

2. *Erosion and the farmer.*
Describes how wind, rain and melting snow can erode valuable farmland and assesses the extent of agricultural losses from these causes in Northern Europe. Discusses possible solutions, namely the alternation of grain crops with soil-conserving grasses and the use of trees and terraces as windbreakers.

3. *Aerial photography and what it can do.* (Based on an article appearing in *Smithsonian*, March 1984, pp. 150-155.)
Reviews several possible uses of aerial photography, including satellite photography, military surveillance, disarmament verification, the study of archaeological sites, census applications (e.g., the counting of homes), weather and flood forecasting, and mapmaking (photogrammetry).

4. *The end of the sugar maple?* (Based on articles appearing in *Blair & Ketchum's Country Journal,* March 1986, pp. 46-49 and *American Forests*, November-December 1987, pp. 26-34.)
Large numbers of sugar maple trees in Canada and the Northern United States are dead or dying, causing a serious reduction in sugar production. Acid rain, causing defoliation, is suspected to be the principal cause.

5. *Can a plane fly forever?* (Based on an article appearing in *Newsweek,* September 28, 1987, pp. 42, 47.)
A prototype of an electric-powered aircraft, requiring no conventional fuel, is to be tested in Canada. Electricity is tranmitted from the ground as microwave energy and reconverted to electricity by "rectennas" on the plane. Theoretically, the plane could remain aloft for months without pilots. Applications might include scientific research, surveillance (military, police, or civilian), weather forecasting, and passenger transport. Microwaves might also power spacecraft. Possible health hazards from the microwaves could deter widespread application.

6. *Nutrition education in child feeding programs in the developing countries.* (Agency for International Development 1974, 44p.)

This simply-worded booklet, supplemented by many cartoon drawings, is intended for village workers and others involved in child feeding in the developing countries in assisting them to teach mothers and children about the foods children need for growth and health and how to use local foods to improve their diets. Chapters cover: The Double Purpose of Child-Feeding programs; What you Should Know about Food; Setting Goals to Fit Your Community; Some General Rules for Teaching; Working with Mothers of Preschool Children; and Teaching Children in School Feeding Programs. It is felt that the nutrition education which grass roots workers provide may have a more lasting effect and may do as much for the prevention of malnutrition as the actual foods contributed, important as these are to the health of the mothers and children receiving them.

7. *Improvement of the nutritive quality and productivity of barley for semi-arid regions; annual report, 1975/1976.* (Montana State University, College of Agriculture 1976, 70p.)

This is the second annual report for a three-year project designed to increase the nutritive value of barleys consumed in less developed countries, increase barley yields, and decrease losses caused by barley diseases. During the first year of work, several LDC's were visited to establish contacts and collect isolates of the major disease organisms. The work with diseases has progressed to the point where a significant outreach program can be initiated. In work on nutritive value, the microbiological assay technique for determining lysine has been perfected to the point where it is a reliable screening tool. No significant differences were found in the feed value of waxy and normal Compana isogenic pairs due to starch type or amino acid composition of the protein. Preliminary results indicate that peoples who consume primarily rice would much prefer and probably consume more of a waxy endosperm barley than the normal endosperm barley. The High Amylose Glacier variety was slightly lower in energy value than normal Glacier but the former has a higher quality protein due to an increase in the protein of several amino acids. Animal performance data (Growth, PER, and BV) support the chemical analyses for protein and amino acid composition of Hiproly and Hiproly Normal barleys. Lysine content of the protein has been found to be environmentally influenced differentially, dependent on the gene present, and is reflected in animal performance. Animal performance is highly correlated to the essential amino acid content of the barleys. Lysine usually accounts for over 50% of the animal variation in growth and PER and 60% of the variation in biological value. A double translocation has been located that should be effective in transferring the Hiproly gene to a population as well as disease resistance genes (scale, net-blotch, barley yellow dwarf) on chromosome 3. Fertile, plump, high-lysine lines from Hiproly crosses have been developed to serve as parents in further variety development work with this gene.

8. *African women in agricultural development, a case study in Sierra Leone.* (Spencer, D. S. C., 1976, 41p. Department of Agricultural Economics, Michigan State University.)

A study of the labor effects on farm families of an I.A.D.P. loan for developing inland swampland for rice production. The study was a small part of a national study of rural employment problems in Sierra Leone. One village, Benduma, in one of the three operational areas of the I.A.D. project was selected for intensive study of the daily work performed by males, females, and children in 23 selected households. From May 1974 to June 1975, interviews were conducted twice a week at selected households, and an input-output questionnaire was used to provide daily records of hours worked per family member and non-farm output, farm and non-farm sales, loans given and received, and gifts given and received. From these data were calculated household income by source and its distribution, labor utilization, returns to labor, and seasonal profiles of farm and non-farm enterprises. The author concludes that women worked slightly harder in the development project than women not participating in it, but that the increase in their work load was much less than the increase in the work load of adult males and children. Women play a substantial role in the cultivation of a "development" crop (swamp rice) using improved technology. However, the results of the study negate the hypothesis that such agricultural development projects place an uneven burden on women vis-à-vis men.

9. *Science and technology policy, research management and planning in the Arab Republic of Egypt 1976, 103p.* (National Academy of Sciences, National Research Council, Washington, D.C. 20418).

Report of a Symposium on Science Policy Planning and a Workshop on the Management and Planning on Research. The conference focused on scientific and technology policy, planning, and research of management. A "workshop" format was chosen as the best method to bring together a representative group of Egyptian and American physical, natural, and social scientists, economists, engineers, and development planners. It was found that although Egypt lacks a formally enunciated national . science policy, the various science-oriented agencies it has established and the funds it provides for research and science education constitute a significant, implicit national policy. Management of this large and complex set of organizations is a formidable task, and every effort should be made for their effectiveness and efficiency. Managing university research is a very different problem from managing applied research institutes and should be solved as quickly as possible. Even though Egypt's applied research program is a sizable effort, its execution probably requires considerable restructuring and redirection if it is to be fully effective. Transfer of technology to Egyptian industry from other nations and from multinational corporations has been and will continue to be a major element in Egypt's industrial development. To ensure effective transfer of technology and to minimize its costs there should be appropriate revisions of national legislation and practices.

10. *Utilization of underutilized marine species for human consumption* (Constantinides, S. M.; Figueroa, Jose; Kaplan, Harvey, 1974, 11p. International Center for Marine Resource Development, University of Rhode Island).

At a time when the prices of fish are rising and protein malnutrition is prevailing in many developing countries, fishermen around the world are throwing back millions of tons of protein-rich fish to die. These fish are thrown back because they are considered "trash" or "discards" or are unfamiliar species of no economical value. In the United States fishermen throw back up to 70% of the fish trapped in the nets while fishing for other market species such as flounder and shrimp. Man cannot afford any more to ignore the protein-rich marine species. Markets for under-utilized species have to be created and expanded as alternative resources to the declining supply of commercially established species, thereby augmenting the industry, encouraging resource conservation and revitalizing the familiar and long-exploited species. Conventional and nonconventional ways can be employed to utilize these species which are considered discards. The utilization of these species can be developed along these main lines: minced fish flesh (mixed species or single species), fish pastes, and dried fish products.

The production of minces from many small and medium-size fish is made possible by the use of separators, which produce meat free of bones. The meat is washed and then frozen in blocks. A combination of fatty and non-fatty fish may yield a desirable end product acceptable to the consumer. Fish pastes, shrimp pastes, and crab pastes can be prepared by various methods. To the washed, minced flesh, salt, starch, and polyphosphates are added to produce a paste from which sausages and other products can be prepared. Other products can be made such as fish mixed with potatoes, fish in spreads, dips, and soups, or several kinds of minced fish mixed together or with other ingredients to produce exciting new flavors. Species that have not been exploited yet by man must be utilized in the future and all so-called trash species must be regarded as edible species fit for direct human consumption.

11. The use of peer tutoring and programmed radio instruction: viable alternatives in education (Hannum, W. H.; Morgan, R. M. 1974, 38p. Florida State University, College of Education).

Educators in developing countries are likely to achieve more by applying the principles rather than the things of educational technology. The principles of programmed learning have been shown to be effective in promoting learning in a wide variety of circumstances. The most effective instructional materials can be developed through use of the principles of programmed instruction and mastery learning. Radio, when combined with the use of peer tutors, can be an effective educational tool in developing countries. The concepts of programmed learning and mastery learning can be incorporated in the design of educational radio programs. Such programs, accompanied by peer tutors, can accomplish the total educational effort within the resources of many developing countries. This type of educational system is a viable alternative to traditional formal education. Such a system should be tried in several developing countries to explore its full potential.

12. Cultural and social factors affecting small farmer participation in formal credit programs (Gillette, Cynthia; Uphoff, Norman 1973, 40p. Rural Development Committee, Center for International Studies, Cornell University).

This paper presents three basic assumptions which, with one exception, are its focus. The exception is the issue of "economic rationality," which is familiar to all concerned with development in the Third World, but which is seen as warranting a brief discussion in the introduction. Part II deals with the cultural context of small farmers as borrowers, i.e., various factors affecting the demand for credit. Following this, Part III treats the cultural context of credit programs as lenders, i.e., factors conditioning the supply of credit available in functional terms to small farmers. Part IV shows various implications of the preceding Parts II and III—what happens when these two cultural systems interact and what are the likely points of difficulty. Part V concludes by comparing general differences between formal and informal sources of credit.

13. *Development of low-cost roofing from indigenous materials in developing nations; annual report, 1974/1975* (Monsanto Research Corporation, Dayton, Ohio, 1975, 335p.).

This report discusses the second phase (May 1974 through September 1975) of a three-phase, 3.5 year research effort to produce improved roofing for developing countries by matching indigenous fibers and fillers with low-cost binders. The ultimate goal of the program is to make available, in at least three countries, one each in Latin America, Asia, and Africa, an economically and technically acceptable roofing system that requires less foreign exchange than existing alternatives. The program objective is to be demonstrated within each of the participating countries through construction of at least four prototype roofs and transfer of the necessary technology to qualified organizations. Current collaborating countries are Jamaica, the Philippines, and Ghana. The project emphasis during Phase III was on development of roofing materials and establishing the mechanism for the technology transfer. Primary objectives of the materials development included establishing a generalized set of criteria for roofing; defining composite material ingredients; determining the most promising sets of materials, processes, and products; and analyzing the cost and practicality of the candidate systems. Four candidate composite roofing material systems were defined that use from 70 to 100% indigenous material. Outstanding as a filler is the sugar cane residue, bagasse. The primary candidate binders include natural rubber, phenolic, and commercial thermoplastic resins. Accelerated and outdoor aging are demonstrating the viability of the candidate systems. The objectives of the technology transfer aspects included defining potential collaborative institutions and individuals in Jamaica, the Philippines, and Ghana; forming Advisory and Technical Working Committees in each of these countries that would participate in the roofing development program; and locating qualified organizations interested in future commercial production of the roofing. Those institutions, committees, and working groups were defined in the three countries and are functioning to various degrees, with Jamaica taking the lead. Private industry organizations that may become future manufacturers of the roofing have been located in each of the three countries. During Phase III, October 1975 through December 1976, the program will be brought to completion through material optimization, design, fabrication, testing, and evaluation of prototype roofing; and field manufacture, installation, and evaluation of full-scale roofing.

Author's Indexing and Explanations
(Major descriptors are identified with an asterisk*)

1. Alcohol fuel today.
Alcohol fuels*
Gasohol*
Production costs
Gasoline
Crops
Agricultural wastes
Refuse derived fuels
Domestic wastes
Industrial wastes
Pilot projects
Waste utilization

Ethanol is not a term in UNBIS but is referred to *Alcohol fuels*, which seems the single most pertinent term for this item. If the term *Ethanol* existed in the thesaurus, this term and not *Alcohol fuels* should be used, despite the title, because the abstract indicates that the article deals exclusively with ethanol. Do not rely too heavily on titles; they are sometimes misleading.

The abstract suggests that the article deals quite heavily with gasohol so this term is also used in the selective indexing. The thesaurus does not allow one to express the idea of "alcohol-powered cars." Nevertheless, this is implied quite clearly in *Gasohol* so use of the term *Automobiles,* while not wrong, seems unnecessary. Using the term *Motor fuels* would be quite wrong because the article deals exclusively with gasohol, a type of motor fuel and *Motor fuels* is a broader term (BT) above *Gasohol* in UNBIS.

In more exhaustive indexing it would be necessary to cover the other ideas summarized in the abstract. The sources of ethanol can be well covered by use of the term *Crops* plus several specific "waste" terms. Because specific types of waste are mentioned, it is better to use the specific terms rather than the more generic *Wastes*. To illustrate, suppose someone was looking for information on possible applications of agricultural wastes. This item seems highly relevant but might not be found if indexed under the more general term.

The term *Municipal wastes* does not exist in UNBIS, but municipal wastes are usually domestic wastes (see scope note under *Domestic wastes* in UNBIS) so *Domestic wastes* should be used. If the article deals heavily with the "waste" aspect, *Waste utilization* seems a good term. *Refuse derived fuels* is certainly appropriate.

Since costs of ethanol and gasoline are compared, the term *Gasoline* should probably be included in the exhaustive indexing. *Production costs* certainly should.

In UNBIS terms it is not possible to precisely express the idea of "scaling up" from pilot plant to commercial production. The most relevant term would seem to be *Pilot projects*.

It is also impossible to express the idea of "advantages/disadvantages" or "problems" (associated with gasohol or alcohol-powered cars). Most controlled vocabularies fail to cover more nebulous ideas of this kind.

2. Erosion and the farmer.
   Soil erosion*
   Rain
   Soil conservation*
   Snow
   Crop rotation
   Crop yields
   Europe

The essential term here is *Soil erosion. Soil conservation* is the single term that best covers "possible solutions." Defects in the UNBIS thesaurus make exhaustive indexing more difficult. *Rain* and *Snow* are both appropriate terms, and necessary if one wants to be able to search specifically for articles on erosion of soil by rain or by snow. It is quite impossible to express the idea of wind erosion since *Wind* is not an UNBIS term. Of the specific solutions discussed, only *Crop rotation* can be covered. The term *Trees* could be used but might mislead or cause false associations so it is probably better omitted.

In UNBIS one cannot express the idea of "agricultural losses," but *Crop yields* is sufficiently close to be worth assigning (i.e., the effect of erosion on yields). The term *Northern Europe* does not exist in UNBIS (although *Southern Europe* does!) so the term *Europe* must be assigned. This illustrates an important point: if the precise term needed is not available, use the most specific term that the thesaurus allows.

> 3. *Aerial photography and what it can do.*
> Aerial photography*
> Aerial photogrammetry
> Photographic interpretation
> Aerial surveys*
> Hydrographic surveys
> Flood control
> Military reconnaissance
> Satellite monitoring
> Geodetic satellites*
> Archaeology
> Censuses
> Weather prediction
> Weather maps

This article seems to deal with the use of aircraft and satellites in the performance of various types of photographic surveys. *Aerial photography* and *Aerial surveys* are important terms. The term *Satellite photography* does not exist in UNBIS. The idea could be expressed, however, by combining *Aerial photography* with a "satellite" term. The most appropriate seems to be *Geodetic satellites,* especially since UNBIS links (by RT) the term *Aerial photogrammetry* to *Geodetic satellites.*

As to the applications, UNBIS covers some well and some not so well. *Military surveillance,* per se, does not exist, but *Military reconnaissance* does. *Verification measures* is a thesaurus term that looks appropriate for this article until one discovers that *Satellite monitoring* is a narrower term to *Verification measures. Satellite monitoring* should be used because the type of verification discussed (disarmament verification) could only be achieved through satellite photography. Remember, always use the *most specific* term available in the thesaurus even though another term may "sound" more appropriate. This illustrates another important point: the "context" of a term in a thesaurus may reveal the meaning of a term even if no scope note is given. The context of *Satellite monitoring* in UNBIS makes clear that it is the use of satellites in verification, not the monitoring of satellites, that is intended.

The study of archaeological sites is probably better covered by *Archaeology* than by *Archaeological excavations.* Since "counting of homes" is used merely as an example of a census application, the general *Censuses* is a safer term than *Housing censuses*. Moreover, the latter term is somewhat ambiguous and may refer to the occupancy of buildings rather than the number of homes.

Weather forecasting translates into *Weather prediction* in UNBIS. Since this implies the development of weather maps this term might also be applied, although it is marginal. Flood forecasting cannot be covered as such. The purpose is prevention of floods so *Flood control* should be used. Since the movement of water or ice is implied, *Hydrographic surveys* might also be considered a good term.

Mapmaking is well covered by *Photogrammetry*. Finally, since these various applications all strongly imply the interpretation of photographs, *Photographic interpretation* seems entirely appropriate.

4. *The end of the sugar maple?*
Sugar growing*
Sugar industry
Trees*
Defoliation
Acid rain*
Canada
United States
Plant diseases

The UNBIS thesaurus recognizes only sugar cane and sugar beets as sources of sugar so it is necessary to use *Sugar growing* here. Since no terms for specific types of trees exist in the thesaurus, it is necessary to use the general *Trees*. Pollution is likely to be the cause of the defoliation but it is unnecessary to use *Air pollution* because *Acid rain* is more precise.

5. *Can a plane fly forever?*
Aircraft*
Electric vehicles*
Microwaves*
Scientific research
Prototypes
Spacecraft
Health hazards
Military reconnaissance
Canada

The idea of an electric-powered aircraft using microwaves is well covered by the three starred terms. More attention is given in the article to possible scientific and military applications so an attempt has been made to cover those aspects. Unfortunately, the idea of surveillance in general is missing from UNBIS and even military surveillance must be translated into *Military reconnaissance.* The other possible applications mentioned— e.g., weather forecasting—are touched upon so briefly in this article that they seem unworthy of coverage in indexing. Since the health hazard discussed is microwave radiation, the term *Radiation effects* looks appropriate at first sight. However, the UNBIS scope note indicates that this term is to be used only for *radioactive* (nuclear) effects so it is not correct to use it here.

    6. *Nutrition education in child feeding programs.*
       Child feeding*
       Nutrition education*
       Child nutrition*
       Developing countries
       Infant nutrition
       School meals

The subject of this report can be covered perfectly adequately by terms available in the thesaurus.

    7. *Improvement of the nutritive quality and productivity of barley.*
       Barley*
       Arid zones*
       Nutrition*
       Crop yields
       Developing countries
       Plant breeding
       Plant genetics
       Plant diseases
       Plant protection
       Proteins

Arid zones is as close as one can get in UNBIS to "semi-arid regions."

    8. *African women in agricultural development.*
       Rice
       Sierra Leone
       Women in agriculture*
       Women workers*
       Women in development
       Women's rights
       Hours of work*

> Working time arrangement
> Labour productivity
> Division of labour

Do not be misled by the title. This is about women in Sierra Leone, not African women in general. The main focus of the study is employment conditions of women, not the cultivation of rice. While *Rice* is a relevant term, it is the women worker and hours of work terms that are most important. *Rice* is not a major term because someone looking for items on the cultivation of rice might not be very interested in this type of social study. The term *Division of labor* is probably relevant, since the male/female relationship in labor is discussed, but the scope note in the thesaurus gives a very inadequate indication of how and when this term is to be used.

> 9. *Science and technology policy.*
> Egypt*
> Science and technology policy*
> Science and technology planning*
> Research and development*
> Technology transfer
> Scientific research
> Public administration
> Management
> Science and technology financing

Quite a few terms are needed to adequately cover this report. Note that *Research and development* and *Management* are both needed to cover the idea of "research management." *Egypt* is regarded as a major term because the entire report is about the Egyptian situation. This is quite different from the article on "African women" where the setting (Sierra Leone) is almost incidental to the purpose of the study.

> 10. *Utilization of underutilized marine species for human consumption.*
> Food consumption*
> Fish*
> Fish processing
> Fishery products
> Fishery conservation*

This is an example of an article that cannot be adequately indexed because the thesaurus cannot express the idea of "underutilized fish species." The terms used here do not give a good picture of what the item is about, but they are the best available.

11. *The use of peer tutoring and programmed radio instruction.*
   Educational radio*
   Programmed instruction*
   Developing countries
   Nonformal education
   Teaching personnel

Again, not well covered because the thesaurus lacks terms to express the idea of "peer tutoring" or even of "tutoring." *Teaching personnel* is as close as one can get in UNBIS.

12. *Cultural and social factors affecting small farmer participation in formal credit programs.*
   Credit policy*
   Farmers*
   Small farms*
   Developing countries
   Agricultural credit*
   Cultural values
   Social values

This is an excellent example of a relatively long report that can be well covered by a small number of terms. To express the idea of "small farmers" it is necessary to use both *Farmers* and *Small farms. Developing countries* is assigned because it is obvious that this is the context in which agricultural credit is being discussed.

13. *Development of low-cost roofing.*
   Roofs*
   Traditional technology
   Bagasse
   Fibres
   Building materials*
   Technology transfer
   Rubber
   Plastic products
   Jamaica
   Ghana
   Philippines
   Developing countries

The indexing of this is not completely satisfactory because the thesaurus does not allow us to express "indigenous materials." Nevertheless, indigenous materials can be considered closely related to indigenous technology, so the term *Traditional technology* is justified, if not exactly ideal.

17

Abstracting Exercises

Part 1

To undertake this exercise it is first necessary to assemble the periodical articles listed. Most of these are readily available through libraries. For each article prepare an abstract or abstracts (see note below) and compare what you write with this author's suggested abstracts and notes. How do these abstracts differ from yours? Which are better? Why?

Articles to be abstracted:

1. Can a plane fly forever? (*Newsweek*, September 28, 1987, pp. 42, 47).
2. Pluto: limits on its atmosphere, ice on its moon (*Science News*, September 26, 1987, p. 207)
3. Plastic shocks and visible sparks (*Science News*, September 5, 1987, p. 152).
4. Moscow's chemical candor (*Newsweek*, October 19, 1987, p. 56).
5. Stereotypes: The Arab's image (*World Press Review*, June 1986, p. 39).
6. Ads require sensitivity to Arab culture, religion. (*Marketing News*, April 25, 1986, p. 3).
7. France, racism and the Left (*The Nation*, September 28, 1985, pp. 279-281).
8. Compassion for animals. (*National Forum*, Winter 1986, pp. 2-3).

Note: For item 1, prepare an indicative abstract. For 2, 5, and 7 prepare informative abstracts. For 3 and 4 prepare both. For 6 and 8 use the form that seems most appropriate.

Author's Abstracts

1. Can a plane fly forever? (*Newsweek*, September 28, 1987, pp. 42, 47)

Abstract (Indicative)

A prototype of an electric-powered aircraft, requiring no conventional fuel, is to be tested in Canada. Electricity is transmitted from the ground as microwave energy and reconverted to electricity by "rectennas" on the plane. Theoretically, the plane could remain aloft for months without pilots. Applications might include scientific research, surveillance (military, police, or civilian), weather forecasting, and passenger transport. Microwaves might also power spacecraft. Possible health hazards from the microwaves could deter widespread application.

Notes

Clarity takes precedence over brevity. The phrase "requiring no conventional fuel" is needed to make clear that the craft is *entirely* powered by electricity. The abstract should not go beyond what is claimed in the article. Thus, "is to be tested" is appropriate even if the abstractor knows that the tests have already taken place. Try to avoid use of extraneous words. For example, "Microwaves might also power spacecraft" is shorter than "Microwaves might also be used to power spacecraft" yet is no less clear. Because no real results are presented, it would be difficult to write a true informative abstract for this item.

2. Pluto: limits on its atmosphere, ice on its moon (*Science News*, September 26, 1987, p. 207)

Abstract (Informative)

Recent estimates indicate that Pluto may be no more than 2,290 km across, with its moon, Charon, no more than 1,284 km across. Pluto's infrared spectrum seems to be radically different from Charon's. Pluto has a methane-rich surface but Charon, with relatively little methane, appears to be dominated by water-ice. Charon's average reflectivity is only about one half that of Pluto, suggesting that Pluto has a lower surface temperature: perhaps 50 kelvins for Pluto and 58 for Charon. Vapor pressure on Pluto could be only 3.5 microbars compared with 59 on Charon. Pluto appears to have nonstatic polar caps of methane ice whose coverage of the planet varies with time.

Notes

This is a true informative abstract that tries to summarize all of the major data reported in the article. Try to avoid redundancy. For example, it is accurate but not necessary to say "Infrared spectral measurements suggest that Pluto's infrared spectrum seems to be radically different from Charon's" because the reference to "infrared spectrum" itself indicates that infrared spectral measurements have been made.

3. Plastic shocks and visible sparks (*Science News,* September 5, 1987, Vol. 132, No. 10, p. 152)

Abstract (Indicative)

Describes conditions under which static electricity may cause fires or explosions in the handling of powders or liquids and mentions two recently-developed instruments that can be used to monitor materials handling operations.

Abstract (Informative)

In filling or emptying containers, static electricity may generate sparks that can cause fires or explosions. Plastic bottles containing flammable liquids may receive a charge from a surrounding plastic bag or coat pocket, causing a spark when the liquid is poured. Charges can also occur when chemical powders are conveyed, when plastic-lined metal drums are filled with conductive liquids or receive rags soaked with conductive solvents, or when solvent-based semiconductive coatings are applied to one surface of a nonconductive film. The human body itself can generate sparks that can ignite flammable vapors. New instruments now allow the monitoring of filling and emptying operations involving powders or liquids. Using electronic image-intensification or the measurement of charge polarity and magnitude, they record sparking and identify conditions most likely to cause ignition. Powders with fine particles are more hazardous than coarse ones. The most dangerous liquids have low conductivity, are negatively charged, are highly flammable, and evaporate easily to form a vapor-air mixture that supports ignition.

Notes

This is a good illustration of the difference between indicative and informative abstracts. The former merely mentions what the article is about while the latter tries to be a true summary—which type of operations, what type of hazard, which type of instrument, and so on. Brevity can often be achieved, without sacrificing clarity, by omitting articles or conjunctions. For example, "In filling or emptying containers ..." is shorter and just as clear as "In the filling or emptying of containers...".

4. Moscow's chemical candor (*Newsweek,* October 19, 1987, p. 56]

Abstract (Informative)

The Soviet Union openly admits to a stockpile of chemical weapons but claims to no longer produce them. Western observers have been permitted at the formerly secret Shikhany base but Western experts feel that the weapons displayed are old ones — the Soviets have more modern weapons that they do not admit to. The U.S. claims to have ceased production of chemical weapons in 1969, but Western intelligence believes that the Soviets are still producing them and have stockpiled as much as 300,000 tons. The U.S. has provided a detailed report on size and location of U.S. stockpiles but the Soviets refuse to reciprocate until a treaty is signed. The U.S. proposal of a ban on chemical weapons was not pursued by the Soviets in 1984 but they now claim to want a treaty and on-site verification. The Soviets say that the U.S. decision to produce "binary" weapons will obstruct the signing of a treaty, but the U.S. feels that this new generation of weapons will actually force the Soviets to negotiate.

Abstract (Indicative)

Describes steps the Soviet Union has taken recently to promote a treaty banning use of chemical weapons. Mentions the new generation of "binary" weapons now being produced by the U.S. and the possible effect of this development on the signing of a treaty.

Notes

Again, a good illustration of the difference between indicative and informative abstract. The latter tries to summarize the substance of the article while the former merely indicates what it is about.

5. Stereotypes: The Arabs' image (*World Press Review,* June 1986, p. 39)

Abstract (Informative)

The American media, especially television, promotes a negative image of Arabs and Arab countries. Hostility toward Arabs, exacerbated by the Arab-Israeli conflict and the oil crisis of the 1970s, extends to the more than 1 million Arabs living in the United States. The interests of truth, peace, and brotherhood require that steps be taken to change this image.

Notes

The abstractor must decide what is significant and what is not. The substance of this brief article seems well covered by these three sentences. It is unnecessary to summarize the details on the stereotypes, which occupies about half of the article. Inclusion of the names of organizations mentioned in the article would make the abstract too detailed.

6. Ads require sensitivity to Arab culture, religion (*Marketing News,* April 25, 1986, p. 3).

Abstract

Because of the decline in oil prices, spending by Arab countries must be stimulated by effective advertising. Advertisers must understand the religious, social, and cultural mores governing Arab life. Some examples of things to avoid are presented.

Notes

Despite being very brief, this is less an indicative abstract than one attempting to summarize what the author says, rather than describing what the article is about. Only the last sentence is truly indicative. This illustrates that abstracts can be made to combine informative and indicative elements.

7. France: racism and the Left (*The Nation,* September 28, 1985, pp. 279-281)

Abstract (Informative)

The ultrarightist party, National Front, actively promotes racial hatred in France, especially against North Africans, but the Communists and Socialists have done little to fight racial prejudice. Campaigns against racism are organized by unofficial groups, mostly youth groups.

Notes

As in the previous example, this abstract is more informative than indicative. A comparison of abstracts 5-7 with abstracts 1-4 will show that it is more difficult to write true informative abstracts in the social sciences than it is in the sciences. Articles in the social sciences tend to be more abstract and to contain less hard data.

8. Compassion for animals (*National Forum*, Winter 1986, pp. 2-3)

Abstract

The close bond between humans and animals, which tended to exist in earlier times, has been eroded by urban development and industrialization, leading to a disregard for animal life in many quarters. But a strong people-animal bond is essential for the health of the individual, the community and society. Suggests ways in which society could improve its sensitivity and compassion toward animals.

Notes

Again, a combined indicative/informative abstract seems most appropriate. The first two sentences, by trying to encapsulate the message of the authors, are really informative, while the last sentence is clearly indicative. The abstract could be made fully informative by summarizing all of the methods for raising compassion, as mentioned on page 3 of the article, but these are so diverse that a rather lengthy abstract would be needed and this seems unjustified by the brevity of the article itself.

Part 2

Reproduced below are eight abstracts that appeared in *Irricab* (April 1980, volume 5, number 2), an abstracting publication in the field of irrigation published by the International Irrigation Information Center. Can you find anything wrong with these abstracts? How can you improve them? See the author's notes on each below.

Abstracts

[The abstracts are reproduced by kind permission of the Agricultural Research Organization, Ministry of Agriculture, State of Israel, and Pergamon Press Inc. The selection of these abstracts was made from this source as a matter of convenience and in no way implies that the abstracts in *Irricab* are of low quality. In fact, they are usually very good and it is difficult to find any that could be greatly improved.]

1. Anon. Clarification of highly turbid waters by means of acoustic filters (Rus) Gidrotekh Melior, 1977, (9): 98-99

Development of a method for water clarification with acoustic filters is briefly reported. Hydraulic characteristics of various screens were studied with and without vibration and the resistance coefficient of various screens was determined. The method is proposed for water clarification without the use of chemical reagents.

2. Vaneyan, S.S.; Makoveev, V.P. (Volzhanka side roll sprinkler for irrigation of vegetable crops) (Rus) Gidrotekh Melior, Mar 1979, (3): 67-68, 1 photo, 2 tab (All-Union Research Institute for Vegetable Growing, USSR)

Experience obtained with the irrigation of various vegetable crops using the Volzhanka sprinkler are reported. The paper contains an equation for calculation of the duration of irrigation and the number of sprinkler units necessary for irrigating a given area. Data are given on crop damage by the sprinkler wheels.

3. Rhoades, J.D. Determining soil salinity and detecting saline seeps using an inductive electromagnetic soil conductivity sensor (Eng) In: *Agronomy Abstracts: 1978 Annual Meeting of the Soil Science Society of America:* 183 (USDA, SEA, Riverside, CA, USA)

A new instrument has been developed for determining soil salinity and detecting saline seeps from the measurements of soil electrical conductivity without probes or ground contact using an inductive magnetic technique. The conductivity can be directly read on the instrument and measurements can be made by walking over the ground. Equipment and results are discussed. Advantages and limitations of the new and previous methods are discussed.

4. Gisser, M.; Pohoryles, S. Water shortage in Israel: long-run policy for the farm sector (Eng) *Water Resour Res,* Dec 1977, 13(6): 865-872, 1 fig. 10 tab, 4 ref (University of New Mexico, Dept of Economics, Albuquerque, NM 87131, USA)

Israel faces a situation of a limited amount of water supply and increasing demands. Since agriculture uses a large fraction of the water available, one potential policy is to reduce allocations of water to agriculture in order to permit the growth of use in other sectors. Estimates of the total loss in income to agriculture from reduction in current allocations are made by using a linear programming model.

5. Debrivna, I. Ye. (Sulfate reducing bacteria of rice irrigation systems in the southern Ukrainian SSR] (Ukr, summary Eng) Mikrobiologii Zhurnal, 1977, 39(5): 627-629, 2 tab, 9 ref (Academy of Sciences of the Ukrainian SSR, Institute of Microbiology and Virology, Kiev, USSR)

The studies reported have shown a very intensive development of sulfate-reducing bacteria in the subsoil of the rice irrigation systems characterized by a high water table. It is suggested this may account for the reduced rice yields under these conditions.

6. Koo, J.W.; Ryu, H.Y. (A study on the determination method of pumping rates in tubewells for irrigation] (Kor, summary Eng) *Journal of Korean Society of Agricultural Engineers,* Dec 1976, 18(4): 1-9, 8 fig, 4 tab, 20 ref (Seoul National University, Suweon, Republic of Korea)

In order to find a method to calculate the pumping rates in tubewells for irrigation, pumping tests were conducted in 12 tubewells. A 3″ centrifugal pump, a 5 hp motor, and a 90 degree V-notch were used in the test and the depths, static water levels, pumping levels, and yields of tubewells were measured. A negative correlation between pumping rate and drawdown, and a positive correlation between pumping rate and the coefficient of transmissibility were found. A formula derived from Thiem's theory was found to be satisfactory for calculation of the pumping rates from tubewells.

7. Shanmugarajah, K.; Atukorale, S.C. Water management at Rajangana scheme—lessons from cultivation—Yala 1976 (Eng) *Jalavrudhi (Sri Lanka)*, Dec 1976, 1(2): 60-65, 5 tab (Water Management Division, Irrigation Dept. Sri Lanka)

This is a description of how it was proven that rice farmers of a certain area had always been wasting water. Water managers were called in during a drought because of the fear of crop failure, and by improved water use efficiency, consumption was drastically reduced without reducing crop yield.

8. Arbarb, M.; Manbeck, D.M. Influence of lateral depth and spacing on corn yield and water use in subsurface irrigation system (Eng) *Annual Meeting, ASAE, North Carolina State University, Raleigh, NC, USA, Jun 26-29, 1977, Paper No. 77-2012,* 21 p. 8 fig., 1 tab, 9 ref. Available from ASAE, POB 410, St. Joseph, MI 49085, USA (University of Nebraska, Agricultural Engineering Dept, NB, USA)

The aims of this experiment were to study the influence of different lateral depths and spacings on corn yield and water use, and to study the practical use of a subsurface irrigation system and the water distribution pattern.

Author's Notes

1. The first sentence adds nothing to the title. The abstract could be further condensed, with no loss of meaning, as follows:

   Proposes a method that requires no chemical reagents. Hydraulic characteristics of various screens were studied, with and without vibration, and their resistance coefficients were determined.

2. Again some duplication of the title. Could be made more compact, as follows:

   Experiences with various vegetable crops are reported. Presents an equation for calculating, for a given area, the required number of sprinkler units and duration of irrigation. Gives data on crop damage by the sprinkler wheels. (NB. Would be much better to identify the crops—e.g., "Experiences with cabbages, beets and carrots are reported").

3. Unnecessary duplication can be avoided and the abstract made more "tight":

The new instrument described operates by measuring electrical conductivity of soil without probes or ground contact. Conductivity can be read directly and measurements made by walking over the ground. The instrument and its results are compared with previous methods.

4. Unnecessarily verbose. Could be reduced to:

Reducing the allocations to agriculture (a major consumer), to allow increased use in other sectors, would be one way of alleviating water shortage. A linear programming model is used to estimate agricultural income that would be lost were present allocations reduced. (NB. Since the title provides the context—water shortage in Israel—it is not necessary to repeat it in the abstract. Title and abstract complement each other; the latter should not exist separately from the title. This abstract is quite longwinded: "a limited amount of water supply and increasing demands" is a roundabout way of saying "water shortage," which is already explicit in the title).

5. This one can be reduced almost 50 percent:

A very intensive development of the bacteria in the subsoil of high-water-table irrigation systems may be responsible for reduced rice yields.

6. Can be further abbreviated:

A 3″ centrifugal pump, a 5 hp motor, and a 90 degree V-notch were used to measure the depths, static water levels, pumping levels, and yields of 12 tubewells. Pumping rate correlates positively with the coefficient of transmissibility and negatively with drawdown. A formula derived from Thiem's theory can be used in calculating the pumping rates.

7. A very longwinded abstract. The substance can be stated as follows:

Water managers, called in during a drought, showed that efficiency in water use could be greatly improved, leading to drastically reduced consumption without reducing rice yield. (NB. Various parts of the original abstract are superfluous. The first sentence is implicit in the later "by improved water use efficiency." The "because of the fear of crop failure" is self-evident and adds nothing to the abstract. On the other hand, because the title is nonspecific, the particular crop (rice), rather than "crop" in general, should be specified. Of course, one could not replace "crop" with "rice" without seeing the original article.)

8. A rare example of a very poor abstract in *Irricab*. It adds essentially nothing to the information in the title. It would not be possible to improve on this without seeing the original.

APPENDIX 1

Summary of abstracting principles as presented by Payne et al. (1962). Reprinted by permission of the American Institutes for Research.

General Principles

1. No restriction should be placed on absolute length of the abstract. The abstract should be of the length necessary to make it the most direct, concise, unified statement possible, which includes all the plus information from the article and none of the zero information. By zero information is meant: (1) that material which is judged to have no reasonable likelihood of directly or indirectly supporting any job decision; (2) that material which is redundant to other material already included; and (3) that material which is common knowledge to those competent in the field.

2. Short, well-written, complete sentences are required for easy access to the information.

3. The abstract may either paraphrase the original article or selectively and carefully lift from it. The better organized, the more well-written the original article, the more dependence may be placed on the latter method, a form of "extracting."

4. Technical words and phrases should be those currently used in the science under consideration.

5. New terms or names should be reported with definitions.

6. To avoid confusion and provide readability, only the most common abbreviations and standard symbols should be used.

Content Principles

1. If not apparent from the title, the introductory statement should give an accurate indication of the subject dealt with and the methods used. However, this statement is wasteful redundancy if the title has well represented the subject matter and method of investigation.

2. If not apparent from the title and/or the introductory statement, the following statement should indicate the article's scope and author's purpose and objectives. If the abstract-user is seeking some specific information, these two statements should indicate to him the likelihood of finding his information.

   In effect, these opening statements should constitute a concise descriptive abstract used in most cases to help the reader determine whether he should go back to the original article, but in this instance to determine for him if the information contained is what he is seeking or appropriate to his task.

3. Whether the article is experimental or theoretical in nature, the author's hypothesis should be explicitly stated if not apparent from the opening statements.

4. The investigative methods used should be identified. If standard techniques or procedures are used, these need not be described. If the procedures are new or contain novel characteristics applied to well-known procedures, these features should be clearly described. The basic principles of new methods or technologies, their uses and qualities, operational ranges, and degrees of accuracy should be stated.

5. Data gathering methods, methods of measurement, rotation of variables, method of isolating the data, identification of indices, data summarizing techniques, etc., must be explicitly described. The abstracter must depend upon the data collection method, along with the method of investigation in evaluating the quality of the author's work and the reliability and validity of the results and conclusions.

6. Data, whether a collection of experimental results or theoretical arguments, must be presented to the extent, and only to the extent, that they fully represent all significant aspects of the article, and must be sufficient to lead logically to the author's conclusions. Data of an absolute nature should be presented in sufficient detail to satisfy the anticipated use to be made of it in projected scientific endeavor.

Data may be presented in any form, the criterion for format being: use the most economical yet most lucid presentation possible. Precisely labeled tables, charts, graphs, etc., may be included, but data presented in this fashion should be self-sufficient, i.e., understandable without reference to the text of the abstract.

7. Qualitative and/or quantitative data manipulation methods, when used, should be indicated. Standard, well-known techniques need not be described. Variations or special applications of known techniques should be presented to the extent necessary to completely represent the significant aspects of the study and to fully substantiate the conclusions drawn.

8. The logical conclusions must be presented. Hypotheses and theories must be re-examined as proven or disproven, accepted or rejected. At this point, the abstracter has the responsibility for discriminating between substantiated and unsubstantiated conclusions and real conclusions vs. inferences. Above all, he must not present conclusions that cannot be verified from the previous sections of the abstract. Erroneous statements contained in the article must not be included unless accompanied by a statement sharply calling attention to the error, and the error correction, if possible.

9. Valid and significant interpretations the author makes of the results and/ or conclusions presented can be included if they further knowledge in such ways as showing new relationships or reaffirming old relationships.

10. Throughout the abstract, the abstracter must exercise his right to clarify and simplify material contained in the article.

APPENDIX 2

Modular Content Analysis With Subject Modules*

Citation

STOLL, A.M., CHIANTA, M.A., and MUNROE, L.R. Flame-contact studies. Transactions of the ASME, Series C, Journal of Heat Transfer, vol. 86, No. 3, August 1964, pp. 449-456.

Abstract

Flame impingement heating apparatus and methods, applied successfully to determine destruction temperatures and thermal characteristics of fiber-type and plastics materials, are described. Test results confirming the analysis are presented. Results for a polyamide fiber, and for the insulation effect of air spaces between fabric layers, are given.

Composite slab models were injected into the flame of a Meker burner and the backside wall temperatures determined optically or by thermocouples. The heat flux to the surface was determined optically. On the flame side of the composite wall a polyamide fabric (du Pont HT-1) of varying weights per unit surface area (3 oz-5 oz/sq yd) was evaluated. The backside, or reference material, in the wall consisted of a resinous compound (simulated skin) with known thermal and optical properties. Destruction temperatures of the HT-1 fabric were 427±3°C as determined optically and 423±27°C as determined by thermocouple measurements. Flame temperature was 1200°C. Burn-through occurred in 3-6 seconds depending on the weight. In investigating the use of air spaces as insulating layers between layers of the fabric, 4 mm. gaps appeared to be optimum for the 3 oz/sq yd material. It was concluded that for short-time, high-temperature applications, insulating materials of this form would tend to be optimum for personnel protection. Very thin (.050-.100 cm) RTV-20 silicone rubber samples were used in validation tests of the mathematical analysis. Excellent agreement was obtained between calculated and measured wall temperatures (percent difference of 0.5 percent); the analysis used was that of Griffith and Horton.

The use of these analytical and experimental techniques is discussed in relation to determining thermal diffusivity and thermal conductivity from flame-contact type tests. It is concluded that the techniques provided a sensitive and accurate means of determining thermal properties.

Specialized Subject Modules (paragraphs supplementary to basic abstract)

*Reproduced by permission of Saul Herner.

Physiology and Medicine

Apparatus is described, and mathematical expressions developed, which may allow an analysis of tissue damage, due to exposure to flame, from knowledge of the properties and temperature-time history of an overlying fabric layer. This constitutes a relatively simple means of studying thermal properties (including diffusivity and conductivity) of intact living tissue without alteration of the tissue itself.

Plastics Industry

HT-1, an experimental heat-resistant polyamide textile fiber of du Pont, was exposed to flame impingement in a Meker burner with a flame temperature of 1200°C. Destruction temperature of fabrics of 3, 4, 5, and 6 oz/sq yd weight was 427±3°C, as measured radiometrically. Burn-through occurred in 3-6 seconds, depending on the weight.

Rubber Industry

Transient heat flow through a two-layer assembly of RTV-20, a silicone rubber manufactured by General Electric, backed by simulated skin, was measured by means of a flame-impingement calorimeter. Three-second temperature rise for rubber layers of 0.95, 0.55, and 0.52 mm was measured within the backing layer and agreed excellently with theoretical values.

Protective Clothing and Aircraft Industries

The experiments described, on the destruction temperatures and thermal characteristics of fabrics under flame impingement heating, are of great significance to the design of clothing for burn protection. In particular they help to explain why, in experiments on flight coveralls, greatly increased burn protection is offered by double-layer clothing as compared to single-layer suits.

Index Entries

Authors
STOLL, A.M.
CHIANTA, M.A.
MUNROE, L.R.

Affiliations
Aviation Medical Acceleration
    Laboratory, U.S. Naval Air
    Development Center,
    Johnsville, Pennsylvania

Glossary

Many terms used in this book are defined when they first occur. Definitions can usually be located through the index. The purpose of this brief glossary is simply to define some terms that are used throughout the book without necessarily being defined explicitly when they occur in the text. The definitions refer to the way the terms are used in this book and do not necessarily correspond to how these terms may be used by other writers or in other contexts.

Database—A collection of items that can be searched to reveal those that touch upon a particular subject. The database can consist of artifacts, such as books (a library collection is certainly a database), or of records representing the artifacts, such as bibliographic records appearing on printed pages, on cards, or on electronic media.

Depth—This term tends to be used very loosely in the literature of information retrieval. In effect it refers to the number of access points provided. In this book the terms *exhaustivity* and *specificity* are preferred.

Exhaustivity—The extent to which the breadth of subject matter discussed in a particular document is covered in a representation of that document. It will correspond roughly to the number of index terms assigned or some other measure of the number of access points provided (e.g., the length of an abstract). Contrast with specificity.

Pertinence—The relationship that exists between a source of information and the information need that some individual has at a particular time. One can refer to a journal article as "pertinent" to the information need if the individual decides that it makes some contribution to satisfying the need (e.g., solving a problem or making a decision). By this definition, only the person having the need can decide what is pertinent and what is not.

Precision—The extent to which the items retrieved in a search of a database are considered relevant or pertinent. A search achieving high precision will be one in which most, if not all, of the items retrieved are judged

291

relevant or pertinent. The precision ratio, a measure of the extent to which precision is achieved, is the number of relevant (pertinent) items retrieved divided by the total number of items retrieved.

Recall—The extent to which all of the items in a database that are considered relevant or pertinent are retrieved in a search of that database. A "high recall" search will be one in which most, if not all, of the relevant (pertinent) items are retrieved. The recall ratio, a measure of the extent to which the retrieval of relevant (pertinent) items occurs, is the number of relevant (pertinent) items retrieved divided by the total number of relevant (pertinent) items in the database.

Relevance—Refers to a relationship between statements of information need and potential sources of information. For example, a journal article can be considered relevant to a statement of need if it discusses the problem or situation covered by the statement. The relationship is a subjective one since different individuals will make different decisions on which items are relevant to which statements or to what degree they are relevant to these statements. A special form of relevance, relevance to an information need, is referred to as *pertinence* in this book.

Representation—A record that is intended to indicate what subjects are dealt with by some bibliographic item. An abstract is one form of representation; a set of index terms is another.

Specificity—The level of detail with which a topic discussed in a document is covered in a representation of that document. The level of specificity possible is determined by characteristics of the vocabulary used in indexing, although an indexer (probably erroneously) may represent a topic less specifically than the vocabulary allows. Contrast with *exhaustivity*.

REFERENCES

Aitchison, J. and Cleverdon, C. W. *A Report on a Test of the Index of Metallurgical Literature of Western Reserve University.* Cranfield, College of Aeronautics, 1963.

Aitchison, T. M. et al. *Comparative Evaluation of Index Languages.* London, Institution of Electrical Engineers, 1969-1970. 2 vols.

Ajiferuke, I. and Chu, C. M. Quality of indexing in online databases: an alternative measure for a term discriminating index. *Information Processing & Management,* 24, 1988, 599-601.

Albright, J. B. *Some Limits to Subject Retrieval from a Large Published Index.* Doctoral thesis. Urbana, University of Illinois, Graduate School of Library Science, 1979.

Alt, F. L. et al. *Integration of Primary and Secondary Production Systems.* New York: American Institute of Physics, 1974. PB 244 771.

American National Standards Institute Inc. *American National Standard for Library and Information Sciences and Related Publishing Practices—Basic Criteria for Indexes.* ANSI Z39.4-1984. New York, 1984.

American National Standards Institute Inc. *American National Standard for Writing Abstracts.* ANSI Z39.14-1979. New York, 1979.

Anderson, M. D. *Book Indexing.* Cambridge, Cambridge University Press, 1971. (Reprinted with corrections in 1979.)

Armitage, J. E. and Lynch, M. F. Some structural characteristics of articulated subject indexes. *Information Storage and Retrieval,* 4(1), 1968, 101-111.

Armstrong, C. J. and Keen, E. M. *Workbook for NEPHIS and KWAC.* Boston Spa, British Library, 1982. British Library Research and Development Reports Number 5710. (Microcomputer Printed Subject Indexes Teaching Package, volume 1)

Artandi, S. *Book Indexing by Computer.* Doctoral thesis. New Brunswick, N.J., Rutgers, the State University, 1963.

Austin, D. *PRECIS: a Manual of Concept Analysis and Subject Indexing.* Second edition. London, British Library, 1984.

Austin, D. and Digger, J. A. PRECIS: the Preserved Context Index System. *Library Resources and Technical Services,* 21(1), 1977, 13-30.

293

Azgaldov, E. G. A framework for description and classification of printed subject indexes. *Libri,* 19, 1969, 275-291.

Baker, D. B. The determining characteristics of the time-space framework of our environment and the special nature of the information that will be needed. In: *Information Demand and Supply for the 1980's,* pp. 63-77. Paris, International Council of Scientific Unions Abstracting Board, 1978.

Baker, D. B. Recent trends in chemical literature growth. *Chemical and Engineering News,* 59(22), 1981, 29-34.

Baker, S. L. Will fiction classification schemes increase use? *RQ,* 27, 1988, 366-376.

Baker, S. L. and Shepherd, G. W. Fiction classification schemes: the principles behind them and their success. *RQ,* 27, 1987, 245-251.

Bakewell, K. G. B. Reference books for indexers. *The Indexer,* 15, 1987, 131-140.

Barlow, D. H. A & I services as database producers: economic, technological and cooperative opportunities. *Aslib Proceedings,* 28, 1976, 325-337.

Barlow, D. H. Information techniques and mechanisms for the 1980's. In: *Information Demand and Supply for the 1980's,* pp. 115-123. Paris, International Council of Scientific Unions Abstracting Board, 1978.

Bates, M. J. Subject access in online catalogs: a design model. *Journal of the American Society for Information Science,* 37, 1986, 357-376.

Bates, M. J. System meets user: problems in matching subject search terms. *Information Processing and Management,* 13, 1977, 367-375.

Baxendale, P. B. Machine-made index for technical literature—an experiment. *IBM Journal of Research and Development,* 2, 1958, 354-361.

Bearman, T. C. Secondary information systems and services. *Annual Review of Information Science and Technology,* 13, 1978, 179-208.

Bearman, T. C. and Kunberger, W. A. *A Study of Coverage Overlap Among Fourteen Major Science and Technology Abstracting and Indexing Services.* Philadelphia, National Federation of Abstracting and Indexing Services, 1977.

Beghtol, C. Bibliographic classification theory and text linguistics: aboutness analysis, intertextuality and the cognitive act of classifying documents. *Journal of Documentation,* 42, 1986, 84-113.

Belkin, N. J. Anomalous states of knowledge as a basis for information retrieval. *Canadian Journal of Information Science,* 5, 1980, 133-143.

Belkin, N. J. et al. ASK for information retrieval. *Journal of Documentation,* 38, 1982, 61-71, 145-164.

Bernier, C. L. and Yerkey, A. N. *Cogent Communication: Overcoming Reading*

Overload. Westport, Conn., Greenwood Press, 1979.

Bernstein, L. M. and Williamson, R. E. Testing of a natural language retrieval system for a full text knowledge base. *Journal of the American Society for Information Science,* 35, 1984, 235-247.

Bhattacharyya, G. The effectiveness of natural language in science indexing and retrieval. *Journal of Documentation,*30, 1974, 235-254.

Bhattacharyya, G. Elements of POPSI. In: *Indexing Systems: Concepts, Models and Techniques;* ed. by T. N. Rajan, pp. 73-102. Calcutta, Indian Association of Special Libraries and Information Centres, 1981.

Blair, D. C. and Maron, M. E. An evaluation of retrieval effectiveness for a full-text document-retrieval system. *Communications of the Association for Computing Machinery,* 28, 1985, 289-299.

Bonham, M. D. and Nelson, L. L. An evaluation of four end-user systems for searching MEDLINE. *Bulletin of the Medical Library Association,* 76, 1988, 22-31.

Borko, H. Toward a theory of indexing. *Information Processing and Management,* 13, 1977, 355-365.

Borko, H. and Bernick, M. Automatic document classification. *Journal of the Association for Computing Machinery,* 10, 1963, 151-162.

Borko, H. and Bernier, C. L. *Abstracting Concepts and Methods.* New York, Academic Press, 1975.

Borko, H. and Chatman, S. Criteria for acceptable abstracts: a survey of abstractors' instructions. *American Documentation,* 14, 1963, 149-160.

Borkowski, C. and Martin, J. S. Structure, effectiveness and benefits of LEXtractor, an operational computer program for automatic extraction of case summaries and dispositions from court decisions. *Journal of the American Society for Information Science,* 26, 1975, 94-102.

Bourne, C. P. *Characteristics of Coverage by the Bibliography of Agriculture of the Literature Relating to Agricultural Research and Development.* Palo Alto, Calif., Information General Corporation, 1969a. PB 185 425.

Bourne, C. P. *Overlapping Coverage of the Bibliography of Agriculture by Fifteen Other Secondary Sources.* Palo Alto, Calif., Information General Corporation, 1969b. PB 185 069.

Boyce, B. R. and McLain, J. P. Entry point depth and online search using a controlled vocabulary. *Journal of the American Society for Information Science,* 40, 1989, 273-276.

Brenner, C. W. and Mooers, C. N. A case history of a Zatocoding information retrieval system. In: *Punched Cards: Their Applications to Science and Industry.* Second edition, ed. by R. S. Casey et al., pp. 340-356. New York, Reinhold, 1958.

Brenner, E. H. et al. American Petroleum Institute's machine-aided indexing and searching project. *Science and Technology Libraries,* 5(1), 1984, 49-62.

Breton, E. J. Why engineers don't use databases. *Bulletin of the American Society for Information Science,* 7(6), 1981, 20-23.

Brittain, J. M. and Roberts, S. A. Rationalization of secondary services: measurement of coverage of primary journals and overlap between services. *Journal of the American Society for Information Science,* 31, 1980, 131-142.

Burchinal, L. G. The ST communication enterprise in the United States: status and forecasts. *Library Science with a Slant Towards Documentation,* 14(2), 1977, 53-61.

Burke, F. G. The application of automated techniques in the management and control of source materials. *American Archivist,* 30, 1967, 255-278.

Byrne, J. R. Relative effectiveness of titles, abstracts, and subject headings for machine retrieval from the COMPENDEX services. *Journal of the American Society for Information Science,* 26, 1975, 223-229.

Caren, L. and Somerville, A. Online versus print sources in academic scientific and technical libraries: supplement or replacement? *Science & Technology Libraries,* 6(4), 1986, 45-59.

Carroll, K. H. An analytical survey of virology literature reported in two announcement journals. *American Documentation,* 20, 1969, 234-237.

Chu, C. M. and Ajiferuke, I. Quality of indexing in library and information science databases. *Online Review,* 13, 1989, 11-35.

Clemencin, G. Querying the French Yellow Pages: natural language access to the directory. *Information Processing and Management,* 24, 1988, 633-649.

Cleverdon, C. W. *A Comparative Evaluation of Searching by Controlled Language and Natural Language in an Experimental NASA Data Base.* Frascati, European Space Agency, Space Documentation Service, 1977.

Cleverdon, C. W. et al. *Factors Determining the Performance of Index Languages.* Cranfield, England, College of Aeronautics, 1966. 3 vols.

Cluley, H. J. *Analytical Abstracts:* user reaction study. *Proceedings of the Society for Analytical Chemistry,* 5, 1968, 217-221.

Coates, E. J. *Subject Catalogues: Headings and Structure.* London, Library Association, 1960.

Coco, A. Full-text versus full-text plus editorial additions. *Legal Reference Services Quarterly,* 4(2), 1984, 27-37.

Collison, R. L. *Abstracts and Abstracting Services.* Santa Barbara, ABC-Clio, 1971.

Collison, R. L. *Indexes and Indexing*. Fourth edition. New York, deGraaf, 1972.

Conaway, C. W. *An Experimental Investigation of the Influence of Several Index Variables on Index Usability and a Preliminary Study Toward a Coefficient of Index Usability*. Doctoral thesis. Rutgers University, Graduate School of Library Service, 1974.

Conrad, C. C. Status of indexing and classification systems and potential future trends. *Journal of Chemical Information and Computer Sciences,* 16, 1976, 197- 201.

Cook, M. *Archives and the Computer.* London, Butterworths, 1980.

Cooper, W. S. Expected search length: a single measure of retrieval effectiveness based on the weak ordering action of retrieval systems. *American Documentation,* 19, 1968, 30-41.

Cooper, W. S. Indexing documents by gedanken experimentation. *Journal of the American Society for Information Science,* 29, 1978, 107-119.

Cooper, W. S. Is inter-indexer consistency a hobgoblin? *American Documentation,* 20, 1969, 268-278.

Craven, T. C. NEPHIS: a nested-phrase indexing system. *Journal of the American Society for Information Science,* 28, 1977, 107-114.

Craven, T. C. *String Indexing*. Orlando, Academic Press, 1986.

Cremmins, E. T. *The Art of Abstracting*. Philadelphia, ISI Press, 1982.

Creps, J. E., Jr. Remarks made at the National Information Conference and Exposition, NICE III, Washington, DC, April 1979.

Crowe, J. D. *Study of the Feasibility of Indexing a Work's Subjective Viewpoint*. Doctoral thesis. Berkeley, University of California, 1986.

Cuadra, C. A. A brief introduction to electronic publishing. *Electronic Publishing Review,* 1, 1981, 29-34.

Cutter, C. A. *Rules for a Dictionary Catalog*. Washington, D.C., Government Printing Office, 1876.

Dabney, D. P. The curse of Thamus: an analysis of full-text legal document retrieval. *Law Library Journal,* 78, 1986a, 5-40.

Dabney, D. P. A reply to West Publishing Company and Mead Data Central on *The Curse of Thamus. Law Library Journal,* 78, 1986b, 349-350.

Dahlberg, I. On the theory of the concept. In: *Ordering Systems for Global Information Networks;* ed. by A. Neelameghan, pp. 54-63. Bangalore, International Federation for Documentation, 1979.

Davison, P. S. and Matthews, D. A. R. Assessment of information services. *Aslib Proceedings,* 21, 1969, 280-284.

Defense Documentation Center. *Abstracting of Technical Reports.* 1968. AD 667 000.

Diodato, V. P. *Author Indexing in Mathematics*. Doctoral thesis. Urbana,

University of Illinois, Graduate School of Library and Information Science, 1981.

Doszkocs, T. E. CITE NLM: natural-language searching in an online catalog. *Information Technology and Libraries*, 2, 1983, 364-380.

Drage, J. F. User preferences in technical indexes. *The Indexer*, 6, 1969, 151-155.

Dronberger, G. B. and Kowitz, G. T. Abstract readability as a factor in information systems. *Journal of the American Society for Information Science*, 26, 1975, 108-111.

Drott, M. C., et al. *Cooperative Use of Machine Readable Database by Publishers of Primary and Secondary Journals—A Preliminary Study.* Philadephia, Drexel University School of Library Science, 1977. PB 276 622.

Dubois, C. P. R. Free text vs. controlled vocabulary; a reassessment. *Online Review,* 11, 1987, 243-253.

Dutta, S. and Sinha, P. K. Pragmatic approach to subject indexing: a new concept. *Journal of the American Society for Information Science,* 35, 1984, 325-331.

Dym, E. D. Relevance predictability: I. Investigation, background and procedures. In: *Electronic Handling of Information: Testing and Evaluation;* ed. by A. Kent et al., pp. 175-185. Washington, D.C., Thompson Book Co., 1967.

Earl, L. L. Experiments in automatic extracting and indexing. *Information Storage and Retrieval,* 6, 1970, 313-334.

Ebinuma, Y. et al. Promotion of keyword assignment to scientific literature by contributors. *International Forum on Information and Documentation,* 8(3), 1983, 16-20.

Eco, U. *The Role of the Reader: Explorations in the Semiotics of Texts.* Bloomington, Indiana University Press, 1979.

Edmundson, H. P. New methods in automatic extracting. *Journal of the Association for Computing Machinery,* 16, 1969, 264-289.

Edmundson, H. P. et al. *Final Report on the Study for Automatic Abstracting.* Canoga Park, Calif., Thompson Ramo Wooldridge, 1961. PB 166 532.

Edwards, T. A comparative analysis of the major abstracting and indexing services for library and information science. *Unesco Bulletin for Libraries,* 30, 1976, 18-25.

Elchesen, D. R. Cost effectiveness comparison of manual and on-line retrospective bibliographic searching. *Journal of the American Society for Information Science,* 29, 1978, 56-66.

ERIC Processing Manual. Section 7: Indexing. Washington, D.C., U.S. Department of Education, Educational Resources Information Center, 1980.

Fairthorne, R. A. Automatic retrieval of recorded information. *Computer Journal,* 1(1), 1958, 36-41.

Falk, J. D. and Baser, K. H. ABC-Spindex: a subject profile, rotated string indexing system. *Proceedings of the American Society for Information Science,* 17, 1980, 152-154.

Fangmeyer, H. *Semi-Automatic Indexing: State of the Art.* Neuilly sur Seine, North Atlantic Treaty Organization, Advisory Group for Aerospace Research and Development, 1974.

Farradane, J. A comparison of some computer-produced permuted alphabetical subject indexes. *International Classification,* 4, 1977, 94-101.

Farradane, J. Concept organization for information retrieval. *Information Storage and Retrieval,* 3, 1967, 297-314.

Farradane, J. Relational indexing. *Journal of Information Science,* 1, 1980, 267-276, 313-324.

Farradane, J. and Yates-Mercer, P. A. Retrieval characteristics of the index to Metals Abstracts. *Journal of Documentation,* 29, 1973, 295-314.

Fedosyuk, M. Yu. Linguistic criteria for differentiating informative and indicative abstracts. *Automatic Documentation and Mathematical Linguistics,* 12(3), 1978, 98-110. [English translation of Nauchno-tekhnicheskaya informatsiya, Seriya 2, 12(9), 1978, pp. 11-17.]

Fidel, R. Individual variability in online search behavior. *Proceedings of the American Society for Information Science,* 22, 1985, 69-72.

Fidel, R. Writing abstracts for free-text searching. *Journal of Documentation,* 42, 1986, 11-21.

Fridman, E. P. and Popova, V. N. Otrazhenie mirovoi literatury po eksperimental'noi primatologii v *Referativnykh Zhurnalakh SSSR. Nauchno-tekhnicheskaya informatsiya,* Seriya 1, No. 2, 1972, 34-36.

Fried, C. and Prevel, J. J. *Effects of Indexing Aids on Indexing Performance.* Bethesda, Md., General Electric Co., 1966. RADC-TR-66-525.

Frohmann, B. Rules of indexing: a critique of mentalisms in information retrieval theory. *Journal of Documentation,* 46, 1990, 81-101.

Fugmann, R. The five-axiom theory of indexing and information supply. *Journal of the American Society for Information Science,* 36, 1985, 116-129.

Fugmann, R. Review of second edition of *Vocabulary Control for Information Retrieval* by F. W. Lancaster. *International Classification,* 14, 1987, 164-166.

Fugmann, R. Toward a theory of information supply and indexing. *International Classification*, 6, 1979, 3-15.

Fuhr, N. Models for retrieval with probabilistic indexing. *Information Processing and Management*, 25, 1989, 55-72.

Fum, D. et al. Forward and backward reasoning in automatic abstracting. In: *COLING 82, Proceedings of the Ninth International Conference on Computational Linguistics;* ed. by J. Horecky, pp. 83-88. Amsterdam, North Holland Publishing, 1982.

Funk, M. E. and Reid, C. A. Indexing consistency in MEDLINE. *Bulletin of the Medical Library Association*, 71, 1983, 176-183.

Gilchrist, A. Documentation of documentation: a survey of leading abstracts services in documentation and an identification of key journals. *Aslib Proceedings*, 18, 1966, 62-80.

Goldhar, J. D. Obtaining and using information in the year 2002. *IEEE Transactions on Professional Communication*, PC-20, 1979, 126-129.

Goode, D. J. et al. Comparative analysis of *Epilepsy Abstracts* and a MEDLARS bibliography. *Bulletin of the Medical Library Association*, 58, 1970, 44-50.

Hagerty, K. *Abstracts as a Basis for Relevance Judgment.* Chicago, University of Chicago, Graduate Library School, 1967. Working paper no. 380-5.

Hahn, U. and Reimer, U. Heuristic text parsing in 'TOPIC': methodological issues in a knowledge-based text condensation system. In: *Representation and Exchange of Knowledge as a Basis of Information Processes;* ed. by. H. J. Dietschmann, pp. 143-163. Amsterdam, North-Holland, 1984.

Hall, A. M. *Case Studies of the Use of Subject Indexes.* London, Institution of Electrical Engineers, 1972a.

Hall, A. M. *User Preferences in Printed Indexes.* London, Institution of Electrical Engineers, 1972b.

Hanson, C. W. and Janes, M. Coverage by abstracting journals of conference papers. *Journal of Documentation*, 17, 1961, 143-149.

Harris, D. et al. *The Testing of Inter-Indexer Consistency at Various Indexing Depths.* Chicago, University of Chicago, Graduate Library School, 1966. Working paper no. 380-2.

Hawkins, D. T. Six years of online searching in an industrial library network. *Science and Technology Libraries*, 1(1), 1980, 57-67.

Haygarth Jackson, A. R. What the large users expect from secondary services producers. *Aslib Proceedings*, 28, 1976, 347-353.

Henzler, R. G. Free or controlled vocabularies: some statistical user-oriented evaluations of biomedical information systems. *International Classification*, 5, 1978, 21-26.

Herner, S. Subject slanting in scientific abstracting publications. In: *International Conference on Scientific Information, Washington, D.C., Proceedings.* Volume 1, pp. 407-427. Washington, D.C., National Academy of Sciences, 1959.

Herring, M. Y. King College Library: online databases vs. hard copy subscriptions. *Library Hi Tech,* 1(1), 1983, 63-68.

Hersey, D. F. et al. Free text word retrieval and scientist indexing: performance profiles and costs. *Journal of Documentation,* 27, 1971, 167-183.

Hitchingham, E. et al. A survey of database use at the reference desk. *Online,* 8(2), 1984, 44-50.

Hodges, P. R. Keyword in title indexes: effectiveness of retrieval in computer searches. *Special Libraries,* 74, 1983, 56-60.

Holm, B. E. and Rasmussen, L. E. Development of a technical thesaurus. *American Documentation,* 12, 1961, 184-190.

Holst, W. Problemer ved strukturering og bruk av den polytekniske tesaurus. *Tidskrift for Dokumentation,* 22, 1966, 69-74.

Hooper, R. S. Evaluation and analysis of indexing systems. In: *The Second Institute on Technical Literature Indexing,* Session 1. Washington, D.C., American University, Center for Technology and Administration, 1966.

Hooper, R. S. *Indexer Consistency Tests—Origin, Measurements, Results and Utilization.* Bethesda, IBM, 1965.

Horký, J. Shoda mezi zpracovateli pri výběrů kličových slov z odborných textů, [Agreement in the selection of keywords from specialised texts]. *Československá informatika,* 25, 1983, 275-278.

Horty, J. F. Experience with the application of electronic data processing systems in general law. *Modern Uses of Logic in Law,* 60D, 1960, 158-168.

Horty, J. F. Legal research using electronic techniques. In: *Literature of the Law—Techniques of Access.* (Proceedings of the 5th American Association of Law Libraries Institute for Law Librarians, pp. 56-68.) South Hackensack, N.J., F. B. Rothman & Co., 1962.

Humphrey, S. M. and Chien, D-C. *The MedIndEx: Research on Interactive Knowledge-Based Indexing and Knowledge Management.* Bethesda, MD, National Library of Medicine, 1990. PB 90-234964/AS.

Humphrey, S. M. and Kapoor, A. *The MedIndEx System: Research on Interactive Knowledge-Based Indexing of the Medical Literature.* Bethesda, National Library of Medicine, 1988. PB 88-243902/AS.

Humphrey, S. M. and Miller, N. E. Knowledge-based indexing of the medical literature: the Indexing Aid Project. *Journal of the American Society for Information Science,* 38, 1987, 184-196.

Hutchins, W. J. The concept of "aboutness" in subject indexing. *Aslib Proceedings,* 30, 1978, 172-181.

ISO 5963-1985 (E). *Documentation—Methods for Examining Documents, Determining Their Subjects, and Selecting Indexing Terms.* Geneva, International Organization for Standardization, 1985.

Iivonen, M. Interindexer consistency and the indexing environment. *International Forum on Information and Documentation,* 15, 1990, 16-21.

Jacoby, J. and Slamecka, V. *Indexer Consistency Under Minimal Conditions.* Bethesda, Md., Documentation Inc., 1962. RADC-TDR-62-426.

Jahoda, G. and Stursa, M. L. A comparison of a keyword from title index with a single access point per document alphabetic subject index. *American Documentation,* 20, 1969, 377-380.

Jonak, Z. Problémy informačníanalyzy prí popisu beletristického díla. (Problems of information analysis in describing a work of fiction). *Knižnice a vedecké informácie,* 10(1), 1978, 16-21.

Jones, K. P. Towards a theory of indexing. *Journal of Documentation,* 32, 1976, 118-125.

Jonker, F. *Indexing Theory, Indexing Methods and Search Devices.* New York, Scarecrow Press, 1964.

Kaiser, J. O. *Systematic Indexing.* London, Pitman, 1911.

Karasev, S. A. Abstracting scientific and technical literature: elements of a theory. *Automatic Documentation and Mathematical Linguistics,* 12(4), 1978, 1-7. [English translation of *Nauchno-tekhnicheskaya informatsiya,* Seriya 2, 12(10), 1978, 1-4.]

Keen, E. M. On the generation and searching of entries in printed subject indexes. *Journal of Documentation,* 33, 1977a, 15-45.

Keen, E. M. On the processing of printed subject index entries during searching. *Journal of Documentation,* 33, 1977b, 266-276.

Keen, E. M. A retrieval comparison of six published indexes in the field of library and information science. *Unesco Bulletin for Libraries,* 30, 1976, 26-36.

Keen, E. M. and Digger, J. A. *Report of an Information Science Index Languages Test.* Aberystwyth, College of Librarianship Wales, 1972. 2 volumes.

Kehl, W. B. et al. An information retrieval language for legal studies. *Communications of the Association for Computing Machinery,* 4, 1961, 380-389.

Kent, A. et al. Relevance predictability in information retrieval systems. *Methods of Information in Medicine,* 6, 1967, 45-51.

Kessler, M. M. Bibliographic coupling between scientific papers. *American*

Documentation, 14, 1963, 10-25.

Kessler, M. M. *Bibliographic Coupling Extended in Time.* Cambridge, Massachusetts Institute of Technology, 1962.

Kessler, M. M. Comparison of results of bibliographic coupling and analytic subject indexing. *American Documentation,* 16, 1965, 223-233.

King, R. A comparison of the readability of abstracts with their source documents. *Journal of the American Society for Information Science,* 27, 1976, 118-121.

Klingbiel, P. H. *The Future of Indexing and Retrieval Vocabularies.* Alexandria, Va., Defense Documentation Center, 1970, AD 716 200.

Klingbiel, P. H. *Machine-aided Indexing.* Technical progress report for period July 1969-June 1970. Alexandria, Va., Defense Documentation Center, 1971. AD 721 875.

Klingbiel, P. H. and Rinker, C. C. Evaluation of machine-aided indexing. *Information Processing and Management,* 12, 1976, 351-366.

Knapp, S. D. BRS/TERM: database for searchers. *Online '83 Conference Proceedings,* pp. 162-166. Weston, Connecticut, Online Inc., 1983.

Knapp, S. D. Free-text searching of online databases. *Reference Librarian,* 5/6, 1982, 143-153.

Knight, G. N. *Indexing, the Art of : a Guide to the Indexing of Books and Periodicals.* London, Allen & Unwin, 1979.

Knorz, G. *Automatisches Indexieren als Erkennen abstrakter Objekte.* Tubingen, Max Niemeyer Verlag, 1983.

Korotkin, A. L. and Oliver, L. H. *The Effect of Subject Matter Familiarity and the Use of an Indexing Aid upon Inter-Indexer Consistency.* Bethesda, Md., General Electric Company, Information Systems Operation, 1964.

Korotkin, A. L. et al. *Indexing Aids, Procedures and Devices.* Bethesda, General Electric Co., Information Systems Operation, 1964.

Krieger, T. *Instructor Influences Versus Text Influences in the Selection of Subject Descriptors by Undergraduate Students.* Doctoral thesis. Urbana, University of Illinois, Graduate School of Library Science, 1981.

Kuhlen, R. Some similarities and differences between intellectual and machine text understanding for the purpose of abstracting. In: *Representation and Exchange of Knowledge as a Basis of Information Processes;* ed. by H. J. Dietschmann, pp. 87-109. Amsterdam, North-Holland, 1984.

Kwok, K. L. A probabilistic theory of indexing and similarity measure based on cited and citing documents. *Journal of the American Society for Information Science,* 36, 1985a, 342-351.

Kwok, K. L. A probabilistic theory of indexing using author-provided relevance information. *Proceedings of the American Society for Information Science,* 22, 1985b, 59-63.

LaBorie, T. et al. Library and information science abstracting and indexing services: coverage, overlap, and context. *Library and Information Science Research,* 7, 1985, 183-195.

Lancaster, F. W. *Evaluation of the MEDLARS Demand Search Service.* Bethesda, National Library of Medicine, 1968.

Lancaster, F. W. *Information Retrieval Systems: Characteristics, Testing and Evaluation.* Second edition. New York, Wiley, 1979.

Lancaster, F. W. Some considerations relating to the cost effectiveness of online services in libraries. *Aslib Proceedings,* 33, 1981, 10-14.

Lancaster, F. W. Some observations on the performance of EJC role indicators in a mechanized retrieval system. *Special Libraries,* 55, 1964, 696-701.

Lancaster, F. W. *Vocabulary Control for Information Retrieval.* Washington, D.C., Information Resources Press, 1972.

Lancaster, F. W. *Vocabulary Control for Information Retrieval.* Second edition. Arlington, Va., Information Resources Press, 1986.

Lancaster, F. W. and Goldhor, H. The impact of online services on subscriptions to printed publications. *Online Review,* 5, 1981, 301-311.

Lancaster, F. W. et al. Evaluating the effectiveness of an on-line, natural language retrieval system. *Information Storage and Retrieval,* 8, 1972, 223-245.

Lancaster, F. W. et al. *Modular Content Analyses.* Final report to the National Science Foundation. Washington, D.C., Herner and Company, 1965.

Leonard, L. E. *Inter-Indexer Consistency and Retrieval Effectiveness: Measurement of Relationships.* Doctoral thesis. Urbana, University of Illinois, Graduate School of Library Science, 1975.

Lerner, R. G. Electronic publishing. In: *New Trends in Documentation and Automation;* ed. by P. J. Taylor, pp. 111-116. London, Aslib, 1980.

Lerner, R. G., et al. *Data-Descriptive Records in the Physical Sciences.* New York, American Institute of Physics, 1976. PB 266 770.

Lilley, O. L. Evaluation of the subject catalog. *American Documentation,* 5, 1954, 41-60.

Loukopoulos, L. Indexing problems and some of their solutions. *American Documentation,* 1966, 17-25.

Luhn, H. P. The automatic creation of literature abstracts. *IBM Journal of Research and Development,* 2, 1958, 159-165.

Luhn, H. P. *Keyword-in-Context Index for Technical Literature (KWIC Index).* Yorktown Heights, N.Y., IBM Advanced Systems Development Division, 1959.

Luhn, H. P. A statistical approach to mechanized encoding and searching of literary information. *IBM Journal of Research and Development,* 1, 1957, 309-317.

Lunin, L. The development of a machine-searchable index-abstract and its application to biomedical literature. In: *Three Drexel Information Science Research Studies;* ed. by B. Flood, pp. 47-134. Philadelphia, Drexel Press, 1967.

Lynch, M. F. and Petrie, J. H. A program suite for the production of articulated subject indexes. *Computer Journal,* 16, 1973, 46-51.

Magill, F. N., ed. *Masterplots: 2,010 Plot Stories & Essay Reviews from the World's Fine Literature.* Revised edition. Englewood Cliffs, N.J., Salem Press, 1976.

Magill, F. N. ed. *Masterplots II: American Fiction Series.* Volume 1. Englewood Cliffs, N.J., Salem Press, 1986.

Marcus, R. S. et al. The user interface for the Intrex retrieval system. In: *Interactive Bibliographic Search: the User/Computer Interface;* ed. by D. E. Walker, pp. 159-201. Montvale, N.J., AFIPS Press, 1971.

Markey, K. et al. An analysis of controlled vocabulary and free-text search statements in online searches. *Online Review,* 4, 1980, 225-236.

Maron, M. E. Depth of indexing. *Journal of the American Society for Information Science,* 30, 1979, 224-228.

Maron, M. E. On indexing, retrieval and the meaning of about. *Journal of the American Society for Information Science,* 28, 1977, 38-43.

Maron, M. E. Probabilistic design principles for conventional and full-text retrieval systems. *Information Processing and Management,* 24, 1988, 249-255.

Maron, M. E. and Kuhns, J. C. On relevance, probabilistic indexing and information retrieval. *Journal of the Association for Computing Machinery,* 7, 1960, 216-244.

Maron, M. E. et al. *Probabilistic Indexing—a Statistical Technique for Document Identification and Retrieval.* Los Angeles, Thompson Ramo Wooldridge, 1959.

Martin, W. A. Toward an integral multi-file on-line bibliographic database. *Journal of Information Science,* 2, 1980, 241-253.

Martinez, C. et al. An expert system for machine-aided indexing. *Journal of Chemical Information and Computer Science,* 27, 1987, 158-162.

Martyn, J. Tests on abstracts journals: coverage, overlap, and indexing. *Journal of Documentation,* 23, 1967, 45-70.

Martyn, J. and Slater, M. Tests on abstracts journals. *Journal of Documentation,* 20, 1964, 212-235.

Mathis, B. A. *Techniques for the Evaluation and Improvement of Computer-Produced Abstracts.* Columbus, Ohio State University, Computer and

Information Science Research Center, 1972. OSU-CISRC-TR-72-15. PB 214 675.

Mathis, B. A. et al. Improvement of automatic abstracts by the use of structural analysis. *Journal of the American Society for Information Science,* 24, 1973, 101-109.

McCain, K. W. et al. Comparing retrieval performance in online data bases. *Information Processing and Management,* 23, 1987, 539-553.

McDermott, J. Another analysis of full-text legal document retrieval. *Law Library Journal,* 78, 1986, 339-343.

Metzner, A. W. K. Integrating primary and secondary journals: a model for the immediate future. *IEEE Transactions on Professional Communication,* PC-16, 1973, 84-91, 175-176.

Minecci, C. M. and Hodge, G. Machine-aided indexing productivity and organizational implications. *Information Services and Use,* 8, 1988, 133-138.

Montague, B. A. Testing, comparison and evaluation of recall, relevance and cost of coordinate indexing with links and roles. *American Documentation* 16, 1965, 201-208.

Montgomery, R. R. An indexing coverage study of toxicological literature. *Journal of Chemical Documentation,* 13, 1973, 41-44.

Mullison, W. R. et al. Comparing indexing efficiency, effectiveness, and consistency with or without the use of roles. *Proceedings of the American Society for Information Science* 6, 1969, 301-311.

Myers, J. M. Computers and the searching of law texts in England and North America: a review of the state of the art. *Journal of Documentation,* 29, 1973, 212-228.

Neufeld, L. What's ahead for secondary services: a look at the issues and the ways technology is changing the field. *Bulletin of the American Society for Information Science,* 9(2), 1982, 40-43.

O'Connor, J. Automatic subject recognition in scientific papers: an empirical study. *Journal of the Association for Computing Machinery,* 12, 1965, 490-515.

O'Connor, J. G. and Meadows, A. J. *Physics Abstracts* as a source of abstracts in astronomy. *Journal of Documentation,* 24, 1968, 107-112.

Olafsen, T. and Vokac, L. Authors' reply to R. Moss. *Journal of the American Society for Information Science,* 34, 1983, 294.

Oliver, L. H. et al. *An Investigation of the Basic Processes Involved in the Manual Indexing of Scientific Documents.* Bethesda, Md., General Electric Co., Information Systems Operation, 1966. PB 169 415.

Oppenheim, C. The patents coverage of *Chemical Abstracts. Information Scientist,* 8, 1974, 133-138.

Oswald, V. A., Jr. et al. *Automatic Indexing and Abstracting of the Contents of Documents.* Los Angeles, Planning Research Corporation, 1959. RADC-TR-59-208.

Paice, C. D. The automatic generation of literature abstracts: an approach based on the identification of self-indicating phrases. In: *Information Retrieval Research;* ed. by R. N. Oddy et al., pp. 172-191. London, Butterworths, 1981.

Pao, M. L. Term and citation searching: a preliminary report. *Proceedings of the American Society for Information Science,* 25, 1988, 177-180.

Pao, M. L. and Worthen, D. B. Retrieval effectiveness by semantic and citation searching. *Journal of the American Society for Information Science,* 40, 1989, 226-235.

Payne, D. et al. *A Textual Abstracting Technique: a Preliminary Development and Evaluation Support.* Pittsburgh, American Institutes for Research, 1962. 2 volumes. AD 285081-285082.

Pejtersen, A. M. Design of a computer-aided user-system dialogue based on an analysis of users' search behaviour. *Social Science Information Studies,* 4, 1984, 167-183.

Pejtersen, A. M. The meaning of "about" in fiction indexing and retrieval. *Aslib Proceedings,* 31, 1979, 251-257.

Pejtersen, A. M. and Austin, J. Fiction retrieval: experimental design and evaluation of a search system based on users' value criteria. *Journal of Documentation,* 39, 1983, 230-246; 40, 1984, 25-35.

Pemberton, J. K. Winds of change in the online world. *Online,* 12(2), 1988, 7-9.

Perez, E. Text enhancement: controlled vocabulary vs. free text. *Special Libraries,* 73, 1982, 183-192.

Perry, J. W. and Kent, A. *Tools for Machine Literature Searching.* New York, Interscience Publishers Inc., 1958.

Petrarca, A. E. and Lay, W. M. The double-KWIC coordinate index: a new approach for preparation of high-quality printed indexes by automatic indexing techniques. *Journal of Chemical Documentation,* 9, 1969, 256-261.

Pfaffenberger, A. and Echt, S. Substitution of SciSearch and Social SciSearch for their print versions in an academic library. *Database,* 3(1), 1980, 63-71.

Piternick, A. Searching vocabularies: a developing category of online search tools. *Online Review,* 8, 1984, 441-449.

Preschel, B. M. *Funk & Wagnalls New Encyclopedia Indexing Manual.* New York, Funk & Wagnall, 1981. (Unpublished)

Preschel, B. M. *Indexer Consistency in Perception of Concepts and in Choice of Terminology.* New York, Columbia University, School of Library Service, 1972.

Price, D. S. Possible impact of electronic publishing on abstracting and indexing. *Journal of the American Society for Information Science,* 34, 1983, 288.

Raitt, D. Recall and precision devices in interactive bibliographic search and retrieval systems. *Aslib Proceedings,* 32, 1980, 281-301.

Rasheed, M. A. Comparative index terms. *International Library Review,* 21, 1989, 289-300.

Rath, G. J. et al. Comparison of four types of lexical indicators of content. *American Documentation,* 12, 1961a, 126-130.

Rath, G. J. et al. The formation of abstracts by the selection of sentences. *American Documentation,* 12, 1961b, 139-143.

Reisner, P. *Evaluation of a "Growing" Thesaurus.* Yorktown Heights, N.Y., IBM, Thomas Watson Research Center, 1966. Research Paper RD-1662.

Resnick, A. Relative effectiveness of document titles and abstracts for determining relevance of documents. *Science,* 134, 1961, 1004-1006.

Ro, J. S. An evaluation of the applicability of ranking algorithms to improve the effectiveness of full-text retrieval. 1. On the effectiveness of full-text retrieval. *Journal of the American Society for Information Science,* 39, 1988, 73-78.

Robertson, S. E. The parametric description of retrieval tests. *Journal of Documentation,* 25, 1969, 1-27, 93-107.

Robinson, J. and Hu, M. DOE's Energy Database (EDB) versus other energy related databases: a comparative analysis. *Database,* 4(4), 1981, 10-27.

Rodgers, D. J. *A Study of Inter-Indexer Consistency.* Washington, D.C., General Electric Co., 1961.

Rolling, L. Indexing consistency, quality and efficiency. *Information Processing and Management,* 17, 1981, 69-76.

Rowlett, R. J. et al. Relationship between primary publications and secondary information services. *Journal of Chemical Documentation,* 10, 1970, 32-37.

Runde, C. E. and Lindberg, W. H. The curse of Thamus: a response. *Law Library Journal,* 78, 1986, 345-347.

Rush, J. E. et al. Automatic abstracting and indexing. II. Production of indicative abstracts by application of contextual inference and syntactic coherence criteria. *Journal of the American Society for Information Science,* 22, 1971, 260-274.

Salisbury, B. A., Jr. and Stiles, H. E. The use of the B-coefficient in information retrieval. *Proceedings of the American Society for Information Science,*

6, 1969, 265-268.

Salton, G. *Dynamic Information and Library Processing.* Englewood Cliffs, Prentice-Hall, 1975.

Salton, G. A new comparison between conventional indexing (MEDLARS) and automatic text processing (SMART). *Journal of the American Society for Information Science,* 23, 1972, 75-84.

Salton, G. *A Syntactic Approach to Automatic Book Indexing.* Ithaca, New York, Cornell University, Department of Computer Science, 1989. Technical Report TR 89-979.

Salton, G. and McGill, M. J. *Introduction to Modern Information Retrieval.* New York, McGraw Hill, 1983.

Salton, G. and Zhang, Y. Enhancement of text representations using related document titles. *Information Processing and Management,* 22, 1986, 385-394.

Sapp, G. The levels of access: subject approaches to fiction. *RQ,* 25, 1986, 488-497.

Saracevic, T. Comparative effects of titles, abstracts and full texts on relevance judgements. *Proceedings of the American Society for Information Science,* 6, 1969, 293-299.

Saracevic, T. et al. A study of information seeking and retrieving. *Journal of the American Society for Information Science,* 39, 1988, 161-216.

Sekerak, R. J. A comparison of journal coverage in Psychological Abstracts and the primary health sciences indexes: implications for cooperative serials acquisition and retention. *Bulletin of the Medical Library Association,* 74, 1986, 231-233.

Seloff, G. A. Automated access to the NASA-JSC image archives. *Library Trends,* 38, 1990 (in press).

Selye, H. *Symbolic Shorthand System.* New Brunswick, N.J., Rutgers State University, Graduate School of Library Service, 1966.

Selye, H. and Ember, G. *Symbolic Shorthand System for Physiology and Medicine.* Fourth edition. Montreal, Université de Montreal, 1964.

Sharp, J. R. The SLIC index. *American Documentation,* 17, 1966, 41-44.

Shirey, D. L. and Kurfeerst, M. Relevance predictability: II. Data reduction. In: *Electronic Handling of Information: Testing and Evaluation;* ed. by A. Kent et al., pp. 187-198. Washington, D.C., Thompson Book Co., 1967.

Sinnett, J. D. *An Evaluation of Links and Roles Used in Information Retrieval.* Dayton, Air Force Materials Laboratory, Wright Patterson Air Force Base, 1964. AD 432 198.

Slamecka, V. and Jacoby, J. *Effect of Indexing Aids on the Reliability of Indexers. Final Technical Note.* Bethesda, Documentation Inc., 1963.

RADC-TDR-63-116.

Small, H. Co-citation in the scientific literature: a new measure of the relationship between two documents. *Journal of the American Society for Information Science,* 24, 1973, 265-269.

Smalley, T. N. Comparing *Psychological Abstracts* and *Index Medicus* for coverage of the journal literature in a subject area in psychology. *Journal of the American Society for Information Science,* 31, 1980, 143-146.

Snow, B. et al. Grateful MED: NLM's front end software. *Database,* 9(6), 1986, 94-99.

Soergel, D. *Indexing Languages and Thesauri: Construction and Maintenance.* Los Angeles, Melville, 1974.

Soergel, D. *Organizing Information: Principles of Data Base and Retrieval Systems.* Orlando, Academic Press, 1985.

Solov'ev, V. I. The aspective method of abstracting. *Automatic Documentation and Mathematical Linguistics,* 5(1), 1971, 30-35. (English translation of *Nauchno-tekhnicheskaya informatsiya,* Seriya 2, Number 2, 1971, pp. 14-17.)

Solov'ev, V. I. Functional characteristics of the author's abstract of a dissertation and the specifics of writing it. *Scientific and Technical Information Processing,* 3, 1981, 80-88. (English translation of *Nauchno-tekhnicheskaya informatsiya,* Seriya 1, Number 6, 1981, pp. 20-24.)

Sparck-Jones, K. *Automatic Indexing 1974: a State of the Art Review.* Cambridge, University of Cambridge, 1974.

Sparck-Jones, K. Does indexing exhaustivity matter? *Journal of the American Society for Information Science,* 24, 1973, 313-316.

Spencer, C. C. Subject searching with *Science Citation Index:* preparation of a drug bibliography using *Chemical Abstracts, Index Medicus,* and *Science Citation Index* 1961 and 1964. *American Documentation,* 18, 1967, 87-96.

Stanley, W. G. Changing revenue patterns from online use. Paper presented at the National Information Conference and Exposition, NICE III, Washington, DC, April 1979.

Stevens, M. E. *Automatic Indexing: a State-of-the-Art Report.* Revised edition. Washington, D.C., National Bureau of Standards, 1970.

Stiles, H. E. Machine retrieval using the association factor. In: *Machine Indexing: Progress and Problems,* pp. 192-206. Washington, D.C., American University, 1961.

Swanson, D. R. Searching natural language text by computer. *Science,* 132, 3434, 1960, 1099-1104.

Swanson, D. R. Subjective versus objective relevance in bibliographic retrieval systems. *Library Quarterly,* 56, 1986, 389-398.

Swift, D. F. et al. 'Aboutness' as a strategy for retrieval in the social sciences. *Aslib Proceedings,* 30, 1978, 182-187.

Tancredi, S. A. and Nichols, O. D. Air pollution technical information processing—the microthesaurus approach. *American Documentation,* 19, 1968, 66-70.

Tell, B. V. Document representation and indexer consistency. *Proceedings of the American Society for Information Science,* 6, 1969, 285-292.

Tenopir, C. *Retrieval Performance in a Full Text Journal Article Database.* Doctoral thesis. University of Illinois, Graduate School of Library and Information Science, 1984. (Condensed versions appear as: Tenopir, C. Full text database retrieval performance. *Online Review,* 9, 1985, 149-164 and Tenopir, C. Searching *Harvard Business Review. Online,* 9[2], 1985, 71-78.)

Terminological Data Banks. Munich, K. G. Saur, 1980.

Thompson, C. W. N. The functions of abstracts in the initial screening of technical documents by the user. *Journal of the American Society for Information Science,* 24, 1973, 270-276.

Thorpe, P. An evaluation of *Index Medicus* in rheumatology: coverage, currency, and efficiency. *Methods of Information in Medicine,* 13, 1974, 44-47.

Timour, J. A. Use of selected abstracting and indexing journals in biomedical resource libraries. *Bulletin of the Medical Library Association,* 67, 1979, 330-335.

Tinker, J. F. Imprecision in indexing. *American Documentation,* 17, 1966, 93-102; 19, 1968, 322-330.

Tong, R. M. et al. *RUBRIC: an Environment for Full Text Information Retrieval.* Mountain View, Calif., Advanced Information and Decision Systems, 1985.

Torr, D. V. et al. *Program of Studies on the Use of Published Indexes.* Bethesda, Md., General Electric Co., Information Systems Operation, 1966.

Troitskii, V. P. An extrapolation approach to the concept of information. *Automatic Documentation and Mathematical Linguistics,* 13(6), 1979, 49-60. (English translation of *Nauchno-tekhnicheskaya informatsiya,* Seriya 2, 13(12), 1979, 1-7.)

Troitskii, V. P. Text, information and epistemology. *Automatic Documentation and Mathematical Linguistics,* 15(1), 1981, 20-27. (English translation of *Nauchno-tekhnicheskaya informatsiya,* Seriya 2, 15(2), 1981, 1-5.)

Trubkin, L. Auto-indexing of the 1971-77 ABI/INFORM database. *Database,* 2(2), 1979, 56-61.

Trubkin, L. Migration from print to online use. *Online Review* 4, 1980, 5-12.

Ulhmann, W. A thesaurus *Nuclear Science and Technology:* principles of design. *Teknisk-Vetenskaplig Forskning* (TVF), 38, 1967, 46-52.

UNHCR Refugee Documentation Centre. *A Guide for Abstractors.* Geneva, United Nations High Commissioner for Refugees, 1985.

Van der Meulen, W. A. and Janssen, P. J. F. C. Automatic versus manual indexing. *Information Processing and Management,* 13, 1977, 13-21.

Van Oot, J. G. et al. Links and roles in coordinate indexing and searching: an economic study of their use, and an evaluation of their effect on relevance and recall. *Journal of Chemical Documentation,* 6, 1966, 95-101.

Vickery, B. C. The structure of semantic coding: a review. *American Documentation,* 10, 1959, 234-241.

Vinsonhaler, J. F. Some behavioral indices of the validity of document abstracts. *Information Storage and Retrieval,* 3, 1966, 1-11.

Virgo, J. A. An evaluation of *Index Medicus* and MEDLARS in the field of ophthalmology. *Journal of the American Society for Information Science,* 21, 1970, 254-263.

Vleduts-Stokolov, N. Concept recognition in an automatic text-processing system for the life sciences. *Journal of the American Society for Information Science,* 38, 1987, 269-287.

Wanger, J. et al. *Evaluation of the On-Line Process,* Santa Monica, Cuadra Associates, 1980. PB81-132565.

Weil, B. H. Standards for writing abstracts. *Journal of the American Society for Information Science,* 1970, 351-357.

Weil, B. H. et al. Technical-abstracting fundamentals. *Journal of Chemical Documentation,* 3, 1963, 86-89, 125-136.

Weinberg, B. H. Why indexing fails the researcher. *The Indexer,* 16(1), 1988, 3-6.

White, H. D. and Griffith, B. C. Quality of indexing in online data bases. *Information Processing and Management,* 23, 1987, 211-224.

Wilkinson, D. and Hollander, S. A comparison of drug literature coverage by *Index Medicus* and *Drug Literature Index. Bulletin of the Medical Library Association,* 61, 1973, 431-432.

Williams, M. E. Experiences of IIT Research Institute in operating a computerized retrieval system for searching a variety of data bases. *Information Storage and Retrieval,* 8, 1972, 57-75.

Williams, M. E. Highlights of the online database field—statistics, pricing and new delivery mechanisms. In: *Proceedings of the National Online Meeting 1984;* ed. by M. E. Williams and T. H. Hogan, pp. 1-4. Medford,

N.J., Learned Information Inc., 1984.

Williams, M. E. Relative impact of print and database products on database producer expenses and income—trends for database producer organizations based on a thirteen year financial analysis. *Information Processing and Management,* 17, 1981, 263-276.

Williams, M. E. Relative impact of print and database products on database producer expenses and income—a follow-up. *Information Processing and Management,* 18, 1982, 307-311.

Williams, M. E. and Brandhorst, T. Future trends in A & I data-base publication. *Bulletin of the American Society for Information Science,* 5(3), 1979, 27-28.

Wilson, P. Situational relevance. *Information Storage and Retrieval,* 9, 1973, 457-471.

Wilson, P. *Two Kinds of Power: an Essay on Bibliographical Control.* Berkeley, University of California Press, 1968.

Winter, D. C. et al. *A Technology Assessment of Advances in Scientific and Technical Information Services.* Pasadena, CA, Xerox Electro-Optical Systems, 1977. PB 265 839.

Wood, J. L. et al. Overlap among the journal articles selected for coverage by BIOSIS, CAS, and Ei. *Journal of the American Society for Information Science,* 24, 1973, 25-28.

Wood, J. L. et al. Overlap in the lists of journals monitored by BIOSIS, CAS, and Ei. *Journal of the American Society for Information Science,* 23, 1972, 36-38.

Wooster, H. Optimal utilization of indexing personnel. *Research Review* (U.S. Air Force, Office of Aerospace Research), 3(4), 1964, 22-23.

Yerkey, A. N. Models of index searching and retrieval effectiveness of keyword-in-context indexes. *Journal of the American Society for Information Science,* 24, 1973, 282-286.

Yu, K.-I. et al. Pipelined for speed: the Fast Data Finder system. *Quest* (TRW Defense and Space Systems Group), 9(2), 1986-1987, 5-19.

Zholkova, A. I. Applying facet analysis methods in abstracting. *Scientific and Technical Information Processing,* 2, 1975, 70-74. (English translation of *Nauchno-tekhnicheskaya informatsiya,* Seriya 1, Number 6, pp. 26-28.)

Zunde, P. and Dexter, M. E. Factors affecting indexing performance. *Proceedings of the American Society for Information Science,* 6, 1969a, 313-322.

Zunde, P. and Dexter, M. E. Indexing consistency and quality. *American Documentation,* 1969b, 20, 259-267.

INDEX

(Because the entire volume is about indexing and abstracting, the use of these terms as entry points has been minimized in this index.)

Brevity in abstracts, 97-98
British Education Index, 160-161
British Technology Index, 53, 55, 159-160
Brittain, J. M., 120, 126, 296
Burchinal, L. G., 252-253, 296
Burke, F. G., 51, 296
Business Periodicals Index, 130
Byrne, J. R., 210, 296

-C-
Card catalogs, 41-42
Caren, L., 251, 296
Carroll, K. H., 130, 296
CATLINE, 243
Chain indexing, 52-53, 147-149, 159-160
Chatman, S., 98, 295
Checktags, 21, 32-35, 66-67
Chemical Abstracts, 48, 94-96, 111-112, 120, 123-124, 126, 149, 153-155, 251
Chemical Biological Activities, 126
Chemical formula indexes, 149, 155
Chien, D-C., 245, 301
Chu, C. M., 84, 293, 296
Citation indexes, 47, 85, 160-166, 232-236
Citation linkages, 232-236
Citation order, 52-56, 94, 151, 157
CITE system, 243-244
Claims of author, 29
Class labels, 16
Classification: analytico-synthetic, 52-53; automatic procedures, 229-236; bibliographic schemes, 14-18, 51-53; defined, 14-16; in printed indexes, 51-58, 146-160; of fiction, 186-187
Classified catalog, 15, 51-53
Classified indexes, 146-160

Clemencin, G., 244, 296
Cleverdon, C. W., 176, 203-204, 207-208, 293, 296
Cliques, 230-231
Cloze criterion, 108
Cluley, H. J., 136, 296
Clumps, 232
Clusters, 230-233
Coates, E. J., 53, 296
Co-citation, 85, 166, 234
Coco, A., 210-211, 296
Coefficient of Index Usability, 130
College of Aeronautics, 203
Collison, R. L., 59, 98, 296-297
Colon Classification, 52
Combinations of terms, 18, 27, 41-43, 161, 163, 165-166
Company abstracts bulletin, 111, 113-114
Compatibility in purpose of abstracts, 109-112
COMPENDEX, 118-119, 210; see also Engineering Index
Complementarity of indexing and abstracting, 6
Computer-generated printed indexes, 43-51, 53-56
Computerized Information Transfer in English, 243-244
Conaway, C. W., 130, 297
Concept, defined, 10
Concept Headings, 171, 226
Conceptual analysis, 8-13, 15-18, 21, 182; consistency in, 68, 70-72; failures of, 76; in abstracting, 106-109
Concordances, 195
Conference paper coverage, 126
Conrad, C. C., 254, 297
Consensus in indexing, 71, 83-84, 171